AS A TALE THAT IS TOLD

By the same author:

The Life of Lord Mount Stephen
Vol One Awakening Continent
Vol Two The End of the Road

Hardback copies of both, also flexi
copies of Vol 2, available from
Aberdeen University Press

AS A TALE
THAT IS TOLD

A Church of Scotland Parish
1913-1954

HEATHER GILBERT

ABERDEEN UNIVERSITY PRESS

First published 1983
Aberdeen University Press
A member of the Pergamon Group
© Heather Gilbert 1983

British Library Cataloguing in Publication Data

Gilbert, Heather
　As a tale that is told: a Church of Scotland
　parish, 1913-1954
　1. Church of Scotland—History 2. Parishes—
　Scotland—Lumphanan (Grampian)—
　History 3. Lumphanan (Grampian)—
　Church history
　I. Title
　285′.2412′32   BX9073.R7

ISBN 0 08 030365 X
ISBN 0 08 030366 8 Pbk

PRINTED IN GREAT BRITAIN
THE UNIVERSITY PRESS
ABERDEEN

PREFACE

This record of the ministry of my father, the Reverend Francis Cantlie Donald, in the Aberdeenshire country parish of Lumphanan from 1913 to 1954 is based partly on documentation and partly on the personal memories of my brother, Craig Donald, and myself and of a number of our parishioners. Some of the latter are mentioned by name in the text; I should like to record my particular gratitude to Mrs A. H. Irvine who, over many years, recalled for me both her own memories and anecdotes of earlier days. I would also like to thank my husband, Ian Gilbert, himself the son of a Church of Scotland missionary and for some years Session Clerk at Crown Court Church of Scotland in London, for his helpful criticism of my work.

The list of chapter contents indicates the topics covered and gives some idea of the still slowly changing parish life of the period. Change has since then accelerated: even the Lumphanan entry in the Third Statistical Account, written in 1952, has indeed become history.

The photograph on the front cover of my father at Michael Fair is by courtesy of *The People's Journal*; I am grateful also to Alex. Morrison, Lumphanan's printer and photographer, for permission to use one of his photographs of St Finan's Church, manse and steading, and to Mrs John Christie for providing a photograph of her grandfather, George McDonald, and his wife.

January 1983   Heather Gilbert

CONTENTS

PREFACE

LIST OF ILLUSTRATIONS

Chapter 1   IN THE BEGINNING: The vacancy and the induction.

Chapter 2   I WILL PLEAD WITH THEM FOR MY HERITAGE: The heritors; stipend and the Law of Ann; manse, steading and glebe.

Chapter 3   HIS PEOPLE, AND THE SHEEP OF HIS PASTURE: The parishioners, present, past and historical; parish history: economic, social and medical.

Chapter 4   CHANGES AND WAR: 1914–1918.

Chapter 5   AND HE PREACHED THE WORD UNTO THEM: Sermons; exchange of pulpits; young communicants' class; the Sacrament; Bible Class; Sunday School; Sabbath observance; Church of Scotland reaction to post-war economic depression.

Chapter 6   INITIUM SAPIENTIAE TIMOR DOMINI: General Assembly: 1930's Youth Committee debates; *Young Scotland* articles; sermon on the 'lapsed'.

Chapter 7   LABOUR NOT TO BE RICH: Working the glebe; 'minister's grass'; horse and other transport: statistics; visiting the blacksmith; sheep, poultry and bees.

Chapter 8   AT ALL SEASONS, SERVING THE LORD: Manse and parish; baptisms, marriages, funerals; hospital visiting; churchyard management; severe winters; the Presbytery.

Chapter 9   WHATSOEVER THY HAND FINDETH TO DO: Assembly time; manse children's tasks; garden and grounds; recreations; the minister's wife; condition of manses; dependants' grants: award and withdrawal.

Chapter 10   THE DEFENCE SHALL BE PREPARED: 1939–1945: Evacuees; Home Guard; parishioners on war service; casualties; German prisoners of war.

Chapter 11   THE THINGS WHICH MAKE FOR PEACE: Education: Lumphanan school; evening classes; campaign for secondary school on Deeside; entertainments; holidays; Harvest Thanksgiving; Christmas.

Envoi   UNTO THE END: Retirement 1954–1974.

ILLUSTRATIONS

between Chapters Five and Six

1 ALEX FORBES WIGHT, Camphill

2 GEORGE McDONALD, Bellman and Gravedigger

3 ALEX REID, Merchant

4 JOHN KING, Knappyround

5 JOHN GLENESK, Craigton

6 WILLIAM G McROBBIE, Joiner and Carpenter

7 DAVID G WATT, Inspector of Poor

8 JAMES MICHIE, Cairnbeathie

9 ROBERT R ANDERSON, Milton

10 ROBERT D DONALD, Banker

11 WILLIAM A DAVIE

12 ST FINAN'S CHURCH, Manse and Steading

Front cover The Minister at Michael Fair
Back cover The Donald family, 1922. *Photo by Andrew Lawson*

CHAPTER ONE

In the beginning

The vacancy and the induction.

AS A TALE THAT IS TOLD

Chapter 1

At one-forty-five p.m. on Thursday the thirteenth of February 1913, some forty
men sat down to luncheon in the Parish Hall of Lumphanan, Aberdeenshire, following the service of ordination and induction of the new parish minister, the
Reverend Francis Cantlie Donald, Master of Arts of the University of Aberdeen.
In the chair, as host and to guide the company, which included presbyters,
elders, and family and friends of the new minister through the fourteen toasts
and replies, was the chief heritor, the laird of Finzean, the Right Honourable
Robert Farquharson, Privy Councillor, Doctor of Medicine, Doctor of Laws and
Liberal Member of Parliament for West Aberdeenshire. Also there was his
brother, Joseph Farquharson, A.R.A., and the Clerk to the Heritors, Francis
J. Cochran.

The first toast (after loyal tributes to the King, George V, to Queen
Mary, to the Queen Mother, Queen Alexandra, and the Royal Family had been
given by the chairman) was 'The Church of Scotland', proposed by Mr A. Forbes
Wight of Camphill, heritor and chairman of the vacancy committee, and replied
to by the minister of Coull, the Reverend Alexander McKenzie. What was upper-
most before the churches, said Mr Wight, was at that time the question of
union. He was sure it was their desire that union should be accomplished
between the two churches, and that very soon. (Applause). He often thought
they owed a deep debt of gratitude to the Old Free Church for what it did for
them in 1843. If the system of patronage had then been abolished, there
would never have been a Free Church at all. At present a committee of the
Established Church and the United Free Church was discussing the question of union,
and he was sure they all hoped that the members of the committee would come to
some definite settlement so as to be able to submit their finding to the next
General Assembly. (Applause). He was quite prepared to admit that the
questions of disestablishment and disendowment were rather difficult subjects

to determine, but still, by adopting the principle of give and take on both sides, he thought an arrangement could be come to satisfactory to all parties. (Hear, hear).

Following the toast to the Presbytery of Kincardine O'Neil, given by the senior Lumphanan elder, William Davie, farmer in Bogentassie, and the response by the moderator of presbytery, the Reverend Andrew Tweedie of Strachan, the chairman rose to propose the health of the new minister and to wish him long life, happiness, prosperity and godspeed in the heavy responsibility that had been laid upon him of looking after their spiritual interests. Dr Farquharson said that he never went into a Presbyterian church without listening to a carefully thought out, logical, spiritual and useful sermon. Important though preaching was, however, there was something more important, and that was the work a man did outside by going among the people and showing them the example of an upright, straight-forward, honourable life. He read a letter from Dr Adam Semple, parish minister at Huntly, stating that Mr Donald's services as assistant there had been much appreciated; his personal qualities and the assiduous discharge of his duties had made him a general favourite. Mr Donald came to Lumphanan with almost the unanimous acceptance of the people, and he had got before him a splendid sphere of work. It was a poorly paid job that of a minister, but although badly paid in money, ministers were paid in kind by the affection, love and confidence of their people.

Although Dr Farquharson did not in this speech refer to the question of union (a later toast to Other Churches was gracefully acknowledged by the minister of the United Free Church at Lumphanan, the Reverend J. Galbraith Smith) he had in a book of memoirs In and Out of Parliament, published two years earlier, recalled that at the age of six he had watched from an Edinburgh window the 1843 Disruption procession out of the Assembly into George Street and down to Tanfield Hall and the first Free Church Assembly. 'Four hundred ministers, at the call of conscience and what they considered their duty, deliberately abandoned their churches and their manses and their incomes, and trekked out, so to speak, into the desert to begin their lives anew. I have often wondered, in the case of some of these poor men, suddenly evicted and having, like their great Master, literally nowhere to lay their heads, when the warm glow of exalted sentiment had been cooled down by the chill dawn of the coming day, whether they did not repent of their rash action, and if the game really seemed to be worth the candle... The whole question at issue was whether a clergyman should be chosen by the patron or by the people. The new Act had already been passed, which gave a congregation the right to veto a bad or unpopular appointment, but it had not received full official sanction, and the extremists would be satisfied with nothing less than the absolute abolition of patronage. On this once vehemently disputed point opinions must differ... But the method by popular election, too, has its drawbacks. A "short leet", as it is called, of from five to six competitors preach in succession, and a small committee is appointed to decide. This generally means that they are led by the nose by the most loud-voiced and dogmatic among them, and some little experience tells me that very insufficient inquiry is made into the candidate's character or personality, or probable capacity of fitting comfortably into a round or square hole, as the case may be'.

The extent to which these latter views applied to the election campaign just concluded can presently be judged from the surviving evidence. Sixteen years later, the first United Assembly in Edinburgh was attended by the Reverend Francis C. Donald, by his U.F. neighbour, then the Reverend David Lawson and by a U.F. elder William Christie, farmer in Nether Tillylair, Lumphanan. This time the procession, on 2 October 1929, assembled separately and came together near the 'heart of Midlothian'. The Minister of St Giles' met the two moderators on the steps of his church saying 'Peace be unto you. Now is the Son of Man glorified'. Ten years after that the two Lumphanan

churches were united. By this time the only visual presence of Robert
Farquharson in the parish was a monument on the very top of Craiglich, and
his brother Joseph, the painter, reigned in his stead.

Long life, happiness, prosperity ... the affection, love and confidence
of his people. My father lived to be over ninety-one. When in his latter
years he spoke in the happiest of terms of his forty-one years in Lumphanan,
I think we imagined that this euphoria was the concomitant of old age; we
remembered more clearly the difficulties and discomforts. But my father,
unknown to us, had, at least from 1929, at first intermittently and then
more regularly, been keeping diaries - a record of activities rather than
comments thereon - and together with other evidence these testify both to
the happiness he found in 'going among the people' and to the affection,
love and confidence that were his reward. The speeches at that induction
luncheon indeed set the tone for the years that followed. The 'give and
take' principle was certainly prominent in presbyterial activities.

Prosperity - no. That he did not seriously look for and certainly
never achieved. He began at a disadvantage of which he was fully aware, and
initially hoped to avoid. On coming to the parish of Lumphanan he was
caught by the law of Ann. Dating from the Reformation, and regulated by an
Act of Parliament of 1672, Ann laid down that if the previous incumbent had
died in office, the stipend for that half-year went to his widow and children.
This obtained until 1925, and was known to be the case at Lumphanan in
1912-13. His predecessor, the Reverend Matthew Charteris Thorburn, died
after thirty years in the parish on 2 October 1912, my father's thirtieth
birthday: he read of this in the newspaper at a time when, having served
two years as assistant at Huntly to the Reverend Dr Adam Semple ('the wisest
man ever I knew') he was beginning to look around for a church of his own.
He had taken his course in Divinity some years after graduating in Arts;
in the interval he had been teaching, first at Aberchirder (he is still

remembered in Foggieloan) then at Laurencekirk, where he had met his bride-to-be Mollie Reid. It had been a long engagement; he had no private income, and the prospect of beginning under the law of Ann was not appealing.

Until now he had never even heard of Lumphanan, but the following Monday he chanced to call on the Reverend James Jolly Calder, a bachelor in his sixties, minister at Cairney, three miles from Huntly. Mr Calder had no doubts whatsoever: 'Lumphanan ... just the place for you'. It was near Aberdeen — he had a cousin a farmer there, Andrew Calder of Cairnton. Eventually my father agreed to let his name go forward, fully expecting and indeed confident that nothing more would come of it.

On 7 November 1912 the Lumphanan congregation met to appoint a vacancy committee. In the chair was the interim moderator, the Reverend Gavin E. Argo, Kincardine O'Neil. Later we were to know Dr Argo as the soul of benevolence. Somewhat portly, he rode a tricycle. He loved children, claiming a special relationship with my sister Betty whom he had baptised: 'You see, Betty, I'm your father' he would say earnestly, much to the amusement of my mother. In the church at Kincardine O'Neil there is a plaque to his memory with the unexpected but appropriate quotation from Browning's

Epilogue to Asolando:

> One who never turned his back but marched breast forward,
> Never doubted clouds would break,
> Never dreamed, though right were worsted wrong would triumph,
> Held we fall to rise, are baffled to fight better,
> Sleep to wake.

On his return home that evening he wrote in his characteristic script a careful minute of the meeting which he sent with a covering note to the newly appointed clerk of the vacancy committee, John Clarke, Craig Cottage: '...You might just buy a penny School Exercise Book to write in this minute and the minutes of Committee... you will get on nicely with Mr Wight as Convener'. The laird of Camphill, advocate in Aberdeen, had the previous month been registered an adherent; there were four hundred names on the newly-revised Communion Roll.

The vacancy committee numbered twenty. Four were from the Kirk Session: William Davie, Bogentassie; John Glenesk, Craigton; John Esson, wood merchant, Kintocher Mills, and John B. King, Knappyround. The others were James Michie, Cairnbeathie; John Forbes, Mains of Auchlossan; Robert R. Anderson, Milton of Auchenhove; John Grant, East Mains; Andrew Calder, Cairnton; Alex. Reid, merchant; Mrs Robert Anderson, Alex. Esson, joiner; Mrs John Glenesk, Mrs John Esson, Mrs John Clarke, Mrs Leslie, Whitehouse; James Ritchie, Newtown; Peter Dickson, blacksmith; and George Merchant, clothier. Mr Michie was elected vice-convener.

As soon as Mr Argo had left for home that November day, the vacancy committee got down to business. To date there had been twenty-three applications. Several of the testimonials were read aloud by Mr Wight, but soon it was agreed that all should lie meantime in the hands of the Session Clerk, John Glenesk, and be open for inspection by members of committee at Craigton Farm. The committee was to meet again on Saturday 16 November in the church at 4.30 p.m. A subsequent note from Mr Wight to the clerk adds a touch of cold reality: 'After the meeting was over I called at the Manse and saw Mrs. Thorburn. She was kind enough to offer the Committee a room in the Manse for our next meeting and to give us a fire, and I think we should accept it. The Church will be very cold and will starve us'.

At the more comfortable meeting in the Manse on 16 November Mr Wight suggested that following the precedent of thirty years ago they appoint a sub-committee of five – two from the Kirk Session and three others – to inquire more fully into the merits of the applicants and to draw up a leet not to exceed six for the committee's approval. It is clear that throughout the convener was only too anxious to bow to the wishes of the members, while trying to be helpful. Normally resident during the week in Aberdeen, he was told that inquiries were already being made, and it was agreed to draw up a short leet of five. (My father later discovered that not only had Andrew Calder been active on his behalf, but an elder's wife had written to a sister in Huntly whom he did not know but who had reported favourably. Moreover the senior elder's son, William A. Davie, destined to be Director of Agriculture and Forests in the Sudan, had sat next him one year in the English M.A. class at University.) The leet was voted upon; two applicants having equal votes there was a second vote, the loser being listed as reserve, and was in fact called upon later. These were then invited in alphabetical order to preach in the Parish Church at noon and also in the afternoon on the five Sundays of December. The convener had proposed that the second service should be in the West End Hall, a small meeting house some two miles away where a monthly evening service was normally held. It was pointed out, however, that this hall was too small. The vice-convener offered overnight hospitality at Cairnbeathie, and he and the Session Clerk undertook to meet the candidates at Lumphanan station on the Saturday afternoons. The latter were requested to forward their choice of Psalm tunes etc. in advance to Alex. Reid, merchant, who was choirmaster.

On 20 November Mr Argo wrote to Mr Clarke enclosing a form of intimation and emphasising the need to make it clear, Sunday by Sunday, who was to preach next, adding 'You are doing nicely, and I trust all will go on well'. Inevitably some dates had to be switched, so that as Mr Wight wrote to the clerk on 21 November, it was most important that the congregation should not mistake one preacher for another. The convener also thanked Mr Clarke 'for the deep interest you are taking in the Lumphanan vacancy'.

My father duly faced his trials on 8 December. On the Saturday he was met at the station and driven the half mile to Cairnbeathie in James Michie's trap. Passing the manse, the pony suddenly swerved as if to enter the drive, drawing forth a jocular comment from Mr Michie that the pony had already decided on the outcome. By this time one applicant had got another church,

so that the reserve was added to the short leet. On 3 December Mr Wight
wrote to the clerk regarding a proposed congregational meeting on 30
December, by which time all the candidates would have been heard, to nominate those for election. He would wish Mr Argo to be present 'to keep us
right in form'. The latter wrote on 5 December that he would be 'very
glad to come over the hill on the 30th at 4.30'.

The manse had by now been vacated, and on 10 December Mr Wight wrote
to the clerk '... Surely some temporary seating accommodation can be
managed in the Manse, and a fire put in the same room as we had before,
so as to make the Congregational Committee comfortable. It would never
do to invite them to a cold cheerless room...' He went on 'I note what
you say in regard to the Rev[d.] - as also the Rev.[d.] F.C. Donald, and will
be glad to hear from you from time to time the views of the parishioners
regarding the different Candidates'. On the same day another applicant
wrote that he had been elected to another parish.

Until now (as he recalled nearly half a century later) my father had
been viewing the prospects with great equanimity. On the short leet were
two very likely young men - one of them with a strong local connection;
next, an Aberdeen assistant, well spoken of in the city; the fourth, a
fine scholar, honours degrees in Arts and Divinity - unfortunately with
physical defects which included an impediment in his speech, yet a very
fine fellow; and himself. He was sure one of the first three would get
the charge. But after the first two had withdrawn a rumour went round that
the Aberdeen man had a German wife, which in 1912-13 was a handicap.
'Result: I was elected at the first vote'.

The candidate who was to have preached on 29 December having withdrawn,
the vacancy committee met on 23 December 1912, the interim moderator, Mr
Argo being present, to nominate 'one or more persons to be voted upon by
the congregation'. It was moved and seconded that only two names be

submitted, but after general discussion it was agreed by 11 votes to 6 that all the candidates who had been heard (at that point there were four) should be voted on. The ballot was to take place in the manse on 6 January 1913, from 11 a.m. to 3 p.m. and from 5 to 8 p.m. The moderator asked that the church officer should be in attendance during election hours, presumably more in order to stoke the fire than to prevent irregularities. Mr Glenesk, as representing the Kirk Session, and Messrs Michie and Calder as members of committee were appointed scrutineers during the counting of the votes, the clerk to be present ex-officio.

The four nominees were notified and wrote in confirmation: 'I send my formal consent to stand for election...' 'I shall only be too glad to stand...' 'I shall be very glad...' My father's choice of phrase was 'I am quite willing to allow my name to be voted on'. On 26 December Mr Wight, writing to the clerk regarding voting papers, was disturbed that an election for Portsoy was to take place a week earlier than theirs: 'I do not see how they could have made the election so soon, if they had complied with the regulations as laid down in the Year Book, which we did'. On 31 December one of the Lumphanan candidates wrote that he had just been chosen for New Pitsligo. A series of vacancies at the time was in fact causing such repercussions as Mr Wight feared and keeping suspense high among my father's generation of students. On 3 January one of these, William Browne, wrote to acknowledge my father's letter of congratulation on his election at Portsoy: 'I am sorry I haven't helped your position for Lumphanan so far as - is concerned. But you know I withdrew from New Pitsligo, and John McWilliam has got it. So your leet will be simplified to three'. Browne wrote also to David Anderson who in turn told my father 'He is in great form over Portsoy. He is the man for the place, I think, as he should suit the fisher folk, and certainly he will work hard among them. I am trying to wait patiently now for the result of Rothiemay'. One of the guests at Dr

Farquharson's luncheon was the Reverend David A. Anderson, 'minister-
elect of Rothiemay'.

On 6 January James Michie, Cairnbeathie, wrote to my father:

> This is a very important day for the Parish of Lumphanan being
> the day for the election of our Minister. I fondly hope you will
> be found at the top of the poll with a good majority over all.
> So far as I can judge such will be the result but no one can be
> over confident – however a few of us are doing what we can.
>
> I will arrange to have a wire sent you Tuesday morning as soon
> as the post office will be open. The poll does not close till
> 8 o'clock Monday.

At 8.25 a.m. the wire was handed in, being received at Huntly 8.48:
'Hearty congratulations 107 votes majority. Michie'.

But now the winter storms which were to become a feature of life in
the parish of Lumphanan were clogging the machinery of procedure. Mr Argo
wrote to the clerk of the vacancy committee on 16 January 1913:

> I herewith send you the form of Call to Mr. Donald, and will you
> do your best to get as many as possible to sign it before Sunday.
> Then on Sunday, will you bring it to Church, where, after Service,
> an opportunity can be given to any. You might bring pen and ink and
> blotter with you. Then it can be intimated that the Call will lie
> during next week in the Shop of Mr. Christie for signature. I can
> get it there to lay before the Presbytery when it meets.
>
> Owing to the snowstorm, Mr. McKenzie of Coull found it impossible
> to get to Lumphanan to read the edict about the meeting of Presby.
> so that will cause a delay of a week.
>
> Please tell any you can that I hope to preach on Sunday first
> at 3.30.

Fortunately by 13 February weather conditions had improved, and at the
service of ordination there were fourteen members present of the eighteen
(excluding Lumphanan) parishes in the Presbytery of Kincardine O'Neil.
Although Ballater and Braemar were absent, the Reverend James A. Lowe
managed to come from Glengairn. There was also a large congregation of
parishioners and others in Lumphanan Parish Church. In the pulpit was the
Reverend Robert Robertson, Logie-Coldstone, (in accordance with custom, the
minister last inducted in the Presbytery) who preached from Ephesians iv,
12: 'For the edifying of the body of Christ'. He pointed out the part that

had to be taken by the church in the regeneration of society, and said Religion should enter into every phase of life. After the ordination ceremony the Reverend William Sawers, Dinnet, addressed the new minister, conveying the congratulations of the Presbytery, then turned to the congregation who 'had called Mr. Donald to take up that heavy duty among them, and such success as might follow him was largely dependent upon them. They must give him their loving and helpful sympathy. There must be sympathy for the man, sympathy for the message, and sympathy for the cause he championed'.

Promptly on 8 January my father had received congratulations from an Aberdeen firm of robemakers with the members of which he appeared to be already acquainted. 'I suppose you know that we made Dr. Semple's Robes, also Rev. James Smith and others so I thought that it might be that you would have a say in the matter regarding your own...' The firm obviously assumed that new robes would be presented to the incoming minister. This was to prove a knotty problem for the vacancy committee, since the deceased minister's widow had given Mr Thorburn's robes to the Kirk Session. This was apparently not generally known, when on 3 February James Michie, the vice-convener, who was not then an elder, called on the convener in Aberdeen to discuss arrangements. Mr Wight, writing that day to my father about his guests and the toast list at the luncheon which Dr Farquharson was to give the Presbytery, added 'There is some word of Pulpit Robes being presented to you, and I have arranged with Mr. Michie that you will be here on Wednesday 5th curt at 2.30 p.m. to meet the Tailor in order that he may take your measurements'.

Later that day the question arose at a meeting of the vacancy committee. 'The clerk gave a resume and explanation regarding the Robes presented by Mrs. Thorburn to the Kirk Session, pointing out the difficult position in which she, Mrs. Thorburn, had thereby placed them with regard to their new

minister. They could not present Mr. Donald with them, they could not robe
him, and so far as he could see, if they insisted on the old set, the only
way out of the difficulty was for the Committee to place themselves entirely
in Mr. Donald's hands'. Mr Michie, who was chairing the meeting, reported
his interview with Mr Wight. One member considered there was no difficulty
at all, the robes were quite good, scarcely any the worse, and there was no
need for new ones at all. 'Questioned on the matter the Clerk said the
figures were not in the least alike and that the Robe as it was would not
fit Mr. Donald.' Mr Clarke himself was a tailor, his shop being in the house
below Craig Cottage; it was he whom Mr Wight had invited to take measurements,
these presumably to be passed to robemakers. Someone moved that Mr Donald
get the old robes and a purse of sovereigns, and that he be not consulted in
the matter. This was approved by a show of hands, and it was then agreed
to issue subscription lists, first to the Parish Church heritors and thereafter to collectors.

Three days later Mr Wight himself presided at a further meeting at
which the whole matter was gone over again. Alex. Reid moved that Mr Donald
be presented with a new set of pulpit robes, Mr John Esson seconding. There
followed an amendment in favour of the old robes and a purse of sovereigns.
These were voted on, eight being for the motion and nine for the amendment,
two members abstaining. Nothing further emerges on the subject, but it
seems from the Press that new robes were in fact purchased by 'friends of
the congregation' and presented to the new minister by Dr Farquharson after
his toast at the luncheon.

Mr Thorburn's robes lay untouched for some twenty years in a brown
paper parcel in the manse linen room. Eventually my father, having himself
resisted for some time my mother's pleas that he ask the Kirk Session's
permission to burn them, agreed that she herself might mention the matter
while serving tea in the interval of a Kirk Session meeting. Until the

union with the Free Church, which possessed a small hall in the village,
these meetings took place in the minister's study, we children being kept
on our best behaviour at the opposite end of the manse. Listening to the
heavy tread of feet from the front door we would say with hushed solemnity
'It's the Session'. On this occasion I was helping with the tea when my
mother said her piece; smiling permission was readily granted. Although in
most respects a 'saving woman', this parcel had for her lain like a ghostly
presence in the house. The new robes served my father for many years. When
they became threadbare he wore those of a deceased friend and neighbour, a
taller man.

At the meeting of the vacancy committee on 3 February 'it was unanimously
agreed to hold a Social meeting in the Parish Hall on the evening of the 13th
inst. at 7.30 p.m., admission 6d.' Mr Reid undertook to supply the musical
items, and the Kirk Session along with the vice-convener were appointed as a
sub-committee to carry out the necessary arrangements. 'The Ladies Church
Committee had previously decided as to the recipients of certain gifts, the
expenses of which were to be defrayed out of their funds and Mrs Esson and
Mrs Glenesk were empowered to purchase these along with Mr Donald's purse
and they made their arrangements for going to Aberdeen accordingly. Mr
Wight was unanimously appointed to make the presentation to Mr Donald, Mrs
Davie a similar honour to Mr Argo, Mrs Esson a like duty to Rev. J.G. Smith,
Mrs King a presentation to Mr Glenesk and Mrs Glenesk a tribute to the Clerk'.
On 6 February, following the committee's 'robes' discussion, 'Mr Davie
objected to the Ladies going to Aberdeen to purchase the gifts, holding that
in matters of this kind, local traders should be supported, and that better
value for the money would be got at home. Mr Esson seemed to consider this
a question of integrity towards the Ladies and objected to the remarks of
Mr Davie'. The latter moved, seconded by Mr John Forbes, that the gifts be
bought locally; Mr Michie moved, seconded by Mr Esson, that they be got in

Aberdeen, the meeting voting 8 to 4 for Aberdeen'. In the event the interim moderator received an arm chair and travelling rug, the United Free Church minister a walking stick, the session clerk an umbrella and the clerk to the vacancy committee, like the new minister, a purse and sovereigns. The minister's purse contained twenty-seven pounds, ten shillings; the spectre Ann receded a little. Although practically anything, from a mangle to a meal girnel, could in those days be obtained from the local merchants on due notice being given (we had a mangle bearing the choirmaster's name 'A. Reid, Auchenhove') there is no doubt that these gifts could hardly have been bought locally at such short warning.

More detailed plans were made at the next meeting on 10 February for the Social. 'Arrangements were also made for a platform party. The Choir were granted free admission and the Clerk was instructed to prove passes for them. Messrs. King and Davie were appointed doorkeepers and Messrs. Esson, Glenesk and Merchant seating stewards. Messrs. Alex. Esson and John Forbes were appointed to distribute the Bread and Jugs at the door'. These were substantial half-pint mugs with LUMPHANAN PARISH HALL and a date in black letters on a pink ground. 'The Clerk was authorised to order from Mr. Milne, Baker, 350 Bags of Bread, bags to contain 2 $\frac{1}{2}$d. pieces, 3 $\frac{1}{4}$d. pieces or thereby, and 3/- value in fancy Bread for the platform party'. The 'pieces' in the bags would have been perhaps a German bun (from 1914 to 1918 the Baker Milnes renamed these Belgian buns; in 1939 we called them Patriotic buns), a square cut-off of sponge with pink water-icing or a macaroon, a cherry bun (actually a biscuit with granules of sugar and a cherry on top) and a 'knuckle' biscuit. Those actually known as 'farthing biscuits' were butter biscuits which later became 'Three-a-penny biscuits'. The clerk was also to instruct Mrs Mitchell, Hall Cottage, (later the hostess of Cameron's Inn) to make tea for a minimum of 350; fully 350 actually came, judging from the number of tickets sold. He was to provide her with the necessary quantities required, 'the same to be equally divided between Messrs. R. Moir and G. Christie'. The bills from the two village merchants, the former's bearing a coloured advertisement for Fels-Naptha, 'The Soap with a way of its own!', the latter's one for Lipton's Tea, 'The finest the world can produce', were otherwise identical: $1\frac{3}{4}$lbs. tea - 3/6; $10\frac{1}{2}$lbs. sugar - 1/$10\frac{1}{2}$; $\frac{1}{2}$lb. loaf sugar - $1\frac{1}{2}$. total: 5/6. Thomas Milne's bill showed that in fact 385 bags were supplied, also a cake and fancy biscuits (2/- each: total 4/-) for the platform, the total £3.8.2, less discount 8/2 (which covered the additional 35 bags): £3.0.0. The tea-making cost 5/-. The use of the hall and council room, including lights, came to 11/-, the bill receipted by George Spark, clerk to the Parish Council. At the meeting on 10 February the vacancy committee arranged provisionally for a supply of cream for the tea, the clerk being instructed to 'write the Ladies who were expected to give assistance with this'.

The committee met only once more, after the induction, on 20 February to approve the accounts. As Mr Michie had declined to charge for accommodation and attendance for the various candidates during their stay at Cairnbeathie it was unanimously agreed that 'under these circumstances some tangible token should be given the Misses Michie for their trouble. Mr. Michie was asked to retire, when it was agreed that the sum of £1..2..9 be expended on umbrellas, Mr. Reid being instructed to purchase to best advantage'. That left a balance of one pound and a halfpenny, which it was unanimously agreed to allocate to the Church funds.

Mr Wight sent his last letter as convener to the clerk on 11 February 1913, two days before the induction:

> I am today favoured with your letter, with rough Draft of Programme for Thursday evening.
>
> I have taken the liberty of altering it, and you will see that after the Presentations are made by me, I propose that the Rev.[d] Mr. Donald should take the Chair, and conduct the Meeting afterwards.
>
> You might shew my Programme to some of the Members of your Committee, and if they approve of it, please forward it to me by

the morning post, and I will get it at dinnertime, and will get
half-a-dozen typewritten copies of the Programme thrown off, and
I will take them with me to Lumphanan on Thursday morning.

I hope my proposal will meet with approval.

Of course you are at full liberty to make any alterations on
my Programme you think proper, or you can stick to your own one,
if you prefer it.

The office clerk who penned the above also transcribed the programme

incorporating Mr Wight's suggestions. Even then the latter was not entirely

satisfied, and inserted further pencilled amendments; he added the names of

the ladies who were to make the other presentations, and substituted for two

'Choir Selections' an additional solo by Miss Milne of the Bakery and one by

Alex. Reid. The Milne family were for at least two generations to con-

tribute to the musical life of the parish; as for Alex. Reid, while he was

among us (he emigrated to New Zealand, becoming a merchant in Lower Hutt)

he was famous for the songs he sang and even composed (mostly comic). Mr

Wight's final version, which was no doubt accepted, was as follows:

<u>Lumphanan Parish Church Social Meeting</u>

<u>13th. February 1913 at 7.30 p.m.</u>

<u>Programme</u>

7.30   Chair Taken.
           Old Hundredth Psalm.
        Chairman's Remarks.
           Mr. Donald ask a Blessing.
7.45   Tea Service.
8.15   Choir Selection.
        Address by Revd. W. Sutherland B.D. Gartly.
        Solo – Miss Milne.
        Address by Revd. J.G. Smith M.A. U.F.C. Lumphanan.
        Quartette by Choir Members.

Mr. Wight   Presentation to Revd. Mr. Donald.
Mrs. Davie   ..   Revd. Mr. Argo.
Mrs. Esson   ..   Revd. J.G. Smith.
Mrs. Anderson   ..   Mr. Glenesk.
Mrs. Glenesk   ..   Clerk of Committee.

        At this stage, the Revd. Mr. Donald will take the Chair,
        and conduct the Meeting afterwards.

Mr. Reid – Solo
Address by Revd. G. McWilliam B.D. Peterhead.
  ..   by Revd. Mr. McGregor, Torphins.
Solo – Miss Milne.
Address by Revd. Mr. McKenzie, Coull.
  ..   Revd. D.A. Anderson, Minister-Elect of Rothiemay.
Anthem by Choir: "I have set a Watchman".

Votes of thanks to Mr Wight and Chairman – Mr Michie.

Mr Sutherland, Gartly, represented the Presbytery of Strathbogie, from
which, as assistant at Huntly, my father came. George McWilliam, a fellow-
student, later for many years at Auldearn, was to be best man at my
parents' wedding.

My father's election to Lumphanan had been promptly reported in the
Scottish press, including the Edinburgh and Glasgow papers, as of course it
would have repercussions far beyond its local significance. Over seventy
messages of congratulation poured into his lodgings at Springbank, Huntly,
some reflecting the various stages of his life and career to date, others,
read now in retrospect, providing interesting connections with what was
still to come. Some were serious, some witty, some included sly references
to a future lady of the manse. Few were merely formal. From the Divinity
Students' Residence at 24 Spital, Old Aberdeen, where my father had served
his turn as 'Pope', wrote James T. Soutter, son of the minister at Echt:
'Dear Father Donald, Do not be too hard on me when I come up for licence'. Soon
he was to go to Nairobi, then in 1917, after acting locum tenens at Dunbar, to
Whitekirk. Some forty years later they were to recall together the occasion
of the installation of Mr Asquith, then Prime Minister, as Lord Rector of the
University when Soutter, most daintily dressed in 'drag', had shouted 'Votes
for Women!' in the Mitchell Hall. The order of the Principal, the Very
Reverend Sir George Adam Smith, to 'Put that woman out!' was frustrated by
the fact that the row of Divinity students had tied the legs of their chairs
together, but equilibrium on the platform was restored when a sacrist mur-
mured 'Only a Divinity student, sir.' A similarly united front later assured

the Principal that rustication of Soutter would mean that of the whole
Residence. The matter was amicably settled when my father, then Vice-
President of the Students' Representative Council, found a form of words
in which the quite unrepentant Soutter could subscribe regret that the
platform party had not accepted as fun a demonstration such as was then
recognised as legitimate on such occasions. I used to be told when a student at Aberdeen 'You people don't have half the fun we used to have.
Rectorials aren't worth going to nowadays'.

Ivo Clark, who had just begun his 37 years' ministry at Farnell, wrote
from Brechin '...Lumph. is justified of its wisdom. We've all been going
it at a run recently – Heughan, Urquhart, McEchern, J. McWilliam and now
you'. Less than four months after reading his poem 'Atween the gloamin an
the mirk' to their Arts Class reunion in October 1949, Ivo was to die at
66. From the manse of Kilchoman wrote Angus Boyd: 'My heartiest congratulations to thee thou bishop of Lumphanan! .. Well you'll be now 'settling
down' eh? .. Isn't Aberdeen doing well? The Residence for ever!' Some
twenty years later their daughters, Betty and Catherine Boyd, were to be
students together, living in the old Womens Union. By then Boyd was at
Kilmore, where after 25 years' ministry he died in January 1946. The
following year my father made a pilgrimage to his grave at Urquhart.

Another sample from the bunch of fellow-students' greetings came from
Henry Coulter: 'Heartiest congratulations! Our year is doing well. I am
to be the last of the Mohicans'. Soon he was to go to Newport, and later
to Bellahouston. I used to be teased as a child because when still lying
in my pram little Tommy Coulter took the cherry off his cherry bun and
put it in my mouth.

I cannot judge whether my father's generation were unusually congenial
as a group; student life in those days had a quality which, about the 1930's,
it began to lose, possibly because of the larger numbers involved. Distance

separated them for most of their careers, but I myself was to find how long
in some cases memories of each other lasted. In 1975, the year after my
father died, I happened to be for the second time in a quarter of a century
in Winnipeg, Manitoba, and called once again on the Very Reverend Dr W.
Gordon Maclean, now retired - in a manner of speaking; he was still a kenspeckle figure in his shovel hat in the streets of the city and active among
war veterans. I asked him 'Do you remember Louis Imre?' Imre Lajos, a
Hungarian, had spent the year 1910-11 at the Divinity Residence and in 1971,
although in absentia, had received an Aberdeen D D. in recognition of the
help he had given Church of Scotland missionaries in Roumania as well as of
his academic distinction. Dr Maclean said merely 'Come and see'. He took me
into another room - only the more treasured contents of the manse had been
retained in his new apartment home - and pointed to a group photograph on
the wall: their Divinity year. 'Can you tell which is Imre?' I could,
because a year or two earlier he and my father had exchanged photographs.
Dr Imre had written from Cluj: 'Your venerable beard of course is a little
unusual for me but the face, the eyes and the whole countenance with the kind-
hearted glance are very acquainted to me and make me remember you in the times
we have been together in the Residence'. In July 1914 Imre had been elected
minister in a small village near Kolozsvar, then after a difficult war period
had become in 1921 professor in the Theological Faculty at Kolozsvar, now
Cluj since Transylvania had been transferred from Hungary to Roumania. Writing at the age of 85 he could say they 'always felt the hand of the Lord
above us defending us not to despair. So lived we in much affliction with
joy'. He still remembered 'most of them who lived together in Residence
Spital'. He recalled my father 'clearly as if you were here, having been the
- so to say - senior, the oldest and most respected by us. I liked very much
Anderson too a tall man to whom the Bohemian student Valis gave the name
Longfellow, Davidson the youngest and a very sympathetic boy, his grandfather

Cunningham - as I heard there - was a great scholar in Church History.
I remember the two Irish students Coulter and Brown. Maclean was having
a room with Valis. I am sorry I cannot remember the football match with
MacEchern...' Victor MacEchern who had played regularly for Aberdeen Football Club, had just been recalling with my father at Creetown (Kirkmabreck)
Louis' excitement at Pittodrie: 'Come on Victor!' My letter to Cluj telling
of my father's death crossed one from Louis' widow.

'The recent quartette of elections in the north has given great satisfaction to our Hall' wrote the Reverend Professor Henry Cowan of the Chair of
Church History at Aberdeen. He thought Lumphanan would be 'a very agreeable
charge, particularly in the summer - sufficient work to keep you busy but not
too much to prevent study and that exercise of continual influence on individuals for good which yields the most encouraging spiritual harvest'. Similar
sentiments were expressed by the Professor of Systematic Theology, William
A. Curtis, and by Dr Thomas Nicol of the Chair of Biblical Criticism. My
father took exception to the latter's saying 'I was glad to have given a
little help at the very early stages of the business' and drafted a letter
in reply: 'Please convey to Mrs. Nicol and accept my best thanks for your
kind letter of congratulation and advice. I am more than pleased with the
result of the election at L.: especially since I did nothing to have my
name brought for$^{d.}$ but send in a formal letter of applic$^{n.}$ to the S.C.'
There is no indication as to whether or not this was ever sent.

The Divinity students were accustomed to being made welcome in the
'manses' of their professors, and in one case their visits continued long
after student days were past. Mrs Gilroy, wife of the Professor of Hebrew
and Semitic Languages, was younger than her husband and lived on in Old
Aberdeen to be over a hundred. To take another backward glance at the
Asquith Rectorial: the day before the installation, when James Soutter was
merely trying on his feminine garments in the Residence in the afternoon

preparatory to joining the torchlight procession, the others, thinking this vision was too good to be consigned to semi-darkness, (there was at this stage no thought of a suffragette demonstration) said 'Let's go and call on Mrs. Gilroy'. In the latter's drawing room the lady was introduced as being on a visit from the Church Offices in Edinburgh. All were settled down with their teacups when suddenly Mrs Gilroy burst out: 'James Soutter, you wretch!' Some years later, when on holiday in the Lumphanan area, the Gilroys came to morning service in the Parish Church, the occasion being chiefly remembered by the fact that my brother and sister, Craig and Betty, then aged about five and four, warned to be on their best behaviour, both succeeded in dropping their collection pennies with a clatter on the wood floor before the 'ladles' came round.

Another lady in Old Aberdeen had the welfare of her students very much at heart: Miss Isa F. Campbell, matron - or 'lady superintendent' - of the Divinity Students' Residence. Her card of congratulation bore no address, but the Aberdeen postmark, and references to other students. She is identi-fied by a reference in one of Louis Imre's letters: '...dear Miss Campbell the death of whom I heard from Dr. Curtis on one of the Conferences' (of the World Alliance of Reformed Churches). A former matron Miss Mary E. Neil wrote from Fasandarach, Ballater with good wishes from her sister and herself. Daughters of a former Glengairn minister, they were to write and illustrate the first short book on the parish Glengairn Calling, the next being by Mr Lowe's daughter, Amy Stewart Fraser, The Hills of Home.

Congratulations from the older generation of clerics came from all the parishes with which my father had been connected: from the Reverend James Smith of St George's in the West, Aberdeen, where both my father and Angus Boyd had been assistants in 1909-10; from the Manse of Marnoch, harking back to Aberchirder days, and from that of Laurencekirk; from Old Deer, where he had briefly assisted the Reverend (later Dr) Robert S. Kemp at the associated mission kirk of Fetterangus; from the Reverend William Grant of

Drumblade in Strathbogie (who a few years later was to marry my future parents-in-law) and from Dufftown a telegram from the Reverend John Barr Cumming of his native parish church of Mortlach.

More than one letter from old neighbours at Mortlach and Auchindoun expressed the sentiment 'if only your dear Mother had been alive, how proud she would have been...' and pleasure that his father had been able to attend the ordination, and that his sister Janet was now nearby, wife of David Burnett of Balfeddie on the Finzean estate. (Dr Farquharson made a graceful reference to the latter in his speech). Messages from Keithmore and the Mains of Clunymore recalled his Cantlie ancestors; a card from young Frederick Bain, later Deputy Chairman of I.C.I., who was to marry Isabel Adami, daughter of Mary Cantlie of Montreal and of Dr George Adami, Vice-Chancellor of the University of Liverpool. The son of his old schoolmaster John Shand (to whom my father paid tribute in his speech at the induction luncheon) wrote from the Schoolhouse at Glass; from Fordyce (a picture postcard of the Academy where she taught many generations in the 'Qualifying Class' - including my husband) wrote Miss Jean W. Campbell, an old classmate at Auchindoun.

A link between past and present came with a card from R.D. Donald, then a bachelor accountant, later to be agent, at the North of Scotland Bank in Lumphanan, after being at Aberchirder: 'We will now be looking forward to having you with us and if you are to have Mr. McWilliam or any of the Aber-chirder folks at your induction I would be delighted to have them with me in my lodgings'. A positively historical document of one sentence came from a U.F. member of Roadside of Glenmillan, Lumphanan: 'Heartiest congratula-tions and good wishes, J. Grant, Colporteur'. From East Newport, Dundee, came a kindly letter from the late Mr Thorburn's widow:

> You will excuse me writing you but I wanted to congratulate you on being chosen for 'our' Parish. I saw it in the Dundee Advertiser today so wish to tell you how pleased I feel that they have got settled and that it apparently has been an agreeable settlement.
>
> I remember you told me that it was your first experience of preaching on a leet so you are very lucky surely for I don't think many young ministers get the first Parish they preach for.

I hope you will be very happy in your new Home and be a successful Minister in every sense of the word. The Lumphanan folk are
warmhearted and kindly and I only hope you will be as happy with
them as Mr. Thorburn and I were.

God bless you in your new work.

From Edinburgh wrote Louis E. McVicker, soon to be at Monigaff and
later at Macduff: 'I hope there is a very nice manse in your place with
Virginia creepers and Tropaeolum roses and ivy and things like that for
I think Mrs. Donald would like them when she comes. Don't you think so
too? Of course you do. Now don't be telling stories! I'll be looking in
another column of the 'Scotsman' steadily from the day of the Ordination
onward, and I'll trust you not to keep me waiting too long, for I might get
tired. Verb. sap.' Among other similar references, some were better
informed than others, particularly if the writers had contacts in Laurencekirk, as had John Edmonston, a childhood friend from Auchindoun, soon to
join the Congregational Union of Scotland. A connection of the Kemp family
of Findhorn (Janet Donald's first husband, Captain George Kemp, master of a
new Donaldson liner on the Atlantic run, had been lost at sea) wrote:
'I suppose the next thing will be the wife. I have not forgotten my promise.
Remember I promised to give you a teacloth but you will have to give me due
warning'. My father's future brother-in-law wrote of his regret at not
being able to attend the ordination: George Reid, a graduate in Arts of
Edinburgh University, was teaching at Falkirk, his parents having just
settled in Larbert. 'We expect Mollie tomorrow evening for a week. Father
has got some considerable difference made on the look of things outside,
since she was before. But he is really only finding out yet how much more
there is to do before the garden is set anything like in order'. George
was to do his turn at a similar task in the manse garden at Lumphanan before
being killed in action in France. Some of our garden plants and equipment
came from Larbert when after the war my grandparents moved north to
Stonehaven.

Thus came the end of the beginning. To bring this chapter to a
close we go back to an undated but no doubt timeous communication headed
'Manse of Cairney, Huntly, N.B.' If the devil could cite Scripture for
his purpose, the Reverend James Jolly Calder felt justified in misquoting
Shakespeare: 'Congratulations! It is splendid! There is "a providence
that shapes our ends"'.

CHAPTER TWO

<u>I will plead with them for my heritage</u>

The heritors; stipend and the Law of Ann; manse,
steading and glebe.

Chapter 2

In 1913, and until the reunion of the old Church of Scotland with the
United Free Church in 1929, the heritors of a parish were - within certain
statutory limits - responsible for the maintenance of churches, manses and
glebes, as well as for the payment of teind-stipend. Although arrangements
varied from one parish to another, incumbents being asked to preserve their
stipend records for the information of successors, the principle was that
teinds represented a tenth part of a laird's income from his lands, by which
the ministry and the basic fabric of church buildings were maintained by the
local landowners. This is no place for even a summary of the history of
patronage and teinds; I can only indicate the position as it faced my
father in 1913.

Stipend was divided into money stipend, due at Lumphanan at Whitsunday
and Michaelmas, and victual stipend, not payable until in the Fiars Court
of the County, the prices of the various grains of the previous season had
been 'struck' by the Sheriff in February or March. The relevant grains for
Lumphanan were mostly oatmeal and barley; only on Pitmurchie was bear still
grown, regarded as an inferior class of victual. The rules dictated that
where bear had ceased to be produced, a minister was entitled to the highest
price of the superior grains.

The changes brought by the twentieth century to local landowners resulted in a gradually diminishing total of heritors; it may be of interest
therefore to quote the position in Lumphanan, and the dues paid, in 1914-15,
the first 'normal' year after my father's induction. His first year was of
course governed by the law of Ann. The Church of Scotland Yearbook for 1909
pointed out that if a minister were admitted after the 29th September he
might have to serve his parish for 17 months before getting any portion of
the year's stipend. My father was rather more fortunate: on 15 May 1913
he received £4 from the Great North of Scotland Railway in feu-duty (the

Deeside Line ran through what had been part of the glebe); in July he got
£6 from the Church's Smaller Livings Fund; on 29 September his first instalment of teind money stipend came to £56.8.7$\frac{1}{2}$, and on 11 November the Railway
paid £5. The following March he got £19.19.5 in victual stipend: in all,
£91.8.0$\frac{1}{2}$. In addition the glebe and steading were assessed at £9.8 and the
manse at £23, although as the latter was not fit for occupation for seven
months this was a nominal figure. On the notional total he had initially to
pay income tax at about a shilling in the pound, but could reclaim nearly
half of this on an earned income basis. The statistics which he drew up
annually until 1935 were mainly for income tax purposes and only exceptionally
do they reveal that the minister himself paid owner's and occupier's rates.
A rebate was received for insurance paid, and for communion elements provided.

(table attached)

In my own recollection, the very word 'heritor' had an ominous ring;
it implied a concept that had little connection with the term 'laird'. It
seemed they wore quite different hats. When still very young I knew all
about heritors' hats; heritors wore long pointed hats swathed in cobwebs,
as well as long cloaks printed with strange symbols (the prototype probably
came from Grimm.) They disapproved of small girls playing 'hitchy' up against
the harling. Some of our heritors were of families long established in the
area, others had acquired their estates more recently. Personal relations
with them were amicable, but business, conducted mainly through the Clerk to
the Heritors, Francis J. Cochran, of the firm of Cochran and Macpherson,
Advocates, Aberdeen, was on a rather different footing. Mr Cochran himself
was laird of Balfour in the parish of Birse, and was anxious to be helpful,
but in the last instance matters of maintaining the property were referred to
a heritors' meeting which took place in the church. Occasionally matters
were delayed because notice of such a meeting, which was attended also by

Meal 18/- (boll)	Barley £1.9.10 (Imperial quarter)	(My.–May; Sp.–September; V – Victual) No.–November
1. Finzean	My. £28.15.0½ Sp. 28.15.0½ V. 39.10.8	£97. 0.9
2. Craigievar	My. £ 6. 0.6½ Sp. 6. 0.6¼ V. 4.16.9	£16.17.9¾
3. Auchenhove	My. £ 8. 9.11 Sp. 8.10. 0 V. 1.12. 3	£18.12.2
4. Findrack	My. £ 4. 1. 9 Sp. 4. 1. 9	£ 8. 3.6
5. Glenmillan	My. £ 3.15. 4. Sp. 3.15. 4 V. – 11. 7	£ 8. 2. 3
6. Camphill	My. £ 2.19. 3 Sp. 2.19. 3	£ 5.18. 6
7. Pitmurchie	My. £ 1.15. 1 Sp. 1.15. 1 V. *	£ 3.10. 2 (plus £6.13.2½)
8. Burnside	£ 1. 3. 2¾ 2. 3	£ 1. 5. 5¾
9. G.N.S. Ry. (feu-duty)	My. £ 4. 0. 0 No. 1. 0. 0	£ 5. 0. 0 x –£171. 3.10

*   'Pitmurchie Victual Stipend for 1914–1915 was not paid till
    Whitsunday 1915. Mr Bower was absent on Military duty and his factor
    apparently was not fully versed in the question of payment of stipend.
    In the circumstances I did not press for payment earlier – £6.13.2½'.

x   'The usual payment of Feu duty in Nov. was withheld pending
    negotiations with Presbytery re liability of Minister to pay for
    Manse Repairs on the Burnside Feu'.

Note: Neither Findrack nor Camphill paid Victual Stipend; Burnside
       paid once a year.

       After 1929 stipend was standardised at the county average value
       of grains from 1875–1922 plus 5 per cent; present incumbents could
       opt either for this or to continue – as my father did until 1935 –
       to be paid according to the current annual prices.

local feuars, had to be given from the pulpit three weeks in advance.

Two of the lairds we have already met in the previous chapter.
Dr Farquharson of Finzean was by far the largest landowner, while Mr Wight
had a quite modest estate, part of the Camphill lands being vested, along
with those of Kintocher, in Lord Sempill of Craigievar. I can recall my
father's meeting the latter's aeronaut son, the Master of Sempill, while
visiting in 1932, and coming home with the news that the Graf Zeppelin
would overfly Lumphanan next day. The Smiths of Glenmillan, advocates in
Aberdeen, had been lairds for a century, but the last, R.F. Marshall Smith,
died in April 1914 and the estate was purchased by Peter Cameron, of the
family long-established at Mill O'Campfield, Glassel. Mr Cameron was in
business in Aberdeen and lived at Bieldside. In his younger day a champion
lightweight, he used to come on his bicycle to pay his share of teind-
stipend. On one occasion my father had a letter from him the following day
enclosing half-a-crown with an apology for having paid him short the day
before. (Also a redoubtable cyclist was his sister Agnes who for many years
played the organ at the United Free Church at Lumphanan and gave music
lessons locally, cycling the five miles from Glassel. Sometimes after
piano lessons she left us quite late at night, and her rather unreliable
acetylene lamp had to be lit for the return journey. Once at least it failed
on the way; going through Torphins she spied the policeman but called out
reassuringly 'It's all right, officer, it's only me!' and pedalled on. She
used to inscribe our practice notebooks: 'Speech is silver, silence is
golden'.)

Pitmurchie had been in the hands of the Lamond family, Hary Lamond
having married Margaret Shand, daughter of the Reverend William Shand,
minister at Lumphanan 1772-1826. After Mrs Lamond's death in 1882 it was
sold by her son to an Aberdeen granite merchant James Haddon Bower, whose
son, Colonel George Haddon Bower, was laird in our time. The latter's wife

was a sister of Mary Garden, then with the Chicago Opera Company. One
Sunday morning in the thirties - my father happened to be away - there
was a flurry of excitement when the two sisters came to morning service,
entering the normally vacant Pitmurchie pew. But although the schoolmaster
thoughtfully provided the opera singer with one of the choir's books, we
were not to hear the famous voice, which remained silent throughout the
service.

Ownership of the estate of Auchenhove was in 1913 in the hands of the
last of the Duguid family there, Charles Stephen Leslie Duguid, a Leslie
of Balquhain. The old castle, to the west, was burned down during the '45,
as was the castle of Balquhain in the Garioch. The present mansion house
was the second to be built on the more easterly site near the loch, the
remains of the first being referred to as the 'aul' wa's'. For some years
the estate was to be in the hands of trustees; during the early twenties
it was rented by Lord Lawrence of Kingsgate, a merchant banker, then it was
purchased by Colonel H.J. Kinghorn, owner of a family store in Aberdeen,
his elder son Alastair running the Home Farm.

The Lumphanan part of the estate of Findrack, formerly part of the lands
of the Frasers of Tornaveen, was owned by Mr David M.M. Milligan, advocate in
Aberdeen, son of the Reverend Dr William Milligan, Professor of Biblical
Criticism in the University of Aberdeen. The small estate of Burnside, near
the church and originally containing the village of Lumphanan until the railway station was built half a mile away, was owned by Robert Stuart, who lived
in Aberdeen. The son of the previous laird, he had been born at Lumphanan
where his father Harry was banker. A letter he wrote my father on 28 March
1913 suggests that he wore his heritor's hat with a difference:

> I have to thank you for your letter of 25th inst. with enclosures
> as stated.
>
> Believe me, I am truly sorry that you should have had so much
> trouble with the small mite I was due; and you really should not
> have even thought of sending me the trifling sum I paid for

remitting. The legal ways of doing things are often hard to understand; they wind, and wind, and one has often difficulty in seeing
their weary end. I think you were quite right, under the circumstances, in letting the Dundee limbs o' the law fork for themselves.
Collecting the various items due, I fancy, would have been no joke.
[This presumably referred to payment of rent for land leased by the
previous incumbent from the Burnside estate.]

I have often heard my friend, Miss Jeannie Anderson, late of
Gartly, speak of you. The late Mr. Anderson and his lamented
daughter, Miss Anderson, were my near neighbours here, having lived
in this street. [The Reverend Alex. Anderson was ordained and
inducted to Gartly in Strathbogie in 1858.] Miss Jeannie, who has
been residing at the Manse, Ythan Wells, for sometime, is coming back
to town at Whitsunday, having leased a flat in Forest Avenue. Poor
thing! she has passed through a great deal of sorrow of late and much
anxiety.

Sometime when you are in town of an afternoon with a little leisure,
I shall be very pleased if you will call for me here anytime after
three p.m.

With kind regards, and wishing you a happy, peaceful and successful ministry in the place of my nativity.

Mr Stuart died in 1935, leaving a legacy to the United Free Church. He was

succeeded at Burnside by Mr Mitchell Kemp, farmer at Chirdhillock, Countess-

wells, who came to live in the top house.

Since 1861 when the railway went through, the land on the north side

of it had been physically cut off from the glebe, and was sold to the laird

of Burnside, but part of the Burnside estate had been rented by previous

ministers. To the south, across the public road, were fields which had been

rented from Finzean. There on the flat land, before a steep rise to a wood

of conifers and birch, had once stood the cottage of the minister's man, who

had looked after glebe and cattle. I can recall the former minister of

Deskford, the Reverend George M. Park, then an octogenarian, standing in

the manse garden and pointing out to me the site of his father's house,

directly opposite.

From the day of his induction, the new minister was of course entitled

to take up residence in the manse. In fact it was something like seven

months before the Lumphanan manse was fit to live in; matters more mundane

than Virginia creepers and ivy - let alone tropaeolum roses - had to be

dealt with. On the Thursday following his Induction, 20 February 1913, my father wrote to Mr Cochran:

> After very careful consideration I have decided not to be an offerer for the lands rented by the late Mr. Thorburn. My original intention was to become lessee — not because I desired to work the lands myself but simply in order to keep them attached to the Church, in the interest of my successors in office. However on consideration I do not feel myself called upon to undertake the worry &c. of managing said lands in the interest of a party who more likely than not will look upon them, as I do, as a burden and not as a source of pleasure or profit. I have therefore informed the present sub-tenants Mr. Michie and Mr. Glenesk of my decision.

> Also, I understand that you are Clerk to the Heritors of this Parish. I have been looking over the Manse and offices and find that a good deal of minor repairs will have to be executed on both buildings. So far as I can see these repairs though fairly numerous will not be of a very expensive nature. However I think it will be most satisfactory if you will send out a competent architect who will go over the buildings with me and report to the heritors.

> I shall be from home from Wednesday to Friday of next week but shall be free to meet the architect at the Manse any other day on receiving due notice of his coming. I trust this course will meet with your approval.

As his future brother-in-law was writing from Larbert on 21 February: 'Mollie will be with us tomorrow for a week' it seems likely that that was where my father was going to be from the 26th to the 28th. His letter to Mr Cochran, drafted the previous day, was written from Cairnbeathie, where he was staying; later he moved to lodgings in the village.

Mr Cochran replied on 21 February that he was passing on the request to the heritors; he had no doubt they would be quite agreeable to send their regular architect out to report. He wrote further on 25 February that he had now been instructed to arrange a date with the architect, who had dealt with repairs to the manse etc. before 'and you may be satisfied that he will give matters every attention'. My father accordingly made out a list of what he himself considered required attention, under the heads 'Indisputable', 'Necessary' and 'Sundries'.

The architect in turn wrote to my father on 28 February: '...If quite convenient for you, I propose coming to Lumphanan on Monday week the 10th prox., by the train which arrives there at 1.23. This will enable me to return by the 4.8 train...' The inspection of the premises duly took place, and left my father very much on his guard. He wrote to Mr Cochran on 13 March that he found the architect exceedingly courteous and willing to listen to his suggestions, but was bound to confess that he considered him 'rather too much of what one would call a "Heritors' man"'; it needed at times more pressing than he cared to exercise to get him to admit as "competent" certain improvements that he regarded as obviously necessary. He therefore did not bind himself to accept the architect's report until he had had an opportunity of examining and considering it. 'I do not wish to be unreasonable in my demands. Still I think that the present is a suitable time for the Manse &c. to be put in proper order, and it is apparent to the passer-by that the "amenities" of the place have been somewhat neglected of late'. He hoped, however, that mutual agreement would be amicably arrived at with the heritors.

Mr Cochran agreed that he was not bound in any way without having seen the report: he would call a meeting of the heritors by circular when it came, sending the minister a copy of the latter to read from the pulpit. On 18 March he wrote that he now had the architect's report; at least three weeks' notice was required for a heritors' meeting, so that Thursday 24 April was the earliest suitable date for the architect. He added 'A minister, as you are no doubt aware, has no locus standi at a heritors' Meeting, but, at the same time, I feel sure that the Heritors will wish to make your acquaint-ance, and no doubt will like to have an opportunity of discussing matters with you. I will, therefore, be glad to know whether the date mentioned is one that would suit your convenience'. My father replied next day agreeing the date and asking if he might have the architect's report to study for a day or two before the meeting. Mr Cochran wrote that he was accordingly calling the meeting for 24 April, and was submitting his request in regard to the architect's report to a few of the principal heritors and would write him again.

A copy of the report, dated 15 March 1913, was duly furnished. It was in the form of a letter to Messrs Cochran & Macpherson, and the preamble was as follows:

> As requested in your letter of 25th ult., I visited Lumphanan Manse by appointment with the Rev. F.C. Donald, and made an inspection of the Manse, Offices, Church, &c., with the view of advising the Heritors as to what repairs are necessary to be carried out, together with a probable estimate of the expense of same.
>
> I thought it desirable to note all the Minister's demands along with those items which I considered were really required, and in estimating the cost to show these separately for the information of the Heritors. It will accordingly be noted in the aftermentioned details that the inner column estimates those requirements asked by the Minister, and which in my opinion are not essential, although no doubt several of them may be desirable; while the outer column estimates the repairs and improvements which, in my opinion, are really necessary to be carried out.

The report was in four sections: I Manse, II Offices (i.e. steading, wash-house etc.) III Church, IV Grounds, Glebe etc. That on the manse had 24 paragraphs, 17 consisting of recommendations by the architect, 7 by my father; that on offices 6 by the architect, 2 by my father; that on the church 4 by the one, 3 by the other; that on grounds and glebe six by my father only. Opposite the particulars of work listed were the two columns with estimates of costs, one headed 'Asked by Minister but not really essential', the other 'Considered necessary by Architect'. At the end of each section the estimates were added up, the totals for the four being set out at the end of the report.

At the heritors' meeting at Lumphanan on 24 April (it is not clear who was in the chair) the minister would not have been allowed to speak at all but for the intervention of Mr Cochran. He then confined himself to stating his doubts as to the architect's impartiality, adding that the 'minister's requests' in the report did not include all that he had asked for: these were therefore now the minimum that he could in conscience see his way to accept. (My father was conscious throughout that he had become custodian not of his own interests only but also of those of possible successors and indeed of the church and parish). When the heritors set out to examine the buildings

for themselves, they apparently agreed to certain items not mentioned in
the report - these included, perhaps, the "indisputable" rat hole in the
servant's bedroom - and as a result my father withdrew one or two other small
requests not then urgent. These agreed items were not all, however, added to
the final report. When the heritors reassembled in committee my father expected to be heard again in support of his proposals. In the event most
debatable points were left to a committee which met later in Aberdeen and
to which he was not invited.

The present manse had been rebuilt alongside, and some twenty years
after, the rebuilt church of 1762. It replaced one from which a turf roof
had been replaced by slates in 1747, following some difficulty over rights
of 'feal and divot'. It is possible that some part of the original was left.
Originally the new house was a long straight building of three storeys facing
south; later the top floor was removed in order to heighten the ceilings of
the first floor rooms; those of the ground floor remained low. In 1828 the
eastern part of the south side was built out several yards while west of
this a new two-storey wing with a large high-ceilinged room up and down was
built out further towards the south, leaving at the west end, next the church,
the breadth of a room on each floor. The 'front' door now faced the church
at the angle of the old west part and the new wing, in the shadow of the
high churchyard wall and four feet below grave-level. To the north, a new
two storey wing was built out in 1869 with two smaller rooms and by 1913
including also a water closet and recently installed bath on the ground floor.
The cold water tank was in a small apartment above: there was no hot water
system. It was possibly also in 1869 that the built out east section on the
south side was retracted a little. It appears on an ordnance survey map
showing the new railway line (i.e. post-1861) and what may have been the
foundations of the built-out section as it originally was became apparent
during the pre-1929 Union renovations, although some stones (about 18 inches

by 15) had sloping tops. Having two parallel wings so far out to the south
probably created a damp channel between: as it was, the small cavity left
there remained a rather dank spot.

The house in 1913 had the maximum number of outer walls of rooms facing
east and north; moreover more than half of the south-facing windows were
those of corridors, linen-room, cellar, milk-house and the entrance-lobby
of the 'back' door which itself faced east. The two rooms in the old west
section had west windows facing church and churchyard walls, and south
windows overshadowed by either the latter or the mainly blank wall of the
new south wing. In the new north wing it was the corridor windows that faced
west. There were in all 36 windows, two skylights, 14 chimneys and fifty
yards of corridor. The elegantly curved staircase with its mahogany rail
was opposite the new 'front' door at the west end; a clear window, high in
the stair wall, looked out on to the wall of the cellar. On the landing was
a window of obscured glass, mainly opaque white, with coloured edge; through
small red panes one could peer over the churchyard to the western hills.
Even windows which faced south had to contend with the rising ground and wood
already described, not to mention a number of tall trees immediately in front;
in my father's time thirteen out of eighteen trees in the proximity of the
house were felled, and the tops taken off the copper beech and elm which
still remain as leafy umbrellas. Young trees were later planted. One of
the drawingroom windows bears an interesting memento: sometime in the mid-
nineteenth century young Rachel McCombie must have been sitting there and
with perhaps a knitting-needle scratched her name on a pane. She was to
marry John Duthie of the Aberdeen shipbuilding firm, and died in Colorado
in 1891.

On 16 May 1913 Mr Cochran wrote my father with the heritors' decisions.
They agreed, as regards the manse, to carry out sixteen - all but one - of
the architect's recommendations as they stood. In the case of the seventeenth,

they had bowed to my father's plea on the day of the meeting that the walls
and ceiling of the diningroom be papered instead of 'coloured', paper to be
at 2/6 a piece. None of the seven requests put to the architect at his
first visit had been immediately approved; at times the terminology used
by the latter in the report seemed calculated to discourage approval. For
example, my father was said to have demanded 'Modern grate, hearth, and
chimney-piece for Diningroom in place of existing which are old-fashioned'.
(Cost £15). In the margin my father had pencilled: 'Grate is "done".
Chimney piece shaky'. The heritors agreed to a new grate and to having the
existing chimney piece strengthened. Then again 'Minister desires wallpaper
of staircase and passage changed as he considers present paper unsuitable,
although it is not nearly worn out'. (Cost £12.10). In the margin 'Torn at
stair'. Again the heritors were prepared to 'patch up the broken parts of the
wallpaper on the staircase and in the passages'. 'Minister desires paint on
staircase and passages freshened and made of uniform colour, including the
floor margin'. (Cost £4.10). Marginal comment 'Paint badly blistered'.
This request was turned down.

But the main bone of contention was the bathroom, downstairs at the
extreme and northern end of the house with the tank in the similar position
upstairs The report stated that 'The position of Bathroom is objected to
on ground floor, and the Minister desires it transferred to the Bedroom on
first floor immediately over the servants bedroom, all as after detailed and
estimated, leaving the closet, however, in its present position for the use
of servants. This change would involve considerable alteration [queried in
margin] on the drains, soil pipes &c., also repairs, painting and papering
of the present bathroom, after removal of the fittings, which are estimated
to cost, exclusive of fitting up the new bathroom afterwards noted ...£17.10'.
Marginal note: 'Painting and papering required in any case!' Later, 'Convert
bedroom over servants' bedroom into bathroom, fit up bath from present

bathroom, also closet in apartment at end of passage on first floor.
Provide new lavatory basin; paper walls, whiten ceiling, paint woodwork,
and provide stove in existing fireplace opening ...£17.10'. In the margin
is pencilled the one word 'Frost!' This was enlarged upon later. Then
'Hot water circulation with the cylinder placed in bathroom, including
alterations on cold water supply, and new kitchen range with H.P. Boiler
complete ...£47.10'. Marginal note: 'Range is done and leaking'. The
existing bath, incidentally, had only a cold water supply.

Mr Cochran wrote that in regard to these three items 'the Heritors are
prepared to provide a hot water circulation if you agree to the bathroom
being left where it is. In coming to this resolution, the Heritors had in
view the fact that the present bathroom was fitted up so recently as only
four years ago'.

Two proposals agreed by all provided that the old parlour by the west
'front' door be made the study, and the bedroom above made into the parlour,
both redecorated and with new grates and hearths. The latter was known to
us as the little drawingroom; the big drawingroom was not furnished until
at the time of the handover from heritors to General Trustees it was redecorated
by the former and furnished partly with items from the 'parlour' and partly by
purchases at a roup when the House of Tillyfour changed hands.

The little drawingroom, with its red wallpaper, white paint and green-
tiled hearth, has many comfortable memories. There we had our first piano
lessons by lamplight from Miss Cameron, and I can remember one of her sisters,
Miss Anna, attired in Edwardian white satin, singing to us there 'Jessie's
Dream', that haunting ballad of the Relief of Lucknow. Craig recalls a
professional singer, Jessie Robertson, visiting with Professor and Mrs Duff
Watson, singing at the piano in the little drawing-room. After 1929 it
became a bedroom. The study below with its red-brick hearth and one wall
lined with books could also look comfortable, although the record contains

such items as 'thermometer in study window 46'. Indoors or out, even in the 1950's the long cold winters would be reflected in the single word 'gealed'. (On 5 May 1884, the minister of Echt, whose manse was of similar design, writing on Presbytery business to the minister of Aboyne, concluded: 'I fully intended to be at Torphins at Mr. McGregor's ordination, but I got so ill with cold as to be nearly helpless and altogether useless'). Only in March 1919 was it discovered that at Lumphanan there was neither felt nor roofing paper on the manse roof under the slates, neither was the wood-lining jointed. In parts, my father then told Mr Cochran, the lining had shrunk so far that a pocket knife blade could be put between the boards. 'This openness in the roof would account in part at any rate for the bitter cold in the Manse in winter. I must therefore add to my list of repairs to the Manse a request that the slates be removed and the roof lined with felt as is now always done in barns as well as in dwelling houses'. There was actually at the bottom of the stairs in an alcove an anthracite-burning stove for space-heating; when tried by my father, however, the flue proved faulty, and even at that time it was realised that anthracite fumes were harmful.

But to return to the 1913 list: again, as to the report on the steading, all the architect's proposals were approved. As this section has perhaps more historical significance it may be of interest to quote in detail:

Door between byre and turnip shed, also
improve the lighting [i.e. skylights] and ventilation ...£4:10

Make good the stable trevisses, replace splits awanting
in the mangers, and improve ventilation   ... 2:10

Move wooden partition in open shed, so as to increase
size of poultryhouse, improve the light and lay cement
floor in place of existing earthen floor   ... 9:10

Repair wash-house boiler, make good damaged waste
pipe of tubs, and whiten the walls   ... 3.15

Repair outside wood and iron work, the pointing and harling
where necessary, also overhaul roofs. &c.   ... 7.10
                              [later estimate £17.10]
Paint the outside wood and iron work   5:10

The two requests added by my father were turned down:

> Provide two of the three cartshed openings with doors
> [pencilled in margin: 'gig-shed']   ... 8.10
>
> Change dung-pit from the present position at Steading
> to outwith the North-East corner of Steading   ...13:10

The heritors considered the doors to cart sheds to be not 'in any way necessary' nor did they 'see their way to change the position of the dung-pit, but they are willing to repair, where necessary, the dung court dyke and the causeway to the byre, to supply a spiked gate at the front of the dung court in such manner as (the architect) may advise'. Opening on to the dung-court there were, besides byre and barn doors, those of the 'chaumer' and adjacent dry closet, intended for a man-servant. The former had a fireplace and cement floor, whitewashed walls and a deep-silled large window facing east.

In the 'Church' section the heritors, as well as agreeing to the architect's four suggestions, were prepared to accede to my father's request that the enclosing wall dividing churchyard from manse be lowered about eighteen inches in the section immediately outside the west study window; they declined, however, to make good defects in the pointing. This meant a little more light let into the new study. About 1927-8 there was a similar lowering of a section further south; by then the front door was being moved actually to the front of the house, the former cellar becoming a sunny vestibule. In 1913 the heritors also agreed, reluctantly and 'on the understanding that it form no precedent for the future, - some of them being of the opinion that this was a matter of cleaning which would more properly fall to the Kirk Session to see to' - to expend £3 on whitening the ceiling and colouring the inside walls of the church (which the architect had admitted were 'at present somewhat dirty'.) It does not emerge whether or not 'Heating' as pencilled in by my father was discussed. Heating of the church was by a coal-fired boiler with hot water circulation, approached by ladder down into

what we called the bellman's hole, in a corner of the church. About 1919
there was an explosion there which scalded the bellman, and a new boiler
was installed. In his later years my father, to help the bellman, habitually
lit the furnace, sometimes on the Saturday night in very wintry weather,
normally on Sunday morning. On 22 December 1946 he noted triumphantly
'Furnace to 60°'. This followed some maintenance the previous week by a
local mason; the previous day – Saturday – he had himself worked on the
furnace from noon until 7 p.m.: by 9 p.m. it had reached 50°. The following
Saturday evening, in more intense frost, it took until 9.30p.m. to reach
50° and next morning, having dropped overnight to 43°, 50° remained the
maximum. Sometimes the oil-lamps would be lit early to help take the chill off.

The last section of the architect's report, 'Grounds, Glebe &c.', was
made up entirely of my father's proposals:

Post and wire fence along the sides of Steading road, and re-hang iron gate at entrance	...£9
Split fence to connect the above fence with Manse, so as to divide the Steading from the Manse, provided with suitable gate for access	... 4:10
Dwarf split fence by the path round Manse to Church entrance	... 8:10
Repair defects in the drystone walls of Glebe using lime for binding the stones at gates	... 3:10
Fence along the sides of back approach	... 7:10
Gravel the walks, yards, &c.	... 1.10

My father had pencilled in 'Draining of Glebe' but again this is not
mentioned at this time: it was not one of the heritors' statutory responsibilities. This applied also to maintenance of boundary walls, once provided;
my father's contention was that if these had been neglected by previous
incumbents it was as if, as far as he was concerned, they had not been provided. Oddly enough, heritors were bound to maintain garden walls: a substantial one encircled the manse garden.

The heritors considered that, 'apart from the Churchyard and garden, their obligations in regard to fencing do not extend at the most beyond any necessary fencing to the approach to the Church. In that view, they are prepared to rehang the gate at the entrance of the main approach from the public road, and renew the fencing along the East side of the main approach as far as the steading, but not beyond it, but not the fencing on the West side, seeing there is already a hedge there, nor any other fencing'. They would have nothing to do with the drystone walls of the glebe, nor with the gravel. Mr Cochran concluded his letter 'I have got the Heritors' instructions to ask (the architect) at once to carry out the above proposals, subject to your approval. These proposals cover all that the Heritors are legally bound to do, and probably considerably more, and I trust that they will meet with your approval, and that we may have the works proceeded with at once. I will be pleased to hear from you at your early convenience'.

My father replied to Mr Cochran on 19 May, reluctantly declining to accept what the heritors offered. He had taken counsel with an authority on Church law who advised him that a minister had no right to be involved in a personal dispute about repairs with heritors or with a committee of heritors: any dispute must properly be transferred to the Bar of the Presbytery. He told Mr Cochran, therefore, that he was placing the whole matter in the hands of the Presbytery, although no meeting could now be held until after the General Assembly. My father had, not unnaturally, already been consulting some of his more experienced fellow-presbyters, one or two of whom had not hesitated to suggest other more costly improvements. He himself did not expect dealings with heritors to wear the nature of horse-trading. Mr Cochran's letter of 20 May rather indicated that some further approach by the minister direct to the heritors would have been expected. In a further letter of 28 May Mr Cochran feared that because the matter had been referred to the Presbytery it would be out of place for him in his official capacity to offer advice, at the same time 'should you care to have a talk I will be glad to see you at any time'. He added 'You spoke of Manse Maill at Lumphanan after the Heritors' Meeting. I think it right to say that the Heritors consider that no such question can arise, the Manse being quite habitable in its present state'. Manse Maill was an allowance payable by heritors to a minister when a manse was not fit to live in. My father had mentioned to Mr Cochran that he might shortly have to leave Cairnbeathie and find other more costly lodgings in the village.

The following weekend he had arranged to exchange pulpits with the then Moderator of Presbytery, the minister at Braemar; this would give Mr Saunders an opportunity to inspect the manse before a meeting of Presbytery was called. On the Friday forenoon my father went into town in the hope of seeing Mr Cochran, but was disappointed. (It was not then possible to telephone from Lumphanan, although telegrams could be sent.) He did, however, manage to see the senior partner in the firm of architects; the latter had been at the Lumphanan heritors' meeting. From him he learned that on that occasion the heritors had not heard him say that what was entered in the architect's report as 'minister's requests' was the minimum that he could see his way to accept. Relating this to Mr Cochran on Tuesday 3 June, my father wrote 'I was under the impression that I did make that statement at the meeting here, but as I was a little nervous then and as I was very much put about by the reception I received when I stood up to make my explanation I may not have said just exactly what I intended to say. Still I fail to see what else I could have said on that occasion as the one argument I wished to make plain was that seeing so much required to be done to the Manse I had asked only what I considered to be absolutely necessary, and there seems to me now to have been no point in my saying anything else'.

To the end of his days, and after long experience of actual horse-trading, my father entertained a firm preference for sheep-men. Now he prepared to give the heritors another chance, and the rest of his letter of 3 June 1913 was a detailed commentary on their decisions regarding the architect's report, which he asked Mr Cochran to lay before them. He agreed to accept the amended proposals for the diningroom. Next came the vexed questions of bath, bathroom, hot water supply and kitchen range:

(1) The Bath as it at present stands is practically speaking inaccessible from the Bedrooms. It is 36 yards plus the stairway distant from the door of the best bedroom and almost as far from every other bedroom. On a journey thither the intending bather has to pass every door in the house except the outside kitchen door.

(2) There is no room in the present bathroom for a lavatory basin, and I consider that a basin is the most important article in a bathroom. In present day terminology a "bathroom" is invariably meant to include a basin.

(3) Suppose a Hot Water Circulation is to be introduced to the present bath, there is no room in the present bathroom for a storage Hot Water cylinder. That cylinder would have to be placed in the kitchen. Now a kitchen is usually warm enough without the addition of a tank of boiling water in the corner.

Also, the cold water cistern would remain where it is at present in the small apartment containing the W.C. immediately above the present bathroom. There it hangs within three feet of a large north window immediately above the burn. A more unsuitable place for it could not have been found in the house. It is just in the very place for the water to get frozen. In winter it would be necessary to burn a very powerful lamp there day and night to prevent the water freezing. Suppose that lamp went out or suppose someone neglected to place it there then one night's frost with a burst pipe or two would do as much damage to paper and paint as would cover the cost of transferring the whole plant according to my plan.

What I propose is to have the bathroom fitted up upstairs. Then the bath can be placed in one corner of the room, a basin in another, the H.W. cylinder in a third while if the cold water cistern were fitted up immediately over the latter, the hot air from the cylinder which in the kitchen would be a nuisance would here be used to good purpose in raising the temperature of the cold cistern and thus would absolutely prevent freezing. Further, if the present W.C.s be left where they are at present with their syphons supplied by one pipe from the mains as now downstairs there could be a stop cock introduced into the pipe with a tap immediately above it for running off all water during the night in times of severe frost. In this way the danger of pipes bursting and destroying paper and paint would be reduced to a minimum.

The expense of fitting up a bathroom properly equipped upstairs as I have suggested would in my opinion be at most from £10 to £15 more than that of introducing Hot water to the bath as it stands...

Besides, there is in the house no housemaid's pantry i.e. place to store carpet sweepers, brooms, dustpans &c. The place where the bath now stands would in my opinion be very suitable for that purpose.

Then as to the stairway and passage wallpaper:

I may say that there are at least 9 or 10 different parts torn
apart from the stair which is torn all up and down. Patching in
such conspicuous places I could not agree to. Besides the paper
is not suitable for a hall and passage paper. What such parts of
the house require is a suitable sanitary paper which can be made
new at any time by being simply washed down with a damp cloth.

Regarding the paintwork on stair and passages:

The heritors surely had not examined the painted parts very closely
else they would have seen this... The stair is blistered with the
paint peeling off from top to bottom, and all along the door posts
and skirting boards the paint is chipped and broken. Besides the
following is the colour scheme. The doors are stained "pine". The
door posts are enamelled white. The skirting boards are black and
the passage and stair margins light brown, while the wallpaper is
green on a yellow background. I do not profess to have an artist's
eye, but it makes my flesh creep every time I look at the place.

He then repeated a plea to have the obscured glass window on the landing

replaced by one of clear glass which would open. 'I am told on all hands

and I can believe it true that the house is inclined to be damp, therefore

it seems only reasonable to have a window which will open in the only place

where all these long passages can have more than a passing blink of the sun...'

The inner hall door, too, was giving trouble. The architect had recommended

oil but 'I fear something more will have to be done to it as I have oiled it

liberally and it behaves as badly as ever. Also - there was no mention in

the committee's decision of the kitchen sink: the report left it in the

kitchen [but a porcelain in place of an iron one] but he now found that the

more suitable place for it would be in the scullery. It seems that he meant

'pantry' which under the proposed scheme would be under the new bathroom; it

was near the kitchen and was to have shelves for dishes. In fact, the porce-

lain sink remained in the kitchen until 1928 when a new lath and plaster

dividing wall with sliding door created a scullery off the kitchen. There

were installed a new sink and two porcelain tubs with teak draining boards,

and adjacent china pantry. Further sub-division of the kitchen then provided

two more shelved cupboards (one for cleaning materials) and the cement floor

was replaced by a not entirely satisfactory composition one. In fact, prior

to the 1929 'Union' handover, a number of my father's 1913 ideas were carried

out (and carried further) without question, and much else besides was granted:
this on a property which the powers that were taking over regarded as 'not
worth spending money on'. There was, of course, a different architect involved.

As to 'offices' in 1913, my father still thought that it would have been
just as cheap and much more satisfactory to have removed the dung-pit altogether, but if the proposed improvements were carried out he would agree to leave
it where it was. He reserved the right to object to it as insanitary if
at any time he might require to use the man's sleeping house. (The dung-pit
was in our time regularly cleared for garden manure, and once completely
removed, after the heritors had handed over, when a neighbouring family were
temporarily housed in the chaumer and their household effects in the barn
while their thatched cottar-house was being re-roofed and modernised. No
manservant was ever accommodated there - nor were our wartime evacuees, as
some thought!) On the provision of a door for the gig shed he remained
adamant: 'A gig shed is surely regarded as an absolute necessity to a country
minister. I cannot consent to withdraw the claim for doors to be hung on the
present opening for the purpose of making it a gig shed. I may say that that
opening had at one time been provided with doors. At least there remain very
clear traces of hinges and door fastenings'.

Next as to Grounds, Glebe &c. It had been said that the front entrance
needed no west fence as there was a hedge there. 'I may say that the present
hedge is no protection. Like everything else it has been neglected and is
full of gaps. Sheep come wandering through it and destroy my rhododendrons
every time they pass along the public road. To make it a very pretty and
useful hedge will take 5 to 6 years. In the meantime it must be cut down level
with the ground. Therefore a fence there will be necessary till the hedge
grows. Then 5 or 6 years hence that fence could be removed and erected at the
back approach to the Church. The fence there is pretty shaky even now but may
hang together for that time'. Then as to the split fence requested between

steading and manse: 'I may say that I have already had on several occasions
to chase away passing cattle from my front door. The whole house is open
to the four winds and has not even the appearance of privacy. Therefore a
fence such as I suggested from the end of the hedge to the kitchen door,
10 yards, is 'surely a necessity'. He agreed that a dwarf split fence from
the back door round to the church entrance was not so necessary, although
desirable. 'The church goers I may say pass close past the kitchen and
bedroom windows and do not all refrain from looking in. However the purpose
of the fence proposed might be served by erecting a single rail with posts...
a small gate between the manse and churchyard wall at the NW corner of the
manse however would be necessary'. As regards the fences, he wrote: 'I
showed the estimates to a practical fencer who simply laughed at them. He
offered to take the whole contract at half the estimate given and assured
me that he would not lose by the transaction. Therefore if the heritors
could see their way to allow me £10 in lieu of all fences and gates required
I think I could erect same to their satisfaction. Any extra expense incurred
I would pay myself'. One gets the impression that the estimates for
'minister's requests' tended towards exaggeration.

He pointed out also that the gate at the public road west entrance to
the church had fallen to pieces: this led through the glebe by what we knew
as the 'green road' to an iron gate and flight of steps through the churchyard
to the west door of the church, and was a right of way for pedestrians
approaching from the west side. 'A new gate with a wicket for church goers
there is sorely needed'. A gate, too, at the public road end of the back
(north) entrance would be a great convenience. 'Now that an auction mart
has been started in the village there are many cattle being driven along that
road and as I said already I have had more than once to drive stirks away
from the front door'. He believed too that it fell to the heritors to provide
a glebe boundary fence. 'The enclosing fence here is a dry stone dyke which

has fallen in parts into slight disrepair. If this dyke were put in order

I should undertake to keep it up from year to year during my incumbency

but I do not see that I should be called upon to repair the neglect of

former ministers'. (The architect had estimated the cost of this at £3.10).

He now offered to do without the gravel for walks and yards.

My father concluded his letter:

> I am very sorry to have to worry the heritors with all this long
> list of repairs &c. but I can assure you that it is no less worry
> to me and on the whole I think it would be much more satisfactory
> to have the place put in proper order now. It would save much trouble
> on both sides in future [the wisdom of this became apparent when manses
> and churches had to be handed over from the heritors to the General
> Trustees 'in a tenantable state of repair' in 1929. See Note.] and I
> can honestly say that all that I have asked for seems to me to be
> necessary and reasonable. I shall have a good deal of trouble and
> expense in getting garden and grounds seen to and put into a present-
> able condition and if I make a permanent improvement in that direction
> as I hope to do I think it is only fair that the heritors should help
> me with the Manse.

> As to Maill I may say that in consideration of the heritors having
> to expend so much on improvements I had not intended to raise the
> question of Maill unless driven to do so. However I may point out
> that water is still running through the kitchen grate, and during the
> last heavy rain water came freely through the south wall and lay in a
> pool in the kitchen passage, that being so and other things as they
> are I consider that the house cannot be said to be habitable and that
> therefore in law I am entitled to Manse Maill. Whether I claim it or
> not depends entirely on the attitude which the heritors take towards
> me...

> I shall certainly prefer to come to terms with the heritors directly
> but I feel so strongly that I have been very moderate in my requests
> that I shall have no hesitation whatever in placing the whole matter
> in the hands of the Presbytery if I find it necessary to do so.

Mr Cochran acknowledged this communication on 6 June and undertook to

submit it to the heritors' committee. He added that, their proposals having

earlier been declined, they were no longer in any way committed to them.

Note: After the Union of 1929 the heritors, under the Church of Scotland
       (Property and Endowments) Act, 1925, transferred to the General Trustees
       all existing rights of church and manse property and all powers and
       duties with respect to their maintenance and repair. In cases where
       such property was considered by the Trustees not to be in 'a reasonable
       state of tenantable repair' the heritors were obliged either to under-
       take such repair or to pay over to the Trustees an agreed sum in lieu.
       Responsibility for churchyards was transferred to Parish Councils.
       This Act provided also for the heritors' surrender of teinds, stipend
       to be payable thereafter from Church headquarters.

'While this is the official aspect of the matter, I may be allowed personally to express the hope that we may come to a settlement, although I fear, notwithstanding, that your requirements are beyond what the Heritors will feel themselves justified in falling in with'.

After a further meeting of the committee Mr Cochran wrote on 20 June itemising their decisions. First, however, he mentioned that the architect's inspector, along with a slater would be at the manse 'on Monday forenoon for ascertaining the cause of your complaint about the water coming through the kitchen grate and through the South wall of the Manse'. The committee were now prepared to recommend the heritors to meet my father's requests regarding the bathroom, hot water supply and new kitchen range, also repainting of woodwork on stair and passages, but not repapering of the latter, nor alteration to the landing window. They would advise the heritors to agree to supply one door to a cart shed to enable it to be used as a gig shed, 'on the understanding that you undertake to arrange with the parishioners to give them sufficient accommodation otherwise on Sundays. The reason for this proviso is that the Heritors understand that this cartshed is in the way of being used by the parishioners for their traps during service'. (Horses were unyoked and put into what we called the big stable next door in the close.) The committee were also to recommend that the heritors accept the minister's offer 'to erect the whole fencing and gates asked for by you for the sum of £10, on the understanding that you complete the work to [the architect's] satisfaction, and that when completed, the fencing and gates, etc., belong to the Heritors. The fencing to be put up by you would include the fencing and gates noted under the Items referred to, and in particular the fencing along the west side of the main approach to the Church in substitution for the hedge which you say is done'. They still firmly declined to have anything to do with the dry stone walls of the glebe.

As to the additional items mentioned in my father's letter of 3 June,

they advised the heritors to have the matter of the inner hall door put
right and had instructed Mr Cochran to get the architect's estimate for
moving the sink from kitchen to scullery. They would also submit the
request 'in regard to the gate at the North-west corner of the Churchyard'.
(This was misunderstood: all that this iron gate required was a knob; my
father was talking about the gate from the public road into the field.)
The clerk's letter ended: 'I think the Committee in coming to this decision
are now willing to meet you on all the main points of difference, including,
as you will see, the removal of the bath to the upstairs room. In doing so,
however, they consider the Heritors would be going considerably beyond their
legal obligations, 'and, that being so, they feel that it is necessary the
proposals be approved by the Heritors at a Meeting properly called. Meantime,
however, it will facilitate matters if you will kindly let me know whether
or not you would be prepared to come to an agreement on the above lines. In
the event of your not agreeing to these terms, then it is understood that
the offers already made are withdrawn'.

My father replied to this letter, which he would have received on Saturday
21 June, on the following Thursday. He apologised for the delay but gave no
reason; he was probably consulting with his future wife, either at Larbert
or at Montrose whither she had been transferred from Laurencekirk some years
earlier. He wrote from the lodgings in the village to which he had moved:
Albert Cottage was a pleasant villa owned by Miss Mary Laing and adapted to
enable her to sublet the upstairs floor to summer visitors. With her lived
one of her three brothers; of the other two one was a crofter and one a
shepherd, the latter, Alick, becoming a flockmaster and later residing with
his sister. Known locally as 'the Provost' because of his substantial figure,
he may well have had some influence on my father's decision to start keeping
sheep.

'I am very pleased to find that the Committee have seen their way to meet

me so far', my father wrote. 'I cannot altogether agree with you when you
say that in offering what they have the committee have gone beyond the
Heritors' legal obligations. I recognise however that, now, the Committee
are showing themselves willing to meet these obligations in a generous spirit.
Therefore, I think, it will now be possible for us to come to an agreement'.
As earnest of his willingness to cooperate, he offered to supply a suitable
paper for stair and passages if the heritors would undertake to put it on.
(The 'recent spates' had resulted in further damage from damp coming through
the wall from broken spouts.) Regarding the gig shed, he wrote that the present
one had been used by parishioners simply because it happened to be empty.
'I have never seen at any church sheds provided for gigs. Parish stables
are common. But both at kirk and market so far as I have ever seen gigs are
left in the open, unless there happen to be some shed unused and handy. I
shall however be quite willing to allow parishioners to use whatever accommodation can be spared for protecting their gigs but I cannot bind myself to
provide a substitute for the present shed'. One of the other two open sheds
was presently to house the minister's cart; the other was the only suitable
cover for firewood. It did once shelter the apparatus of an itinerant grinder.
Nearly forty years later, when the minister's daughter-housekeeper acquired a
car, a meeting of Kirk Session <u>ad</u> <u>hoc</u> after a morning service agreed to covering in the cart shed, and by Monday the joiner was on the spot taking measurements. The car still required some protection from resident swallows.

My father restated, in case of mistake, the terms of his offer regarding
fences and gates, making clear that this did not include fencing on either
side of the north approach to the church from the Burnside road: this had
been withdrawn at the heritors' meeting on 24 April. He was pleased that the
committee were to recommend acceptance. 'I may say', he added, 'with regard
to these gates and fences that last Monday forenoon I had to turn away three
separate droves of cattle from the front door of the Manse within half an

hour'. Monday was mart day at Lumphanan. In the event he himself made and erected the split fence with diamond-shaped heads from the top end of the hedge to the manse wall beside the back door, including a wicket gate. This fence was moved eastward and double gates added when the new front entrance was built pre-1929. He once astonished my mother by going out at the back door and taking a running sideways leap over it, saying afterwards 'If only I'd had these boots on yesterday I'd have beaten Alex Reid at the school picnic'.

The hedge west of the main front entrance was to be cut down right to the ground; although for long there were a number of blanks, it was remarkable how this drastic action produced eventually an effective barrier and pleasant feature. My brother remembers when it was only two to three feet tall. As to the glebe walls, my father continued in the above letter 'as the Heritors consider that this ring dyke does not belong to them, I presume that if they do not see their way to recommend the repairing of it, they will not object to my selling a part of the tumble-down portion to the Road Authorities for road metal to cover the expense of repairing the remainder of the dyke and of erecting what gates are necessary'.

After pointing out their error concerning the west churchyard approach gate he recapitulated the points still at issue, now reduced to five and including 'some loads of gravel for the area in front of the manse'. 'I have offered to bear part of the cost of No.1 (papering). The other four items are obviously necessary. But for the sake of a speedy settlement I shall offer further to renounce all claims for Manse Maill if the Heritors agree to do these five items'. If the heritors sanctioned the committee's main recommendations he would then give his consent to the work being proceeded with at once and renounce his claim to Manse Maill if there were likelihood of the manse being ready for occupation by the end of August at the very latest. The delay in receiving or answering Mr Cochran's letter meant there was little time left before Sunday to call a meeting of heritors. 'If you can, however, fix a date for

a meeting and send me an intimation to be read on Sunday I shall be much
obliged as I should like to get the Manse made ready as soon as possible
now'. He was obviously anxious to fix the date of his wedding while equally
determined to have the manse made as habitable as possible before bringing
his bride home.

Mr Cochran wrote next day that the earliest date possible for the
meeting would be in the week commencing 27 July: would 29 July suit him
should the heritors wish to see him to discuss matters? He added 'In regard
to your proposal about the Glebe dyke, I do not fancy the Heritors will consider they have any right to give you permission to remove a part of it, and,
on the other hand, I do not think you have any right to remove it yourself'.

On 30 July 1913 Mr Cochran wrote to the architect: 'The Heritors at a
meeting yesterday at Lumphanan came to an agreement with the Minister as to
the works to be carried out, it being understood that they should be put in
hand without delay. The Minister's desire was that they should be completed
by the middle of September, but it was explained to him that this might not
be possible, but you will, no doubt, do your best to meet his wishes'. There
was now, in fact, a fairly comprehensive list of works to be done, those the
architect had originally recommended and most of what my father had requested.

The main item the heritors still refused to tackle was the glebe dyke:
this came up again in 1918, along with the fencing on either side of the north
approach to the church. A new gate and new stile bars at the public road at
the old approach on the west side of the churchyard were promised under the
1913 agreement, and the walks, yards &c. were to be gravelled. A copy of Mr
Cochran's letter to the architect was sent to my father on 31 July, with the
addition of the points accepted as at 20 June. The clerk added 'It is also
understood that, in view of immediate instructions having been given for the
works to be carried out, you waive any claim which you might otherwise have
put forward - but which, of course, the Heritors have never in any way entertained

- for Manse Maill'. The last sentence indicated the more relaxed relations now obtaining: 'I think you were also to send me a Memo. of the small items which you mentioned on Tuesday for the first time, but possibly you may prefer to state them direct to (the architect). If that is so, it is all the same to me'.

In acknowledging this letter and copy of the letter to the architect on 1 August my father noticed only two slight omissions — alterations on the latter's report agreed at the April meeting — one regarding refreshening the paint in the small bedroom between the new parlour and new bathroom, the other concerning wood-lining the walls at the back of both church entrance doors. As regards Maill, 'I think that my offer to waive claim for Maill was to be on condition that instructions for a commencement be issued at once. For a reasonable time I suggested six weeks but as it seems to be difficult to tie down workmen to a definite date I am quite willing to allow for any necessary delay, but I should certainly like to get entry by the end of September at the very latest as being in rooms I find is inconvenient for myself, and seriously interferes with the efficiency of my work'.

On the same day the architect wrote my father that having now received instructions from Messrs Cochran & Macpherson to procure estimates for the improvements agreed on by the Heritors, 'In order that no time may be lost in connection with the matter, I am arranging to meet Contractors at the Manse on the forenoon of Monday first [4 August] at 11.30. I trust it will be convenient for you to attend as there will be some points in regard to which we shall require to consult with each other'.

Mr Cochran wrote on 2 August confirming both the two items of work mentioned by my father and his contention about Manse Maill. He was asking the architect to hurry on the Manse work in preference to the rest 'which, I suppose, is what you would wish'. This 'full and correct' statement of the agreement entered into with the heritors at the meeting on 29 July was acknow-ledged by my father on 5 August. The architect had been at the manse the day

before to meet contractors; he had pointed out to him several of the
additional items which he had mentioned: 'These he noted for submission
to your sub-committee. Other minor items will no doubt crop up in course
which [the architect] says will be duly dealt with by him'. The latter had
promised to have the works carried out as fast as possible 'so that now
everything seems to be going smoothly'.

On 8 August the architect wrote that he had that day accepted the offers
of contractors and asked them to arrange to get the work put in hand at once.
They were:

> Mason Work - P.R. Leslie, Torphins
> Carpenter Work - W.G. McRobbie, Lumphanan
> Slater Work - Edward Waldie, Banchory
> Plumber Work - William Reid, Banchory
> Painter Work - John Mason & Son, Aberdeen

The letter ended: 'I shall be glad if you can come to Aberdeen any day next
week for the purpose of selecting the wall papers and the grates. The forenoon of Wednesday or Friday would suit me best'.

The notice read from the pulpit calling the meeting of heritors for
29 July 1913 had included, as second item on the agenda, 'To receive Report
by said Committee as to the liability as between the Real Rent and the Old
Valued Rent Heritors for works at the Church and Manse &c.' The third item
was 'To transact any other business competent to be considered by the Meeting,
including the imposition of an assessment if so resolved'. It was in fact
resolved at the meeting to levy an assessment in the parish according to the
Real Rent and the Old Valued Rent. This emerges from a formal letter of 28
August 1914 (sic) from the Clerk to the Heritors, Mr Cochran, to my father
as Session Clerk. It continued:

> The works in respect of which the assessment was to be made having
> been completed, I have now made out the Account which amounts to
> £478:1:9, of which £444:14:2 is payable by the Real Rent Heritors and
> I make this intimation to you as Clerk to the Kirk Session in terms
> of Sec.II of the Ecclesiastical Assessments (Scotland) Act 1900.

> I have also to point out that Sec.III(2) of the above mentioned
> Act is in the following terms:- "The rental on which each Heritor

shall be assessed shall be his total rental within such Parish as appearing in the Valuation Roll (whether such rental consists of one or more subjects) but subject to the deduction of the sum of £50 when the amount of the deficiency which would be created in the total amount of the assessment by allowing such deduction to every Heritor has been paid to the Collector of the assessment by the Kirk Session". You will thus see it is optional to the Kirk Session to pay a proportion of the assessment, and I have prepared and send you herewith Copy of a Scheme of Allocation among the Real Rent Heritors of the £444:14:2 to be assessed for, from which you will see that the proportion of the assessment to be contributed by the Kirk Session would, if so resolved, be £74:16:11. I will be glad to hear from you as early as you possibly can whether or not the Kirk Session are to make this payment   I think it right to point out that Sec.III of the said Act contains the following further provision "provided always that no Heritor who by reason of any exemption or deduction allowed by this Section is relieved altogether from assessment in respect of the execution of any work shall be entitled at any Meeting of Heritors to take part in the discussion of or to vote upon any question concerning any plans for or the execution of the said work or the defraying of the expenses of the same".

Over twenty of the Old Valued Rent heritors or 'feuars' were private individuals who owned business premises and/or their own dwellings or additional houses, whose 'real rent' according to the Valuation Roll ranged from £76 downwards. At £1 was 'James Emslie, Labourer' (of whom more anon) who had a tumble-down stone cottage in the wood opposite the manse, due to pay 1s.5d. towards the assessment unless this were paid by the Kirk Session. Even lower stood a lady against whom no rental at all was hazarded, nor any assessment levied; she later disappeared from the list into more comfortable rented accommodation.

Other Old Valued Rent heritors were the Deeside District Committee of the Aberdeen County Council (Waterworks and Sewers), the Great North of Scotland Railway Company (Houses, Ground and Deeside Railway Extension), Lumphanan School Board (School and Schoolhouse &c.), the Parish Council óf Lumphanan (Poorshouse at Knowehead, Parish Hall and house, and Burial Grounds), James Duguid, Sub-Postmaster (Houses, Offices and Yards, Oldbank), Aberdeen Commercial Co. Ltd., Aberdeen Lime Co. Ltd., Northern Agricultural Co. Ltd., all three having Stores at Lumphanan Railway Station, Alex. Middleton & Sons Ltd., (Auction Mart), North of Scotland & Town and County Bank Ltd. (Bank

offices and House), the Parish Minister himself and the Trustees of the
United Free Church, the former on account of 'Glebe, Manse & Offices &
Steading' real rent £32.8, the latter for 'Church Hall, United Free Church,
Manse, Offices & Garden', real rent £71. These two were however granted
exemption under the Ecclesiastical Assessment, Scotland, Act of 1900.

It is not proposed to pursue the matter of payment of the various assess-
ments except to note that the solicitors of the Great North of Scotland Railway (formerly the Deeside Railway) chose to revive an earlier (contested)
claim that they were entitled to relief from the Presbytery as Superiors of
their ground from payment of a proportion of their share. Their contention
was that they paid a feu-duty of £8 per annum to the minister in respect of
a clause in the 1859 Feu Disposition in the Deeside Company's favour by the
former Superior Mrs Margaret Lamond of Pitmurchie which freed them from all
further parochial burdens. The Heritors' legal advisers — and the Presbytery
of Kincardine O'Neil — considered this claim to be ill-founded. The £8
feu-duty (which was part of the minister's stipend and which the Railway now
proposed to withhold until their claim was settled) resulted from the invest-
ment arranged by the Rev. M.C. Thorburn in 1885/6, and approved by the Court
of Teinds, of £200 realised from the sale to Mr Harry Stuart, father of Robert,
of the part of the Glebe across the railway and surrounded by the Burnside
lands of the latter. The feu was then purchased from Mr Stuart. In the end
the Railway lost its case and continued to be assessed as before.

The wedding was now fixed for 4 October 1913, and it was a question of
getting a minimum of furniture to be going on with. My mother wrote on
9 September: 'Once I saw the place I would be able to say what was wanted at
moment and what could be done without... It is not the struggle I mind a bit ...
It isn't just money that makes one happy at home', adding cheerfully 'If we
can't afford sofa for a wee bit we can share basket chair as we have done
before — Eh?' She was glad he was pleased with the 'red room' so far. What

is paint? ... Oh! I see parlour has white paint. - Carpet not too much of
any colour would be best. Wallpaper would be changed long before carpet...
The bedroom next must be very nice indeed, I think. [There was a communicat-
ing door between it and the parlour; I can only think of it with frost
flowers on the window-panes.] And the one over kitchen is all right too.
That is good... I fear towels are the most suitable things for the bathroom
press - clean towels I mean. Anything damp would not do. Where is the rail
for damp towels to dry now?...' From this letter it emerges that my father
was already keeping bees and taking off his first honey crop. His first
nucleus came I think from Alex Reid, merchant. There were always wild bees
under the roof, as at the manse of Glengairn. A last-minute meeting for
shopping in Aberdeen was arranged for Saturday 13 September before my mother
left Montrose for Larbert to fulfil the 15-days residence qualification.
Her sister Ann had wanted her to come to Glasgow that day, probably to choose
the traditional bridesmaid's gift of a china teaset.

The wedding took place at the Alexandra Hotel in Glasgow. Among the
telegrams received was one from Lumphanan Kirk Session, and later my mother
received a large silver tray inscribed: 'Presented to Mrs. Donald along with
[silver] tea set and kettle on the occasion of her marriage by the Congregation
of Lumphanan Parish Church. Oct. 4th.1913'. This, and the bridesmaid's
Foley china teaset, of an unusual vertical rose pattern, are still in the
family. And still in use is the parlour carpet 'not too much of any colour'.

CHAPTER THREE

_____

His people, and the sheep of his pasture

The parishioners, present, past and historical; parish
history: economic, social and medical.

Chapter 3

'Going among the people': my father lost no time after his induction in 1913
in beginning his rounds of the parish, and maintained thereafter a systematic
visiting schedule. As parish minister, he was of course responsible for
everyone within the ecclesiastical boundaries, whether communicant members
or not. To the end of his long life, which included twenty years of retirement, his care of his parishioners never really stopped. Many of these, and
their descendants, were by that time living, as he later was, outwith the
parish, and it seemed natural to maintain the link. This was something very
much in tune with the character of Lumphanan itself; in a parish where the
same names, of people and of places, recur for centuries, although there was
a good deal of movement within this framework, continuity mattered a great
deal. At the same time newcomers were made welcome. My father once reported
a conversation he had had with the mother of two sons — call them James and
John — one of whom had just taken a farm in Lumphanan and the other a place
in another county where the average holding was larger. Said the mother,
visiting the new Lumphanan farm: 'James got a very different reception here
frae John in his new place. Here James wisna mony days sattlet fin the
neebors cam' drappin' in aboot, ane aifter anither, a' speirin' fit they cu'd
dee t' help him on wi' his wark on the lan', that wi' the flittin' an' things
hid fa'en a bittie ahin' for the time o' the year. Whereas wi' John, nae a
craitur' cam' near him 'cep' a man that aince hid a ferm hereaboot, an' the
minister'.

Mr Thorburn's widow had been right when she wrote: 'The Lumphanan folk
are warmhearted and kindly'. My father found, too, that some of the most
genuine neighbourliness was practised by parishioners not noted for regular
church attendance. At a distance of forty years one may perhaps quote (as my
father never did, to my knowledge) the case of the young artisan-crofter who
died and was buried one wintry day leaving a widow and young family and the

three fields unploughed. My father was confident that at least there would be no difficulty about the latter, and he was not disappointed. Two farmers, regular church attenders, elders respectively of the parish church and of the U.F., readily responded in the vein 'We're just about finished ourselves: I'll get the man to go over with a pair as soon as we're done'. The third, working singlehanded a more remote holding and in consequence seldom seen in public, was more than ready to help: 'I'm not begun our own yet so I'll just take the pair over tomorrow and do the widow's first'.

As had been his custom when assistant at Huntly, the new minister kept a small notebook in which he entered the address of each home with a list not only of its occupants but also of absent members of the family. The latter might be employed quite nearby or might be very far away indeed: the drift across the Atlantic or to the Antipodes was still prevalent. Some went abroad to settle, others worked for a time and returned. The records of the Loanend Mutual Improvement Society which flourished in the West Side of Lumphanan in the 1890's show that three members read papers on their experiences in North or South America. That of James Gordon, Loanend Farm, recalling his period of work on the Canadian Pacific Railway in the late 1880's after completion of the main line, has been deposited in the Public Archives of Canada, having been found among his papers after his death in 1947. This trend was obviously regarded as nothing very unusual, and no hint of a romantic if laborious past hung over the Jimmy Gordon we knew, driving in to the village with his small green-painted cart and chestnut pony, or seated in his pew on Sundays, his wife with him in sober black. I recall as a very small child, accompanying my parents to Loanend with pony and trap, rather taking exception to Mrs Gordon's addressing our beloved pony Dandy in what I thought a disparaging tone: 'You're just a petted thing!' (patting the pony's neck and slipping her a peppermint). James Gordon's gravestone in the Craigton cemetery records his being of the third generation of the family at Loanend. The first and second are interred in the old churchyard at the Loch of Aboyne.

There was a tale - probably not apocryphal - about a Lumphanan man who emigrated to New Zealand and on disembarking ran into another Lumphanan man strolling along the quay. In 1964 I had a letter from a Montreal businessman who the previous day had given a cousin of ours a lift from St James Street, the main banking sector of the city, up to the residential area on the mountain. Both were interested in some historical work I was doing and my name came up in conversation. Whereupon the chauffeur 'begged to inquire whether this was the same lady whose father was a Presbyterian minister and who lived for a long time at Lumphanan, Aberdeenshire ... she had a brother named Craig'. Eight years earlier, and two years after his retirement, my father had indeed had a long letter from the wife of the chauffeur, Hardy R. Grubb. The latter who with his brother James had been in the Shanghai Police, had been offered his job by the Canadian when the latter was on a fishing holiday on Deeside, and his wife's letter, giving a vivid account of life - including church life - in Franco-Scottish Montreal, was in acknowledgement of my father's circular Christmas letter to former parishioners. Hardy's mother Jessie, Mrs James Grubb, formerly of Wardhead, was one of a score of individuals (as distinct from families of the same name and relatives) who had contributed to the 'testimonial' to my father on his induction in 1913 and also to the farewell gift in 1954. The second list, complete with addresses, was kept up-to-date by my father until about 1971 (sometimes with the help of Lucy Grant, daughter of another 1913/1954 survivor, Robert R. Anderson, Milton of Auchenhove) and for over ten years he cyclostyled a Christmas letter to each. (As this involved posting some 300 letters, he would take these along to the GPO in Edinburgh to be franked. On one occasion he got into conversation with the counter hand and explained what it was all about. The latter asked if he might take a copy of the circular letter home to show his wife.) This list was of course much longer than that of 1913, including not only descendants of original parishioners but former U.F. members and their families and other contacts over the years, thus giving the lie to my father's occasional remark that he had more friends in the churchyard now than walking about.

Another 1913 parishioner and elder who had worked in the United States was John B. King of Knappyround, by training a gardener. Again no one would have guessed from the sober demeanour of this tall, bearded man that his early life had included a spell in Kansas. Recalling this when about to visit him once when he was approaching ninety, I took along one of Henry D. Thoreau's books (not 'Walden' - I think it was 'Winter') which as I write are being featured on radio, bringing to the groove-bound a breath of fresh air from the New World of the 19th century: '...How worn and dusty, then, must be the highways of the world - how deep the ruts of tradition and conformity! I did not wish to take a cabin passage, but rather to go before the mast and on the deck of the world, for there I could best see the moonlight and the mountains ... Why should we be in such desperate haste to succeed, and in such desperate enterprises? If a man does not keep pace with his companions, perhaps it is because he hears a different drummer. Let him step to the music that he hears ...' Mr King examined the volume slowly, and finally said 'I think I have this book upstairs'.

He had a fund of recollections which, if not exactly in the category of 'tall stories', tended to have an element of narrative exaggeration. My mother, stirring her own strawberry jam on the kitchen range, would recall Mr King's tale of how one Saturday night he was landed with a vast quantity of surplus strawberries and decided the only solution was to make jam himself. But the jam, as the experienced strawberry-jam maker well knows is liable to happen, got out of control, and was soon running over the kitchen floor and out at the door ... My father used to repeat some of the stories Mr King told of his experiences nearer home while a farm servant in the parish of Cushnie. Going home one moonlight night he was suddenly aware of a ghostly apparition, white

and writhing, just ahead of him and which he must pass. His hair stood on
end, lifting his cap right up off his head. Then, as suddenly, recognition
dawned: it was only Mrs - taking in her washing. 'My bonnet came down with
a dunt!' Another tale he told was of Dr Salvesen, Tarland, (later of Glassel
House) who when the snow in the fields was level with the top of the dykes,
had had the bright idea of using a pair of skis to get around the practice.
A farm servant on the Braes of Leochel - also named John - had been taken ill
and was awaiting the doctor in the chaumer when the small boy of the farmhouse,
looking out, spotted the approaching apparition, cloak flying out behind it.
Running into the house he cried 'The devil's comin' fleein' doon the park,
loupin' the dykes!... d'ye think he's come for John?'

At the beginning of the century - and indeed earlier - a popular form of
charitable money-raising was the compilation of books of quotations, the names
of contributors being printed alongside the quotation of their choice. In
1910, for example, the Aberdeen University Missionary Association, of which my
father was at one time President, had published a Birthday Book of this kind.
One might think that each contributor's choice was a serious indication of
personal character, leanings or interests. and this was often the case; on
the other hand many thought that this was a suitable occasion for frivolity,
especially if the book's saleability were to be considered. Shakespeare and
Burns were perhaps the most popular choices for exerpts, along with the current
writers of the 'Patience Strong' school. For the U.M.A. book my mother,
'M. Reid, Montrose', had chosen Alice Carey:

> How much we take, how little give,
>   Yet every life is meant
> To help all lives; each man should live
>   For all men's betterment.

whereas my father's 'Saxonised' verse was

> Exams are noucht but senseless crams
>   They drive me fair dementit;
> The path to poesie once was mine
>   But thro' exams I tint it.

In 1912, more as a personal autograph book 'from friends far and near' than

for any stated charitable purpose, one of the well-known sons of Lumphanan,
John Don, then headmaster of Carrick Academy, Maybole, (of whom more anon)
son of John Don, blacksmith at Peelbog (1807-74), had brought forth such a
collection entitled 'Musings from Lumphanan'. Whatever it may prove regarding the contributors - and, as a rule, the men, especially the younger ones,
maintained a lighthearted style while the women were more serious - one
contribution was uninhibitedly genuine and characteristic:

> 'Tis the greatest folly
> Not to be jolly;
> That's what I think!!

Thus, Mrs John King (Fanny Reid) of Knappyround. She attributed it to
Longfellow: I wonder! Mrs King gave herself unstintingly to the service of
God and her neighbour until she died at the age of 62 after a short illness,
but did so in a spirit of unfailing cheerfulness. Knappyround, home of the
Reid family, had indeed once been an inn, but was now a moderately-sized
croft only. Mrs King, discovered late one night by my father on the short-cut
down to the Hillock, explained that she had just been down feeding their cat
as they were away. Found with a bandaged hand, she had been trying to slice
an old heel of a loaf because another neighbour had run out of bread and she
had given her the new loaf. On a Saturday evening she would sweep through
John's greenhouse and a basket of prize begonias would arrive at the manse for
next day's church service. I can just remember her in person, sitting opposite
me in the local bus, the bright, bobbing cherries on her black **straw** hat
reflecting the pink cheeks and sparkling eyes.

One day she gave a tea party for some local ladies and surprised them by
suddenly asking brightly 'Well now, what would you all like me to leave you
in my Will?' Responding in the spirit in which the question was asked, each
guest stated her preference; my mother fancied a farmhouse Hepplewhite chair;
Jean Thorburn, the late minister's daughter, opted for the brass kettle which
Mrs King habitually brought to church socials. The Will was a joke, but when
after Mrs King's death her husband prepared to share the house, and some of

these possessions were sold at auction, my mother bought the Hepplewhite chair which is before me as I write, and has remained 'Mrs King's chair'. My mother also sought the divided bon-bon dish which Mrs King would bring to socials, but it could not be found and Mr King said 'I believe she broke it herself'. This illustrates very well the spirit in which many roups were attended; people were looking more for mementoes than for bargains, and this took the rough edge off what might have seemed almost a second funeral. It was a friendly duty to attend.

The Kings had no children but habitually kept a young man (we used to call him 'the King's butler') who helped generally on the croft and with messages. Incidentally, John King's contribution to the Don 'Musings' came from Shakespeare:

> How poor are they that have not patience:
> What wound did ever heal but by degrees?

He became our senior elder, and lived well into his nineties. In due course he discussed with my father the making of his Will. He wished half of what he left to go to Aberdeen Royal Infirmary where he had recently had the most kindly treatment; the other half to go to the Kirk Session. Following the inauguration in 1948 of the National Health Service the former clause was reconsidered, and after consultation with the almoners' department a codicil was added in 1950 directing that this half-share be divided equally between the Infirmary's Nurses' Welfare Fund and their Good Samaritan Fund, providing comforts for patients at the almoners' discretion. He particularly wanted the nurses to benefit. The Kirk Session legacy, yielding initially £14 annually, was 'to preserve the amenities of the Church and Manse Grounds of St Finan's by trimming Hedges, cutting and raking the Grass of the Manse Grounds and Church Approaches and keeping the Walks tidy - not for keeping the vegetable garden soil - in so far as this does not fall to be met by the Churchyard Authority then existing'. The sum was generally used in our time for the maintenance of hedges and grass by a measure of hired help, but on one occasion

my father did all the grasscutting himself for a season so that the legacy
money could go towards repairing a causeway in the steading.

John Don, who collected the <u>Musings from Lumphanan,</u> was born in 1861. He
took an M.A. Degree at Aberdeen and B.Sc. at London, becoming a Consulting
Chemist and Water Engineer (F.I.C., A.M.I.Mech.E.) He studied also at Leipzig.
In 1894 he was appointed Principal of the Technical and Art School at Inverness,
in 1898 Rector of Peterhead Academy. Thereafter from 1905 he was Rector of
Carrick Academy, Maybole, writing various textbooks and being joint author of
<u>Modern Methods of Water Purification.</u> His mother, Eliza Birnie, was a daughter
of the Reverend Alexander Birnie, schoolmaster at Lumphanan from 1804 to 1856.
Mr Birnie kept diaries which unfortunately have disappeared, although John
Don's sister Mrs M.H. Kennedy had made a few extracts which she ultimately gave
to my father. The most noteworthy local reference is 'April: 1822. Rode to
Findrack and got cowpox matter off Adam Farquhar's natural son Robert for
Jessie'. Jessie was his eldest daughter, who died in 1845. Eliza's other
son, Alexander Birnie Don, had been Boxill Prizeman in Mathematics at the University of Aberdeen, and from 1890-98 was Rector of Dunfermline High School, but died
early. John Don and his sister Charlotte, who lived with him at Maybole, kept
on the family cottage at Peelbog next to their father's forge. A timber garage-
cum-laboratory was built to house the Model T Ford with its gleaming brass lamps.
This would occasionally be taken out for an airing, John Don driving accompanied
by James Benzies, whose neighbouring croft was a few yards up the hill known as
Benzie's Brae. James might next day be seen on the glebe, walking up and down
sowing corn broadcast, to left and right, from the measure which hung from his
shoulders.

John Don's own quotation in 'Musings' was taken from Chaucer:

> The firste vertue, sone, if thou wilt lere,
> Is to restreine and kepen wel thy tonge.

while Charlotte contributed 'What a blessing to have ready wit ... and ready
money to back it'. (Dickens). I remember one afternoon coming home from school

down Reid's Brae to Peelbog for some reason lagging behind my schoolmates,
and meeting Mr Don who remarked 'You're the hin'most!' (Reid's Brae was so
named because it bordered Roadside, farmed by the Reid family for two or more
generations; they were related to the Reids of Wartle.) Later, when I was
in my first year at Banchory, my mother over tea in our drawingroom, was
telling Mr Don how I was in close competition there with two boys. He begged
me to hold back: 'Just imagine one of those boys having to go home and admit
he'd been beaten by a girl!' I never did beat either of those two, but not for
want of trying.

John Don's sister Mrs Kennedy, whose late husband – formerly schoolmaster
at Strathdon – had been Registrar, lived at Rose Villa in the village. Her
quotation was 'Tinsel may impose upon one for a time, but sterling coin alone
will always and everywhere pass current', and it immediately brings back the
little lady in black, a very private person, very firm in her views. She had
a great sense of history, and of family: the blacksmith's daughter and the
granddaughter of the schoolmaster merged most happily. From her house she
could hear the sounds of the village smithy at Faburn, comparing one smith's
hammer with another's. It may well have been she who inspired my father, many
years later, to tackle the well-known smith of Campfield, Glassel, James C.
Forbes, on the subject. Part of his reply was incorporated in a letter from
my father, signed 'Rhythm', to the Inverurie Advertiser of 9 July 1954:

> The custom of beating in time on the anvil's heel is a very ancient
> one... Firstly, as the blacksmith, the muscles of his brawny arms in
> full play, beats the iron into shape his brain is also functioning at
> full speed. Sometimes, however, he must think twice before he hits
> the iron again, so to mark time he musically taps the anvil once, or
> twice or thrice as the case requires... As the job or piece of hot
> iron is being turned, it is necessary to miss a stroke or so, and
> every smith with any sense of rhythm must perforce beat in the time
> on the anvil; this operation, if the sledge is being used, can be
> done very beautifully if the smith possesses the soul of music...
> The light rhythmic taps on the anvil are a positive relief to the
> arms of the smith, who, although his muscles are "like iron bands"
> cannot strike the iron continuously with herculean strokes without
> the relief given by the practically effortless tap, tap, tap on the
> anvil ...

Forbes himself played the fiddle, and sang in the choir at Torphins U.F. Church.

Mrs Kennedy possessed, I believe, the first wireless receiving set in the village, and we children would be invited to go and 'listen in' with headphones. I still have a book which she gave me initialled on the flyleaf 'M.H.K.' - Jane Austen's Sense and Sensibility. She always sat in the Peelbog pew, and in her Will made a bequest to the church from which a silver individual communion set was purchased for taking the sacrament to elderly or sick parishioners in their homes; it also provided Bibles for Sunday School children.

At Wellbank next door to Mrs Kennedy in 1913 lived Mrs Stuart, widow of a merchant in the village, a relative of the laird of Burnside, and her maid Miss Lizzie Keith. The latter was noted in my father's visiting book as being a U.F member but I seem to recollect her as being a familiar figure in our very young lives. One of Mrs Stuart's books, too, is still in my possession: entitled Cookery and Domestic Economy it also has her name on the flyleaf 'Maggie Adams, 1888'. Published by William and Robert Chambers, 'The present work has been designed and written entirely with a view to practical utility, and for the information of those young Housewives in the middle ranks of society, who have not had the benefit of regular instructions in the affairs of the kitchen'. The author - merely 'H.S.C.' - a Mrs. Chambers? - says 'The circumstance of having lived a number of years in Scotland, has enabled me to give a variety of receipts for SCOTCH DISHES, the accuracy of which may be relied on.' Indeed, she gives a receipt for potted head ('Take the half of a bullock's head and clean it; soak it in warm water, with a cow heel ...') and instructions for broiling salmon 'on a gridiron over a clear fire'.

My father once asked Mrs Stuart whether she was related to Dr Francis Adams (1796-1861), medical practitioner at Banchory, Greek scholar and translator of Hippocrates, of Aretaeus of Cappadocia and of Paul of Aegina. 'Hooch aye, ma uncle Francie'. Both had been born at Auchenhove, where it seems Francis' father was gardener at the 'Aul' Wa's'. In 1961, the centenary of Adams' death, he looked up Francis Adams in the Edinburgh Register House:

'Adams, 19.3.1796 – James Adams in Auchinhove, a son baptised Francis, witnesses Francis Black and Alex Cromar'. Adams' centenary was being marked in various ways. My father listened to a BBC broadcast by Dr Douglas Guthrie on 17 February 1961, and on the 25th an illustrated article by Guthrie appeared in The Scotsman. The same day an article by Professor John Craig was printed in The Lancet. It so happened that my father was staying with us in London shortly afterwards and had mentioned Adams to our neighbour, an Italian doctor; she immediately recalled the Lancet article and produced her copy. Guthrie had suggested that before going to the University of Aberdeen Adams was self-taught; there was another assumption that he had attended the Grammar School in Aberdeen. My father doubted this, since Alexander Birnie was by then schoolmaster at Lumphanan, and 'could have given Adams all the Latin he needed for University entrance'. I have now confirmed, having consulted their record, that he never was at the Grammar School. Born on 13 March 1796, he would have been 13 when he entered University in 1809; he graduated M.A. in 1813. There was then little medical teaching at Aberdeen; one chair was founded in 1700. For that he went on to Edinburgh, then took the examination of the Royal College of Surgeons of London. In 1846 the University of Glasgow awarded him the degree of LL.D., and in 1856 Aberdeen an honorary M.D. He had been offered the Chair of Greek at Aberdeen, but preferred to remain a country doctor. Requiring little sleep, he managed to devote many hours a day to his Greek translations, although it is said he tended to fall asleep on horseback on his rounds. He died in February 1861 just before his 65th birthday, having contracted pneumonia following a visit to a patient one winter's night. He is commemorated by an obelisk in Banchory bearing the Latin inscription composed by Principal Sir W.D. ('Homer') Geddes of Aberdeen University, translated thus by my father:

> Bereft of a most venerated leader his friends have erected this to
> the memory of Francis Adams, M.D., LL.D., who of all the physicians
> whom Scotland has produced, possessed, without exception, the richest
> stores of erudition in Letters as well as in the Sciences. He lived
> long in this secluded valley, far from Princely Hall or Seat of Learn-
> ing, a veritable Apollo amongst men, faithfully serving Medicine and
> the Muses. Born in Lumphanan 1796. Died at Banchory 1861.

After his retirement my father continued to take the Aberdeen Press and Journal daily and press cuttings about Lumphanan folk and connections, even to the third and fourth generation, circulated continually within the family. The 1963 headline 'Kemnay man wins Scottish ploughing championship' with accompanying photograph of James Grant of Nether Mains was annotated 'Grandson of Johnnie Grant East Mains [of Auchenhove]. Do you remember your interest in his father and George setting out to Ploughing Matches with grand decorations and ribbons flying?' Four years later James had a third in one event at the national ploughing matches at Ross-on-Wye, Herefordshire, and this cutting reported that he would take part next day in the final to decide the national champion who would have a place in the world final in Rhodesia in April 1968. The Grants of East Mains were an example of the same family in the same place featuring in both my father's testimonials, 1913 and 1954. This also applied to the Leslies of Whitehouse, and young Gordon Leslie – his father Charles (auctioneer with Reith and Anderson) was then at Wester Durris – was another noted ploughman of the third generation. There is a letter from him acknow- ledging my father's congratulations after an event in 1958.

The Grants' farm, East Mains of Auchenhove, stood on the edge of the Loch of Auchlossan. Driving my mother round the parish not long after their marriage, my father happened one day to take the road past the loch. My mother was delighted: 'A lake! Then there'll be boating!' 'Boating!' was my father's withering reply, 'That's a farmer's lands under water!' The name Auchlossan (pronounced with a long 'o' and one 's') may have derived from the Gaelic Achadh-an-losgainn, the field of the frog. There was a legend that long ago a huge frog dwelt in the loch, consuming one cattle-beast daily until the neighbouring farmers combined to slay the monster. In fact, fields from three estates – about 250 acres, including 60 acres of marsh – lay under the waters of the loch, which had been partially drained near the end of the seventeenth century. About 1860 a business man from Aberdeen, James W. Barclay (later M.P. for Forfarshire, 1872-92) came to terms with the lairds of Finzean, Auchenhove and Aboyne, agreeing that for a 25 year lease on easy terms he would drain the loch and leave it drained. Barclay rented the adjacent farm of Mains of Auchlossan, carried out his bargain and put practically the whole of the loch lands under the plough. Thus was fulfilled the prophecy of the Reverend William Shand. writing his piece on Lumphanan for the first (Old) Statistical Account of 1743 '(one day) the plough may be seen going where the ugly and voracious pikes are now lying, and corns growing instead of almost useless weeds'. With the great demand for fodder for horses, especially during the Deeside season when Queen Victoria was at Balmoral, this was a profitable venture. After Barclay's time, however, the outlet drain and the open ditches which carried off the surface water were neglected, and nature gradually reasserted itself. By the early 1920's the loch had returned to its former level. During the second world war the Department of Agriculture, by arrangement with the proprietors, repaired the ditches and cleared the outlet tunnel, so that again crops were grown on the dry loch. Then in 1954 heavy rains broke the banks of the Aboyne burn, so that the water once more spread over the loch area. 'The loch' became quite a regular feature to be reported on in parishioners' letters: either it had filled up again or had again been drained; November 1954: 'the loch of Auchlossan is back in its original form - in fact it was extra big on Saturday...' One of the lairds had been out duck-shooting. By 1959 the main drain had collapsed. In October 1960: 'The loch of Auchlossan is in being again and most of Taggart's (Drumduan) large crop in stook standing waist high or floating wantonly...' February 1972: 'Auchlossan has filled again'. August 1972: 'We have almost re-drained the Loch of Auchlossan'. In May 1974 the Press and Journal pictured Frank S. Allen of Auchenhove with his boat high and dry by the dry loch. Certainly in January 1974, bringing my father back on his last journey to Lumphanan and purposely choosing the 'Poorshouse Brae' route with its

magnificent view from Knowehead, overlooking the loch area, the late afternoon sunshine lay only on dry fields.

John Forbes, farmer in Mains of Auchlossan until his death in 1929,
(at first in partnership with his brother William who died in 1930) was a
philosopher with whom the minister spent many a happy evening. Not long
after he came to Lumphanan my father was at Auchlossan and happened to mention
how put out he had been at some remark made to him by another farmer. 'Never
ye min'' said John Forbes, 'the skitteriest coo has aye the loudest lowe!'
On another visit John had a tale to relate illustrating the subtle class dis-
tinctions maintained by some of the 'travelling people'. Early one morning
he had encountered in the close at Auchlossan a wandering character who was
in the way of turning up occasionally for a day's work and night's lodging in
the loft. Sensing that this man was in a somewhat disgruntled frame of mind,
Forbes asked 'What's ta'en ye the day, John?' The other pointed balefully
northwards in the direction of the cross-roads known as the Pole, and related
how the previous evening, making for Auchlossan but being weary and the night
fine, he had decided just to doss down under a tree in the Pole wood. In the
morning, on the way to the farm, he passed a 'wigwam' with a tinker woman
outside it. He shouted some greeting but received no very enthusiastic response. A man's voice from within the tent was then heard demanding to know
to whom his wife was speaking. It was her reply that had caused the disgruntle-
ment. 'Some puir deevil been sleepin' at the back o' a dyke'.

John Forbes (the accent is on the second syllable) has a particular claim
to inclusion in the annals of the parish. He it was who located that early
Christian relic the Lumphanan baptismal font, mentioned in the Old Statistical
Account as being at the manse in 1743 but removed by Margaret, daughter of the
Reverend William Shand, on her marriage to Hary Lamond of Pitmurchie in 1820.
According to the late Sir Owen Morshead, formerly the Queen's librarian, whose
lecture in 1967 on the impact of the Victorians on Dorset churches my husband

and I heard at Dorchester, many old fonts had been rescued from farmyards and vicarage gardens. This was indeed to be the case with 'our' font. On coming to Lumphanan my father had heard about the font from Robert Stuart of Burnside: the latter had often seen the stone at Pitmurchie where, with a lead pipe introduced through the bottom, it had served as a watering trough for bestial, but it had since disappeared. My father happened to mention this to John Forbes, whose simple response was that if the font were to be found he would find it. This was an attitude later to be displayed by his younger son, Commander Ian Forbes of the Metropolitan Police, the detective who solved all his cases including that of the Cannock Chase murder. Writing in 1967 to thank me for a cutting from The Times about Ian, my father said 'He has been getting praise in most of the papers for his recent works and seems to be quite a chip from the Old Block — his father. I am hoping to tell the Moderator [about to visit the Presbytery of Deeside] how old John found for us the lost Baptismal Font...' In fact, the Very Reverend Dr Roy Sanderson went to see the font.

After several false trails had been followed up, John Forbes discovered the stone at the farm of Stranduff on the Kincardine O'Neil estate, whence it had been removed by the forester, John Urquhart, on the instructions of Mr Lamond when the Pitmurchie estate was sold to the Bowers. It was again being used as a watering trough by the forester. There my father and John Forbes saw it. On being asked whether he would accept a substantial larch trough for the font so that the latter could be restored to the Church of Lumphanan, the forester replied that only the proprietor of the estate, Mrs Pickering, could give the necessary consent. Negotiations were begun through the Kincardine O'Neil minister. Dr Argo, with Mrs Pickering, but before they had got very far the latter died. In due course my father sent a memorandum regarding the font to the heir, Mrs Pickering's daughter Mrs Vaughan Lee, who then returned the font to the church. Unfortunately John Forbes did not live to see this. The actual removal was carried out by a cart and horses from the neighbouring Dess estate by arrangement with the laird, Mr Walter R. Davidson, an architect by training and an elder at the church of Kincardine O'Neil. The font, of rough-hewn granite, is estimated to weigh about 15 cwt. and may have been used by Finan himself in the late sixth century. Being too heavy to be placed within the church - Finan would have baptised in the open air on the church site - Mr Davidson had imagined it would be placed in the churchyard at St Finan's. (After the 1929 Union names had to be chosen for all churches in parishes where the Parish Church and the former United Free Church both became members of Presbytery. At Lumphanan the latter was named the Stothert Memorial, after the Reverend Thomas Stothert who was instrumental in raising the present building, and the parish church St Finan's.) My father, who had already surveyed the churchyard with this in mind, therefore invited Mr Davidson to suggest where the font should be placed. It was, of course, impossible to find a suitable place that had not been used for sepulture. He could only suggest that it be returned to the manse garden, thus concurring in the minister's own conclusion. There it was placed on the site of one of the elm trees which had been felled some years earlier, and there it remained until 1971 when the manse at St Finan's was sold. By then it was becoming clear that eventually one of the two churches would be closed. My father had fore-seen such a contingency, and was fairly certain that this would be St Finan's. ('The young folk prefer the Stothert: it makes a better wedding photograph'.) He had therefore suggested that in that event the font be removed to the Stothert Memorial Church, where it now is. St Finan's was closed after a final service in 1980.

There seems to have been almost a tradition among Lumphanan ministers' sons that they should seek their fortunes - or at least their livelihoods - overseas. John Don's book of 'Musings' includes two lines of Robert Burns received from George Thorburn, then in Rangoon, Burma:

Frae the friends and land I love,
Driv'n by Fortune's felly spite.

George did return to his native land, but died in 1924. An early death
abroad had been the fate of Tom McCombie, son of Mr Thorburn's predecessor,
the Reverend Dr Charles McCombie of Tillyfour, who served the parish for 49
years, his brother William (for a time M.P. for West Aberdeenshire) taking
over the famous cattle-breeding estate. Born in 1856, Tom had gone to South
Africa, where he edited the <u>Cape Lantern</u>. He was drowned while on a journey
into the interior, crossing a swollen river. But he has left a legend in
Lumphanan. When aged about 11-12 he and some classmates at the parish school
had been suffering the attentions of the school bully, an older boy. Finally
they decided they could put up with this no longer, and Tom was chosen as
their champion to challenge the bully to a fight. But lest the Dominie should
interfere, it was agreed that the duel must not take place at the school but
be fought to a finish in the stackyard at Bogloch farm on Saturday after
Catechism in the school. The challenge was duly issued and accepted. By this
time Tom McCombie was beginning to have some doubts about his ability to beat
the bigger boy, but, undaunted and resourceful, he evolved a plan of campaign.
First he borrowed from farm-servant friends half a dozen gully knives. Then
he abstracted from manse drawers lint, bandages and various medicaments, and
was ready at Bogloch ahead of his opponent. When all had assembled Tom rather
ostentatiously opened his knife blades and set them out in a row. Next he
handed round his surgical equipment amongst his allies. Then he deliberately
took off his jacket, rolled up his sleeves, and approaching the bully with a
determined aspect commanded 'Now choose your weapon!' Whereupon the big boy,
victim of that element of surprise recommended in the manuals of warfare,
could only mutter 'A didna think it wis t' be a fecht o' that kin'.' He then
turned tail and made off, followed by the jeers of the whole school. Needless
to say, the bullying ceased. This event of 1866 or '67 may seem ancient
history, rather before our period. The tale was told to my father by John

Don. But in Lumphanan in our day, as has been said, continuity was important
and the present stretched back a good way. It occurred to my father to ask
one of the older generation, George Cromar, Milton of Auchlossan, who might
have been about five years old at the time of the fight, whether he had ever
heard of this event. At once George's face was lit by a radiant smile:
'Man, I wis there!'

A resourcefulness similar to that of Tom McCombie was to be shown in
the early days of World War II by George's great-nephew James Cromar. Notable
in his early schooldays as a successful truant, my later recollection of Jimmy
at school was as an expert in mental arithmetic. Miss Robertson would draw a
circle of numbers on the blackboard and ask him to demonstrate this expertise
as she quickly moved her pointer from one figure to another. Quick as light
Jimmy followed. His quick-wittedness stood him in good stead when his
battalion of the Gordons was captured at St Valery after the evacuation at
Dunkirk. The convoy of prisoners was passing through Belgium when they
chanced to stop for a meal on a roadside bordering a cornfield. Unobserved
by their guards, Jimmy and a companion slipped into the tall corn. The latter
unfortunately was later recaptured, but James got away. He was cared for by
friendly Belgians until he escaped to Spain: he was the very first to do so
by way of 'Dédée's' Comet Line.

It is tempting to skip back over two hundred years to the tale of another
enterprising Lumphanan escapee: Peter Williamson, eldest son of James
Williamson farmer in Hirnley, later in Upper Balnacraig, who as a boy of
twelve in 1742 was kidnapped on the harbour in Aberdeen by agents of a con-
sortium of 'worthy' citizens, and shipped to America to be sold as an inden-
tured slave. The apparent digression is legitimate not only on the grounds of
historical parallel. Peter's plantation servitude under a Scotsman who had
undergone the same experience was entirely beneficial, but in 1754 when settled
on his own land he was captured by marauding and murderous Indians. After some

months he escaped one day by slipping into a hollow tree. Later he survived
a period of military service against the French, who were supported by the
Indians in North America. This time when he became a prisoner of war in 1756
he was shipped with others back to Portsmouth; the French didn't want to be
bothered guarding them. Discharged from the army on account of a hand wound,
he was given six shillings to find his way back to Aberdeen. He supplemented
this by selling a chapbook 'The Curious Adventures of Peter Williamson' to
which, of course, the above 'worthy' citizens of Aberdeen took exception and
the book was burned at the Castlegate. His subsequent adventures in Edinburgh,
where he was known as 'Indian Peter', are less relevant to this chronicle,
but the final connecting link is coming up. Determined to pursue by litigation
his former captors in Aberdeen (he had already brought a successful case
against the magistrates for wrongful imprisonment on his return) Peter caused
evidence to be collected within the parish of Lumphanan and elsewhere concerning the activities of the kidnappers' agents. The latter tended to frequent
the markets such as Michael Fair at Aboyne, Bartle Fair at Kincardine O'Neil
and Briac Fair at Tarland. One of the Lumphanan witnesses was Peter Cromar,
then of Burnside. Parallel branches of the Cromar family had continued in
the parish, either at Bogloch or at Milton of Auchlossan, producing some
notable schoolmasters, one rector of the Grammar School at Aberdeen.

One difficulty regarding names is in sorting out the correct generation
referred to, if there is no date to give a clue, especially as the same
Christian names tend to recur; both sons and daughters when christened would
be given the names of a respected forebear. A wife would wish sometimes to
have her maiden surname perpetuated in a child's forename, and this in itself
can be a historical clue. John Forbes's wife was Betsy Durward, and Durward
history in Lumphanan goes back many centuries. Their granddaughter was therefore christened Betsy Durward Anderson — her father, James R. Anderson, later
took over the family meal mill at Auchlossan — although she is always known
merely as 'B.D.' Towards the end of his time at Lumphanan, or it may even

have been later, my father received by post from outwith the parish a request for a testimonial from – he imagined – a member of the youngest generation of the name and forename. He responded with enthusiasm: besides knowing this man he had known his father and his grandfather – 'all splendid workers'. He was unperturbed when presently he received a letter of thanks from the 'young man's' father, saying that he had been chosen for the post in question out of a hundred applicants. 'Well, well, it was still perfectly true what I wrote'.

The inescapability of the distant past is less worthily illustrated in the lingering attitude towards our witches. The gean tree that marks the spot, or guards the rickle of stones where stood a cottage later 'condemned' as uninhabitable, would once – and may still – be side by side with a rowan tree. When I took over an aunt's cottage in Dorset my father actually said 'You'll need to plant a rowan to keep the witches away': I did, and we have not been troubled. Lumphanan featured in the post-Reformation witch-hunts, the best-known practitioner of the occult being Margrat Og, her victim Agnes Ross, the lady of Auchenhove (the 'Aul' Wa's'). A latter-day believer in the power of witchcraft was 'Butter Jess'. When I first heard of her I imagined that because of her mode of life she belonged to the fairly distant past. Her one-roomed cottage – the original building which, adapted in 1906 and extended in 1934, is now Woodlands, in the village – had an earthen floor, on which she slept on a pile of straw. It was the Free Church minister, the Reverend A.S.A. Bishop, who provided her with a proper bed, but Jess wouldn't have it. Mr Bishop was at Lumphanan 1889–1910 (being at first colleague then from 1893 successor to the Reverend Thomas Stothert) so this roughly dates 'Butter Jess'. In the middle of the earthen floor, it is said, grew a tree, on which she dried her washing. As her nickname suggests, she sold butter, going around on foot – probably for long distances – collecting and retailing. Her belief in witchcraft entailed even longer detours, for Jess wouldn't cross a straight

line. To tease her, farm servants would draw a straight line on the road
with a rake or hoe so that to avoid it poor Jess had to climb over dykes,
fences and ditches.

It was, no doubt, not only in rural Dorset that in former days peasants
shared their dwelling with their livestock. There a stone and rubble [rouble]
built thatched cottage of the 17th century had two parallel beams running
from front door to back supporting wooden screen walls separating humans from
animals; it was known as a 'screen' cottage. Traces of an even cosier arrangement could be found in our day in the cottage above Cairnbeathie to which
Jessie and Annie Milne retired. They were the survivors of the three Miss
Milnes whom my father first visited in 1913 at the other Milton of Auchlossan
(although like George Cromar and his sister they were U.F. members). Some
callers at the cottage once heard from a corner of the kitchen the sudden
cackling of a hen, and out from the meal girnel flew the triumphant bird.
'That's Gertie – she aye lays in the meal girnel', explained Jessie. The
latter was easily recognisable in her rather pointed black felt hat on the
road to the village. At one time her invariable remark on meeting the banker's
wife there would be 'Oh hullo, Mrs. __ I didna' ken ye. I thocht ye were a
lady visitor'. Meeting my brother one day when he was home for his school
holidays, she surprised him by her sibilant greeting: 'It's very refreshing
to see you!' I recall as a child being sent up by my father with a press
cutting which he thought would interest the sisters: I think it was a photograph of Lincoln Cathedral; Jessie was very proud of having the Bishop as a
customer for eggs when he was on holiday in Aboyne. This was received (prior
to closer examination) with great solemnity: 'It's a circular!' In due course
Annie died and Jessie – almost entirely retaining her composure and presence
of mind – made nearly all the necessary arrangements. When the undertaker
went up and asked about the coffin, however, Jessie was momentarily nonplussed:
'Oh I forgot aboot the kistin o' Annie!'

In the manuscript version of the Lumphanan article in the Third Statistical

Account (much shortened by the editors) writing about 1950, my father observed that it was becoming exceedingly difficult to get reliable information as to former days: fewer traditions remained as regards the parish in the past. We were fortunate in that we still had a few people endowed with a sense of history and who delighted in describing how things were. The introduction of electric lighting was for most households long delayed, partly by the second war, and that of reliable electric power even longer, especially in the remoter areas. We took our paraffin lamps as a matter of course, but one or two enterprising people installed their own electric light. I can well remember, however, the fascination with which as children my sister Wendy and I listened one day to James Cockie of Mill Farm describing a rush lamp and how it worked. We had often peeled rushes, revealing the white taper inside (no one ever quite succeeded in eliminating these intruders from the part of the glebe known as the rushes field) but had never suspected such possibilities of illumination. Maggie Adams in her youth at the 'Aul' Wa's' — within sight of Mill Farm — would no doubt have been quite familiar with this; if not, her book of cookery and domestic economy would have rectified this: under the heading 'Directions for servants' was the cautionary paragraph:

> Never leave a candle burning at your bedside, or on a table when you go to bed, except it be a rush-light burning in a basin at a considerable distance from the bed. The burning of candles at bedsides has often caused fires.

It was Mr Cockie who gave my father the copy I have of Henderson's <u>Aberdeenshire Epitaphs and Inscriptions</u>, originally a presentation copy from the author. Published in 1906, it contains a good deal else of local historical interest.

One of those who made their own electricity — possibly the first — was Andrew ('Postie') Lawson of the Old Schoolhouse, Craigievar, grandson of Andrew Lawson, last schoolmaster there. Best remembered now as the builder of the first steam car in Aberdeenshire in 1895, his history has from time to time been written up in the local Press. His distinctive signature appears in the list of contributors to my father's 1913 testimonial. Postie had hydro-electricity, operated from the nearby burn, which among other things drove his wife's butter-making churn. Born in 1854, he trained as a joiner but soon took over his father's postal round, Craigievar to Whitehouse. In 1914 he retired and devoted himself to the seven-and-a-half acre croft and to his quiet technological revolution. Our pony-trap was no stranger to Postie's close, and visits to this house of wonders were a special childhood treat. In a sort of studio-cum-workshop between house and byre was set up the magic lantern, and from the vivid impression left to this day (and given Postie's ingenuity) the pictures on the screen might well have been both moving and three-dimensional. There sat Diogenes, a rugged old ruffian rather like the story-teller in the 'Boyhood of Raleigh', at home in his barrel. Enter two mischievous boys, intent on teasing the philosopher. Came retribution: the barrel set a-rolling, ironing out the hooligans as flat as pancakes.

Postie himself in old age was a fine-looking, broad-browed, white-bearded man, the slight droop at the corners of eyes and mouth seeming to emphasise his questing, speculative aspect. I was always convinced that a picture which hung in my father's study of a white-capped old lady, sitting at a spinning-wheel by the light of a deeply-recessed cottage window was a portrait of Mrs Lawson. She once showed us over Craigievar Castle, with its exciting and sometimes grisly relics including medieval instruments of torture such as branks for the over-garrulous, and its reputed ghost. But I preferred the more kindly spirits of Old Schoolhouse. There was 'The Whistle', an almost life-size statue fashioned by Postie of the poet Charles ('Hamewith') Murray's herd lad, who 'cut a sappy sucker from the muckle rodden tree' and so enchanted himself with the music he made that all else went by the board until - tragedy! - winter came, and back at school 'the maister brunt the whistle that the wee herd made'. Then there was the Sailor, now at Oldmeldrum, larger than life in stone with a massive anchor - not Postie's own work. More likely to be a Lawson creation was the bas-relief frieze depicting 'Shouther-the-wind', the

hunch-backed horse-dealer of Hamewith's poem 'The Packman'. We read that
the packman, getting on in his career, 'bocht fae Shou'der-win' a hardy
cleekit shalt' - a transaction that would be appreciated by natives of Craigievar and of Hamewith's nearby Alford. There were the friendly faces, too,
of grandfather clocks in all stages of internal investigation; there were
spinning-wheels and sundials: the sundial still at the manse was Postie's
work, set up in our time. Then there was the photography: this ranged from
large-scale coverage of public occasions to family groups; we were lined up
in the garden, or placed sitting or kneeling on a plaid rug while Postie,
his tripod set up, got under his black cloth and operated the shutter. And
what good clear pictures they still are! Postie would sometimes admit that
one of these was 'a good tak'. He developed them himself. In these more
recent days Postie drove a conventional motor car with a tourer hood, one of
only a handful owned locally in a still largely horse-drawn community. The
steam car the 'Craigievar Express' - thus named, I feel sure, not by its
builder but by irreverent locals - achieved national fame when, restored by
its new owner, it took part in the London to Brighton RAC veteran car run
in November 1970. The Times described it as a 'Lawson Steamer mail cart'.
There is some difference of opinion locally as to whether Postie actually
used it on his rounds, farmers contributing a shovelful of coal as necessary.
Never having actually seen it myself, I once asked my father whether he had.
'Seen it? I've been in it!'

Some time after Mrs Lawson died, a roup was held with a view to reducing
the glorious clutter at Old Schoolhouse. But Postie, unwilling to see his
treasures dispersed, kept withdrawing items until the object was all but
frustrated. At the final roup, after Postie's death in 1938, the main characters were still present: The Whistle, The Sailor and Shouther-the-wind.

What was that? not the merchant's Model T Ford...? no, a lady on a
motor-bicycle! The first time that Miss Margaret Robertson, of Mains of

Findrack, passed the manse on her motor-bike (perhaps about 1920) my mother, full of admiration. said 'I should like to do that!' My father's response was 'Bold Bess!' When I asked my brother recently why Miss Robertson rode a motor-bike. he replied that. so far as he knew. in order to get about! Her two brothers didn't have a gig and were dependent on push-bikes; she was by nature a rather independent. emancipated woman.

Andrew Lawson's successor on the croft was Miss Annie Macgregor. who had retired from Craigmill. Leochel Cushnie. on the Craigievar estate, having succeeded her father, Duncan Macgregor, there when he died at 92 in 1908. At Craigmill her 'grieve' for 34 years had been Jimmy Brown. and he took up the same role at Old Schoolhouse, inheriting the croft when Miss Macgregor died. In his 92nd year, after having for many years scythed all his corn crop by hand, he began to resort to a binder. He never married, although on one occasion when getting a little weary of being interviewed by the Press, he informed a reporter that his wife had died two years earlier. This news was duly printed. Jimmy died eight months before his 100th birthday, having been in hospital for three years.

Electric lighting from a dynamo was a feature of the croft Kirkbrae, at Burnside, of the Sherriffs family. They too had one of the earliest wireless sets as well as a gramophone with a large green horn. Alex. Sherriffs – another contributor to the 1913 testimonial whose family are still in the same house, was politically minded and for some years, when collecting our milk there. we exchanged our Press and Journal for his Daily Herald. Craig recalls being taken by my father to an election meeting in the village in 1924 which was being addressed by C.M. (later Sir Malcolm) Barclay-Harvey, the Conservative candidate. When questions were invited Alex. Sherriffs half-rose from one of the long wooden benches on the floor of the Parish Hall and said: 'Maister Harvey, I am awfa' against they subsidies'. 'Oh, but', said Barclay-Harvey, 'I think that subsidies are very useful in appropriate

circumstances, such as encouraging the production of oats and potatoes'.
'Taaties!' replied 'Shirras', 'Ye're gaun tae gar us eat taaties an' mair
taaties: ye'll seen hae us a' grumphin' like pigs!' Mr Sherriffs once told
me, as a child, how in his own childhood the family had to take sour milk to
their porridge (the milk 'went off' relatively quickly in older days, especially in warm weather) the fresh milk going to customers. 'We used to
plead for fresh milk', he added.

I regarded it as a special treat when going for the milk if I were in
time actually to see a cow being milked and then to watch the subsequent
straining process in the kitchen with its flagstone floor, the dresser hung
with decorative jugs, next to it the rack of ancient-looking guns on the wall,
and its open fire complete with 'swey'. On one side of the fire was Mr Sherriffs' traditional farmhouse armchair, on the other his wife's rocking-chair.
The deep sunny window-ledge on the east wall would be filled with pot-plants;
at right angles, beyond the wall-clock, was another deep, much smaller window,
facing south. Once the house had been an inn, the ale being sold through
this tiny window. Burnside was, in fact, the original village of Lumphanan.
I recall Mrs Sherriffs making us a dish of 'calfie's cheese', a custard made
with the first rich milk after a cow had calved. I met it again during the
last war while posted near a Scottish farm; the maker called it 'beastie
milk pudding', my southern-speaking colleagues called it chericot tart. The
coming of the Milk Marketing Board in the thirties was the beginning of the
end of such neighbourly arrangements, with milk at twopence a pint.

But there were other comings and goings, mostly concerning sheep. Mrs
Sherriffs was particularly devoted to animals and would willingly adopt a
motherless lamb that we happened to have. She survived her husband for some
years. At her funeral my father (so he wrote to me) 'said a few words about
how good she had been to her beasts'. She had a great love of beautiful things,
and kept an enchanting flower garden with a row of beehives up on the Craigton

hill at the extreme end of a long neck of their land. It was like an illustration in a seed catalogue. From her we got the delphiniums which appear in later photographs of the manse.

At an earlier period milk had been fetched from Cairnmude, on the top of the south hill opposite, farmed by the Sutherland family. On this errand my brother absorbed much farming lore. Mrs Joseph Sutherland, like her daughter Mary after her, was extremely skilled in domestic matters if sometimes a little slap-dash in procedure. On asking, once, for one of her recipes my mother was told: 'Tak' a gowpen-fu' o' flour...' When asked what was a gowpen, Mrs Sutherland just made an all-embracing circular gesture with her hands, repeating 'a gowpen-ful''. Her extravert nature made her wish to share anything she had - even a secret. On one occasion she arrived at the manse all agog to share (with the utmost discretion) some important secret that had been divulged to her. On her way down, she related, she had met her neighbour Miss Helen Laing, 'so I told _her_ the secret' (this with lowered voice). That she was entirely justified in her choice of confidantes is manifest: while retailing the story, my mother never mentioned what the secret was.

We got fresh butter - and sometimes a crock of salt - from Cairnmude, and Mary used to win prizes at shows for her dainty dishes of shaped butter. She had a great sense of history: writing to my father after his retirement she noted that it was the 38th anniversary of her mother's death: 'the 7th in 1920 was on a Friday and a lifetime in between. She used to tell us of the hard work and the small wages when her father died a young man in 1872 and she would have said the world is turned upside down since then. Think on the upside down since 1920... Here is the cottar situation at present. They have a modern house with bathroom and electric light, double sinks with hot and cold in both, £8.8 a week, $\frac{1}{2}$ ton o' tatties, and 3 pints of milk daily ...' We still got fresh butter by the pound, neatly stamped, when Mary married Fred Christie, a Free Kirk stalwart, who in 1927 became tenant of

Leyhead on the opposite northern hill. Fred was an intellectual, despite
having left school at 11 to herd cattle. The bookshelf in the kitchen con-
tainedGibbon's <u>Decline and Fall of the Roman Empire</u> in several volumes.
Latterly, when he became housebound, my father would bring him books from
the Public Library in Aberdeen: one was a history of India. On one occasion
Fred was in the village and got into conversation with an ex-London policeman
and a young man up on holiday from his London job at Scotland Yard. They fell
to talking about London and eventually the young man, Ian Irvine, said 'You've
surely been a lot in London, Mr Christie. You seem to know a lot about it'.
Fred's reply, given with a typical 'wag' of his arm, was 'Never been in't
but I can read, can't I?'

Leyhead tended to be the first port of call of my brother Craig when on
vacation from Cambridge. They would get involved in deep discussions by the
kitchen fire; occasionally Mary would be appealed to for an opinion and
would pause, arms akimbo and head on one side, to consider her answer. I never
recollect her actually sitting down at home. One day in the mid-1930's during
the summer vacation one of Craig's Cambridge friends, Keith Conn, later, until
his death, Professor of Physics at Exeter, came looking for him. I knew where
he would be and together we drove in Keith's Riley 9 up the old road past
Brankholm to Leyhead. Soon we were all sitting out in front of the house
in the sun - except, of course, Mary, still on her feet handing round a box
of sweets. Fred and Keith got into a mathematical discussion, the latter
somewhat hampered by confusion over the term of measurement 'quarter'. Neither
Fred nor the Sutherlands had contributed to John Don's 'Musings', but I can
remember Mary, just before her marriage, sitting (yes) in our drawing room
writing in our family autograph album:

> Courage, brother! do not stumble.
> Though thy path be dark as night;
> There's a star to guide the humble:
> 'Trust in God, and do the right.'

My father used to say of Lumphanan - and the records frequently prove him right - that if there was one death there were likely to be three. In January-February 1974 he himself, Fred Christie and Jean Davie, late of Bogentassie - all over 90 - died within five weeks. The last-named. Mrs Arthur Cousin, lived in Surrey, but to assist in proving the rule a fourth nonagenarian, an in-comer, passed away locally.

More will be written presently about our older local burying grounds. First to be interred in the new cemetery at Craigton in 1928 was James Fyfe, aged 86, a tall, solemn and bearded dyke builder who had earlier lived alone near the fountain at the north entrance to Glenmillan House. His contribution, unattributed, to John Don's book of quotation was

> No matter how lowly or lonely our lot,
> Our wish is that others may thrive.

A bachelor with a dog, he was one day about Knappyround when Mrs King, roused for once to indignation, ran out from the kitchen where she had been churning to tell him 'Your dog's just taken a pound of my butter!' Jamie was unperturbed: 'Oh aye, he wid dee that. Gweed for's teeth!' Some years ago I was recalling this tale with Elizabeth Davie (Mrs William Davie) sister-in-law of Mrs Cousin; she had been telling me how Mrs King had always sent Christmas roses to the latter at Godalming. She then told me how about 1923 Jamie Fyfe had come into the house at Bogentassie where her elder daughter Armorel, a baby, lay on the sofa. The tall dyke-builder looked down at the baby and tears welled up in his eyes.

One of Jamie Fyfe's sayings used to be quoted in the district: 'What comes after death? The pairtin' o' the gear'. The Last Will and Testament was in fact an important preoccupation of those who felt they were nearing their end, and frequently the minister would be involved in the ceremony, whether the document then passed to a lawyer or remained in holograph. Few had great possessions, and generally the desire was to make appropriate provision for family and dependants; often a word of gratitude was incorporated in the text. '...In recognition of her services to my mother...' marked the devotion of a quite young girl who had not only cared for her elderly grandmother but had cheerfully kept house for the latter's two middle-aged bachelor sons on a farm. Occasionally there was ill-feeling and even confusion when it transpired that another Will had been made at a later stage, perhaps to the advantage of some comparative stranger whose help had been essential at the end of the day. The record for the simplest - and by implication pleasantest - Will goes to Alexander Robb: 'I, Alexander Robb, Collieston Croft, Lumphanan, hereby declare that I leave all of which I die possessed to my housekeeper, Helen Laing'. This was witnessed on 11 October 1919 by Francis Cantlie Donald and Mary Donald. (It was even written on a sheet of my mother's writing paper.)

Miss Helen Laing had been one of the first to call at the manse after my parents were married. My mother had been anxious that all parishioners should feel free to call without specific invitations being issued. There was initially some reluctance, but not in the case of Miss Laing. Going from the kitchen one day through the house towards the front door, my mother was surprised to encounter a strange lady in the passage. Miss Laing explained that she had aye been in the wye o' jist comin' in thus in Mrs. Thorburn's time, and soon she was equally well established as a welcome visitor in ours. I can recall her, sometime in the 1920's, sitting at tea in the nursery (which became more a family sittingroom) remarking 'Aye, the warld's ill pairtit'. I cannot now recall what was under discussion. Actually Miss Laing was given to making quite irrelevant pronouncements. Meeting the new banker's wife in one of the village shops, the old lady looked into her face and said 'The nearer the kirk the faurer fae gweed!' As has been mentioned, she was a neighbour on the south hill of the Sutherlands at Cairnmude, and occasionally on a Sunday evening my brother would call upon her, living in modest comfort on her inheritance and a ten shilling pension, keeping a few hens.

In the same area, further west, lived in 1913 three generations of the
Emslie family. The one we got to know best was second-generation Robert;
everyone called him 'Robbie' but to our family he was always 'the Bellman'.
As well as farming Newton Croft he later became foreman surfaceman on the railway, and for many years he was also - one might well say 'primarily' - bellman
at the 'auld kirk', receiving on his retirement a gold watch from the Kirk
Session and congregation. A man of immense dignity when carrying in the Bible
on a Sunday - he did this with the same slight rocking motion as he shifted
from one foot to another which I was later to note in the Sunday procession
of University staff at King's College Chapel, Aberdeen - Robbie's 'keckle',
far from the laughter of fools, was instantly recognisable on less formal
occasions. Once on a pouring wet day at the station, waiting for the 8.22
up-train, he put his head in at the ticket-window: 'A ticket to Dryland,
please!' (Keckle). My father used to say he was a master at the soft answer
that turneth away wrath. On Sunday mornings before service, having got the
furnace going, he habitually sat on a table gravestone near the east door
doling out clove-centred sweets to the Sunday School children or smoking his
metal-capped pipe. At one time he took a Sunday School class, and at any time,
if during church service unaccompanied children were creating a disturbance,
Robbie would leave his pew near the door and go and sit between them. On
Communion Sundays he would wear his best navy blue suit instead of his usual
dark tweed, and, having a steady hand, he would be entrusted with the task
of filling the individual glasses. The wine would first be poured into two
china bowls, then measured out into the glasses with a silver spoon. Until 1928
there had been no vestry in the church, the minister's study being virtually
next door; then one of the square pews, that of Findrack, was enclosed for
the purpose, Robbie's comment being that the new vestry was 'just big enough
for me and the minister'. Occasionally Robbie would help out at Craigton farm
which had land near the village, and once had to point out to a lady that her
hens were invading her neighbour's cornfield. 'It's no' my hens', came her swift

denial. 'It's the innkeeper's deucks'. Robbie put his hand in his pocket and (no doubt with a twinkle) brought forth his evidence: a hen's egg. 'Did the innkeeper's deucks lay that?'

Another 'Robbie' who made his mark as a personality in Lumphanan was Robert Moir. Starting his grocery career as an apprentice with the late husband of Mrs Stuart, Wellbank, in the Square, he presently had his own store further up the village. A member for a time of the Parish Council, he was a leading Liberal and an adherent of the Plymouth Brethren. Craig liked to hear his tales of the past in Lumphanan: on one occasion he asked Mr Moir how someone he had described had been so successful. 'Push, man; jist push!' (rhyming with 'rush'). His son David followed on, and presently they exchanged dwellings, David living adjacent to the shop and Robbie retiring to the bungalow behind. The latter was somewhat disappointed to lose the lean-to greenhouse at Bridgeview, being heard to say regretfully 'Here we have no abiding city'.

Chapter 1 mentioned the memorial to Dr Robert Farquharson of Finzean erected on the top of Craiglich. It is equally a memorial to William Fraser. He had been present at the meeting of tenants and others, chaired by my father, held at the auction mart in the village on 22 July 1918 (there were 23 men there and one lady, Miss Jessie Milne, then of Milton of Auchlossan) to discuss a memorial to the laird. Five proposals were put forward: a bursary to help a local schoolboy to attend a college of Agriculture; a tablet in the Parish Church; a water fountain and trough in the village; preservation of the Peel Ring; and a monument on the top of Craiglich (pronounced Craigliach). The last proved the most popular suggestion and a subcommittee including William Fraser, mason, and William G. McRobbie, joiner, was appointed to visit Craiglich and report on the accessibility of building materials and the approximate cost of a monument of stone and concrete which would be visible on the summit. At a meeting on 13 June 1919 Mr McRobbie submitted plans for a cairn 30 feet high and 12 feet at base and specifications for same. He was then asked to get offers for erecting this from one or two local contractors. But at the next meeting on 27 June Mr McRobbie reported that no offers were forthcoming. After discussion, Mr Fraser was asked if he would undertake the task, payment to be made for time and material, and he agreed to do so.

The sketch that he submitted was for a cairn 12 feet high on a 10 foot base, tapering to 3 feet at the top, with an inscription tablet a third of the way up. His specification was as follows:

> Foundation - the surface to be dug of to the hard and the Foundation
>   to be Laid with large flat stones and solide packed at the
> Back the Building to be of Drie stone Roubles work joints to be all
> Broken and the stones to be all Built end Long and put close together
> and Built to the taper shown and finished on tope with concrate say
> 2 cwts of cement & five cwts of good clean sand the Contractor to do
> all Labour afford all Material and halage the stones will be got on
> the Finzen Estate unles otherwise arranged a inscription Stone will
> be Built in where directed but will be suplied.

In July 1920 Mr Fraser submitted his account as follows:

	hours			
Wm. Fraser	245	à	1/8	£20 – 8 – 4
E. Stuart	72	..	1/8	6
A. McGregor	72	à	5/	18
James Benzie	78	..	1/-	3 –18
A. Greig	100	..	1/2	5 –16 – 8
Tom Mearns	45	..	1/-	2 – 5
18 cwts cement			7/-	6 – 6
Sand Holed			7/6	7 – 6
				£63 – 1 – 6
		Tablet		4 – 5 – 2
				£67 – 6 – 8

The subscription list shows that the blacksmith at the West Side, James Nicoll, Marywell, contributed a weather guide. The monument was unveiled on a day of pouring rain: Craig recalls watching the participants from a west-facing manse window with my mother, my father of course being in the procession. The most quoted feature was that the farmer in Tulloch, Lewis Strachan, drove his phaeton right to the top of Craiglich. To begin with the monument was very prominent: it is still visible from a distance, more so from the Coull direction. On the neighbouring Mortlich hill is a memorial to the tenth and last Duke of Gordon; this apparently was never more than a cairn of stones with an inscription slab at the foot.

The Fraser family featured both on the 1913 testimonial list and on that of 1954; although by then not at the same place, they were represented by both second and third generations. Making his first rounds of the parish in 1913 my father had found them at Boghead, on the Perkhill under Meall Maud. I remember William Fraser, generally known as Fraser - the - mason, in later years as a slightly bent figure with a characteristic felt hat and fluffy beard stumping up the village at great speed with the aid of a stick. The list of Frasers in my father's notebook included 'Alick 16 horseman At home'. Presently he was on the list of young communicants and then, like most of his contemporaries, he was off to the war, later to be one of the original members of the local sub-branch of the British Legion. In the late thirties he became postman for our area, which included the scattered West Side of the parish.   Early in the day he had absorbed the headlines of the day's newspaper (wearing a large pair of horn-rimmed spectacles he could be seen with the <u>Press and Journal</u> spread out on the handlebars of his bicycle) and was ready to discuss world affairs. I well remember the day on which his main headline was on the dropping of the first atomic bomb at Hiroshima; Alex. reckoned it was the Bible prophecy of the burning of the world coming true.

Eventually giving up the croft he came to live at Ashfield, at Burnside; later he was to move into the village. But this was not yet retirement. Before the latter event, after forty years in the service of the Post Office, and marked by a public presentation, came perhaps the most alarming of his postal experiences. In the severe winter of 1959-60 came a day of blizzard when it was realised in the village that Postie Fraser hadn't returned from his rounds in the West Side. My father wrote from Edinburgh after a visit to Lumphanan: 'Alick had a terrible day in a snowstorm in January. He lost

himself in a drift about Tillylair and at the Pole met a County snow plough
coming to meet him after dark. The plough had been turned out by Williams
of the Bank after they had stopped for the day. That was the storm when a
girlie from Inverurie perished in a field on her way home from school'. I
recalled coming out of my London office to find a newsboard at Charing Cross
with the legend: 'Inverurie girl lost in snow'. Alex. was indeed in a state
of collapse when met by the plough, and appropriately when his presentation
was featured in the Press and Journal Henry Williams was in the photograph.
It was the latter who wrote to me later when Alex. acquired the old bakery as
a retirement home: 'Our new baker is "Postie Fraser" but I am afraid we shall
never see his bread'. As treasurer for many years of the local British Legion,
Mr Williams always wrote a summary of the local news, first to my father, then
to me, along with our receipts. Alex. Fraser died in hospital in April 1971;
the obituary cutting from the newspaper which I found among my father's papers
was I think the last press cutting he made.

> Frame your mind to mirth and merriment —
> Which bars a thousand harms, and lengthens life.
> — Shakespeare.

This cheerful contribution to the Don 'Musings' came from Miss Bella Coutts,
then at the Howeburn, another of the individuals who contributed both to my
father's 1913 testimonial and to that of 1954, the latter with her husband.
When we think of Bella we see first a neat navy-and-red uniformed postwoman,
complete with broad-brimmed hat, deftly delivering mail. She was not our usual
'post' but occasionally brought the afternoon mail; ours was the last house to
have a second delivery in our direction. The usual postman — before Alex.
Fraser we had another ex-serviceman James Dowers — left our letters on the table
inside the back door; Bella always made a point of putting them inside the
front door: that was when the front door later really was in front. She always
seemed to have a smile on her weather-tanned face and a twinkle in her eye.

Off-duty she was even jollier, and in her youth evidently very jolly indeed.

She lived with her mother, Isa Coutts, a cripple for many years, and also
nevertheless of a cheerful countenance. From Howeburn they moved to Cloak
Cottage and later to one of the smaller houses at Glenanan. Bella loved parties,
and a 'sauty bannock party' that she gave at Cloak one Saturday night has passed
into legend. Their neighbour at Cloak House, Andrew Low, who had earlier been
at a wedding, was teasing one of the Miss Milnes from the Bakery, whereupon
she lifted up the bowl of batter and poured it over Andra's head, whence it
quickly spread over his best black suit. Next morning John Riddler, cycling
down from Greenburn, Tornaveen, to the Free Church, noted that Andra's best
suit was 'hingin' on the rope'.

Bella provided us with one of our great delights - a wind-up gramophone
with a large pink horn on a wooden base. She had just acquired a 'portable'.
We went along one evening to Glenanan - my mother, sisters and I - to hear
some of Bella's records on her new 'toy' (I recall 'The weddin' o' MacInnes
and his cross-eyed Peg') not knowing that we were to fall heir to the other.
She gave us a selection of records, too, ranging from large 78's - hymns such
as 'Nearer my God to Thee' and 'A few more years shall roll' through 'Beautiful
garden of roses' to small Woolworths discs 'When I met Connie in the cornfield'
and 'Song of the dawn'.

Late in life Bella married and went to live at Kirkstyle, Midmar, where
her mother also lived before she died. The wedding ceremony took place in the
manse. My sister Wendy and I, having prepared the room and set a vase of
flowers there, retreated to the garden. But after the ceremony Bella came
in search of us, in her pretty blue dress which an American cousin had sent,
to thank us for the flowers.

Most homes in the parish were of a modest size, and one might wonder how
in some cases numerous occupants fitted in, particularly if 'summer visitors'
(sometimes called 'lodgers') were catered for. Children boarded out by the
County Council, too, might be added to an already complete or growing family.

These were by no means regarded as second-class citizens, and would continue when grown up to regard this as their home. The boarded out children wore substantial, if readily recognisable, serge suits and dresses, woollen socks and stockings, with, for the girls, print dresses in summer. Many of us wore cotton pinafores to school, as French children of both sexes still do, which home-laundering and starching kept fresh-looking. And the girls' white broderie-anglaise which was a feature of social occasions such as school concerts may well have been hand-me-downs of long standing. It was not uncommon, however, and quite acceptable, for any boy to explain his absence from school 'My boots were at the souter's', and I have heard in the early 1930's a young farmer in his first place expressing doubts as to the possibility of his children's attendance at Sunday School on the grounds that they didn't have any Sunday clothes: doubts promptly dismissed by my father. I think the children as a whole appreciated character more than clothes, and in many cases there were more 'characters' among the less well-off than among those with a more sheltered upbringing. All clothing would be of a quality that would nowadays be highly regarded. The fact that there were two tailors in the village and at least two dressmakers in the parish is significant. 'Ready-to-wear' was not yet common. Older women wore the same familiar Sunday clothes or 'social' dresses for years, although young unmarried choir members, for example, might wear a new, rather glamorous, gown for performances at Church At-Home or Choir Concert. Many men wore very characteristic headgear, easily recognisable on a passing cart.

It may sometimes be thought that current attempts to make the disabled a normal part of the community are of recent origin. Provision may in some cases have been woefully inadequate by modern medical standards, but on the other hand it was commoner than it is now to find a physically or mentally disabled member of a family, or someone else cared for within a family, sitting by a fireside instead of being relegated to an institution. A half-way house might be the local poorshouse, and at Lumphanan that was for many years the

home of cheerful Joe Grassick, a wheel-chair cripple. When my father came
in 1913 Joe was being cared for by the Grubb family at Wardhead on the West
Side of the parish; on the testimonial list for the induction gift Joe's
sixpence was recorded before the Wardhead subscription. When on the death of
Mr Grubb the family gave up the farm Joe came to the Poorshouse at Knowehead,
up the road from the school, and would be wheeled down to join the fun on such
special occasions as the school picnic. My brother Craig coined for him the
name 'Joe Roe'. He had a lively intelligence and inspired much affection as
is evidenced in the letter received by my father in November 1945 from Mrs H.
Gibbon, matron of Knowehead Home (as it became) when Joe had to be transferred
for more nursing care to Woodcot, Stonehaven:

> Just a note to let you know that I had a long letter from Joe
> Grassick yesterday and I am so pleased he is being well treated and
> very comfortable. There are four trained nurses and two learning.
> He was put to bed when he went there but the Dr. called on Thursday
> so he is to get up every day. The matron has ordered a paper for him.
> He says she is very nice. I just thought I would let you know as you
> have always been so nice calling here from time to time and I had not
> time to let you know before he left here.

For the next few years my father was able to make at least an annual visit to
see Joe at Stonehaven.

The ideal of 'the disabled in the community' is surely realised in the
hospitable home of Miss Maggie Macgregor, niece of Miss Macgregor of Craigmill,
at Moss-side on the old road which runs from the Stothert Memorial Church up
to Parkhill on the Tarland turnpike. When she was a young woman her father
was killed by falling off a hay-cart. At first, in addition to running the
croft to which they had come in 1911, my father had suggested that she might
look after the occasional elderly person recommended by the County Council.
But presently Maggie felt she could do more for a younger age-group, and at
the time of writing is still caring for these, ably assisted now by a long-
standing resident, Miss Jean Mess, a diabetic. One blind girl was with her
for over twenty years, until she died. Under Maggie's care a mongol girl
(they were always known as 'Maggie's girls') was believed to have broken the

record by living to the age of 48. My husband and I happened to look in while the latter was near her end. There she lay, downstairs in the 'best room' to make nursing easier, by her side a bottle of the same grape-juice that we had just purchased for our picnic lunches. Maggie had been lining the ceiling with acoustic tiles, and then, when it was suggested that the tall Tilley-lamp on the sideboard might endanger these, she had brought in the beautiful brass stable lantern. There was no electricity at Moss-side, and in the kitchen the black pot still hung over the open fire, although calor gas was used. No television, therefore, but on the radio Maggie could still listen to dance-music and recall the days when she had her own band. Much music-making went on in remote parts of the parish in those days. Maggie played the piano; she had never taken lessons – not for lack of persuasion by her aunt at Craigmill – but listened to gramophone records and then played by ear, 'vamping' with the left hand. The other members of the band were Sandy Taylor, cornet, and two fiddlers, John Riddler of Greenburn and Willie Little-john, Sunnybrae, Perkhill. Mostly they played Scottish dance music, but I remember one At-Home when Maggie launched into 'Wheezy Anna'. Other popular songs she recalls playing included 'Sweet Hortense' and 'Horsey, keep your tail up'. At one time Maggie had also been a post-woman, and as she knew all the 'locals' she was in demand to keep the records at roups, where speed and accuracy were essential – not to mention neat handwriting.

In the course of his first round of the parish my father had knocked on the door of a croft in a fairly remote area. A small boy came running through to see who was there, stared for a moment at the clerical garb, then shouted 'Come an' see the bloody mannie!' Thus was sown the germ of what turned out to be a happy idea. For many summers a Sunday School was held on Sunday after-noon in the barn of one of the farms, first at Parkgreens, later at Futtie and latterly at Home Farm, Camphill. This was well attended by the children in the area, some of whom were 'boarded out', and the season would end with a modest tea-party in the barn. There was also, on each occasion, a pleasant

tea-party in the farmhouse for the minister, or his deputy - sometimes my
brother would take the class - and the organist, (sometimes me.) A small
harmonium was acquired secondhand from 'Cockie' Hunter's in Aberdeen, and it
seemed altogether appropriate to have as background to 'French' or 'Jackson'
the chink of harness from next door as the minister's pony munched her way
through a nice wisp of hay. Far from having come, as he at first rather feared
from the above encounter, to a heathen land, my father met with nothing but
enthusiasm and co-operation for this venture. The story had an appropriate
ending even for the little boy: some years later my father was paying his
first call on a newly-wed couple, the boy now with a place of his own. The
latter, having intercepted the minister in the close, asked if he would like
to see round the farm. As they passed the kitchen window my father noticed
a signal being exchanged, and when the tour of inspection was over he was invited indoors, to find there a most delicious 'spread' in the best room.

     A warmer initial reception met my father on his first visit to the
lodging house at Moss-side Cottage, down the road from the Macgregors. At
our annual Church At-Home he would make mention of parishioners who had died
during the past year and I can remember his referring thus to Jeannie Smart,
who like her mother Meggie before her had for many years provided overnight
lodging for the wandering people. The old house could be stretched to accommo-
date an extraordinary number of tired pedlars and other pedestrians. Jeannie's
daughter, the late Mrs Mary Paul, once wrote to my father from Canada 'I've
seen my mother sheltering 16 people in that wee but and ben on a night of
blin' drift going out to the little croft for two wisps of straw to make a
bed shift on the floor for her weary bairns'. She recalled that in her
grandmother's time 'one night in particular policemen came looking for some
one suspected of stealing. There were 16 in the house at the time when they
called. "Foo mony bairns hae ye the night Maggie?" In reply she answered
"Come in an' coont them". The answer she got was "God bless you". Although
a stormy night she got up and made a pot of tea to warm them, the Bobbies, on
their rounds'.

Jeannie once told my father that she and her mother 'had kept fowk a' their days an' never had fash wi' ony o' them' – a worthy tribute, surely, he commented, to both guests and hostelry. Actually, other local evidence suggests that occasionally the 'bairns' were glad of a friendly elbow, but this could be given in the knowledge that no harm would come even to a young lady who proffered it. There was a certain ritual on arrival: to the broth-pot on the fire each guest would contribute his morsel of beef, tied with string, each making his own recognisable knot in his string. Each would bring in a peat from the stack. Part of the nearby peat moss was designated 'Minister's Moss', marked by a wooden post at each corner bearing the initials 'M.M'. I have seen one of these, but by the time my father came his moss was practically worked out, and Jeannie was welcome to take anything she could still find there. She hadone permanent lodger, an old man known as 'Moss' who spent the summer in a shack outside and came in to sleep in the fire-house in winter. One afternoon my father called and found Jeannie Smart in bed and the fire out. Earlier that day she had felt so ill that she had told 'Moss' 'I think I'm gaun tae dee'. 'Weel, weel, Jeannie, ye'll jist hae tae dee than', he remarked, and left her to it. My father set to, lit the fire and soon had the kettle boiling. She lived many years after that; born in 1847, she died about the age of 82.

Maggie Macgregor wrote to me in 1973: 'the poor wanderers of the road had not much money amongst their hands at that time. They were so grateful when given an egg or two or a "suppie" milk poured into the blackened jug they used for making their tea in. Commonly a syrup tin with a wire put round to hang on a fire. Then I can mind on the "better class" who went round with their pony and spring-cart. You could buy some bonnie ornaments then from 1/6 maybe 2/6 but they were not the kind that the glaze peels off when you wash them. They were all nicely glazed at that time. There is nobody will even buy "rags" meantime – no bonnie bowl offered for them now'. I can vouch for the 'glaze': we still have jugs from this period.

Jeannie Smart's mantle fell upon Mr and Mrs Geordie Keith. The Keith family came from Lumsden; Mrs Keith was a Mearns, others of the family having settled nearby: William, at Moss-side before the Macgregors, had moved up to Mosshead. Joe was vanman to John Walker, merchant at Parkhill shop, their cousin Maxwell lived with his sister Mrs James Ingram at Perkmoss: some will reappear later in this chronicle. Before the 1914 war Geordie and his twin sons, Angus and John, went round with a cart supplying crockery and glass. The twins, fine-looking young men as my mother remembered them, 'two nice, quiet lads' was Maggie Macgregor's verdict, went off to the war and did not return. One fell at Loos, the other died in hospital at Etaples. A grandson of Jeannie Smart's, then a Canadian, James Mitchell, died at Vimy Ridge. Mrs Keith had an elder son, Maxie, who continued with the cart until the late thirties. Earlier all the Keiths had spent the winters in Aberdeen, then when Jeannie Smart's house became vacant at Moss-side the Keiths took over the care of the wandering folk, Geordie continuing on foot his parish rounds, selling smaller items, his pack on his back. He became very deaf and used to be disgruntled if he did not always make a sale. Some say he took to the bottle quite early on; few who saw him in the village, apparently perennially waiting for the bus at the War Memorial, remembered, or even knew, that among the names inscribed on the long 1914-18 list of 26 were those of his two boys.

The day that Princess Elizabeth was married — 20 November 1947 — it so happened that a young man from the Commonwealth War Graves Commission was visiting the parish to check on the one or two war graves that we had locally. He came to the manse in the morning and my father persuaded him, as he was staying the night at the hotel, to join us all in our local celebration that evening in the Parish Hall. When he demurred on the grounds that he would know no one, my father guaranteed to find him a partner, and I was deputed to fill the role. This caused some mystification locally, especially as the young man was thought to resemble the Duke of Edinburgh. But no-one knew, that evening, what had taken place in the afternoon. My father had been reminded, on thinking of war graves, that he hadn't seen Geordie Keith, then a widower, for some time. So off he went up the old road, only to find at Moss-side Cottage a locked door and then the sound of low moaning inside. Obviously recalling his earlier experience with Jeannie Smart, he went in some alarm to consult the nearest neighbour, Maggie Macgregor. She kept her own counsel but accompanied my father back to Geordie's, where she knew how to prise the door open. When he saw my father Geordie, loyal subject, waved his bottle: 'Ah Mr. Donald, jist celebratin', ye ken!' Geordie died in the Royal Infirmary in July 1953. The old house became a ruin, but their neighbour planted daffodils in the garden, and cows graze among the berry bushes.

We saw many of the 'wandering people' at the manse, filling their tea-tins from the kettle on the kitchen range or spreading 'pieces'. Some made pot-scrubbers from heather which were ideal for cleaning the porridge pot. My father had an arrangement with Mrs Keith whereby anyone asking for a shilling for a bed was given a signed chit; cash too often was diverted elsewhere before the recipient got as far as Moss-side. He would then settle up periodically. When young I once acceded one Sunday afternoon to an apparently innocent request for some methylated spirit for a man's stove. Afterwards I described the recip-ient - a newcomer - whereupon my father, recognising the latter in the village, accosted him 'Ah, you're the man with the stove'. Presently the latter righted the record by appearing in army uniform. Some of the wandering folk were pipers, some proficient, some not. If the former, Craig would get out his pipes and have a tune with them. Some, between the wars, were not true wandering folk at all, but unemployed ex-servicemen, perhaps selling matches. My mother always had a soft spot for these, having lost her brother on the Somme. Families with children tended to camp out either at Dess or at Satan's Den, on the road to Torphins, and sporadically the children attended school, their clothes permeated with camp-fire smoke. Sometimes I was called upon by our teacher to help them

with their reading during the dinner-hour. I can remember a baby being brought
to the manse to be christened, tea being served afterwards as usual. Thereafter when calling the mother always reminded us that this was the baby that
was christened.

One winter's night, on the way up to Moss-side, old Mrs Macphee succumbed
and died in the snow. They came to ask if she might lie in the church hall
until the clan could be summoned for the funeral, and permission was readily
granted. On the day of the funeral the hall was packed. Receiving them on
entry my father recognised a face familiar from his Banffshire youth. His
mother had been accustomed to receive the wanderers at their home at the Bridge
of Fiddich; one of these men had offered to teach my father to wrestle, and he
agreed to learn; the next thing he knew he was on his back on the kitchen
floor, much to the consternation of his mother. But the 'tackle' that he
learned that day was to come in useful on at least two occasions later in life:
once in arresting an intruder at the manse one night and once in ejecting a
troublemaker at the Parish Hall. (On the former occasion he was temporarily
alarmed to hear the male voice of another 'intruder' in the house; this was,
however, my mother's dramatic intervention to deceive No.1 before she sallied
forth to Burnside for help.) At all events my father was delighted to renew
acquaintance with his wrestling instructor. Afterwards he always declared
that Mrs Macphee's funeral was the most reverent that he had ever taken. He
did not relate how, on this occasion, the travelling people were dressed.
After his retirement, at another such funeral in Lumphanan, the male mourners
all wore bowler hats and brown kid gloves. This was told me by Lucy Grant,
who because of her kindness to the deceased had been invited to be present.

For as long as my father was at Lumphanan it was customary for a funeral
to take place on the third day after death. Not long after he came, it so
happened that one Saturday evening he had arranged to take a funeral the following Tuesday; this meant that the grave would have to be prepared on Monday,
so he at once set out in search of the gravedigger in order to give him as long

notice as possible. The previous holder of the office, George McDonald, of whom more will be heard presently, had just retired, and his successor was James Emslie, feuar of Woodside at the east edge of the Cairnbeathie wood. He was always known as 'Postie' Emslie, although it is not clear when he occupied this position. He was employed as a sawmiller with Mr George Spark at Faburn. On this Saturday evening, having drawn a blank at Woodside, my father proceeded to the next most likely place, the bar at the hotel in the village. There, sure enough, was 'Postie' Emslie, but so put out was the latter at having been tracked down to this haunt — and no doubt invigorated by what he had consumed — that he insisted that he commence his task straight away. Absolutely adamant and deaf to all persuasion, he accompanied my father back to the church and got his tools out: the boards, the pick and the spade, the measuringline and edging tool. Somewhat apprehensive of the result, my father stayed to help. It so happened that the new grave was to the west side of the church, in full view of the houses at Burnside, and Alex. Sherriffs, enjoying a quiet pipe on the seat outside his door, looked on with interest from afar. At the initial marking out, my father got the impression that 'Postie', from excess of zeal or other cause, was going slightly off course. Unobtrusively with his foot, he moved the board slightly, and by dint of keeping his foot there ensured regular progress. Suddenly 'Postie' noticed the foot. Raising his implement above his head he advanced on my father. That, fortunately, is where the tale ends: presumably the very act of threatening violence cleared the air.

'Postie' Emslie became, at one remove, part of our childhood lore. At Woodside he kept a goat. My father, before he went visiting of an afternoon with pony and trap, would leave the pony's evening feed ready in the stable. Gradually he noticed that Dandy was showing symptoms of undernourishment. The 'little stable', where she occupied the further of two stalls, away from the single central skylight was dark (the stable later became the coal cellar,

one stall for manse coal, one for church; the 'big stable' was where parishioners could leave their horses; new loose-boxes for ours were later made
elsewhere). Then one evening, returning earlier than usual, my father entered
the 'little stable' to discover, in Dandy's stall, 'Postie' Emslie's goat
having a good feed. For years afterwards we used to repeat the payline: 'And
the goat turned round and said "Beh-eh-eh".' 'Postie' resigned as gravedigger on 28 February 1917; he himself was eventually buried at the U.F.
church where his mother's grave was.

Writing of 'Postie' Emslie leads us on to the lady who eventually became
the last 'feuar' of Woodside. May Wright Thomson (generally known as 'My
Vricht') was both a local character and a piece of social history. When
terminology became more sophisticated it emerged that she was a particular
type of psychopath; while her intellect remained more than adequate she was
subject to occasional bouts of eccentric behaviour. On these occasions she
was perfectly cognisant of what she was doing and saying, but probably persisted out of sheer devilment. There was no question of criminal act or even
intent, and under the more enlightened legislation of later days, when medical
science had advanced and public attitudes changed, she would certainly not
have been treated as she was. Fortunately she did live long enough to benefit
from these at the end. She must early on have completely exasperated her own
family; they were probably the last who could have done anything with her.

She was perhaps what is now known as a 'drop out' yet without most of
the characteristics which the term implies. She was living an entirely independent life — and in fact to the end had means of her own — when the 'system'
descended upon her. There is no saying how long she could have continued to
live as she chose; outside interference resulted in her running up a bill —
which she paid — for her maintenance 'in care' until national legislation
entitled her to become mainly a charge upon the State. She enters the annals
of the parish when nearly fifty, during the first world war. She married a

serviceman (a bricklayer to trade) on leave from the Army. The banns were called from the church door, two surfacemen being summoned off the nearby railway as witnesses. (When, many years later, she heard of the death of one of these, Robbie Emslie the bellman, she observed 'Well, that's ane o' my bridesmaids deid'.) When after the marriage ceremony they arrived at the station she was still carrying her bouquet of yellow broom. Her husband survived the war but deserted her about 1920 and she resumed her former life-style. When 'Postie' Emslie died she moved into his tumbledown cottage, Woodside, which she referred to as 'Emslie's Cottage' (or sometimes 'Emslie's Hovel' or even 'St. James's Palace') and when the roof fell in she moved into the outhouse which he had used as a workshop, naming it Birkenhill. She her-self could use tools and made for herself a splendid barrow - long and narrow, with no sides, as for carrying firewood. She was working on it one day when a local girl, doing duty as postman, passed down the 'old road'. May told her proudly that she had just heard 'Postie' Emslie's ghost say to her 'Ye're makin' a richt job o' that barra, May!'

May kept pretty much to her own side of the wood except perhaps at berry-picking time: she sold her blaeberries and cranberries and contrived a patent device for picking these, a sort of cross between a brush and a comb, with a piece of syrup-tin nailed to the back; she presented one to my brother. She would greet him 'Aye aye minister's son!' - just as she greeted my father 'Aye aye minister!' A newcomer to the parish was once told by his predecessor: 'There's one bit of advice I have for you: never take cranberries from My Vricht; she goes up to the Cloak hill and when both her baskets are full she just takes off her bloomers, ties the legs, and fills them'. To most people she was just good for a laugh, at the same time inspiring a certain respect: someone to be reckoned with. Occasionally she sallied forth to the village for shopping (mostly she would come down to vans on the main road) and on the pound notes she spent would be her name and address (in one of its forms) or the legend: 'This is one of May Wright's beloved pounds which she will never

see again'. She would put her earnings into a Post Office Savings Bank
Account.

In the wood she was said to talk to the birds (which of us who has a
garden does not?) and round her door was a most beautiful pale yellow wild
rambler rose. I recall my brother and his wife Mary, not long after their
marriage in 1945, coming down from the wood with a great armful of the very
prickly stems covered with tiny blooms: years later Craig sent me some small
roots of it; only one 'took', produced thirteen roses on a stem about a foot
high, and died. We still think of them as 'May's roses'. Mostly she kept
herself to herself, always neatly dressed in a long skirt with apron tied
tightly round her waist, and a grey-and-white checked headsquare tied under
what I remember as a stern, white face. (My brother comments: 'it wasn't
always stern - she had quite a twinkle' - which goes to show that it all depended whom she was facing.) Occasionally she would accost a 'trespasser'
in aggressive tones, and this was her eventual undoing. One day in 1932 a
deputation came to the manse, evidently to complain of her. It seems my
father reassured the complainants, accepting responsibility for her future
conduct. But complaints perhaps persisted; I know that from time to time
he would reprove May on this account.

Then one day in the thirties officialdom stepped in. May and her immediate belongings were removed to the Poorshouse at Knowehead. Next day May
fetched her barrow and wheeled them all home again. There was a pause, then
on 1 September 1937 officialdom struck again. Armed with a sherriff's warrant
(for which she was later charged 2/6) and medical certificates in Lunacy
(£2.2s.) she was once more removed, this time to the Royal Mental Hospital at
Aberdeen. (Removal cost to her £1.15.4). She had played their game - as she
so often did - by addressing the Torphins policeman, who was present at the
removal, as though he were the King. This was all done quite without reference to my father, who had of course no official standing in the matter;
perhaps, indeed, to relieve him from the need to intervene, a day was chosen

when he was from home. Someone was to write to him in 1938: '...You have been a good friend to May. As long as she keeps on speaking a lot of silly talk...they will keep her in the Asylum.' To begin with, May was restless. My father visited her on 2 November and again on 28 December 1937 when he noted that she was 'in disgrace'. But she then settled down fairly happily and indeed when she was temporarily removed to Montrose Royal Asylum from April 1943 until May 1944 (late on 21 April bombs were dropped on Aberdeen and again on the 23rd one fell on Craigie Loaning) despite apparently greater freedom there she looked forward to her return. She wrote the following pretty lucid letter to my father from Montrose:

North Esk Villa
Royal Asylum,
Sunnyside,
Montrose.

Monday
24th April
 1944

> I'm writing you this letter to let you know I'm always here in
> Montrose yet but looking forward to be back in Aberdeen Royal Mental
> Asylum Cornhill Road again soon. Just 1 year since I came here on
> the 24th day of April 1943 – how quick time passes. I wrote ––
> months ago ... I told her I was to be back in Aberdeen soon that time
> but did not get so we think we may be there soon again I think but of
> course I'm not yet sure. There has been little snow in this part of
> the world & Farming will be going on in full swing. The farms is
> very large in comparison to where I once came from. Wheat Barley &
> Corn grows here. There is about 60 milk cows Dairy ['milch' stroked out]
> about 250 pigs belonging to this place. Work is done mostly by machinery.
> We get a gran view of Montrose & the sea and other places if we choose
> to go & see them for ourselves no one cares where we go if we be back
> in time for our food an our Bed – but they like us to go to Bed at $\frac{1}{2}$
> past 7 at night rise at 7 next morning not to sleep our heads into train
> oil you know. Well I saw the Revd Mr. Hepburn some days ago I told him
> I was to write to you he is minister for this place he was acquainted
> with you years ago & stayed or met with you in an Edinburgh Hotel. You
> can look over your memory & see if you remember anything about him he
> looks a nice Dark haired fellow hes got a wife & one of a Family he has
> an other church some where in the name of St Cyprus I dont know if Ive
> spelled it right but you excuse me if Im dawft I dont know better. I
> am well tell the Lumphanan folk I am asking for the whole job lot of
> them and I hope your & yours are a fine. Hoping to see you in Aberdeen
> when I get back I'll write when I am over to Aberdeen & let ye ken.
> With best wishes to you & yours from Mrs John Jas Thomson dont answer
> this in case we may be away to Aberdeen.
>
>   Cherrio minister

As the advent of the National Health Service approached there appears
to have been a general settling of accounts, and as May was owing some
£885 – mostly for board at the RMH over the years – the question arose of
appointing a curator bonis who would have access to the £950 odd in May's
Post Office Savings Bank account. Otherwise, the debt would fall to be
borne by the Public Assistance Department. In the event, the only relative
who could be traced declined, even after a visit from my father, to have anything to do with it, possibly – and probably correctly – anticipating May's
wrath should her nest-egg be known to have come under this jurisdiction.
Thereupon, on 10 February 1948, the Chief Assistance Officer 'respectfully
submits to the Court that another person who might properly be appointed
Curator Bonis ... is the Reverend Francis Cantlie Donald, St Finan's, Lumphanan. Minister of the Parish of Lumphanan, who has taken an interest in the
welfare of the said May Wright or Thomson for many years, and who is willing
...' My father went into Aberdeen that day and signed his consent, and was
on 12 February duly appointed.

No sooner were May's debts settled than the inauguration of the National
Health Service, and consequent transfer of the cost of the maintenance and
treatment of patients in the Royal Mental Hospital from the County Council to
the State, did away with the need for the Curatory. Explaining this to my
father in a letter of 9 September 1948, the County Clerk Depute added that of
course there would be no legal objection to his retaining the office of Curator
Bonis if he wished to do so in the interest of Mrs Thomson. 'However, I must
point out to you that the discharge of your duties as Curator Bonis involves
a certain amount of administration such as the preparation of the annual accounts
which have to be lodged with the Accountant of Court, and, to enable you to
carry on that administration to the satisfaction of the Accountant of Court,
I think it would probably be necessary for you to obtain the assistance of
a Solicitor. The fees payable to a Solicitor for work in connection with the
Curatory would, of course, be a proper charge against the Curatory funds...'

By 18 September the firm of advocates selected by my father wrote that the County Council were to send the relevant papers the following week. On 16 May 1946 my father had ascertained in Aberdeen that May's date of birth was 19 December 1867. He had obviously been checking up on her pension rights and noted her pension number as received from the Assistance Board. This had of course not been payable as by the time she was 70 she was already in care. The pension question cropped up again in 1949 and it appears that in the process of assuming the curatory he omitted to cash several weeks of a new Non-Contributory Old Age Pension book and had to make good the amount himself.

Latterly his duties included the replenishing of May's wardrobe. In December 1949 a nurse wrote: 'I find the slippers received from Milne & Munro unsuitable for Mrs. May Thomson. Something soft with a crepe sole would be more suitable. I have returned the slippers to Milne & Munro', He was rather hurt over this, as he had eschewed the 'softie' style in order that May might have something more dressy. His pocket book (undated but corresponding with an engagement diary entry) for 23 January 1950 has an Aberdeen shopping list which includes 'May's rigout'. He had that day been seeing not only May but the hospital's medical superintendent. May had just had her hair cut short and asked my father to take her in a brush and comb next time he visited her.

On 21 May 1952 the Physician Superintendent wrote to the firm of advocates:

> I duly received your letter of 17th May last regarding (Mrs. May Wright or Thomson) and I have to say that prior to that time Mrs. Thomson was not in receipt of any regular allowance for comforts. The only contributions to her welfare were made by the Rev. Francis Donald, when at a very occasional visit he left her a small parcel.
>
> Since then we have arranged for 5s. per week Old Age Pension to be paid to our House Steward on her behalf. This money is expended on weekly comforts such as fruit, sweets, cakes, etc. through our Hospital Shop.
>
> Mrs. Thomson, although now a very feeble old lady, is able to be up and about for a few hours each day. She has virtually no clothing of her own and is not very pleased to wear hospital clothing as she says she can afford to supply herself with clothing. I have asked the Matron to look over the patient's wardrobe and to let me know what clothing she could be suitably supplied with. I am informed that she requires a dress, a cardigan, two sets of underclothing, 4 pairs woollen stockings, slippers, shoes and handkerchiefs.

If you can put me in funds of say £20 out of her own money, I will have the articles provided for her.

My father was to pay one or two more visits to May before his retirement. Going home in the bus after one of these he was asked by a parishioner how May was. His reply is quoted: 'There's a lot o' folk goin' about outside nae half as wise as May'.

CHAPTER FOUR

Changes and war

1914-1918.

Chapter 4

The Great War, when it came, took most people by surprise. As late as 23
July 1914 the House of Commons had been assured by the Chancellor of the Exchequer, Lloyd George, that relations between Britain and Germany were better
than they had been for years. But by Sunday 2 August chain reaction by Euro-
pean countries to the murder by a Serbian of the Austrian Archduke Franz
Ferdinand, and to the subsequent ultimatum, had resulted in a state of war
between the main powers. Britain was not obliged to support France, and at
first the Cabinet was divided on this issue. But the guarantee of the maintenance of Belgium's neutrality became the deciding factor when the German
army invaded Belgium en route for France. Britain declared war on Germany on
Tuesday 4 August.

The following Sunday at the morning service my father took as his text
'The Lord is my shepherd. I shall not want'. The Old Testament lesson had
been Psalm 37:

> Fret not thyself because of evil-doers, neither be thou envious
> against the workers of iniquity. For they shall soon be cut down like
> the grass, and wither as the green herb. Trust in the Lord, and do
> good: so shalt thou dwell in the land, and verily thou shalt be fed...

From the New Testament he read from John 14: 'Let not your heart be troubled
...' The sermon set the scene and reflected the first reactions: calm confidence, readiness to accept sacrifice in a just cause. Later, years of unpre-
cedentedly heart-rending war experience were to raise more complicated issues;
confidence gave way to bewilderment and soul-searching. Objectives became
less clear, realities - social and political - more evident.

> The Lord is my shepherd. I shall not want. These words strike the
> keynote of a Psalm which from beginning to end breathes forth _trust_ and
> _confidence_ in Jehovah - the God of Heaven and Earth. Like the peal of
> Sunday bells rising from an ancient sanctuary which has stood for cen-
> turies peacefully surrounded by green graves and spreading trees it
> proclaims the sweet gratitude of the worshipper for God's gifts of peace
> and plenty. 'The Lord is my shepherd. I shall not want. He maketh me
> to lie down in green pastures. He leadeth me beside the still waters.
> He restoreth my soul. He leadeth me in the paths of righteousness for
> his own name's sake'.

But the Psalmist was no mere man of dreams and pious meditation whose life was spent far from scenes of stir and action, and who vainly called 'Peace peace, when there is no peace'. He had passed through the storm and stress of an active life. In the pursuit of his calling as a shepherd he had been led into those deep and gloomy valleys so plentiful in the upland pasture lands of Palestine where wild beasts lurked in their dens and where the shepherd when he entered to look for straying sheep was continually at the mercy of unseen foes. (It was in a valley such as this - a valley of deep gloom - that young David caught a lion by its beard, and slew it and delivered a lamb from its mouth). Yet even in such a place the Psalmist felt secure in the keeping of the Almighty. 'Yea though I walk through the valley of the deep shadow I will fear no evil: for _Thou_ art with me: Thy rod and thy staff they comfort me'.

He was also a man of war. He had lived on tented fields and had grappled with his enemy in stern grips of deadly strife. Yet in later days he could lift his thoughts to God and say - 'Thou preparest a table before me in the presence of mine enemies; thou anointest my head with oil: my cup runneth over'. 'Surely _goodness_ and _mercy_ shall follow me all the days of my life: and I will _dwell_ in the house of the Lord for ever'.

Thus! under two images equally familiar in Hebrew poetry - that of the 'shepherd' watching over his flock, and that of the 'banquet' where Jehovah presides at the table of the just - the Psalmist expressed the peaceful calm of those who are conscious of the continued presence and the over-ruling providence of God.

So whether we take the Psalm to refer to _temporal_ or to _spiritual_ things it is equally true to life. (1) Take it to refer to temporal things - we can say from our own experience what we read in another Psalm this morning - 'The steps of a good man are ordered by the Lord; and he delighteth in His way. Though he fall he shall not be utterly cast down: for the Lord upholdeth him with His hand. I have been young and now I am old; yet have I not seen the righteous forsaken nor his seed begging bread'.

'The Lord is my shepherd. I shall not want'. We have never seen an honest industrious man in utter want unless he belonged to that senseless class, so common in our own country, who refuse to accept of help from a friend. (Nursing a vain and empty pride they prefer to starve rather than permit a friend the privilege of extending to them a helping hand in a time of need). But apart from such as these, in spite of frosts and storms and unprofitable harvests, in spite of outbreaks of disease, in spite of sudden accidents on land or shipwrecks on the sea, we can each of us truly say that we have not seen a righteous man forsaken nor his seed begging bread. Is it not rather a wonder to us all how some poor people live, and how families of happy, healthy children are reared and brought to manhood and to womanhood, with what one might call 'no visible means of support'. That is the wonder of the world - until we reflect that God is in His Heaven and that 'He giveth the beast his food'. 'He causeth the grass to grow for the cattle and herb for the service of man'.

(2) Or - on the other hand - suppose we take this Psalm to refer to God's gifts in spiritual things - to His guidance through life and His presence at death. We can say with equal truth 'The Lord is my shepherd. I shall not want'. For when troubles gather round us and our outlook upon life is dark - when friends misjudge us, when trusted ones desert us, when we lie in the grip of pain or when death draws near to our door -

where do we turn but to the Word of the Eternal God who whispers in our ear 'Come unto me all ye that labour and are heavy laden and I will give you rest'. Then when we reflect on Him who endures from generation to generation and who knoweth the hearts of the children of men, comfort steals over our minds and we can once more truthfully say 'The Lord is my shepherd. I shall not want. He maketh me to lie down in green pastures. He leadeth me beside the still waters. Yea though I walk through the valley of the shadow of death I will fear no evil, for Thou art with me, Thy rod and Thy staff they comfort me'.

Thus, whether we are faced with the prospect of worldly loss or with the greater calamity, anxiety of spirit, it is a comfort for us all to know that we can lift our thoughts to God, and that He can understand the secrets of our hearts. For at a crisis such as we are passing through at the present moment we need an anchor sure and steadfast to which to lash our hopes.

At the present moment we as a nation are passing through a crisis such as has never been known before since the world began. Only this day week we awoke to a world clad in the pleasant garments of summer and with everywhere around us prospects of an early and abundant harvest fast ripening in the fields. But!! - into the midst of these peaceful scenes (as we were assembling for prayer in the House of God) there was flashed throughout the land the terrible news of war.

We could scarcely believe it true! After 1900 years of the teaching of the Gospel of Christ - the gospel of peace and goodwill - we could scarcely believe it true that any government (conscious of the duty that it owed to its people and conscious of the terrible results that would follow upon the outbreak of war) could take upon itself the awful responsibility of plunging its people into the horrors of war; of war waged with those terrible engines of death now devised by the skill of man for the destruction of his kind.

We could not believe it true! Yet news came upon news, and within two days the whole continent of Europe was seething in the cauldron of strife. The days since this day week have looked like years, so much has been pressed into one short week. For a time it seemed as if God had fallen from His throne in the Heavens and the Devil was set loose upon the earth to ravage and devour.

For fast upon news of war came rumours of famine and want. Prices of food leapt up and for a time it seemed as if the devils of trade were more to be feared than the demons of war. Unscrupulous men - lost to a sense of their country's need - regardless of the miseries of the poor - sought for a time to make private gain at the cost of their country's good. While those who could buy by laying in supplies snatched bread from the mouth of the poor man's child.

Yet this was only for a time. For our statesmen, while engaged in preparations for a war which has been thrust upon them in spite of their most strenuous endeavours to keep peace, have not forgot the needs of the poor at home. By a series of Christ-like laws (not devised in the stress of the hour but carefully prepared) our Government have made sure that the poor man shall not want; that unscrupulous men shall not make gain at the cost of their country's need, but that trade shall be maintained and that all shall receive the necessities of life at reasonable cost, if need be at the expense of the coffers of the State.

Thus even amidst the din and the clash of arms, even through the smoke clouds of war, we can look to our God in Heaven, who giveth the ravens their food and supplieth the wants of the children of men, and say as our fathers said of yore 'The Lord is my shepherd. I shall not want'.

While those who leave their friends and their homes and buckle on their arms in 'defence' of their native land - for let the cravenhearted clamour as they may, so far as the British nation is concerned this war is waged not for offence or aggrandisement but to protect the vitals of the nation from the envy and ambition of a fiend. Therefore while the young men of the nation take up arms and leave their homes to do battle for their country, they can do so firmly confident that their cause is just and good, and assured in heart and spirit that 'Though they walk through the valley of the shadow of death, they need fear no evil; for while they serve their country and their God 'goodness and mercy shall follow them all the days of their life and they will dwell in the House of the Lord for ever'.

<u>All</u> will not come back. We must prepare ourselves for that. Many young lives will be lost, and many a home will be plunged in gloom. 'Yet greater love hath no man than this that a man lay down his life for his friends'. It is far far better and it is a more Christ-like thing to give one's life in the flower of one's age than to spend a hundred years in selfish ease at home. It is a nobler thing to buckle on one's armour in defence of righteousness and honourable dealing than to remain at home in ease while brave men are shedding their blood for the honour and protection of their native land.

And may God's blessing go with all who have gone to the war! May His comfort be found in the homes of those who will never return.

Just over four weeks later, on 8 September 1914, the merchant from the West Side, **Alex** Reid, doing his round with his horse-drawn cart, spread the news of the day: 'There's a wee German got in at the manse an' they canna get rid o'm!' We had never heard this tale of Craig's arrival until sixty years later my brother and I called at Marywell smiddy to ask James Emslie to 'take a cord' at my father's funeral. James remembered the merchant bringing the news to Broomhill farm. Alex had resigned from the post of precentor in March of that year, owing to pressure of business, being succeeded by William D. Harper, Home Farm, Auchenhove. Besides running his business and keeping an excellent garden, with a score of beehives, the merchant had sidelines such as pulling teeth. This was on occasion accomplished merely by leaning out of the cart, pliers in hand; children would then be rewarded with a sweetie out of the jar.

Some time before Craig's birth my father happened to be speaking to the stationmaster, at this time Mr James Stuart, a member of the Free Church.

The latter asked how they were liking Lumphanan, to which my father replied
that he was very happy there but that his wife was a little lonely; she was
expecting a baby and people seemed shy of calling. 'Oh, then, my wife will
call.' Not only did Mrs Stuart call; she it was who was with my mother when
Craig was born. Sixty years later their son Alex, when minister of Banchory
West, took part in my father's funeral service, at which his sister Laura
played the organ.

Craig was baptised by the Free Church minister at Lumphanan, the Reverend
J. Galbraith Smith. My parents had the happiest relations with Mr Smith and
his sister during the time that remained of the former's ministry there.
Many years later, during his retirement, my father did a good deal of research
into Gordon history – both family and regimental – which he recorded in several
hard-back notebooks. He had himself for some years been a Territorial with the
Gordons; the historical link was with his Banffshire ancestors. After relating the possibly apocryphal tale of the origin of the Gordon motto 'Bydand' –
the rallying of his men by Scurdarg at the Battle of Brechin in 1452: 'Back,
boys, we're bidan' (standing firm) – he added what he termed a conversation
which he could guarantee:

> 'My friend the Rev$^{\underline{d}}$ James Galbraith Smith, Minister of Lumphanan
> U.F. Church (1911-1919), joined the Gordon Highlanders at Banchory early
> in 1915 as a Private, was in due course promoted Sergeant, then Lieut-
> enant, and later served as a Chaplain in Europe and at Aldershot
> until he was demobilised in 1920. He had resigned his charge at Lumph-
> anan at the end of the war in 1919 and after demobilisation a year
> later was inducted to the U.F. Church at Balgedie and Portmoak, Kin-
> rossshire, [in 1923; from 1927 Balgedie only.]

> 'Invited to this Induction the writer met there another guest Colonel
> Wm. Robertson, V.C., one of the earliest rankers to rise to command his
> Battalion of the Gordons with whom he had seen much active service in
> different regions of the World.

> 'On our way North that night by a late train, Col. Robertson and I
> were the only occupants of our compartment. We conversed freely until
> subjects for talk grew limited. Then I said to the Colonel that I would
> like to ask him a question – "We in the North East are led to believe
> that the Gordon Highlanders are the crack Regiment of Infantry in the
> British Army – Is that really correct?"

> '"Well", said the Colonel. "I was a Gordon myself, as you know, so

that it is hardly for me to answer that question. But I can truthfully tell you this - I have had long service with the Gordons in India and Africa and elsewhere, and have often been in pretty stiff and dangerous situations, and I can assure you that, if in peace times an officer or a non-commissioned officer treats the lads from the North East fairly reasonably well, and then in war time they are with him in any dangerous crisis he can depend upon them to stand by him and not to run away. They are "bidin" with him."'

In July-August 1942, then retired, Mr Smith was to spend ten days with my parents at Lumphanan during another war. While he was serving in the first, the Reverend Ernest Richards acted for a time as locum tenens at the U.F. Church and in 1916 married Louie Glenesk of the Craigton. Mr Richards then became minister at Midmar and later moved to Bervie.

At a Kirk Session meeting in December 1914 it was agreed that my father should approach Mr Galbraith Smith with a view to arranging for a joint service of intercession on the first Sunday of the New Year. On Mr Smith's suggestion this service was held in the parish church at the usual hour for morning worship. The Kirk Session later recorded in their Minutes their appreciation of the fact that the two congregations were able to join together at the morning service, and thus at the chief service of the day unite in solemn prayer to Almighty God for the safety of the empire and her allies and for success of their cause in the present deplorable war.

A united service was held each January while the war lasted, turn about in either church, with the host minister preaching the sermon. My father's wartime sermons reflected a gradual change in attitude by the Church as a whole towards the war as, far from being 'over by Christmas', the conflict dragged on. On 3 January 1915 he preached on Isaiah 30 v.15: 'Thus saith the Lord God, the Holy One of Israel - In returning and in rest shall ye be saved: in quietness and in confidence shall be your strength' - re-interpreted as 'in returning to rest your confidence in God ye shall be saved'. (My father frequently had recourse, while preparing sermons, to the Greek or Hebrew versions of scripture.) The lessons read were Psalm 33: '...Blessed is the nation whose God is the Lord...', Paul's epistle to Titus 3 vv.1-8: '...Not by works of righteousness which we have done, but according to his mercy he saved us. by the washing of regeneration, and renewing of the Holy Ghost; ...' and that to the Ephesians, Chapter 6. verse 10 to the end: 'Finally, my brethren, be strong in the Lord ... take unto you the whole armour of God, that ye may be able to withstand in the evil day, and having done all, to stand...'

The sermon began by referring to the crisis brought about by the Jewish nation in the time of Isaiah. Once Abraham, father of the Jewish people and the father of our Faith, had come to a realisation that beyond the mighty objects of nature which had been the objects of worship of heathendom - sun, moon and stars. mountains, rivers and seas - was a power which controlled them all, the Jewish nation had been led into the promised land of Canaan and had preserved there the purity of their national life. Conscious of their divine mission they had lived in this narrow country, small but independent, set at the crossroads of ancient movement and commerce, recording their heaven-sent visions of spiritual truth in the books of Scripture. Between Egypt and Assyria, so long as they remained neutral they were assured of the protection of both. But by Isaiah's day they had begun to lose sight of their divine mission; wishing to extend their borders they had made a pact with Assyria in return for military aid; then. seeking to break this irksome bond, they had turned for help to Egypt. Enter Isaiah with his 'Woe to the rebellious children. saith the Lord, that take counsel but not of me...' Isaiah's message was 'In returning to rest your trust in God ye shall be saved'. My father added 'Perish policy and cunning ... Trust in God and do the right'. He went on:

> Four months ago. the rulers of our own country were faced with a similar problem. The relations of the British nation towards its neighbours was different from that of the people of Judah towards theirs: but the problem which faced our rulers was in principle the same.

Were we to be true to the mission given to us by God, were we to be true to our plighted troth, were we to be true to our highest ideals <u>or</u> were we to accept a present easy course and gain a passing advantage to ourselves at the expense of national honour?

For we, like the Jewish people, have a definite mission to perform. (Every nation and every individual has a mission to perform if only they care to look for it.) To the Jewish people was given the task of teaching the nations righteousness, of revealing in their Scriptures and in their national life the All Mighty, the All Merciful, the Holy One of Israel. To the British people has been entrusted the further task of breathing out upon the nations the spirit of freedom, the spirit of trust in democratic government and the spirit of fair dealing between nation and nation... It is true that we have not been always faithful to these high ideals. Sometimes to our shame and to our loss our fair name has been sullied by selfish and self-interested dealing as for example when in the late Boer war of 1900 we interfered with a peaceful and peace-loving nation purely for the sake of commercial gain. But on the whole and at its best the British nation has ever stood for freedom, for democracy, and for honest dealing between nation and nation.

And in the early days of last September, we were faced with the problem: were we to continue true to our ideals and rally to the help of a smaller nation whose integrity we had promised to maintain, against a powerful empire whose creed was 'might is right'... <u>or</u> were we to consult only our own present interests and stand aside reaping the benefits of neutral trade while our neighbours' countries were overrun and ravaged before our very eyes.

To our honour we chose the righteous course, although that course involved us in war - in a war where thousands of our countrymen have already laid down their lives and in which it is to be feared that many brave men will still be sacrificed maintaining a righteous cause. Yet 'in quietness and in confidence shall be our strength'...

That same divine quietness and confidence has been freely manifest on every hand. Our young men are rising to a sense of the nation's need with no undue ostentation or mock bravado. Nowhere in our country has there been tripping of the goose-step or triumphal marches to celebrate our victories but everywhere the best of our manhood is rising quietly and confidently to do their duty to the motherland and to preserve her good name among the nations.

The same heroic spirit animates the wives and mothers who are left behind. By nothing have I been so deeply moved since the war began as by the noble attitude of mothers in this parish. 'Yes' several have said to me, 'we do not like to see the young men go. We would fain have kept them back. But what is our country to us if we cannot rise to defend it when it needs us to do so?'

Even the commercial world, that world which we sometimes regard as wholly given over to the creed of L.S.D., as wholly engaged in self-centred barter, has fully shown that there too are <u>ideals</u>, <u>ideals</u> of patriotism and honour. Sometimes we find an individual's greed gets the better of his conscience. But such cases are the exception, not the rule, and on the whole the commercial world has rallied nobly to the exhortation of our rulers - to exercise self-sacrifice for the nation's good. Prices have risen but they must inevitably do so when the costs of transport and production have been so much increased. We must bear with that...

Now here today we are met a united parish, met in the House of Prayer to invoke the blessing of Almighty God upon our nation and our nation's cause. We are met under no sense of humiliation for our nation's sins. Our nation has her sins and we are sorry for them. But throughout this crisis we have been braced by a sense of power, braced by the knowledge that God is with us and that the divine blessing will follow us and aid us in our efforts to restore a lasting peace upon the earth.

Therefore with quietness and with confidence we can lift our voices unto the God of our Fathers, realising our nation's duty and asking that understanding be given us to discern aright our country's mission to the world, asking that wisdom be given to our rulers to guide them through the many complex problems that arise in a state of war, asking that skill be given to our leaders on land and sea, asking that courage and endurance be given to our men in the army and the navy, asking that patience be given to those who fain would go to fight but who are kept back by necessary ties at home, asking that self-sacrificing love be poured out in fullest measure on the fathers, the mothers, the wives and little children who give their dear ones to their country, asking that mercy and compassion may rest both now and in the dark days still to come upon the homes where loved ones will never return.

On Sunday 4 April 1915, after morning service, the Kirk Session members present met briefly to consider a letter from the corporation of Glasgow asking for help in the disposal of Belgian refugees, the Government having decreed that the City of Glasgow should be the distribution centre for Scotland. At a fuller meeting of Session the following Sunday it was agreed to ask Glasgow if there were among the Belgian refugees persons suitable for agricultural work or domestic service. (My father's sermon at the 1916 harvest thanksgiving service was to refer to the difficulties resulting from shortage of labour on the farms.) Obviously single workers were visualised, whereas it emerged that the need was for the congregation to maintain a whole family. Presumably this involved providing a vacant house: at all events no immediate action was taken. (I have seen only a few rough notes of minutes.) One wonders what the parishioners of that time would have thought of the influx of Glaswegians — the 'evacuees' — which took place during the second world war.

Certainly the church's own finances were not in too flourishing a condition. The balance in hand at 31 December 1912, £12.18.11 (several 1912 items were not settled until 1913) had at the end of the following year been reduced to £1. 7. 2. In 1914 there was a deficit of £3. 15. The whole budget, including contributions to the Schemes of the Church, was in the region of £40, the largest items being the precentor's salary (£5 in 1912, £14.10 in 1913) and that of the beadle (in 1912 £3. 6. 8, in 1913 £8). Coals and paraffin in 1913 came to 13/9. Communion elements were according to custom provided by the minister. In October 1916 the Kirk Session agreed that on account of lighting restrictions there should be no evening service during the coming winter. Fortunately most windows in the manse were fitted with shutters; in some others the dark 'anti-Zeppelin' blinds lasted on until the next war..

On 7 January 1917 it was again my father's turn to preach to the united congregational service of intercession. His text was from Psalm 46: 'God is our refuge and our strength':

> ... as we come before our God today in humble supplication conscious of our needs — conscious of our failings both national and individual — we should yet remember that He is our refuge and our strength, that He will be a never-failing help in times of trouble unto all who place their trust in Him and who seek to obey His will.
>
> Never were we as a nation and as individuals more in need of the guidance of God than now, and perhaps never before did we realise so clearly or so completely that God alone is able to deliver us from the troubles with which we are beset.
>
> Two years ago we met together here to ask God's blessing on our country and our arms. Then our armies had just rallied from the retreat from Mons and turned the tide of battle on the Marne. And to the more optimistic amongst us it seemed as if the day of victory was not far distant. So my message to you then was based upon the text: 'In quietness and in confidence shall be your strength'. Assured of the righteousness of the cause for which we took up our arms, we were prepared to go forward in quietness and in confidence, trusting in our own strength and that of our allies to gain a speedy victory over those powers who so wantonly and so wickedly broke the peace of Europe.
>
> But much has happened since. The conflagration has spread. Other countries have joined in the strife both upon our own side and upon the side of our foes. Therefore the issues which at first were simple and plain to us all have, as the months roll on, become more and more complex and involved, until now it seems as if God alone knew where we stand or how the struggle is to end. Certain it is that now there are few amongst us who profess that confidence in ourselves which we displayed when the war began. Through war and its exactions we have learned as we never did before to look beyond ourselves and our own imperfect vision of realities and our national aims and ambitions to Him and seek to be guided by the counsels of His word and the example of Jesus Christ His Son that we can hope to obtain His blessing and His help. We have learned as we never did before that to Almighty God nations are as a drop in a bucket or as the small dust in the bottom of a balance.

This war and its issues seem to be gradually passing out of men's grasp: yet it is growing gradually clearer every day that over all this struggle of the nations with its conflicting aims and aspirations there can be seen the sure directing hand of God, using the nations and their quarrels as His instruments to work out His own ends - to establish the rule of righteousness upon the earth.

The war is testing the nations as metals are tried by fire. It has exposed their weaknesses - it has laid bare their national sins. Yet it has at the same time revealed virtues which were dormant. It has called forth and given free play to many of the finest qualities of mind and heart and spirit of the men and women of our own and other nations that never had true scope before. We have learned that victory will come to us only if we can rouse ourselves up and shake ourselves free from the trammels that have been hindering our progress and from the sins that have been eating into our vitals. God has got the nations of the world in His fan. He is separating the wheat from the chaff.

Speaking only of our own nation - we have already discovered and overcome many of the evils which for long have hampered us and which since the war broke out have been postponing the day of victory:

eg. (1) The young manhood of our nation was fast becoming sapped through love of ease and pursuit of pleasure but the freewill rally to the colours of the great proportion of the best of our young men proved that the spirit of our fathers was not dead but only sleeping, that our manhood could rouse itself to some effect in time of need. Yet a state decree was necessary to call up those who lagged behind.

(2) Again, we had our many trade disputes. Before the war distrust and bitterness between employer and employed was souring our industrial life, and paralysing our progress in trade. Here too we have witnessed great reforms; in many a workshop a new bond of confidence has been established between master and servant; and where selfishness still holds sway the state has stepped in and said 'Let justice be done between master and man and let not the nation suffer from the selfish wrangling of a few'. There will not in future be the same suffering amongst innocent poor from strikes and trade disputes, between well-paid workmen and money-grabbing proprietors that existed before the war.

(3) Again our tendency to gluttony and luxurious living has been checked. Now it is regarded improper (and in a restaurant illegal) to indulge one's appetite with more than is necessary to maintain the full vigour of one's mind and body.

These and many other evils have been exposed and dealt with either by the pressure of public opinion or by the decree of the state. Yet drunkenness - our nation's greatest and most destructive vice - is still rampant. Some feeble effort has been made to deal with it. But ere victory can be gained our nation's drunkards must be seriously grappled with and conquered. Until now I have never been an advocate of the total prohibition of the sale of strong drink - I have always preferred to look for our nation becoming more sober by self-discipline and self-restraint. But now - delay is deadly. If - as great employers of labour on the Clyde and in other ports - themselves by no means abstainers from alcohol - declare that war work is being retarded by intemperance and shipping held up through drunkenness - then total prohibition is the only cure (with of course due compensation to the interests affected). Each day the war is prolonged and victory is delayed there must be paid a heavy toll in life and limb. If their indulgence in drink must be paid for by

the lives of our soldiers, the flower of our land, then the price is
too dear. Indulgence must cease and cease at once. We must follow the
noble example set by our King, best of all by our own free choice - but
if not thus then by constraint of the state...

Mention of the King's example referred to the latter's renunciation of

all alcoholic drinks in royal residences in April 1915. Referring back, in

his conclusion, to the accepted occasion of the origin of Psalm 46, my

father said:

> King Hezekiah gained an easy victory over the hosts of Assyria
> because he took counsel of God and sought to do God's will. So we -
> as individuals - if we humbly and in true sincerity come to the throne
> of grace, and earnestly enquire what God would have us to do - shall
> receive guidance from His Holy Spirit. And if all be guided by God
> and seek to obey Him each in his separate sphere and station then our
> nation and our rulers will go forward to a victory which will be
> speedy and to a peace which will be secure. God or rather godliness
> will be our refuge and our strength. But unless we accept the Law of
> God as our only standard and guide we can neither hope for victory nor
> for a peace which will be enduring. The war may be brought to an end.
> Hostilities may cease now only to open again fiercer and more bitter
> than before. The sacrifice which so many of our sons have freely made
> will have been offered up in vain...

The General Assembly of the Church of Scotland in Edinburgh in 1916 had

accepted an overture by the Presbytery of Edinburgh 'in view of God's calling

to the earth and His Pleading with His people through recent events and the

present distress, to appoint a Commission of the Church with powers, which

should consider the need and prepare the way, and in due season, by authority

of the Supreme Court of the Church, might in the name of God call the nation

with penitence, faith, and hope to hear and obey His Word'. The Commission

on the War was duly appointed, with powers to confer, inquire and report upon

the spiritual and moral issues involved, and 'generally to take such steps by

way of organisation of conference, evangelisation, devotion, or literature, as

may forward the purpose of preparing the Church and nation to understand the

present visitation, and to meet the requirements of the time according to the

mind of God; ...' It was directed also to 'seek sympathetic action in all or

any of these directions with similar bodies representing other Christian Com-

missions and with the civil authorities'. As regards the other Christian

bodies, the most enthusiastic response came from the United Free Church of

Scotland, and joint congresses were held in the four principal cities. The Commission adopted the motto 'National re-dedication - Scotland's answer to God'.

There were reflections of this movement in the January 1917 sermon quoted above. The year 1915 had seen the spreading of the war in many directions and to other countries. Opening with the Dardanelles campaign it had closed for Britain with the evacuation of Gallipoli. There had been some successes - at a price - in the west including the first battle of Ypres. There had been horrifying incidents such as the sinking of the Lusitania as well as of naval vessels. The Zeppelin bomber appeared on the horizon. By 1916 there was talk of a compromise peace, but American initiatives in this direction, while gaining some support, came to nothing in the circumstances prevailing. Germany and her allies - the 'Central Powers' - were at the time having too much success on land to consider such a possibility. In July 1916 came the great British offensive on the Somme where much progress was made at the cost of many lives. Again there were disasters at sea, including the sinking by the Germans of the hospital ship Britannic. Progress on the Somme was maintained into 1917 although its momentum was threatened by industrial difficulties, mainly the outcome of such grievances at home as dilution of labour (the introduction of unskilled workers, sometimes at piece-work rates which exceeded those earned by the skilled) or just sheer war-weariness with overtones of pacifism. There were heartening successes such as the capture by the Canadians of Vimy Ridge and the second Ypres victory. America entered the war although the Russians, in that year of revolution, withdrew, and Italy was in retreat. Another hospital ship had been torpedoed by the Germans ... but Jerusalem had been freed from the occupying Turks.

The American President Wilson's campaign for peace without victories had continued with little success. A letter to the Press by a former Governor General of Canada, Lord Lansdowne, argued for a compromise peace. On 5 January

1918 Lloyd George, who already had visions of post-war reconstruction calculated to win the support of the multitudes, announced a British 'programme for peace' under which justice would be done to all sides. Ironically, the very improvement and success that lay ahead in 1918 on both home and battle fronts caused this admittedly politically-inspired overture anent peace to be relegated.

Meanwhile the General Assembly's Commission had ordained that for three Sundays in January-February 1918 ministers should in their sermons concentrate on God's message to the nation. No specific guidance as to content appears to have been given. On 26 January my father took as his text Isaiah 26 v.9, having read Chapters 25 to 26 v.14: 'When thy judgments are in the earth, the inhabitants of the world will learn righteousness':

At the present moment God's judgments are in the earth. God is speaking to mankind, speaking in no uncertain voice - with a voice which demands attention. God is speaking to His people with the voice of war. Speaking not in anger, but pleading with His children to listen to His voice. He is speaking to us as He spoke to Pharaoh in Egypt long centuries ago: and He is determined that we like Pharaoh must listen to His voice. You remember that in the several plagues sent upon Egypt God spoke to Pharaoh first in the milder language of personal inconvenience, then through the loss of crops and cattle in the language of personal loss; next when these gentler warnings were disregarded He spoke more sternly in threatened famine and finally, when none of these arguments were of any avail he spoke in a language which compelled response, through the loss of first born sons. Now it seems to me that during the last three years God has been dealing with mankind at the present time much in the same way as He dealt with the Egyptian King. During the last four years our own nation and all other nations have suffered personal inconvenience, and personal loss. We have been threatened with famine. But to all these forms of Divine warning it has been possible for many to turn a deaf ear. However the Almighty has always weapons in reserve, and now in His wisdom He has found it necessary to use a final form of argument which must compel attention - the taking of precious lives, the darkening of homes, the striking down of the young manhood of all lands. The Angel of death has reaped an untimely harvest in many a sorrowing home. None of the nations now at war can refuse much longer to be moved by the appalling total of young lives lost and maimed, a total now mounting into millions.

Soon all the nations must acknowledge that God is speaking to His people - 'and when His judgments are in the earth, the inhabitants of the world must learn righteousness'. God is longsuffering and He is merciful, but He is also just. He pleads and argues with His children - pleads and argues in many ways - gradually growing sterner and more insistent - until finally if men spurn His gentler warnings He must use language which will compel attention. God can be a stern schoolmaster. His voice is hard and exacting now but we must acknowledge that God's actions are just - the severity has been necessary. He is teaching righteousness and He is determined that men will learn. But what a price have we had to pay for our schooling!

'God's judgments are now in the earth'. This war certainly is a judgment sent by God to teach men righteousness and it serves no purpose whatever for us to argue as so many have done and still do that Germany and Germany alone was responsible for the war. Certainly Germany began the war and it seems as if Germany's rulers are more slow to learn the lessons taught by this war than are the peoples of the other nations. But were Germany alone responsible for all the sufferings that war has entailed the Almighty would have raised His arm long ere now to free the world from the tyrant's yoke. Germany began the war - and she has waged it from the start with utter disregard for the principles of morality or mercy. I wish to say nothing in favour of Germany. But what was the state of our own country before war began? We were fast approaching civil strife at home - capitalism versus labour were waiting only for a match to burst into flame, and all our land was unrest and discontent. Four years of war has perhaps caused us to forget these things. No! We misinterpret God's arguments unless we acknowledge that He is dealing with our own nation and with our allies as well as with our foes.

This war, and its consequent suffering and sorrow, is meant by God to teach not only the German people but to teach all mankind what are the natural and inevitable consequences of pride, ambition, jealousy and hate: or to class all under one head, the inevitable consequences of selfishness, self-interest and disregard for God. Until men learn that the affairs of the world cannot be governed by any balancing or adjusting of self interests (however skilfully this balancing or adjusting may be executed) there can be no enduring peace. Until men learn to respect the claims of others as well as to push their own, between individuals there will be strife, between nations war. In private intercourse, man with man or in public dealings, business with business, company with company, nation with nation, if friction, strife or war are to be averted there must be not only insistence on one's own rights but acknowledgment of the rights of others and a genuine desire to give and take in the interest and for the good of all, more of 'neighbourliness' between individuals, between classes and between nations.

The lesson seems simple. It is simple, as all God's lessons are. Yet how loth men are to learn. For example, look at the laws and machinery that have had to be devised for regulating the food supply of our own country. Men, money, brains have been diverted from the prosecution of the war to regulate almost every branch of trade and to fix the price of almost every article bought and sold. Why? Just because buyers would not voluntarily share and share alike, and sellers would not charge a reasonable price. A few - let me be generous and say many - answered the request of our rulers to ration themselves voluntarily, and many were content with fair profits. Others paid no heed. Thus legislation became necessary. The mighty cumbrous machine that now controls our food supply had to be set in motion - the result! Loss of striking power; war dragged on; lives sacrificed because by some, self-interest was placed before the interest of the nation or the interest of their neighbour. God speaks to say that unless we all learn to discipline ourselves and join together for the common good. He must wrestle with us still - He must prolong the war. 'He must judge the earth that the inhabitants of the world learn righteousness'.

Let us however trace the vice of self-interest to its source. We find it rooted in disregard for God. Self-interest springs from refusal to acknowledge that over all men and over all nations is One who is Father of all and who desires that all men should be brothers. That there is a disregard for God in our own land as well as in Austria or Germany is but too clear to us all.

[Here he listed four instances of this disregard, in public worship, keeping of the Sabbath, teaching of the young and reading of the Bible.]

Nevertheless even in the present welter of the nations there is a gleam of hope. So far it is but faint, very faint. Yet in the distance I can see that God's lessons are gradually being learned. Men are seeking for surer foundations whereon to build the future of the nations, the future of society within the nations. In so far as they are doing so, doing so in increasing numbers in our own nation and in other nations both amongst our friends and amongst our foes. In so far is the end of this war drawing nearer, and the spirit of the common brotherhood of man is gaining power.

God is speaking to us plainly, appealing to us, arguing with us, wrestling with us. His judgments are in the Earth. Are we to listen? Are we to help to prolong this terrible struggle? Or are we to learn righteousness?

Thirty years later, on a September Sunday, unknown to my father, his congregation included a distinguished theologian. I had recognised him on the way in because two months earlier the Reverend William Cuming Thom, M.A., B.D., Ph.D. (Aberd.), S.T.M. (New York), Principal of St Andrew's College, Sydney, Australia, had received the honorary degree of Doctor of Divinity at Aberdeen at the same ceremony at which I had graduated M.A. After the service Dr Thom asked my father 'Do you always preach from the Old Testament?' 'Oh — sometimes from the Old, sometimes from the New'. By 1948 Old Testament preaching had fallen somewhat into disrepute, as had Old Testament-based instruction in Sunday Schools. My father's interpretation of the New Testament will be dealt with presently.

In another sermon of the 1918 trilogy 'God's call to the nation' he was still with Isaiah, this time Chapters 59-60, the text: 'The nation and kingdom that will not serve thee shall perish; yea, those nations shall be utterly wasted':

The prophet was here speaking to the Jewish people in the time of their exile: a heathen emperor had descended upon Judah and carried off its population captive. Most of the Jewish people could not understand why this should have happened — why God's people should be harassed and their country harried by a man who knew not Jehovah — a

worshipper of idols. Isaiah had the answer: 'Behold, the Lord's
hand is not shortened, that it cannot save; neither his ear heavy
that it cannot hear; but your iniquities have separated between you
and your God, and your sins have hid his face from you, that he will
not hear'. God had not turned away from them. They had turned their
backs on Him. Nevertheless 'The Redeemer shall come to Zion...'
Isaiah breaks into poetic rapture in declaring the greatness of the
glory that is in store for Zion when her people have been brought to
reason and acknowledge their God as King. (By Zion here as so often
elsewhere in the Prophets is meant not merely the city Jerusalem but
all that that city was understood to represent - the acknowledgment
of God as Jehovah, acceptance of His rule of righteousness and peace.)
Even in the midst of captivity in a foreign land Isaiah could see a
brighter, fairer, grander future for Zion than Jewry had ever witnessed in the past. Isaiah might have been speaking yesterday telling
of the fairer future that it is to be hoped is in store for the ancient
city of the Jews, now rescued from the power of the Moslem Turk, and
(what concerns us more) telling that when all the nations turn from
their transgressions and serve the God who dwelt in Zion and obey the
Gospel that emanated therefrom - Jehovah will once more turn the light
of His countenance upon His children to refresh a weary world.

Isaiah's message ... is for no particular period in time. It was
true for his own people in his own day. It is true for us now. It has
been applied to many a special period of national chastisement in the
past. Perhaps - who can tell - it may be needed yet again in the centuries to come. The end may not be yet. Isaiah mentions no _time_.
Unlike the Book of Daniel or the Book of Revelation he makes no attempt
to calculate the date of the fulfilment of his forecast. He builds
his argument on bed-rock principles of Divine Truth. Therefore it is
true for all time...

Let us apply Isaiah's message to ourselves - to our own nation
today... There _is_ a God, a good, a wise, a powerful God. But we must
confess that we have not served or acknowledged Him as we ought. We
may have professed knowledge of him (the Jews did that!) We may have
rendered him lip-service (the Jews did that). Nevertheless it must be
confessed that the British nation - in spite of its many virtues (and
we have virtues; it were absurd to deny them: look at the manner in
which so many of Britain's sons sprang to the country's service in the
early days of the war; the works of love and mercy of our women; the
freewill offerings of people carrying on Red Cross work, Y.M.C.A.,
Church Huts for rest and recreation; the patient endurance of the
troops: in spite of the services we have rendered to mankind in the
past for the cause of justice and of freedom, we have been drifting
away from God and from Godliness. I do not say that _we_ have as a nation
sinned in the same degree as our enemies - yet we must ponder well on
our past and consider whether _it is not possible_ that we have incurred
the displeasure of God. For example, what are some of the reasons
that have prolonged this war? Think what these are and what they teach.
Two have been publicly admitted by the head of our Government: (1) the
withdrawal from our support of Russia. (2) The lack of a united control
in the conduct of the war. To these two I shall add a third - our failure hitherto to attract to our side the masses of the German and Austrian
Empires. A rising of the German and Austrian people against their
autocratic rulers has always been predicted. It has not yet occurred.
Yet these _three_ causes are not 'three'. Trace them to their source and
you will find that they are 'one'.: a cause which can be definitely and
sufficiently expressed in the one word '_materialism_'. The war has been

prolonged because of the materialism of our own nation and of our allies ... nothing without payment or reward.

(1) What caused the Russian defection? Russia rose in revolt against her former rulers because they ruled for their own ends, for their own glory, and not for the welfare of their people. When that revolt took place the new government gained access to the presses [i.e. cupboards] of the Foreign Office. There they found the agreements - the treaties - signed in secret between Russia and her allies. These treaties told the price for which her sons had to give their lives by the thousand. The aims for which the nation was bleeding and dying. What were they? The overthrow of Prussian militarism certainly - but more. The territorial aggrandisement of the Russian Empire. Constantinople - the City of the Golden Gates - access to the Mediterranean Sea. Territory in Asia Minor and Persia, possibly also at the expense of Austria in Galicia and else-where. At once the question rose. Was it worth it? The answer, almost unanimous, was No! Russia would fight for freedom, freedom from the aggressor from without, freedom from the tyrant within; but to sacrifice her sons for territorial aggrandisement, she would have none of it. She called to us - to her allies - to revise their war aims. We refused. We hesitated. Russia was lost. Russia's aid was lost because the old Russian Government and the allies had prearranged the terms of peace. These terms were national aggrandisement. The war which it was declared to the world was a war of self-defence and of punishment of a wanton aggressor, was found to be also a war of imperial extension.

(2) The lack of a united control in the conduct of the war. Italy's great reverse - a reverse which undid the toil and sacrifice of years - was attributed to lack of a united control. Certainly. But for what reason? Reason simple. Each country was fighting its own war, for its own purpose, its own aims. Only the other day we were told again from Russia what was the bargain made by Italy ere she drew the sword - again territorial expansion: not only recovery of her own, but aggression at the expense of other States. Italy entered the war not only to obtain redress for the wrongs inflicted upon herself in the past but to inflict new wrongs on others now. The allies agreed; a treaty was signed. We accepted Italy's help but at a price. We know now we lost the help of Russia because the Russian people rightly refused to sacrifice themselves for the prize demanded by her former rulers. It is not yet clearly known what was the true reason for Italy's great retreat. I do not know. Yet there always is suspicion that it was because her people refused to fight for the price prescribed. Thus the war has been prolonged... sacrifice incurred because the warring nations sought material reward for their efforts. Had the united war aim been only to defeat and destroy the military caste ... of Prussia it would have been over long ere now.

...There was a third reason for the continuation of the war.

(3) The failure of the allied powers to win the sympathy of moderate men in Germany and Austria. Why this failure? Need I ask? It was because the German people knew our true aims. They knew that we, the allied powers, desired expansion at the expense of Germany's allies. That they were determined to resist. Had we and our allies declared and redeclared with clean hands that we fought only to redress the wrongs of Belgium and France, to destroy the military machine of Prussia, then the German and Austrian masses would have been with us; long ere now the war would have been won...

I have no record of the total number of Lumphanan parishioners who were

on active service during the 1914-18 war, some of whom would have been in the regular army. Considering that twenty-six fell during the war it might seem that the number who took part might have been considerably more, had not casualty lists been in that war so appallingly long. The list of the fallen is as follows:

Charles Park	Robert Davidson
John Coutts	Hugh Gordon
James Farquhar Ingram	William Milne
Thomas McDonald	George McLaren Littlejohn
William Fraser	James Glass
Samuel Durward Watt	Alexander Riddoch
William Flett	John Keith
William McIntosh	Angus Keith
James Mitchell	Harry Shaw
George Riddoch	James Cowie
Joseph Michie	James Cameron
Charles Alexander	John Herd Bisset
Lewis Tavendale	George Florence

Recently I was in correspondence with a resident of Aberchirder, in the pursuit of evidence of my father's time there as a school teacher; she had spoken to one or two women whose memories went back to 1905, but wrote 'his boys would have gone to World War I likely'. That was assumed to be sufficient explanation of why none were still around. Probably typical, statistically, is the evidence of a small book produced in Tarland in 1919 recording the names of men and women of the Howe of Cromar who served in the Great War: 263 men and seven women (nurses) went, 54 men did not return, one was still missing.

Still hanging in the Parish Hall is a group photograph of the Lumphanan Volunteer Detachment 1917-18, local men prevented by being in reserved occupations from enlisting for active service. Most were farmers, one or two railway surface men. In charge as Lieutenant was the schoolmaster, James Maclean; under him were Sergeant John Forbes of Auchlossan, Corporal Charles Leslie, Whitehouse and Lance Corporal John Watt of the Hillock. Their piper was the gardener at Glenmillan, J.A. Reid, the drummer John Scott, Cloak Farm. The photograph included two N.C.O's from the Gordon Highlanders who presumably gave some instruction. Among other local people who contributed to the war effort was W.G. McRobbie, a veteran of the Militia, who spent some time in a factory manufacturing aeroplane parts until an injury forced his retirement from this.

The first front-line casualty to return to Lumphanan was Alex Milne of the Bakery; for many years he was to be our postmaster, his artificial right hand in its glove holding down the book of stamps while his left flicked over the pages. His sister Florence, always known as Fluffy, drove the baker's horse van, dressed in breeches, as her war effort. John Smith of Ardieraar lost a leg, as did David Watt, Gateside, for many years our Inspector of Poor, and clerk to the Parish Council 1922-1930. Both of these used a motor-cycle and sidecar to get about. David Watt's son was named after the fellow-soldier who, at the Front, had saved his life. A victim of shell shock was Albert Reid, Roadside; for a time he was able to work as a postman.

In due course a local branch of the British Legion was formed, at first jointly with Torphins, and one was reminded, on its special occasions, of this improbable episode in the lives of peaceable people. After the second war we ex-service-women were welcomed into the membership, sharing their activities (no mention of a 'Women's section' with a different badge, although our smaller version was on a gilt bar.) At the annual November dinner the two-minute silence in remembrance of 'fallen comrades' brought back very vividly all that one had heard of 1914-18; it was almost too soon to appreciate adequately the rather different but in many cases equally horrific exploits of World War II. After dinner we sat round the table with our glasses enjoying a sort of 'smoking concert'. Peter Sim, senior, would give us the old song 'Oh, lucky Jim'; Jack McGregor would sing 'Flower of Braemar'; all would join in some of the old or newer wartime choruses. A brief business report would be made: we had a separate Earl Haig Fund committee, on which my father and I both served, through which any ex-service people or perhaps widows could be helped. Latterly the most popular form of aid might be provision of a television set for a house-bound invalid. The Scottish organisation of the Earl Haig Fund was different from that of England, with more local control. (I had no difficulty, however, on one occasion in London in getting some help for a West Indian ex-serviceman, whom I met while visiting a Lumphanan man in hospital there, on application to the Legion headquarters in Piccadilly.)

The original membership of the Lumphanan sub-branch was listed by the secretary, James Dowers, as follows:

Col. H.J. Kinghorn, Auchenhove
James Harper, Woodend
Wm. Nicol, The Kennels, Findrack
Alex Wood, Shoemaker
John Hossack, Prospect Ter.
John Stevenson, Glen Road
John Taylor, Kintocher Cottage,
                  Craigievar
George Buchan, The Parish Hall
Alistair Kinghorn, Home Farm,
                  Auchenhove
Alex Milne, Post Office
James Calder, Cairnton

Capt. Cochrane, Findrack
David Abernethy, Bogloch
James Anderson, Auchlossan Mill
Alex Ross, 3 Perkhill Road
Wm. Davidson, Glen Road
Alex Fraser, Boghead
Peter Angus, Hotel
Donald Mitchell, Burnhead
James Dowers, Glenannan

A later President of the Lumphanan branch was Alex Thomson who had been with Fords in Canada and served in the Canadian Army in World War I. He retired to Lumphanan in the thirties (his wife was a sister of Mrs 'Geordie' Buchan) having built the shop at 'the corner' which he named Highland Park after the Ford factory.

During the Depression in the 1930's it was not uncommon in Scotland for localities affected to organise pipe bands as a form of recreational positive activity. In Lumphanan this was not exactly so; it just happened that five pipers were available, and the formation of a branch of the British Legion was a stimulus, as it could play at - for example - their church parades. One of the above-mentioned five was my brother Craig, and he has written a note about it for me.

There had usually been one or more pipers in the parish. During the first war, as has been mentioned, J.A. Reid, gardener at Glenmillan, played for the Volunteers. Then there arrived Pipe-Major John Stevenson, who had been a 'regular' in the Black Watch, serving with them in the Boer War and with the Royal Scots in the Great War; and also Peter Sim, shoemaker and saddler, who had earlier been in the band of the 4th Gordons when my father was a sergeant in the Aberdeen University Company. Peter served in the regiment in the Great War. These three pipers would play at school picnics etc., backed up by John Scott, Cloak, or on occasion by a horseman at Milton of Auchenhove, James West, with the big drum. Mr Reid left in the late 1920's but in the thirties Craig had lessons from the Pipe Major and in due course joined the band with a fellow-pupil, Andrew Gauld, from Torphins, blacksmith in Learney, and George Smith, who lived near Findrack.

The big drum was by now the responsibility of Jack McGregor, Glen Road, while John Grant, former blacksmith, was a kettle-drummer, sometimes joined by Sandy Stevenson, the Pipe Major's son. Particularly as Andrew Gauld was the Honorary Secretary of the British Legion in Torphins the band was styled the Lumphanan-Torphins British Legion Band. It turned out quite frequently on public occasions, perhaps parading up and down the village while some event took place in the Parish Hall, in dress that was reasonably, if not quite, uniform.

The reference in the last sermon quoted above to the 'works of love and mercy of our women' recalls that my mother's sister, Beatrice J.D. Reid, had from August 1914 been on active service with Queen Alexandra's Imperial Military Nursing Service Reserve, so that, allowing for security considerations, some idea of life 'at the front' must have percolated through family channels. Auntie Bee initially kept a diary of her service in France on Ambulance Train No.3; later as sister-in-charge of a casualty clearing station she obviously had no time for this. The diary records, first, the impatient days at Rouen in early August, waiting for orders, with conflicting rumours circulating as to where the nursing sisters would be sent (these even included a tale that they were to be returned to England as it was too dangerous for them in France). All they knew for certain was that the German Army was approaching, with fierce fighting. My aunt meanwhile had heard that her brother George Reid, the youngest of the family and the only surviving son, had joined up and was in training first at the Royal Military Academy, Woolwich, then at Shoeburyness, with the Royal Field Artillery. Having been in the O.T.C. at Edinburgh University he was commissioned on 26 August 1914. On 21 September came an urgent message that six of the nursing sisters were to go right up to the Front: 'our work will be hard and all our strength required mentally and physically' reads the diary, 'We must pray to God to help us. They say it is terrible up there'.

Until 15 April 1915 the routine continued: setting forth to one battle area after another with the ambulance train, collecting the wounded, dressing the wounds on board as the train made either for one of the ports where these could be transferred to hospital ships, or for a base hospital. Even the latter, in spite of the fact that occasional German wounded would be included and cared for, did not escape shelling, or bombing from the air, by the new phenomenon of warfare, the aeroplane. At base, the sisters could visit a German hospital and talk to 'Tommies' there who were too ill to be moved. (My father once accosted one of our Lumphanan men home on leave 'And what do you think of the Germans, Sammy?' Glancing round, lest he be overheard speaking treason, Sammy replied: 'They're just folk like ourselves'.)

Up at the front the ambulance train would be shaken by the noise of the guns, or of bursting shells: 'We see them glisten, then burst...' It was not unknown for a patient on the train to be hit by shrapnel. There would be accidents as trains collided. Besides ambulance trains there were others loaded with refugees, and crowds of the latter would be seen 'hundreds of men, women, children, prams, parcels, dogs &c.' (this near Bethune in late October). The now familiar place names recur: Abbeville, Hazebrouck, Yprès, Bailleul, Poperinghe, Étaples, Amiens ... By October 1914 the Germans were being driven back into Belgium. Among the wounded were Indians, Algerians, later Canadians... but always it was a special treat to come across Scotsmen. The London Scottish were the first territorial regiment encountered, then, after a 'big engagement' about 15 December, 'many Gordons'. In February 1915 there is merely a note

that Sister S. came to congratulate my aunt on being mentioned in despatches;

later an oak leaf was added to her medal ribbon. Unlike my Uncle George, who,

once in France, never brought back any memento of the trenches, Auntie Bee

records getting in November 1914 a German helmet, and later was to supply

the family with brass "cartridge" casings and a part of the howitzer shell

which was responsible for her own wound. On 25 July 1916 Uncle George wrote

to Auntie Bee from No.3 General Hospital, B.E.F.: 'Yesterday morning between

6 and 7 I had a piece of High Explosive shell strike my steel helmet which

saved me, but I have a slight head wound ... You know where the fighting is

thickest now. We were there'. [Vimy] That day the British were to capture

Pozières in the second stage of the advance on the Somme. (We were to have

the helmet at home, with its considerable dent.) On my uncle's last leave, seen

off at the station by his father, he pressed a ten shilling note into the hand

of the latter who, momentarily bewildered, accepted it: 'I didn't need the boy's

money'. George was killed outright at Biefvillers on the Somme on 25 August

1918. Two days earlier he had filled in one of the routine postcards, strok-

ing out the phrases not applicable. On 24 August, date-marked the 25th, he

had written to his parents 'I can only say that I am busier now than I have

ever been before'. The documentation of that last phase must have been dupli-

cated in a score of homes in our parish. His colonel got in touch with Auntie

Bee at her field hospital. She it was who, after hostilities had ceased, went

in search of George's first grave with the wooden cross bearing only his name,

Lieut. Geo. Reid, 27 Coy. R.F.A. and 'R.I.P.' Nearing the spot where he had

fallen, she asked directions of a French level-crossing keeper; he left his

crossing and accompanied her. Later George was reburied in the War Cemetery

near Miramont called Adanac ('Canada' in reverse) because of the many

Canadians buried there.

An interesting document from the home front survives among my father's papers: the Minutes of the Lumphanan War Savings Association, in the

inevitable penny exercise book. The first meeting, called by public intima-

tion, was held on 29 December 1916 in the Parish Hall. The banker, Mr William

Horne, called to the chair, explained that he had been asked by the County

Clerk, Mr William Murison, Secretary to the Aberdeen Local Central Committee

of the Scottish War Savings Association to call the meeting. He then out-

lined the aims of the Association:

> (1) To impress upon communities the great necessity of saving
> every possible penny in order to keep down the national expenditure
> and to provide against a possible period of general depression after
> the war.

> (2) To make known to all the help that individuals can give to
> the conduct of the war by investing their savings in Government
> securities.

> (3) To make generally known the very favourable terms given to
> investors by the Government and especially to small investors in War
> Savings Certificates.

The schoolmaster, Mr James Maclean, was prepared to organise a War Savings Bank

in connection with the Parish School if the community so desired. After dis-

cussion it was agreed that the Lumphanan War Savings Association be formed, with

a branch at the school, if this arrangement were sanctioned by headquarters.

Mr Horne was appointed President and the Rev. Francis C. Donald Hon. Secretary

and Treasurer. Those present, along with the schoolmaster, who was unavoid-

ably absent, were to form the committee. Unfortunately, in the Minutes, my

father mostly noted surnames only: (Lewis) Strachan (farmer at Tulloch),

(W.G.) McRobbie, (John) Glenesk, (R.R.) Anderson, (William) Ferries (farmer

at Leyhead), (John) Scott (farmer at Cloak), (James) Stuart, Stationmaster,

(John) Clarke (tailor), W. (William) Reid (Roadside), (?Andrew) Calder, and

(?) Aitken [?Tornaveen]. It was proposed also to add Alex. Reid, merchant, and

(?Adam) Walker, (merchant at Parkhill), and others as might be necessary. At

the next meeting three others were added: Mr Jamieson, later hall-keeper,

(?Andrew) Low and (Dick) George, roads foreman, Glenanan. Although affiliation

was not yet officially approved, a parcel of Savings books had been received, and those present were enrolled. It was agreed that the committee make a house-to-house visitation throughout the parish to explain the aims of the Association and make known the favourable terms offered: £1 on redemption for 15/6 certificates. 'It was agreed that the Treasurer should be at the Public School on the Evening of the Second Tuesday after Books etc. were issued to the members of Committee for above Canvass for the purpose of enrolling members and receiving deposits.'

By 20 February 1917 when the committee next met at the School the Association had been duly affiliated with the Scottish War Savings Committee and it was arranged that the school branch be worked under the Parish Association with a separate secretary and treasurer (the schoolmaster). The parish treasurer was authorised by the authorities in Edinburgh and London to hold War Savings Certificates in stock on credit. These would be issued at the manse on Mondays from 3-5 and 7-9 p.m. and also at the Mart when convenient. The parish was divided into districts allocated to committee members. By 4 May 1917 at the next meeting it was reported that 36 depositors had purchased certificates: 818 in all, totalling £633.19s. At the school, certificates to the value of £55.10.7 had been taken up. The stationmaster having just left the district after thirteen years there, Mr Jamieson was appointed to the responsibility Mr Stuart had held for signing the appropriate forms in connection with the certificates received on credit.

Thus was launched a project which continued at the school with weekly collections although of course the general public later dealt direct with the Post Office. Eventually 'War Savings' were renamed 'National Savings' which continue to this day.

CHAPTER FIVE

———————

<u>And he preached the word unto them</u>

Sermons; exchange of pulpits; young communicants'
class; the Sacrament; Bible Class; Sunday School; Sabbath
observance; Church of Scotland reaction to post-war
economic depression.

Chapter 5

'Sometimes from the Old, sometimes from the New'. The text my father chose

for his afternoon sermon when 'preaching for' Lumphanan on 8 December 1912

(there is now no record of his mid-day sermon) was John 11, v.35 'Jesus wept'.

He had already preached this sermon, on the story of the death of Lazarus and

of Jesus' visit to the bereaved sisters Martha and Mary, at Huntly and at

Drumblade. The afternoon congregation would have included farm and domestic

servants who were not free to attend the earlier service. The accompanying

readings were Isaiah 53 - itself a prophecy of the life and death of Our Lord -

and John 11, 1-36. The praise list my father sent was as follows: Psalm 23 -

The Lord's my shepherd; and four hymns from the 1898 hymnary: Before Jehovah's

awful throne; Glorious things of thee are spoken; Jesus thou joy of loving

hearts (or, as an alternative, I heard the voice of Jesus say;) and Hark, hark

my soul, angelic songs are swelling.

The subject was neighbourly sympathy: in particular, response to bereave-

ment; Christ had 'walked many weary miles ... that he might comfort two poor

village women who had placed their trust in Him'. It may have been chosen

for this 'Royal Deeside' occasion partly because it contained this reference:

> A beautiful story is told of the late Queen Victoria. On the death
> of the Queen her retainers at Balmoral were telling over the kind deeds
> she had been accustomed to do among them, when an old gamekeeper's
> widow spoke through her tears saying: 'The Queen was right kind to me
> when she cam' to see me after my man died'. 'What did she say to you?'
> was asked. 'Oh! she said naething', was the reply. 'She took my hand
> and juist sat doon an' grat wi' me'. No words were needed. The bond of
> their common widowhood united the hearts of Queen and cottager. And a
> purse of gold would have been as dross to the lonely widow compared with
> the sympathy and the tears of her Queen.

In general, my father thought that acts of sympathy and kindness were more

commonly performed among the poor than between the rich and well-to-do. Often

well-meant overtures were rejected out of pride or a spirit of independence.

Similarly the ever-ready sympathy of God - made manifest in His Son - was not

always readily sought. He quoted another instance from country life:

Not long ago it was my privilege to get a special opportunity for observing the beautiful tie of sympathy which binds the poor man to his neighbour. I was called to take the service at the burial of a ploughman's child - the only boy in a family of five. In the small room of the cottage there were gathered together the sorrowing father and mother, their four little daughters, their neighbour, and their master's wife. Then one by one the-men-of-the-farm came in, big, brawny men; and each took a last, long look at the silent form of the dead, but, ere they went out, one by one, each man tenderly took the hand of the mother and held it for a moment in his own. Not a word was spoken! Those big, rough-looking men went out in silence as they came in, yet it was plain to be seen that the silent shake of their horny hand was enough to convey to the heart of the grief-stricken mother such a message of comfort as even the pen of a poet could never completely express. Heart went out to heart as I never had seen before. And that afternoon I went home firmly convinced that in that farm cottage, small though it was, and poor as the surroundings were, I had stood for a moment in the presence of God. I had certainly seen a vision of the love of my Father in Heaven.

The sermon ended: 'Let us, therefore, in so far as we are able strive to bring Heaven down to earth, by spreading our sympathies around us on all who come within our reach... The more ... that we rejoice with those that do rejoice and weep with those that weep, the more shall we become like unto Him who loved us and Who gave Himself for us ... for it is only by doing so that we ourselves can become worthy to enter the Kingdom of Heaven and to sit down at the table of the Father, along with His Son our Saviour, who Himself was not ashamed to shed tears of love and of sympathy with those who trusted in Him'.

Another of my father's New Testament sermons must have come near to establishing a record, in pre-broadcasting days, for the number of those who listened. Curiously enough, exchange of pulpits seemed commoner in the days when transport was difficult - especially on a Sunday when prejudice as well as economics operated against the running of public transport - than in later, more mobile times. Ministers exchanging pulpits might be accommodated in each other's manses on the Saturday night. When my father first exchanged with the minister at Echt, Mr Soutter's successor 1915-50, the Reverend T.A. Munro, a great favourite with our family, each would set out on his bicycle, complete with clerical hat, to cover the 12-mile distance; they would meet half-way and have a chat, then remount and go their separate ways. Later Mr Munro

had a car and provided transport for both. In this manner not only was
there contact between ministers, but congregations got to know other preachers
or members of presbytery, a great advantage when some of the latter became
involved in supervising vacancies or unions. On one occasion my father was
to preach at Coull; leaving pony and trap at Loanend farm, he 'took over the
hill' on his feet. As he came within earshot of the church he was surprised
to hear the bell already ringing. He said to the beadle 'You're very sure
of your man!' There was a well-known recitation in the North East regarding
a minister who visited in turn all the places on Donside, each time preaching
the same sermon, on the subject of the widow's cruse. There were various
versions but it went something like this:

> Roon by Keig an' Tullynessle
> Aye the wifie an' her vessel.
> Doon by Tough an' up by Towie,
> Aye the wifie an' her bowie.
> Syne by Lumsden an' Glenbogie
> Gaed the wifie an' her cogie.
> Up Glenbuchat an' Strathdon
> Still he drave the wifie on.

Sermons in those days would be much commented on, so that the preacher would
have been in no doubt of the reactions of his hearers. An oft-repeated
sermon would therefore perhaps be more the result of favourable response than
merely a matter of convenience.

My father's record concerned a discourse on Mark 14,v.42: 'Rise up, let
us go', which indeed had relevance to the wider dissemination of the gospel.
This he preached over five years on twenty-one occasions. The first was on
the island of Swona in the Pentland Firth, where, as a student, he was summer
missionary in 1909. The following Sunday he gave it again at the Pentland
Skerries lighthouse. This would have involved a trip by rowing boat; there
was as yet no motor-boat on Swona - more of this anon. The Sunday after he
was similarly conveyed to St Mary's, on the island of Holm, where the sermon
was repeated. The other occasions were as follows: Cairnorrie, Stonehaven,
Aberdeen (at St George's in the West where he was student assistant from

1909-10), Aberdeen Trinity, Fetterangus, Millbreck, Rora School, Forfar St James, Kininmonth, Torry, Huntly — both the parish church and the United Presbyterian; Aberchirder, Kinnoir, Mortlach, Longhill, and on his arrival in Lumphanan, at the Tornaveen meeting-house, and at the parish church in January 1914.

The sermon concerned Jesus' last night on earth, when after the Last Supper He and the eleven disciples went out to the garden of Gethsemane. Christ then went apart with the three who were nearest to Him, Peter, James and John; but again He left them to 'watch' while He prayed. Once more the theme is human sympathy — or, as it turned out, the lack of it. The humanity of Christ is manifest in His need of comfort at this hour: He knew what lay ahead; the disciples had not yet appreciated what was to come, and repeatedly failed Him: always He returned to find them asleep. Finally Our Lord, accepting the frailty of human nature, ended by saying 'Rise up, let us go ...' which meant to the meeting with Judas and those who had come to arrest Him. (Yet John — unlike the author of Mark — records also the words of one of Jesus' prayers in the garden 'I have finished the work that Thou gavest me to do'.) To frail humanity (later galvanised by the promised Holy Spirit at Pentecost) He left the work that seemed scarcely begun. This was a theme which was to emerge in the only published work of theology which my father was to leave. In it also, as in his various dealings with people over his ministry, this acceptance of human frailty — but recognition also of the potentialities — was to be an essential feature.

'Rise up, let us go; lo, he that betrayeth me is at hand. They were His parting exhortation to them as He braced them for the battle to which they were about to go forth — the battle of life alone without the bodily presence of their Master...' But first came the phase when He was alone: 'Alone with God He opened out His soul: "If it be possible let this cup pass, yet not my will, but thine be done". And coming back he found the three asleep, quietly

resting, while His life's blood was dripping out for them and for us ...
"Simon, sleepest thou", He said. "Couldst thou not have watched with me one
hour?... Watch ye and pray lest ye enter into temptation. The spirit truly
is ready but the flesh is weak". Again He went alone and prayed a second
time. And again He found His watchers sleeping, "neither wist they what to
answer Him". But now Our Lord's divinity came forth... He cast Himself on
God alone and from Him He found support... He shrank no more from duty —
but arose prepared and ready now to face it... "Sleep on now and take your
rest":' but the disciples, now bitterly repenting their failure, were wide
awake; they were therefore given another chance: '"Rise up, let us go".
Their work was still before them, and the memory of their backsliding in the
past would but stir them on to greater firmness in the future. And those
disciples did arise and go to work and we, who worship here today, owe this
our meeting to their efforts to take up and carry on the service of their
master...' The sermon ends 'happy is the man whose fall brings home to him
his human weakness and his need for a heavenly father's guidance for the
future'.

My father, when assistant to Dr Adam Semple at Huntly, had frequently
had to take the class for intending communicants. The Doctor — then ageing —
had given him a clear outline of what he had to teach and afterwards demanded
a full report on the meetings. Although the content of my father's teaching
tended in later years to vary, the essence remained the Semple scheme: the
Sacraments, the Old Covenant, the New Covenant. This began with Genesis I
and Question I in the Shorter Catechism (it does not seem to have embraced
more than a selection from the latter) and went briefly through the Bible
ending with Revelation Chapter 22: '...I am Alpha and Omega, the beginning and
the end, the first and the last' — thus showing a clear connection right
through from the beginning to the end.

In an introductory talk on 'joining the Church' he first answered the question: 'What is "the Church"'? It was a body of men and women who, realising their need of a Saviour, believed in the Lord Jesus Christ; in His Gospel they felt that they had all they needed for this life and to prepare them for the life to come. They therefore banded themselves together in a body called 'the Church' and although this might then be separated in practice into, for example, the Church of Scotland, the United Free Church or the Roman Catholic Church, all had the same aims. Church members had both privileges and responsibilities; the former included the opportunity of worship, the feeling of being one of many, participation in the commemoration of Christ's death, the sacrament of baptism of children, and on another plane the right in the Scottish churches to elect a minister. In return they ought to set an example to others and to offer help where needed.

Before each subsequent meeting (perhaps five in all) the intending communicants were asked to read certain portions of Scripture and learn or read selected questions and answers in the Catechism; for example, on the first topic 'What is the Lord's Supper?' they had to read Matthew 26, vv.26-28; Mark 14, vv.22-24; Luke 22, vv.19-20; First Corinthians 11, vv.23-26; to learn from the Catechism 92, 93 and 96: ('What is a sacrament?' 'Which are the sacraments of the New Testament?' 'What is the Lord's Supper?') and read 94, 95, and 97 ('What is baptism'? 'To whom is baptism to be administered'? 'What is required to the worthy receiving of the Lord's Supper'?)

At the end of the course, the intending communicants would be introduced to the Kirk Session before (not during) a pre-Communion service on the Sunday evening prior to Communion Sunday. In those days, I think, to be a central feature of a public service in a full church would have overwhelmed young country people. At the early presentation to the Kirk Session the minister announced that attendance at the communicants' class had been perfect; the lessons had been learned, and that the young people understood fully what they were doing. They promised that they wished to become followers of Christ; that by sitting down at God's Table they wished to show before God and man that they accepted Christ as King; that by their lives and example they would endeavour to be the means of leading others to Him. They were then accepted into the Church with the words 'The Lord bless thee and keep thee ...'; communion tokens were distributed, and in a final address they were reminded that they were now full members of Christ's Church, and exhorted as to attendance at divine service and if possible also at Bible Class.

Craig and I have combined to produce a note on the celebration, as we recall it, of the Sacrament of the Lord's Supper at Lumphanan in our father's time. Communion, or in common parlance 'The Sacrament', twice a year was an event of which the parish was vividly aware. Virtually everyone attended who could, the negligent being stimulated by the sanction that after three years' non-attendance they might be crossed off the roll or at any rate invite a rebuke, understandingly administered in my father's case. In his early years it was preceded by a service on a mid-week so-called Fast Day. This he discontinued as latterly not only was there no fasting, but generally only employers attended after setting their staff to work; instead there was a special pre-communion service the previous Sunday, often taken by a visiting preacher, culminating in the announcement 'The Sacrament of the Lord's Supper will be dispensed here this day week'.

At the preparatory service nickel 'tokens' were handed out (and likewise by elders visiting likely communicants in their area or at the Church door on Communion Sunday) as symbols of eligibility. These were collected before Communion began by elders carrying 'ladles' - baize-lined boxes at the end of long shafts - also used in the early days for taking up the offering. Since the mid-nineteenth century the Lumphanan tokens had been quite large octagonal oblongs. On one side was the name of the parish and the original date of issue; on the other 'This do in remembrance of me'. These were preceded by a very much smaller and thinner token, rather like worn slate, with the letter 'L'. A collection of these came to light in my father's day and were restored to the church. Our tokens were kept, between Services, in the study in a cotton draw-string bag inside a stiff black leather pouch with two handles.

Until motor-transport became common, on Communion Sunday the number of gigs etc. was so great that special arrangements had to be made for stabling. The elders came attired in frock (or morning) coats and top hats, but with black rather than the white ties customary in city churches. They took their places at the beginning round the Communion table, where the beadle had already placed the bread, cut in cubes except for the piece which the minister handed to the elders and then took himself, and arranged on pewter plates lined with white napkins which folded over the top. Behind were the racks of individual glasses of wine which my father had introduced in place of the common cups – an arrangement belying traditional Scots conservatism. The two pewter cups were then used at all services to receive the collection at the doors (placed inside slotted boxes) being carried in by the beadle and placed on the Communion table before service began. (On Communion Sundays he placed them on the table in the square Session pew).

The pews in the body of the church had been covered with freshly laundered linen napery. There was more than the usual solemnity as the beadle fetched first the pulpit Bible and then the minister. The well known and loved ritual then proceeded with, inter alia, paraphrase 35 to the tune Rockingham: 'Twas on that night when doomed to know' and the hymn

> Here, O my God, I see thee face to face,
> Here would I touch and handle things unseen.

We always, I think, had the same praise-list, ending with a few verses of Psalm 103: 'O thou, my soul, bless God the Lord.' The only element of originality was the sermon with which the minister had taken more even than the usual trouble, and an address when he descended from the pulpit to give Communion to the elders, who then dispersed to serve the congregation.

It was not uncommon for a minister to be assisted by a colleague from another parish, though that was not the practice in Lumphanan. In all there

was a great sense of occasion, heightened by the presence of former parishioners who had returned for the service, sometimes from a considerable distance, or who because of their attachment to Lumphanan, had not 'lifted their
lines', which was the common term for the disjunction certificate obtainable
from the minister of membership of the Church.

The senior elder of our early days, William Davie of Bogentassie, –
whom I can visualise now in his frock-coat – is commemorated by the present
Communion table, given by his family and dedicated on 5 January 1930.

After the Communion service everything remained in place in the church
until later in the day (there was only one 'sitting') when the glasses would
be removed to the manse, soaked in pails of cold water and then washed and
dried. The stands with their trays were wiped as necessary; often the latter
were set up to dry on some of our many window-sills so that the American cloth
lining the pockets would not be sticky and impede future removal of glasses.
The church cleaner dealt later on with the linen.

'This do in remembrance of me' was the text of my father's Communion
sermon on 15 May 1932. It was the third of a series on the fundamentals of
the Christian faith; the first had dealt with the preparation for Christ in
the Old Testament, the next with the coming of Christ and His works. Now he
was to stress the necessity for man willingly to do his share. Corroboration
of the first had come unexpectedly in an article in the previous day's
Aberdeen Press and Journal adducing proof beyond doubt that the scriptural
account of the past was true;

> are we then to raise doubts when the Bible speaks to us of the future –
> tells us of a life beyond the grave – of the many mansions of our
> Father's house in Heaven – of the welcome awaiting there for good and
> faithful servants, and likewise of the stern condemnation of the wicked
> and slothful servant who buried his talent in the ground and did nothing,
> when on this earth, to improve his Master's Kingdom? If corroboration
> of our Bible story is secured in unlooked for places and in unanticipated
> ways, surely, we can with confidence place our trust in the teaching of
> our Lord and Master. We can take Him at His word.
>
> Now, today, as we sit down to the ordinance of the Sacrament of the
> Lord's Supper we insert the keystone of the arch which connects the past
> with the present and the future. Christ our Saviour came to fulfil the

past, to tell us of the future. Before He left this world He issued the command "Do this in remembrance of me." Therefore when we do this — when we observe the sacred sacrament of bread and wine — we do this as willing believers in Jesus Christ

<u>Believing in Him</u> as the suffering servant of God who fulfilled in Himself all that had been foretold.

<u>Believing in Him</u> as the Redeemer who willingly gave His life to prove to us (beyond shadow) that death is not the end.

<u>Believing in Him</u> as the risen Lord of heaven and earth who is now on high preparing the Father's mansions there for us and those who will follow us.

This action is the supreme manifestation of our faith — of our trust and of our hope. As we draw near the sacred Table let us look back upon the past, remembering the sacred heritage upon which we have entered — remembering the many who sowed that we might reap — prophets — Christ — missionaries — teachers — parents — those who have sat with us at this Table in the past, strengthening us in faith, encouraging us to follow worthily in their footsteps.

Let us look to ourselves at the present time, appreciating this privilege that is ours of being accepted members of the Christian Church, heirs of this Christian heritage.

Let us look forward — confident in our Faith — confident in our Master's promise — that when we shall no longer be here, we shall be privileged to enter the better lands beyond.

My father would have been cheered to read a letter to <u>The Listener</u> of 8 November 1979 by John May of Lincoln Theological College to the effect that '... even theologians have given up trying to "disprove" Genesis.'

My father's <u>Book of Common Order</u> was variously amended in manuscript over the years (and once even re-bound by a kind friend) and he later also acquired the 1928 revision — and slightly amended that. He held his first class for intending communicants at Lumphanan before the May Communion of 1913. There were 5 girls and 14 young men. One of the girls was a domestic servant at a farm quite near her home, the others were 'at home'. Of the men — all local — seven were farm servants working at varying distances from their homes (three of these were farmers' sons), four worked on their family farm, one was a sawyer in the village and one — son of a sawyer — was a postman, and two were carpenters in their family business. Most of the names are familiar; the last-mentioned carpenters, Charles and James Smith of Bridge of Dubbs, Tornaveen, were excellent craftsmen and when the manse steading and glebe were being put in order before the heritors relinquished responsibility in 1929, it was they

who made the substantial new gates, including those into the dung-court, and
the 'bucht' for the sheep near the north entrance, the last presumably on my
father's account. In the course of this operation, one day, we children
were examining in their presence a dead mole; the Smith brother who remarked
'Look at its wee eyes!' remained to us 'Wee Eyes' to the end of the chapter.
Later there were more 'incomers' employed on the farms, single men who would
have been engaged at the half-yearly Aberdeen feeing market, and thereafter
stayed for shorter or longer periods. They would be seen on free Sundays
cycling to their own homes in their best navy suits, folded raincoats strapped
to their carriers.

A roll book has survived for the Junior Bible Class enrolled in March
1913, 12 boys and 8 girls, their ages ranging from 14-16. Three of the girls
were in service, the rest at home. Four of the boys were 'fee'ed', one worked
for the local butcher, the others worked at home. The average attendance
during the year was 11; on 23 March 'very stormy' only 4 turned up - three
boys and Annie Keith from the Hilton, who had much the most difficult journey.
Again on 28 December it was 'very stormy' and six came. It is worth noting
that of the 20 in the class only 2 came from the village, half a mile away;
the maximum journey was about two miles each way. As there was a vacation from
August to October - the busiest time on the farms - the class was liable to
have the worst weather of the long winter. During the year one boy graduated
to the Senior Class (he had 'joined the Church' in May) two boys and one girl
'deserted', one girl - a maid servant - 'left at term' and a girl and a boy
left the district.

There is no record of what was studied at either senior or junior Bible
Class in those days. Before very long several of the boys of the 1913 junior
class were off to the war, and by 1918 the total given for Lumphanan's
Bible Class (Parish Church) in the Church Year Book was 9. During the twenties
this was to drop to zero, although Sunday School numbers were maintained and
even increased. Early in the decade the Church of Scotland became extremely

disturbed about Sabbath observance as a whole, and the General Assembly exhorted ministers to preach special sermons on the subject. My father complied with a series of three early in 1925 at evening services. In these he tried to analyse the problem and to show what church attendance meant or ought to mean. (The last sermon was based on what he considered the 'perfect assembly for worship' depicted in Acts 10, vv.33-44: Peter's summons to meet those gathered by Cornelius of the Italian band.) At the same time my father asked the Sunday School to write an essay on 'What do we mean by going to church to worship God?' He preserved the piece written by my sister Betty, aged 9, and indeed I recall his quoting it in a sermon many years later:

> We go to church to praise God by singing hymns and thanking Him for sending rain to make the world beautiful to make us happy. We also worship Him by listening to the minister explaining parables in the Bible and difficult things we don't understand. We worship God by praying and asking Him to forgive our sins, and help us to forgive the people who have done wrong to us. We thank God also for sending Jesus His only Son to teach us to be good and try to do better, and after all His hard labour to be crucified for our sakes. We worship Him by reading the Bible and learning how to do better and be kind to one another and try to keep the commandments and learn how to get to Heaven. If we love everybody and don't think much of ourselves we will be pleasing God. We worship God for sending everything He thinks would make us comfortable. Ministers are messengers from God and tell us their message from God, and tell us what we have got to do to please God, and try to get to Heaven. God does not care where we worship Him ...

The last phrase 'so long as we do it properly' was somewhat uncertainly scored out. She may have meant 'God does not care to which denomination we belong' as this idea was apt to recur in my father's teaching. On the other hand she may well have heard him quote Dr Semple's sermon on John 4 v.24: 'God is a Spirit, and they that worship Him must worship Him in spirit and in truth' (generally referred to as 'Semple on Praise', 26 March 1893): 'You can worship God in the open air, or in a barn, for God is everywhere'... but 'Is Christ always to be kept in the stable?' Dr Semple was discussing some of the externals of public worship and the desirability of some element of beauty in it. During the post-1843 Disruption years, of course, many of those who 'came out' worshipped in barns.

Except on Communion Sundays, morning church attendance never recovered its former level, although numbers at the monthly evening services at the West End hall and bi-monthly at Tornaveen meeting-house (one service taken by the Torphins minister) kept up for longer. The congregations at these might include both United Free and Established Church members. The West End hall was used for secular events as well; the Tornaveen building was purely ecclesiastical, the school — and later a public hall — being used for other purposes. I recall my father, returning from a round of calls in the Tornaveen area, reporting that a 'love-darg' had been in progress at the meeting-house, mainly the pruning of the hedge by locals. There was a special kind of community spirit in these outlying areas.

At morning services it was noticeable that particularly in the case of small farmers and crofters, who did not have a 'kitchie deem', it was often the man of the house only who came, with or without children who had already been at Sunday School. For most of our time all continued to use their recognised family pews, the church being divided by charter into heritors' areas according to the size of the estate.

The Bible Class, at least, after the second war picked up again and was at times exceedingly lively. One year my father asked them what they would like to study that winter. After consultation, back came the answer 'Astronomy'. 'Certainly' said my father, 'if you can give me a good reason'. 'The heavens declare the glory of God and the firmament showeth his handywork'. So Astronomy they studied. Having taken down from his own shelves Sir James Jeans' The Mysterious Universe, borrowed from me a book entitled Round the Sun, and made repeated visits to both University and Public Libraries in Aberdeen, the minister succeeded in keeping one jump ahead of the class until the end of the session. Attendance varied in those years from ten to twenty.

In spite of the coined phrase 'war to end war', the years after 1918 brought only uneasy peace. Within the Church of Scotland the twenties saw the commendable, if not quite complete, culmination of the movement to mend the

Disruption of 1843. But on the secular side there was industrial warfare
and economic depression - not only in Britain - which had repercussions even
on a rural community. With hindsight one can perceive the trends which by
the mid-thirties had resulted in, for example, craftsmen in other lines being
employed 'on the roads'. This coincided with the creation of a tar-macadam
road network, meeting the needs of increasingly motorised transport. Ironically,
one of the more promising outlets for young men, apart from the police service
and the regular Army, was the rapidly-developing Royal Air Force. After a
mid-twenties emigration - New Zealand, for example, claimed both the 'merchant
from the West Side' and the clerk to the 1912-13 vacancy committee - a different routine for seeing the world set in. Several of our regular army men
were in the Far East, to be trapped in the next round of hostilities; long
before that young Arthur Watson, only son of Arthur Watson, who succeeded
James Benzies at Peelbog and similarly worked on the glebe and manse garden
at intervals, and his wife, then church and school cleaner, had died while
serving with the Royal Air Force in Iraq. In a civilian capacity John Cecil
Littlejohn of West Kincraigie, whose mother was a Calder of Cairnton, had gone
out to India after an engineering training, and died after a brief illness -
another only son. Neil Cameron and Margaret, one of his sisters, whose father
Hugh was Finzean estate gamekeeper at Knowehead, sought careers in the U.S.A.
Shortly after coming home on holiday in the early thirties (I can recall the
picture postcard he sent us of the Berengaria on his return voyage) Neil died
in America. Margaret was to die there also some years later. Jack Forbes,
son of a 1914-18 veteran in the village, spent some years in South America,
returning eventually to Aboyne to be a helpful County Welfare Officer when the
area of local offices was enlarged and we no longer had an Inspector of Poor
in our village. Hattie Berry, of the family earlier at Cairnbeathie, settled
in Geneva where she had a post with the League of Nations; she made provision,
however, for her ultimate return to Lumphanan: her ashes lie in the old
churchyard. Three of the Leslies of Whitehouse went to Canada early on. In

1937 my brother Craig, on graduating from Cambridge, embarked on a career with the Colonial Administrative Service (later Overseas Civil Service) his first posting being to Cyprus.

All this is anticipating events: there is still much to record of earlier years. But to end a chapter largely devoted to sermons which reflected national events, it would seem appropriate to quote that preached by my father on 20 November 1932. By this time he had ceased to write out his sermons in full; two sides of a sheet of writing paper, with many abbreviations, indicated his train of thought. Later the back of an envelope sufficed.

One of the leading members of the Church of Scotland's wartime Commission on the Moral and Spiritual Issues of the War had been the Reverend John White of the Barony Church in Glasgow. He it was who later suggested the creation of a Church and Nation Committee, to report to each General Assembly on current relevant issues. This was instituted in May 1919. The annual report has become over the years a reference source on various less traditional preoccu-pations of the Church. At the General Assembly of 1931 one of the clauses of the Church and Nation convener's deliverance, as accepted after suggested amendments by Dr John White, read 'The General Assembly record their sympathy with all who are suffering from unemployment through the long-continued trade depression, and their pride in the steadfastness and courage of their faithful people; and, recognising the serious moral and social dangers of the situation, especially to the rising generation, express their thankfulness for public measures that have been taken for the relief of the distress, their earnest desire for the development of such schemes as are calculated to remedy or diminish the evils, and their prayerful hope that, by the blessing of God on our industry and commerce, days of greater opportunity of work and service for all may soon return to our land'. Another clause on the Church's attitude towards peace was, after much discussion, passed: the merits of a defensive war were accepted by the majority. Incidentally, the report by the Maintenance of the Ministry Committee stated that the minimum stipend of ministers of £300 and a manse had been achieved, 'but the coming year would be a difficult one owing to the serious fall in fiars prices [for grain: the heritors still paid their dues, but direct to Edinburgh] and the economic stress in the country'. Their aim was a minimum of £400; this was achieved only after the second world war, although a slow climb began in 1939 with a rise of £5.

At the opening of the Assembly in 1932, the traditional letter from the monarch, King George V, contained the sentence 'In these times of widespread depression, the Churches, no less than other bodies, have difficult problems of their own to face in the fields of finance and organisation, while at the same time their labours are the more needed to carry the banners of hope and faith in the fight against adversity'. The Lord High Commissioner, in his opening address, praised the brave spirit of endurance in which the people of Scotland were meeting the all but unprecedented hardships of the time: 'I can never believe that a nation that can display such qualities is anything but deeply religious. The outward semblance of religious feeling may be small, church attendance lamentably poor, but if the heart is true, then no man need despair, and to you, sir [the Moderator] and your brethren, and to every member of the Church, lies the task not of sowing the seed, but of quickening that which lies dormant...' thus Sir Iain Colquhoun of Luss.

Speaking to the Church and Nation Report, the convener said that unemployment 'still continued to be the nightmare of thinking men and women'. Others thought it inevitable: neither man nor God could govern and direct it. 'Against that materialistic view, his Committee held that unemployment was not an inevitable fate, but a symptom of disease in the body politic...' Certain newspapers had criticised the report of the Church and Nation Committee for its insistence on the place of spiritual and moral forces in the solution of that problem: why? ... while it was notoriously difficult to disentangle the moral issue in the situation, in which the whole world shared, the Church and Nation Committee had made a strenuous endeavour to guide the Assembly and the whole Church to those crucial points, from which they might begin to rethink

the problem. and they had dared to put in the forefront those Christian con-

siderations which it was the Church's business to hold and to apply. Prac-

tically every country in the world was suffering. whatever might be its

government, its politics, its economic and financial theory and practice. In

Germany there were six million over 21 years of age unemployed; in the U.S.A.

ten million - with no insurance; in Great Britain 2.5 million. Without a

change of heart and outlook, without due recognition of moral and spiritual

forces, the best endeavours of statesmen. economists and financial experts

could only end in a postponing of the day of reckoning. Referring to a letter

addressed to the Moderator by the Scottish Independent Labour Party Executive,

hoping that the General Assembly, when considering the report of the Church

and Nation Committee on unemployment. would adopt an emergency deliverance

petitioning the Government to withdraw the means test, and to restore to the

unemployed the cuts in benefit taken away by the National Government, (... 'The

Church of Scotland should give a lead to the whole country, particularly as

the means test is operated on all sections of the unemployed. irrespective of

religion, politics, and nationality'.) the convener could only say that while

the Church would desire that no one be victimised. and that the application of

the law should lean to the side of generosity and sympathy, the Committee had

not had this subject under review and could therefore offer no guidance to the

Assembly. He then passed to the subject of Disarmament. (There was, in fact,

some discussion on the means test with examples given of its provocative

operation).

This then was the background, more lurid in industrial areas, to my father's

November sermon of 1932. Turning once more to Isaiah, Chapter 40: 'Comfort ye,

my people', he described the whole world as being under a cloud, in need of a

message of comfort. Saying 'You know the conditions at home' he referred also

to difficulties in America, Canada, Australia and New Zealand, 'not to mention

India, China, Ireland.' He quoted a conversation he had had recently on a train with an intelligent British sailor: since the war the latter had been in seventeen countries, but had no hesitation in saying that home was best; this was of some consolation. Again there was a parallel with Jewish experience as recorded in Psalm 137: 'By the rivers of Babylon, there we sat down, yea, we wept, when we remembered Zion'. The years of captivity had made Isaiah's countrymen more ready to listen, and he had his message ready: 'Comfort ye, comfort ye my people, saith your God. Speak ye comfortably to Jerusalem, and cry unto her, that her warfare is accomplished, that her iniquity is pardoned: for she hath received of the Lord's hand double for all her sins'. Then came the prophetic vision: 'The voice of him that crieth in the wilderness, Prepare ye the way of the Lord, make straight in the desert a highway for our God. Every valley shall be exalted, and every mountain and hill shall be made low: and the crooked shall be made straight, and the rough places plain: And the glory of the Lord shall be revealed, and all flesh shall see it together ... He shall feed his flock like a shepherd; he shall gather the lambs with his arm, and carry them in his bosom, and shall gently lead those that are with young...'

Although Isaiah was sure that Israel's adversity had come deservedly, he could still hold that God had not forsaken his people, and could confidently foresee this dazzling future offered to the people of Zion: 'Behold, the nations are as a drop of a bucket, and are counted as the small dust of the balance: behold, he taketh up the isles as a very little thing... All nations before him are as nothing; and they are counted to him less than nothing, and vanity... Why sayest thou, O Jacob, and speakest, O Israel, My way is hid from the Lord, and my judgment is passed over from my God? Hast thou not known, hast thou not heard, that the everlasting God, the Lord, the Creator of the ends of the earth, fainteth not, neither is weary? there is no searching of his understanding. He giveth power to the faint; and to them

that have no might he increaseth strength. Even the youths shall faint and
be weary, and the young men shall utterly fall: But they that wait upon the
Lord shall renew their strength; they shall mount up with wings as eagles;
they shall run, and not be weary; and they shall walk, and not faint'. And
Isaiah's confidence was justified; the Lord 'turned again the captivity of
Zion'. Many vicissitudes were still in store for the 'chosen people'; even
in 1932 (although my father could not say this) the end was not yet.

But he asked 'Can we apply the teaching of Isaiah to the conditions of
the world today? to the conditions of our own country, of ourselves?' Present
conditions were due largely – not altogether – to the war, and the economic
and social consequences of war, for example: 1. to the fact that during the
war all nations participating in the war withdrew men from industry to fight,
their place being taken by women. This fact, sometimes overlooked, had caused
an extraordinary upheaval in trade and industry and in work in shops and offices
throughout the world. 2. During the war the nations had borrowed to an unprecedented extent: the war had been largely waged on borrowed capital, mostly
blown wasted into the air. Those who borrowed now had to repay, but money
wasted on unproductive ends could not now be found for repayment. 'This is
one of the fundamental laws of Providence which cannot be escaped'. 3. During
the war, and because of the war, many classes of individuals enjoyed an
unaccustomed prosperity, learned extravagance, and spent unwisely, also on
unproductive ends. Others, to keep pace, like the nations borrowed or committed
themselves to Hire Purchase, the instalment system, and now like the nations
had to repay, or borrow further to repay. Sooner or later, with both nations
and individuals an end must come to this procedure. 4. Other factors were at
work which coincided with the years of war but were independent of it, for
example, the widespread replacement of the horse by the motor car, motor bus
and motor cycle; the accumulated output by mass production of all kinds of
machinery made goods; the awakening of a 'national consciousness' in many
lands that had lived for centuries without change, for example India, China,

Turkey and Russia. Emphasising that 'economics is not our province' he summarised the results of these accumulated circumstances over the world: general
dislocation of trade; uncertainty as to the future, the capitalist afraid
to take risks, the artisan finding no demand or outlet for his skill. Too
many were saying 'Let us eat, drink and be merry for we cannot tell what the
future is to hold in store for us'.

'We see the disease. We understand the canker. Have we a remedy, or
is the recovery of prosperity beyond the capacity of human ingenuity to devise
...We are now paying the natural price for advance in civilisation unregulated
by obedience to the word of God. We may deny the existence of God - a Supreme
Ruler - and live without thought of God. We cannot escape God or evade the
consequences of disregard of His Laws...' The text of the sermon had been
'Comfort ye my people'; Isaiah's words of comfort to the Jewish people, whose
warfare was accomplished and whose iniquity was pardoned provided the timeless
solution: '... they that wait upon the Lord shall renew their strength; they
shall mount up with wings as eagles; they shall run, and not be weary; and
they shall walk, and not faint'.

'Economics is not our province' my father had said. Economic history,
according to Arthur Birnie, for long lecturer in that subject at the University
of Edinburgh, may deal primarily with the material side of human progress, but
it is not therefore a materialistic study. In the introduction to his
Economic History of the British Isles, first published in 1935 and revised in
1938, he writes:

> The part played by the economic factor in moulding human destinies
> runs no risk of being overlooked today... Civilization, in its intel-
> lectual and spiritual aspects, is bound up with the achievement of
> a certain degree of material prosperity. Bread and butter questions
> are important because without bread and butter the artist could not
> paint, the poet dream, the philosopher weave his theories or the
> politician save his country. Indirectly, then, the economic Historian
> is concerned with the highest interests of mankind. He traces that
> material progress without which the noblest activities of the human
> spirit could never reach fruition...

The last chapter of the book assesses the economic position both of the British

Isles and of the world in general after the 1914-18 war. (Birnie had already published an economic history of Europe.) Britain's future, he thought, was bound up with the cause of economic internationalism: 'Her salvation depends on the victory of ideals and policies which will promote and not frustrate economic co-operation between the nations'. But his general Conclusion admits the instability of all forms of social and economic life:

> This is one of the great lessons to be learned from a study of history. Social evolution never stands still; change follows hard on the heels of change; every age is an age of transition. Looking back, we see how one economic system after another has risen, reigned for its brief period and then given way to its successor. Every generation dreams of achieving economic stability, of constructing a system of society which will combine economic efficiency with economic justice. None attains the desired goal. There is something almost painful in this unending spectacle of frustrated efforts and deluded hopes. Yet unless we surrender history to the dreary dominion of chance, we must assume that there is some rational purpose in it all. 'Man', said Kant, 'desires peace, but Nature knows better; she gives him strife'. With the race as with the individual, effort is often richer in blessing than achievement. In wrestling with a stubborn economic environment, in striving after impossible social ideals, mankind perfects its qualities, ennobles its character, and, in some way which we can only dimly perceive, fulfils its high destiny.

The General Assembly debates on the 'Church and Nation' report continued during the thirties to highlight the problem of unemployment; the situation improved latterly partly because of the rearmament programme. The Church's attitude to peace and war was debated annually until 1938 when a fair hearing was afforded the growing pacifist lobby. The relevant committee was then discharged. The following May - when conscription had already been introduced - there was further debate on the subject, one pacifist speaker still maintaining that even a heavy German air-raid should not shake the United Kingdom into reprisals. (He was outvoted). We must leave discussion of the sequel to a later chapter. But the background of the thirties explains the reaction in 1945 of the Vice-President of our British Legion branch, John Hossack, a veteran of 1914-18, to the dropping of the first atomic bomb: if atomic power started revolutionising industry it would only render more people unemployed.

1 ALEX FORBES WIGHT, Camphill

2 GEORGE McDONALD,
Bellman and Gravedigger

3 ALEX REID, Merchant

4 JOHN KING, Knappyround   5 JOHN GLENESK, Craigton

6 WILLIAM G McROBBIE, Joiner and Carpenter   7 DAVID G WATT, Inspector of Poor

8   JAMES MICHIE, Cairnbeathie

9   ROBERT R ANDERSON, Milton

10   ROBERT D DONALD, Banker

11   WILLIAM A DAVIE

12 ST FINAN'S CHURCH, Manse and Steading

CHAPTER SIX

Initium sapientiae timor Domini

General Assembly: 1930's Youth Committee debates;
Young Scotland articles; sermon on the 'lapsed'.

After all the drama attendant upon the union of the churches in 1929, the
General Assembly of 1930 had its own highlights, including the debate on
the report of the 'Youth Committee' - the Committee on the Religious Instruction
of Youth. A similar discussion took place in 1931. Among those attending on
both occasions from what was now the Presbytery of Deeside (basically the
former Presbytery of Kincardine O'Neil together with United Free Church ministers; there were also readjustments of boundaries) were the minister of
Crathie, Dr John Stirton, and my father. The latter, having been from 1927-29
Presbytery Clerk, was now joint clerk dealing with correspondence, the U.F.
minister at Torphins, the Reverend J.M. Carlisle, being in charge of records.
The religious teaching of the young was approaching, or in more sophisticated
areas had reached, a watershed, partly because of the unsettled post-war times,
when 'the old values' were taking a knock, partly because religious instruction
and example within the family had declined or was entirely lacking. Sunday
Schools continued to flourish, if only because it seemed a good way of keeping
the very young out of the way on Sunday mornings. But statistics showed an
unprecedented leakage of youth between the stages of the Sunday School and
the 'Young Communicants' Class. The school-leaving age was, of course, still
fourteen, so that in many cases young people of that age slipped out of the
family circle. The convener of the Youth Committee, among the deliverances
put before the 1930 Assembly, suggested approval of the committee's policy in
preparing suitable courses and notes for Bible Class teachers, so arranged as
to afford a complete system of religious instruction in the essentials of
Christian knowledge for young people.

Among guest speakers invited to address the 1930 Assembly was the Rev.
James Reid of a Presbyterian Church of England charge at Eastbourne. Describing the current attitude of youth in these difficult post-war times, he praised
their 'remarkable honesty' and 'adventurous faith', preface perhaps to 'divine
opportunity'. To the Assembly he said 'When they thought of that young girl,

Miss Amy Johnson, making her adventurous voyage on a monoplane, didn't they just long to win all those qualities for the service of Christ?' Even scientists were discovering that there were more things in heaven and earth than had been dreamed of in their philosophy. The door was open for the possibility of miracle, and a faith in the supernatural grace of God, and His power to move in His own world, such as they found in the New Testament. He found in the young a reaction against materialism (following the realisation of some of their elders in the post-war reaching after material satisfaction that this was a chimera) which had given birth to the phrases 'fed up' and 'bored stiff'. At the same time they tended to be too introspective to be really concerned with social reform. They required first some inner sorting out: they wanted a religion that would clean life up but without hypocrisy; they wanted fellowship within the Church but not just another form of social life. Dr Reid described the reactions of a young boy whose father had taken him to see 'Journey's End', expecting an attitude of revulsion to the horrors of war: 'By God, dad, I wish I had been in it!' Well, there was 'not a more dangerous idea in the world than the forgiveness of sins. The people of Jerusalem on the day of Pentecost said: "These men are drunk"; but the Apostle Peter had replied: "Nay, but this is that of which the prophet spoke when he said the days would come when God would pour out His Spirit upon all flesh, and their sons and their daughters should prophesy, and their young men should see visions and their old men dream dreams"...'

After another guest speaker had dealt with religious education in day-schools, Professor A.A. Bowman, Litt.D., of Glasgow University, described the attitude of educated youth, referring to a 'desire for liberation' yet at the same time a 'yearning for an authority'. Christianity, he felt, had been over-simplified; in every other sphere they demanded a laboured effort of knowledge, yet on the other hand there seemed to be very little information available about the nature and the ways of God. He too referred to religion's own excitements set against the excitements of a 'roaring world', and the possibilities

for those seeking a personalised religion: first, the fear of God, the con-
viction of sin, and then - and only then - the love of Christ.

The 1931 report of the Youth Committee claimed some definite progress
towards providing a systematic 4-year course of instruction for the post-
Sunday School period; four text-books had been commissioned from leading
theologians. (At the 1933 Assembly there was criticism of the first of these
volumes: a Kirkcaldy elder recalled the tale of the professor of theology who,
when asked how he treated his subject, replied 'Oh, I just begin wi' infinity
and go straight on'. A Kirkcaldy minister followed: '...Last autumn they had
been provided with No.1 of a series for junior Bible classes; but the knowledge in it was far too wonderful for them. They sent the books back for the
use of people of greater understanding, because they were a simple folk in
Fife, and betook themselves with more pleasure and more profit to the bare
text of Scripture...') A Leith minister in 1931 found that one solution was
to provide a bridge between Sunday School and Bible Class by taking the 13-
year-olds into a Junior Bible Class. Lord Sands proposed an addendum to the
Youth Committee's 1931 deliverance recommending that presbyteries consider anew
the question of a link between Sunday School and the Young Communicants Class.

It seems clear that there was some private discussion on the subject
between my father and Dr Stirton, Crathie. It happened that the Director of
Religious Education at the Church's Edinburgh Headquarters was then the Rev.
W.M. Wightman, a former headmaster who had turned to Divinity during the war
and after being ordained in 1917 was inducted in 1918 to the parish of Boharm
in the Presbytery of Aberlour. (There, with a modest roll of 236 communicants
he had a Sunday School of 65 and a Bible Class of 33. In 1924 he went to St
Enoch's, Glasgow; three years later he became the Church's Director of Religious
Instruction of Youth (later termed Religious Education). He was awarded a D.D.
in 1937. He died in October 1959. In the 1960 Assembly Report there were two
references to his twenty-one years as Director: he had also been Secretary to
the Youth and Education Department. He had 'brought great enthusiasm and

imaginative leadership to the new movements in the Church after the war').

The outcome was the publication, over seven months in 1932-33, in 'Young

Scotland', the Church's periodical for young people in their teens, of a

series entitled The Minister's Class: Sunday Evening discussions on Religion.

The author was merely stated to be 'A Northern Minister', but was in fact my

father. This was not a course of instruction for 'intending communicants',

but for those at the Bible Class stage who were merely considering 'joining

the Church', - a bridge on which they might pause and consider. Dr Stirton

read the articles in manuscript (his letters are, I think, mis-dated June and

October 1933: it seems they must have been written in 1932, as the first

article was printed in October of that year.) He wrote on 5 June:

> I have read your manuscript carefully through and, without the
> slightest hesitation I congratulate you very heartily upon this effort
> of your pen. I have endeavoured, microscopically speaking, to discover
> serious faults of thought, of style and of grammar, but have been
> baffled at every point. I think you have given food for stimulating
> thought in the youthful mind upon subjects of the highest importance.
> Your expression is clear and capable of being understood by the youngest
> child, however unlettered, and, what to myself has afforded sincere
> pleasure is the clever way in which you impress upon the children
> truths such as those of the Shorter Catechism, as being clear and simple
> as the day in spite of the tendency at the present time to decry all
> such teaching as too heavy and involved for youthful minds to understand.
>
> In this you have wielded the "art which conceals art".
>
> I read your papers with the purpose of detecting faults but the
> faults, if such there be, are of so insignificant a character that it
> would be hypercritical even to mention them. Your friend Wightman is
> quite correct in his estimate of the work and I shall have pleasure in
> re-reading the papers when they appear in the full glory of print.

> On 12 October Dr Stirton wrote again:

> I have read carefully your m.s. and again congratulate you upon it.
> It is very carefully thought out & expressed. I have made a few small
> corrections but they are not of importance. In a literary production
> never say "Very very" - one "very" is enough. Once more congratulating
> you, I am yours sincerely J. Stirton.

There were two postscripts; in the first the Crathie minister wrote:

'Had a pleasant and interesting visit to Glamis Castle'. The second, after

a reference to the short-lived 'Forward Movement', (launched in 1930 to take

advantage of the 1929 union of the churches to revive Christian life and

witness in Scotland) recorded: 'I was at the Synod meeting & heard Cox "slating" you!! J.S.' This was probably in connection with some Presbytery matter. The Rev. Dr J.T. Cox, Dyce, as well as being author of the indispensable Practice and Procedure in the Church of Scotland, also held the office then named Joint-Senior Clerk of the General Assembly, and was clerk to the Synod of Aberdeen. A Deeside Presbytery elder was once heard to say 'If that man Cox comes here interfering again we'll throw him in the Dee'. He was later to become involved in the union of 1939 of the Lumphanan churches.

About the Young Scotland series Mr Wightman also wrote to my father on 12 October 1932:

> I have your letter of 10th anent "The Minister's Class". I have not bothered you about it because I was perfectly satisfied with it. The matter was fresh and well put, and there was a certain grip in the writing of it which I felt would carry on the readers to the end. It is not possible to let you have No.2 as it is already in the hands of the printer. We must keep a month ahead of publication. I shall try to rescue the manuscripts and pass them on to you so that you may compare them with the printed pages. You can take No.1 as a reasonable criterion of the space available: half a column more or less will not annoy me.
>
> I am concerned about the title of No.3. I don't like "God's Purposes in Temptation" as a title. At the same time I feel there should be conveyed the suggestion which it gives of growth through testing and trial. Perhaps you may evolve something in the course of the month, and I shall keep my mind in touch for a possible title.
>
> Don't worry too much about unorthodoxy. I am afraid that the Youth Committee is condemned beyond reprieve in the minds of many people, and certainly I don't think you have transgressed in any way at all. Our aim is to get the truth across, and it is not fair that isolated phrases or expressions should be over-keenly scrutinised.

His reference to the Youth Committee reflected the current discussion on the changing attitudes of the young. It is perhaps significant that during the debate in the 1935 General Assembly on Religious Instruction of Youth, it was the veteran missionary of Blantyre, Nyasaland, Dr Alexander Hetherwick (ordained 1883), who spoke up for Mr Wightman. Speaking, he said, not as a missionary but as an old Sunday School superintendent - he had just returned to his own West Church of St Nicholas in Aberdeen where the minister had given him back his old post '(Applause)' - 'He would like to refer ... to the services of Mr Wightman who had come to Aberdeen to deliver a series of lectures, which had been highly appreciated, and were better attended than many other

lectures delivered there. He had left behind him the gratitude of most of
the teaching-staffs of their schools. Those who wished to get helpful instruction could not do better than ask Mr Wightman to deliver the lectures
which he had delivered in Aberdeen. There was one matter that had lain upon
his soul ever since he came home and that was the great change in the whole
Sunday school work and youth of the Church in the past fifty years; he
referred to the decreased attendance of young people and children at the
services on the Lord's Day...'

Many years later my father had occasion to write to a member of the
Church's Education Department about an expanded version of The Minister's Class
which in his 83rd year he had been revising while living at the Retired Ministers' Residence in Carlton Street. He had just been watching a television discussion 'on Sunday Schools and Religious Education generally, when one speaker
propounded some extraordinary remarks on Adam and Eve and some other items in
Scripture'. He went on to explain: 'The backbone of my writing was given me
by the late Dr Adam Semple, Minister at Huntly 1875-1914. I was very fortunate
to be his Assistant at Huntly 1911-1913, after I finished my Divinity course at
Aberdeen, for I found the then aged Doctor to be one of the wisest and most
widely read men I have ever met...[He] often spoke to me about what he himself
owed [at the University of Glasgow] to Drs John and Edward Caird...' (a somewhat controversial pair.)

A first glance at the Young Scotland articles, seen together as printed,
would no doubt be off-putting to those who were out to change the orientation
of Christian teaching. One can hear the twentieth-century term 'fundamentalism'
mentioned. (The term itself appears to have gathered moss over the years.)
Having been round most if not all of the science classes at University while
spending four years over his Ordinary Arts Degree (his bursary permitted this
four-year luxury) my father was well aware of current theories to date about
the Creation. It emerged that in essentials there was no important divergence

of thought. In the second article he wrote:

> Of late years there has been some considerable controversy over
> the manner in which the heavens and earth came into being. and over
> the age of heaven and earth, e.g. some people calculate the age of
> the heavens and the earth to be a few thousand years; while others —
> whose opinion on this matter deserves respect — have said that they
> are millions of millions of years old. But notice how clearly the
> Bible avoids a controversy of this kind. It states simply that heaven
> and earth were created by God "in the beginning"... The aim of the
> Bible is not to state the time when or the manner in which the heavens
> and the earth came into being, but to place before us God's purposes
> in Creation and particularly his purposes in creating Man.

> If you wish to pursue further the interesting subject of the manner
> in which, or the time when, the universe was made, you must study the
> sciences of astronomy, geology, geography, natural philosophy, and
> natural history. These sciences unravel and explain in detail the
> secrets of the nature and structure of God's works. The Bible simply
> states that these bodies were created by God, and then goes on to tell
> us more fully about Man: its own particular sphere.

The last sentence is the amended version of 1965; today's news

(1979) indicates that the scientists are still revising their theories.

The articles were written for the type of young people he had known,

leading them gradually from what was familiar to the revelation of the whole

truth; showing by simple illustration what the process of 'joining the Church'

could mean both personally and through them for the community, for the Church

itself and perhaps even for the wider benefit of mankind. They show very

clearly the historical sequence of the Creator's plan. Not everyone possesses

a sense of history; many are content to begin at a half-way mark or at the day

before yesterday. Rootlessness has many origins. For someone who has this

historical sense the continuity of Scripture is particularly meaningful: from

the Creation — whether taken literally or not — and the earliest evidence of

the fallibility of the human race, on through the pre-Christian centuries,

with their prophets, priests and kings, and the tales of the vicissitudes of

the chosen race, then to the fulfilment of the prophecies of Christ's incarna-

tion, to His teaching and to the further work of His apostles, until by the

last chapter of the Revelation of St John everything has fallen into place.

What more could the young of any generation demand?

The seven articles of The Minister's Class will now be summarised, with

occasional reference to the revised version. The latter, in 1965, came to the same basic conclusions; as an octogenarian my father would affirm that he still saw no reason to believe otherwise. More space was given in the revision to individual Old Testament prophets and to John the Baptist; on the New Testament, alternative renderings from the recently-published New English Bible version would sometimes be inserted. (When the N.E.B. Old Testament came out my father was obviously disappointed: 'I don't know that it's any improvement on the old one'. I think he missed the resounding phrases which he himself declaimed so memorably: 'Lord, thou hast been our dwelling-place in all generations...' His own copy he placed on the communal bookshelves in the lounge at the Retired Ministers' Residence, instead of on his own shelves.)

Early in the first 1932 article, headed 'Why do we wish to "join the Church"?', we meet the Shorter Catechism, and any whose immediate reaction might now be to sidestep this section would do well to pause and take another look at this historic document. Undoubtedly a gem of compression, this early paperback gave the gist of the most important teachings of the Church. The occasional section jars, but in practice its use was selective. Man's chief end – to glorify God and to enjoy Him for ever – was in my father's teaching simply translated into the individual's task of improving on creation as he found it and being a good neighbour.

The second article 'God's purposes in creation' went on to study the nature of man and the purpose for which he was placed on the earth. The class was urged to forget the proper names, Adam being merely the Hebrew word for 'man' and 'Eden' for 'pleasantness'. Genesis 2 v.15 was 'meant not merely to tell us what happened long ages ago upon the banks of the Euphrates, but also to tell us what is happening amongst ourselves every day'. To illustrate the nature of man, and the essential difference between man, endowed with a conscience, and the lower animals, there is an imaginary dialogue between minister and class in a country setting:

Suppose ... that I turn my horse out to graze on a field of rather poor grass, and suppose that in the next field, belonging to my neighbour, there is a crop of very excellent pasture, what is likely to happen? Answer: The horse stretches over the fence and grazes upon the better grass...

But suppose that at another time these fields are under crop and the poor field has very few sheaves in it, while in the fertile one there is an abundant harvest, and suppose my neighbour discovers my man filling our cart with sheaves from the better field, what will he say to my servant?....What is the difference between my horse grazing in another man's field and my man gathering sheaves from it? Answer: The horse does not know better, whereas the man knows that he is stealing...

Under the altered title 'Do we carry out God's purposes?' the third article pursues man's freedom to enjoy everything in creation provided he does no wrong. The entry of the serpent – the tempter – almost makes one look for the psychologist at its tail. The members of the minister's class might have little difficulty in obeying the ten commandments set out in the Shorter Catechism; the insidious tempter who might almost make a virtue out of the actions he inspired was less easy to resist. The woman even misquotes him, to her further undoing. Here my father introduced a modern Eve, more suited to his teen-age 1932 audience, who exemplifies clearly the successive stages of the Bible incident. But first he asked the class 'Have any of you ever heard the serpent speaking? No? Probably not. The serpent whispers ... Let me tell you, however, a tale about a young friend of mine:

This friend – whom we may call Esther – was maid to a certain Mrs. A., a kindly and considerate employer. One day Esther had arranged to leave work early to go home to her little sister's birthday party. It chanced that Mrs. A. had promised to go on the same day to sit with Mrs. B. – a permanent invalid – while her attendant did some necessary shopping. Early that afternoon Mrs. A. received a wire from friends stating that they were motoring through the town and hoped, if convenient, to spend the night with her. Mrs. A. called Esther, explained the circumstances, and asked if she could arrange two bedrooms for the guests before she left. Esther, who was an obliging girl, agreed, and a wire was sent off to invite the motorists to stay the night. However, no sooner had Mrs. A. gone to pay her visit than Esther began to wonder how she could overtake these extra duties and be ready for her sister's party. Besides, she thought it somewhat hard that those motorists should choose this particular day for their visit. It was not long since they had stayed a night before. She wondered why they did not go to the hotel. It looked as if they were making a convenience of her mistress – imposing upon her good nature. Just, she was sure, as Mrs. B. did. It was scarcely a week since Mrs. A. had spent a whole afternoon reading to

Mrs. B. In fact, she assured herself that it would be a kindness to
Mrs. A. if she were to let both Mrs. B. and these other friends
understand that they must not expect so much from her mistress. But
how could that be done? By omitting certain of the usual preparations.
Were she to do so she would not disappoint her sister by arriving late,
and the motorists would see for themselves that Mrs. A.'s house was
not always ready for guests at a moment's notice. Therefore, to save
time for herself and to protect what seemed to be her mistress's
interests, she decided to omit certain usual preparations and started
off for home.

By now the class were beginning to see what the minister was getting at,
and when he asked: 'Had Esther heard any voices, I wonder, that afternoon?
... As she was nearing home she saw Mrs. A. approaching at some distance.
What, I wonder, did Esther do?' Answer: 'She turned down a side street ...'
The revised text continues thus:

Esther is now beginning to see certain aspects of the situation
which she had previously overlooked - aspects that had been obscured
by the smoke-screen of "promises" suggested to her by the "voice"...
You may think, perhaps, that I have taken, as an illustration of this
deep theme ... a very unimportant peccadillo quite unworthy to be compared to the record of Scripture... (but) the principle involved is
exactly the same, whether the wrong-doing is the misdemeanour of a
serving maid, the defalcation of a man in business, ... or the high
treason of a country's ruler who for short-sighted, selfish ends, or
merely for personal ambition, tries to turn to his own advantage the
sacred trust of government entrusted to his charge.

The printed article ends:

You will not now deny that you have heard this serpent speaking -
whispering - wily - insinuating - making evil look like good...Yet
some people ... tell us that these opening chapters of Genesis are
Eastern myths - legends - that have grown up in the dim and distant
past. Eastern and ancient they certainly are ... But ... nowhere in
modern literature do we find such width of outlook, such accuracy of
perception, such profound philosophy compressed into the space of a
few short verses. These three first chapters of Genesis, upon which
the Bible is built up, form, indeed, a worthy foundation for Scripture -
a foundation well and truly laid. Whether or no the writer or editor
was Moses, the Author was the Spirit of the Living God.

In the fourth article 'Wrongdoing: 1. The Penalty; 2. The Reprieve' the
minister asks the class: '...When we consider all the sorrow, the labour, the
suffering that exist in a world which, but for wrongdoing, might be a veritable
Garden of Happiness', ... was it not a pity that the Creator did not set up
some railing round the Tree of the knowledge of good and evil ... (making it)
impossible for man or woman to reach up to the fruit of that tree?' The class
know the answer: 'No ...because man would then have been like the beasts which

need "fences"'. The minister agrees: God in His wisdom made man on a higher
scale, with a conscience and a soul, capable of enjoying happiness in freedom,
and fit for entering into eternal life. The tragedy of mankind was man's
misuse of this freedom. 'I wonder if Genesis foresaw the Armageddon of
1914-1918, and the world of 1932 groaning under its burden of debts and unemployment?' The revision added 'of 1939-45, and the whole world of today
groaning under those burdens of debts, disillusionments, and dread of disasters-
to-come that wrong-thinking and wrong-doing have laid heavy upon the shoulders
of mankind'.

Having sounded the depths of the outer darkness the article then ends
with the sunrise of reprieve; in Isaiah's words 'to revive the heart of the
contrite ones', or as the Shorter Catechism put it 'God...did enter into a
covenant of grace to deliver them out of the estate of sin and misery; and
to bring them into an estate of salvation by a Redeemer'. But first, in advance
of Jesus Christ, comes John the Baptist, with his call to 'repent' - or, as my
father preferred to translate the Greek, 'change your outlook upon life'. Here
again the revision goes into much more detail, first offering an explanation
of why the Redeemer's coming was so long delayed - and, indeed, of why so
much more of human history was included in the Old Testament - and enlarging upon
the role of John the Baptist as the keystone of the arch between Old and New
Testaments.

The fifth article pointed out how, under the Pax Romana, the time was at
last ripe for the coming of the Saviour. Under the far-reaching communications
system of the Roman Empire conditions were better than ever before for the
spread of the Gospel, and for the establishment of the kingdom of heaven upon
earth. Jesus was able to say to His disciples 'Go ye therefore and teach all
nations ...' The 1965 revision pointed out sadly that even then the idea of
world unity had hardly been grasped: 'The present day troubles of the United
Nations Assembly shows this only too clearly'. But my father did not despair:

'...we may add, in spite of the many problems and perplexities which harass the world at the present time, notwithstanding the dark clouds that, in our own day, still cast their shadows over so many lands and peoples; and in spite of those numerous experiments in conduct and in codes of morality which seem sometimes so precarious and so fully fraught with possibilities of danger to the nations of our world today, History, both sacred and secular, is still recording that slowly, very slowly - painfully slowly - progress continues to be made'.

This article stresses the continuity of Old and New Testaments: as the revision has it 'to place beyond any possibility of doubt the fact that the scheme of revelation presented in Scripture is not a haphazard collection of independent, unrelated incidents and doctrines, but is a well-connected and continuous whole'. The printed article highlights other sayings of Jesus which emphasise the links: 'I am come not to call the righteous but sinners unto repentance... The Son of Man is come to seek and to save that which was lost'. Jesus did not complain unduly regarding the weaknesses or shortcomings of mankind except that, like John the Baptist, he was scathing about self-righteous hypocrites. 'I am come that they might have life, and that they might have it more abundantly... I am come - a light into the world... I am the light of the world: he that followeth me shall not walk in darkness but shall have the light of life'. But also 'while ye have light, believe in the light'. There was light sufficient now, but the process of further enlightenment was to continue: 'I have yet many things to say unto you, but ye cannot bear them now. Howbeit when he, the Spirit of truth is come, he will guide you into all truth... If I depart, I will send him unto you'. Even then, the world was not quite ready to comprehend all that was to be taught concerning God's plans for mankind, but ultimately, the Holy Spirit would come to guide men 'into all truth'. The revision states:

Our God is, as He has always been, a living God... He is still speaking to mankind 'at sundry times and in divers manners'... Century

after century, through the inspiration of the Holy Spirit, mankind
continues to gain gradually a fuller and clearer understanding of
truths which had previously been only partially revealed... But we
can also see at the present day ... the gross darkness that still
broods over many lands, even over many so-called Christian lands -
not excluding our own - and therefore the consequent further need
for the guidance of the Holy Spirit to dispel this darkness ere all
the families of the earth can be accounted truly 'blessed'.

To return to the printed article: the next saying of Jesus to be high-
lighted was 'I am the good shepherd: the good shepherd giveth His life for
the sheep'. Jesus did not expect that men would always receive His teaching
without question; yet He believed that there was to be found in His life
and in His works, but especially in His death, evidence of His messiahship
sufficiently convincing to satisfy every genuine seeker after truth. Jesus'
message was not confined to revealing the possibilities open to man for a
fuller and more abundant life on earth; he taught of a life beyond death.
'Let not your heart be troubled: ye believe in God, believe also in me. In
my Father's house are many mansions ... I go to prepare a place for you...'
This article on the fulfilment of the Old Testament prophecy of the coming
of the Messiah ends with the quotation 'The Son of Man came not to be ministered unto, but to minister, and to give His life a ransom for many'. The
minister's class was told that He came to give - not to receive; - to demonstrate, both by precept and by example, that 'a man's life consisteth not in
the abundance of the things which he possesseth', but in the nature of the
service which he renders to his fellow-men and to God. The final comment,
leading on to the next topic, extended this concept to God's need of the help
of all His children ere His 'blessing' could be spread abroad to 'all the
families of the earth'.

In the sixth printed article, headed 'Eternal Life and the Kingdom of
God', the emphasis in Jesus' teaching changes from 'I' to 'You'. It goes
back to the early days of His mission beginning with His own temptation:

If the Redeemer is to claim men's allegiance and if He is to help
us to avoid the snares of the Tempter, what was more natural than that

He should first show Himself able to resist the Tempter? You remember the baits put forward — a comfortable life with a full table easily acquired; notoriety; unlimited power. Are not these just the type of baits or bribes that appeal to ourselves today, enticing us to devote our lives to enjoying ourselves rather than, as the Catechism counsels us, to glorifying God and enjoying Him? Jesus, however, fortified by Scripture, refused to be diverted from His duty, and the Tempter, admitting defeat, left Him.

The 'class' then discussed why Jesus should have begun his preaching by associating Himself with John the Baptist, repeating his message: 'Repent: for the Kingdom of Heaven is at hand' concluding that it was His desire to demonstrate clearly that He was working in close co-operation with God's human agents, presently assembling round Him the 'fishers of men'. Then comes the surprising Sermon on the Mount, listing the happy ones: the humble, the meek, the merciful, the pure in heart, the peacemakers, even the poor in spirit. 'These were not the classes of people that men had been accustomed to call the happy ones. Jesus was certainly presenting His hearers with a "change of outlook" upon life'. Even more surprisingly He then addressed the assembled crowd 'Ye are the salt of the earth ... Ye are the light of the world'. Instead of denouncing all who heard Him as unprofitable servants 'He begins by turning their thoughts to the secret of true happiness, and then, taking men just as He found them, without upbraiding, He explains to them that their lives are valuable ... to themselves, ...to their fellow-men, ...to God. He assures them that it is only through their active co-operation that the world can become a truly happy place and that glory can then fully redound to God its creator...' We are back to the Shorter Catechism: 'Man's chief end is to glorify God...' Now comes the question of 'enjoying' Him for ever.

About this Jesus was less explicit, but, harking back first to John the Baptist's announcement that the Kingdom of heaven was 'at hand', the article quotes Jesus' reply to the Pharisees: 'The Kingdom of God cometh not with observation: neither shall they say, Lo here! or, lo there! for, behold, the Kingdom of God is within you.' In the revision the New English Bible translation is also given: 'the Kingdom of God is among you'. Then, looking forward to the very close of Jesus' ministry, the article cites the last

evening He spent with His disciples, when He prayed:

> Father, the hour is come; glorify Thy Son, that Thy Son also may
> glorify Thee: as Thou hast given Him power over all flesh, that He
> should give eternal life to as many as Thou hast given Him. And this
> is life eternal, that they might know Thee the only true God and Jesus
> Christ whom Thou hast sent. I have glorified Thee on the earth: I
> have finished the work which Thou gavest me to do.

Under the sub-heading 'Not endless existence but a state of the soul' my

father then quoted practically verbatim extracts from the sermon on eternal

life by his own mentor Dr Adam Semple which had in 1880 been published in the

collection Scotch Sermons. The writers of these now tend to be discredited:

they included John Caird. So far as I can ascertain Dr Semple has not been

singled out for criticism, probably for the simple reason that there was

nothing to criticise. Mr Wightman in 1933 certainly gave his generous approval

to the inclusion of long extracts in my father's article (Semple, like himself,

had been at St Enoch's). He wrote on 24 January:

> I worked through the manuscript of No.6 of "The Minister's Class"
> last night with a jealous eye for any material which could be cut out,
> because it is very long. I read it closely but I can find nothing whose
> removal would not interrupt the continuity of the argument, so I am
> letting it go with the hope that the printer can get it into the four
> pages. It is good stuff and I hope people are reading it. I know some
> are, and there is no harm in finding it a little difficult.

> It may be as well just to leave Semple's own words, although I believe
> that you could have paraphrased it more concisely. Still we have the
> weight of his authority in the article and that is something gained...

> I wonder how many city congregations would listen to sermons so
> closely built up as Semple's are if they were preached today; in the
> country I used to find it different.

In Dr Semple's sermon 'eternal life' is synonymous with 'the Kingdom of

God', something to be aspired to not only in the hereafter but through being

in communion with God in this life, by 'knowing' Christ. What is meant by

'knowing' Christ?

> Is it enough that we are able to tell all the marvels that attended
> His birth, to go through all the incidents of His strange life, to
> recount His miracles, and repeat His parables? No, truly: these are
> not Christ, but the vestments which may even conceal Him from us. The
> mere facts of Christ's life may be known as facts by the atheist and
> the hypocrite as accurately as by the most spiritually minded of men,
> but the life of Christ - the Man Himself - lies deeper than His words

and acts. We must penetrate beneath the surface to the moving spirit, and come into living contact with the heart and mind which prompted the actions.

What avails our knowledge of Christ's miracles, if we feel not the tenderness and love which speak in them and prompted them? Are we better or wiser for our ability to detail all the mysterious agonies of Calvary, and yet be untouched by the spirit of self-sacrifice which breathes through them? What to us are Christ's kindly acts and tender words, if our hearts be cold to the human sympathy which lies beneath them? Not by familiarity with the record of Christ's outward life, not by the knowledge of what is patent to the eye, but by communion with the inward life - that communion which imbues us with the living Spirit - does Christ become known to men. The mind which was in Christ must be in us - we must be able in some measure to make our own that tenderness and love, that purity and self-sacrifice, which distinguished Him.

If we cannot die, as He did, for our fellow-men; if we cannot, by a word, make suffering cease; if we cannot bid the guilt of sin depart, there are still many ways in which we can be Christ-like. We can at least live for our fellow-men, and, in so doing, breathe that spirit of self-sacrifice which produced its noblest fruit in the death of Christ; we can, at least, make suffering less, and so soften the pains of disease; we can at least show the sinner the vileness of his folly, and lead him to that love which will say - 'Thy sins are forgiven thee!'

The coming of Christ did not make the sin and sorrow and suffering of the world vanish - His work still needs to be carried on by those in whom He lives, when each, in his sphere, labours, by active work or by patient example, to leave the world better than he found it. Only when we thus are 'labourers together with God', when we take up, in our own feeble way and according to our opportunities, the work which Christ Himself began - when our hearts throb, though faintly, with the same feelings as stirred the breast of Jesus, and we are re-living (but yet, how far off!) the life which long ago He lived on earth - only then have we attained that state of purity, of love, of self-sacrifice, which is implied in the knowledge of Him Whom God has sent. To know Christ is, if we dare say it, to be Christ.

From the language of the text, ('This is life eternal') thus explained, two consequences seem to follow: (1) Eternal life - or as it is sometimes called, the Kingdom of God - is a state of the soul, and not any outward glory. (2) It seems to follow that Eternal Life is therefore a present as well as a future state...

In the above quotation one or two phrases from the original which were excised from the printed article have been restored from the revised version. My father ended his sixth article by asking the 'class': 'Need I now ask you what is meant by "enjoying God for ever"? Eternal life is present with us here and now. Whenever we make a conscious effort to be pure, as Christ was pure, to help "by active work or patient example to leave the world better than we found it", then the Kingdom of God is within us and we are with Christ inside the Garden of Happiness, having free access to the Tree of Life. We

are <u>living souls</u>, made in the image and likeness of God - enjoying Him for
ever...'

At the opening of the seventh and last printed article, headed 'Life Eternal may be ours - The Church - The Tree of Life', my father was, in imagination,
brought down to earth in a dialogue with his 'class'. He recalled that the
Old Testament taught that Man was made in God's image, endowed with a conscience
and a soul, and that in the New Testament they learned that if Man, following
the example of Christ, refused to listen to the tempter and cultivated his
spiritual nature, he might spend his time in this world in a garden of happiness, 'then finally at his death (as a chrysalis casts its covering and rises
into the air a beautiful insect) shed his natural body and pass with a
spiritual body into the place prepared for him in the mansions of his Father's
house beyond. "There is a natural body and there is a spiritual body"'. The
reaction of the 'class' was 'But do you really believe that this is possible?'
to which the minister responded:

> Well, we agreed that you should test what I tell you by the measure
> of your own experience ... You have, I am sure, <u>seen</u> a caterpillar, a
> worm, a creature of the earth, curl itself up in a corner, then in due
> course burst its shell and fly out a butterfly. Or, you may have <u>seen</u>
> a circle of jelly in a ditch turn first into a tadpole swimming in water,
> then into a frog which stepped out on to the dry land. [For his town
> readers he added 'If you have not yourselves actually observed these
> interesting transformations, you know from the testimony of those who
> have seen them that these, and even more wonderful changes, are well-
> known facts of nature sufficiently vouched for by those who watch for
> and study them'.] If, then, the Creator has, as we know, made provision
> for such wonderful changes in the life-history of the creatures of the
> roadside and the ditches, is it too great an exercise of faith for us to
> believe Scripture when it tells us that He can provide a spiritual body
> in a new and different sphere for the highest of earth's creatures - Man?

The 'class' agreed that God might well make provision for this change in man,
but what were the chances of sinful man qualifying for this promotion?
'Have you not rather been describing an ideal, a state of perfection towards
which we may look or aspire but into which we can never hope to arrive? ...
Does not the Catechism say - "No mere man since the fall is able in this life
perfectly to keep the commandments of God, but doth daily break them in
thought, word, and deed?"'

The minister admits that the Catechism certainly appears to be a little pessimistic but they had already discussed and found reasonable the Bible statement that if we did wrong we would spiritually die: 'We cannot, therefore, I fear, expect to secure the peace of Eternal Life through the perfection of our "works". Let us not, however, forget what our Redeemer has told us regarding the "Grace" of God...' Recalling the familiar phrases of Jesus' teaching ... 'not to call the righteous but sinners to repentance;' the welcome back to the prodigal son; the words of the Lord's Prayer: 'Forgive us our debts...' (was this impossible of attainment?) the growth of the grain of mustard seed, or the leaven hid in the meal, showing the potentialities of very small beginnings,

> 'We may not attain to "perfection" either in character or in conduct, but if we earnestly try to cultivate our spiritual natures we shall "grow in grace" and so become more fit to be regarded as "the salt of the earth" - "the light of the world". Would you care then to test, from your own experience, this further assertion that I have now made, namely, that you can secure eternal happiness and perpetual peace of mind by earnestly endeavouring to cultivate within you the spirit of Jesus Christ - endeavouring not merely to know about Christ, ... but ... to know Him effectually through becoming yourselves Christlike in character and in conduct, or at least as Christlike as you can? ... If, from your own experience, through a conscious knowledge that you have tried to do your duty, you find that you have acquired an abiding peace of mind - that peace which passeth understanding - you will then know that you are fulfilling your true destiny on earth, that you are entering into Eternal Life and are preparing yourselves to glorify God on earth and to enjoy Him for ever. This is a peace that each individual must purchase for himself...

Then comes the final summing up, pursuing the question why one should 'join the Church'. 'The Church ... represents on earth today our Saviour's first disciples whom He called to be "Fishers of Men", and to whom He gave the command, "Go ye and teach all nations"... The Church is a fellowship of men and women - believers in Our Lord and Saviour - called together by Him for mutual strength and encouragement to carry on the work of the Creator and the Redeemer...'

In the revised manuscript there is a section here on the disciples before and after the resurrection. Before Jesus' death they had failed to understand much that He had tried to teach. As Luke put it, they 'trusted that it had been He which should have redeemed Israel', but they expected this to have been achieved rather by physical force, as David had delivered their fathers from the Philistines. They had also been concerned about the 'reward' they were likely to receive: who was to be greatest in the Kingdom of heaven? In Gethsemane they had failed their Master; after His arrest they all 'forsook Him and fled'. After His resurrection 'they began to realise more clearly the true nature of His divinity, and to understand more fully the meaning of much that He had told them... and when at Pentecost the Holy Spirit descended upon them, they all, with the exception of the traitor Judas, rose to a full sense of the responsibilities which had now fallen upon them. They had now neither fear of death nor of what men might say or do to them, but in response to their Master's command to 'go and teach all nations' they entered with vigour upon the work which He had given them to do'. The New Testament could tell only the early history of the spread of the gospel; history since had traced its further penetration to the ends of the earth.

The printed article had cited the references in the Book of Revelation to the 'new heaven and the new earth wherein dwelleth righteousness'. In the midst of this stood the Tree of Life whose leaves 'are for the healing of the nations'. 'You all know ... the need of the nations for healing at the present time [1933]. Possibly there has never been since the days of Caesar throughout the whole of the world such a sense of the need for a cure for the nations' troubles as exists at the present day...' The revised manuscript (1965) expanded this section: 'While this is so ... these nations, in their corporate capacity as sovereign states, seem to be much more unwilling than they might be to test the remedy which Scripture has prescribed...'; from the reports of international conferences 'we gather that it seems as if many, if not most, of their representatives have been more concerned about trying to secure benefits to carry home with them to their own nation, than about trying

to ascertain what services their country could most effectually render to
their neighbours and to the world...' But who, he asked, are the 'nations?'
... 'just ourselves and our neighbours more or less remote. Therefore, since
... "the peace of God which passeth all understanding" can be attained only
by each individual ... so ... peace and goodwill amongst the nations can be
secured only when the citizens who make up these nations become disposed to
goodwill and to peace...' The printed article puts it: 'In the presence of
this need it grows daily more abundantly clear that there is only one sure
remedy ... the leaves of the Tree of Life – to which we have learned only
those have access who, in the spirit of Jesus Christ set service before self;
duty before pleasure; the commandments of God before the enticing but falla-
cious promises of the Devil'.

But 'Why join the Church?' The article says 'In order to take up and
forward the work of Our Lord's disciples by each in his own particular sphere,
and in the way for which he is best qualified and equipped, contributing his
share to the advancement of the Kingdom of God upon earth.

> Our Saviour gave His life, His disciples gave their labour, some of
> them their lives; succeeding generations have followed, some helping
> in one way, some in another, to answer their Master's call. We are now
> reaping the fruits of their labours'.

The revision – written at the end of a long ministry – inserts here: 'The
Church does not pretend to be a reserve for only the pure, the wise, and the
strong in spirit. The Church exists for people as they are – an organisation
in which the strong may succour the weak, the wise guide the wayward, and the
pure reveal to the impure and thoughtless the beauty of holiness which radiates
from those who are imbued with the spirit of their risen Saviour. It exists
in order that all who are associated with it may by their mutual intercourse
in its fellowship, and through their common worship in the sanctuary and the
observance of the sacraments of the Church, influence one another to become
firmer in their faith, purer in life and conversation, richer in love and in
service towards one another'. The printed article continues:

Are you, then, willing to cast your stone upon the cairn of human
uplift and progress - not merely selfishly, for your own eternal
happiness and peace, but rather for the betterment of mankind and the
greater glory of God?

Re-reading this I had a 'flash-back' to a sunny day in, I think, 1956, after

my father's retirement, when Wendy drove us north from Edinburgh over the

Cairn O'Mounth to stay at Torphins. As always, we paused at the crest to

admire the view. and my father picked up a loose stone and added it to the

Cairn.

The last article then ends: 'Your parents at your baptism pledged

themselves to train you up in the faith of Christ and in the fear of God.

Now, when you are come to an age when you can think and reason for yourselves,

it is your privilege to make your own decisions... Therefore, as Joshua placed

before the assembled tribes of Israel the momentous issue, "Choose you this

day whom ye will serve", so it is now my duty to submit a similar question

to you. It is my earnest wish that you will all return to me the answer

given by Israel to Joshua - "The Lord our God will we serve, and His voice

will we obey"'.

As a post-script to this chapter it would seem appropriate to add some

brief extracts from a sermon of my father's concerning the unbeliever or,

more particularly, the lapsed. The text (John 10, vv.24-25) referred to the

Jews who surrounded Jesus asking 'How long dost thou make us to doubt? If

thou be the Christ, tell us plainly'. Jesus had answered them 'I told you

and ye believed not: the works that I do in my father's name, they bear wit-

ness of me'. When preached, the sermon was prefaced by Isaiah's (Chapter 55)

timeless call to faith, to the happy state of the believer:

Ho, every one that thirsteth, come ye to the waters... Wherefore do
ye spend money for that which is not bread? and your labour for that
which satisfieth not?... come unto me: hear, and your soul shall live...
Let the wicked forsake his way, and the unrighteous man his thoughts:
and let him return unto the Lord, and he will have mercy upon him; and
to our God, for he will abundantly pardon ... ye shall go out with joy,
and be led forth with peace: the mountains and the hills shall break
forth before you into singing, and all the trees of the field shall
clap their hands.

In almost every human life, the sermon proceeded, there came a period of doubt, when 'the maturing mind begins to question the faith that was taught it in childhood'. Some escape this; 'others, and perhaps a larger number, on being confronted with the wider issues of life, have their childhood's faith stirred to its depths, and have often to pass through a period of anxious enquiry and vacillating indecision before they can come to rest in the soul-satisfying Gospel of Christ. In every age we have our enquiring Philips and doubting Thomases. But honest doubts are signs of hope - signs that the enquiring doubter is seeking after truth, and it is far better to be an anxious doubter than a careless believer...'

Jesus had answered these Jews abruptly because their questions were merely intended to induce argument. Honest doubters He met with sympathy. But more convincing than words were works: these were listed in the sermon, each proving conclusively that Christ was the son of God in that His perfection and achievement in all things were beyond human powers. Another proof was His love for mankind:

> In history we read of instances of men dying for their friends, for their country or for their faith. But where in history do we read of one who laid down his life for those who hated him, for those who cast him out in spite of what he did for them?... Who but God's son could have done so? ... But above all else we see Christ's sonship in his desire to raise all up to a higher, better, purer and holier life ... to raise men's thoughts above the cares of the day to seek those things which are enduring and eternal. To raise men up to see what it is possible for them to become when the spirit of God dwells in them. In all these works of divinity Christ alone was perfect... And if we put our trust in Him and look to Him for guidance we shall receive that power which makes us sons of God.

CHAPTER SEVEN

─────────────────

<u>Labour not to be rich</u>

Working the glebe; 'minister's grass'; horse and
other transport: statistics; visiting the blacksmith;
sheep, poultry and bees.

In his book <u>Past and Present of Aberdeenshire</u> published in 1881, the Reverend
Dr William Paul, minister at Banchory Devenick from 1826, commented on the
change in the face of the countryside over that time. The land was more
highly cultivated, by improved methods, arable ground being laid out in regular fields and waste land being reclaimed; there was extensive planting by
lairds of suitable timber; altogether the land wore a 'beautiful aspect'.
By the end of my father's life this trend had been much intensified: particularly noticeable was the neat ploughing right to the edges of fields when
after the second war tractors gradually replaced horses. The two wars had,
however, made savage inroads on the woodlands: after 1918 the Glenmillan hill
was bare and not replanted, and by 1945 most of the other woods had been wholly
or partly depleted. One Sunday evening, 31 October 1943, my parents took what
must have been their last walk together up the old road to view the nearly
bare site of what had been the Cairnbeathie wood. Some woods have now been
restored.

By the time my father was inducted to Lumphanan – officially a 'smaller
living' – in 1913 it was already becoming fairly unusual for a minister to work
his own glebe; this was regarded as part of stipend and declared for Income
Tax purposes: 1913-14 'manse £23, glebe and steading £9.8'. Originally glebes
were supplied to support a horse for transport purposes and traditionally two
cows. In practice we never had a milk cow but once had a few stirks on a
temporary basis; my mother would say she could do with the milk and the cream
but couldn't be doing with the cow. 'Minister's grass' was therefore considered
to be of primary importance, although some arable was desirable to produce
winter keep for the horse, unless this were bought in. After the railway feu
was deducted from our glebe rather over four acres remained; this feu had
possibly been mainly grassland, leaving only the steep field between manse
and burn for this exclusive purpose. In practice, the south-west or 'rushes'

field, after rather unsuccessful crops early on, was generally used for grazing only, because of drainage problems. The higher land west of the church was fenced off as arable. The east field – for some years known as the 'football field' as the local club played there until they acquired a pitch in the village – and 'the meadow' between it and the burn were sometimes under crop.

Various considerations affect any estimate of whether, over the forty-odd years that my father worked the glebe, he did so with any pecuniary advantage. His own records are incomplete, although it is quite remarkable what can be gleaned from assiduous study of the available material, putting two and two together from frequently cryptic references in sporadically kept diaries.

For some reason manse gardens had by church law to be perpetually well protected – ours by high stone walls – but heritors, as indicated in Chapter 2, did not consider themselves liable for glebe boundaries; later law declared that these were the shared responsibility of minister and adjoining occupier (in our case, except for one small stretch, the public road authority) and must be left in good order for the next incumbent. As our garden was too large to cultivate in its entirety, part was fenced off for pasture, as also was part of the lower lawn in the 'grounds'.

Despite the fact that the previous incumbent had let the glebe to a dairy-man (as did Dr Argo of Kincardine O'Neil – quite a usual practice) part of the boundary dyke of the east field had crumbled, so that although by law ministers working their glebes were responsible for fencing and draining, my father contended that far from having inherited adequate fencing it was as though this had never been. The heritors did not agree. Late in 1917 therefore my father decided to write for guidance on these two points to the Reverend Dr William Mair, ordained 1861, formerly of Earlston, whose 'Digest' of Church Law was, along with its U.F. equivalent, the fore-runner of 'Cox'. (Mair and Cox had collaborated on the last 'Digest'.) Dr Mair's reply makes it worth while to quote at length from this correspondence, giving some indication of the loopholes to which the fences of the law were liable. First, from my father's letter:

1. Part of a dry stone dyke (60 to 70 yards) separating the Glebe from a public county road is in so bad repair that it is useless for keeping cattle in the glebe or for preventing cattle passing along the road from entering the glebe. Two years ago at a meeting of Heritors called by the Clerk at the request of the Parish Council to consider the state of the Churchyard, I brought up the question of the dyke and asked the Heritors to put it in order, or, alternatively, to allow me to accept an offer from the local Road Surveyor to erect a substantial wooden fence in exchange for the stones to be taken by him and used as road metal. They denied liability for repair and refused to allow me to accept the Road Surveyor's offer. As the matter was not on the card of business, and as the field was then in crop and likely to be so for some time I did not press my request and watched it for the time. Next spring however the field must be sown out to grass and by autumn something must be done to the fence. A stone dyker tells me that the dyke is not worth repairing. It is all bursting out and he says it would be necessary to pull it down and rebuild it. This he says would cost two shillings a yard or £6 to £7. Are the heritors liable for the cost of this? Or if they deny liability can they prevent me accepting the Road Surveyor's offer which I presume will still hold good...

On this point Dr Mair wrote on 10 November 1917:

None of the statutes anent glebes contains any requirement to the effect that the ground designed as a glebe should be fenced or enclosed by the heritors, and no decision imports that walls or fences constitute an integral part of the glebe. A wall or other enclosure for a manse garden has repeatedly been held a necessary adjunct of the garden, mainly on the ground of its being necessary for the beneficial use of the garden. The same argument may be used for your stone wall.

The manner in which you brought the matter before the heritors was from every point of view ill-advised.

So also was your entering into a bargain with the Road Surveyor. The heritors could do no other than disallow it, and it was well for you they did. That bargain implied that the dyke was yours, and that therefore you are responsible for all that concerns that boundary henceforth! One good thing arising from the heritors breaking up your bargain is that they thereby acknowledge responsibility for that dyke.

You say, 'If they deny liability can they prevent me accepting the Road Surveyor's offer which I presume still holds good?' You certainly cannot hold the Surveyor to the bargain after two such years - years which have affected all bargains. But I cannot imagine why you should wish such a bargain - substituting a stone fence for a wooden one, [He obviously meant the reverse.] and taking that boundary upon your shoulders (and, so far as you can, putting it on those who come after you). As for their denial of responsibility (which you seem so ready to accept), denial does not settle the question - this is for a civil court.

My advice is that you should do nothing just now in this
matter. Let the decay of the dyke exhibit its practical results,
and this will bring the question of liability to the test. (Of
course, when things are approaching that point the heritors should
be informed.)...

On the question of drainage my father had written:

Part of another field of the glebe is going into rushes on account
of bad drainage. This field has been in corn crop for two years. Both
years about a quarter of an acre would not plough and had to be left in
rushes and last year the crop on another quarter was very poor on account
of damp and I am told it would be useless to sow turnips on the latter
part next spring. A practical drainer has examined the field and he
reports that there have been old fashioned stone drains in it but these
are all choked up and useless and would have all to be lifted and relaid.
He advised as being cheaper and more satisfactory that instead of repairing the old drains 200 or 300 yards of new tile drain pipes be put
in. This he said would dry the whole field including the part entering
to rushes and would make the whole capable of growing corn, turnips and
grass. Are the heritors liable for the cost of drainage?... In the last
edition of your 'Digest' I see that every parish entitled to a manse is
entitled to a glebe of 4 acres Scots 'arable' land. If the part complained
of is not dried soon scarcely 4 acres (imperial) would be left 'arable'
i.e. capable of being ploughed and growing a crop of corn or turnips... *

Dr Mair's reaction was brief and decisive:

Heritors are not liable for the cost of drainage. It is a matter of
farming, and you are the farmer. You should follow the advice which you
quote of the practical drainer. If you could have done it a year ago,
it would have been well.

As regards the dyke, my father was accordingly writing to Mr Cochran,

the heritors' clerk, on 26 July 1918:

...As regards the Glebe Dyke that I complain of:- As I said part of
it has almost disappeared and the remainder is practically all ruinous.
Both Benjamin Grassick, Dyker, Torphins, and William Fraser, Mason,
Lumphanan, assure me that it would be necessary to take it down and
rebuild it from the foundation - this at a cost of 2/- a yard or £7 for
70 yards - but that even then unless 20 loads or so of stones were added
it would not be high enough to act as a sufficient fence for horses and
cattle. Unless these extra stones were added to replace those which have
disappeared one or two rows of wire would have to be erected above the
dyke.

The dyke as it stands is absolutely of no use as a fence. To enable
me to get the good of my grass after harvest either of two courses must
be taken.
  1. To rebuild the dyke and add one or two rows of wire on posts. Or
  2. To erect a fence inside the dyke. This would have to be 2 or 3
feet back from the dyke to get clear of debris and would have to be every
bit as complete a fence as if the dyke were not there at all.

Now the heritors cannot expect me to choose the latter course and
erect at my own expense such a fence - seeing that at last meeting they
refused to allow me to accept the Road Surveyor's offer to substitute a
substantial wooden fence for the stones of the dyke.

---

* 48 Scottish = 61 imperial acres.

Neither can they expect me to rebuild a dyke which I found going to ruin when I came to the Parish and make it good for 2 or 3 generations of ministers.

On the other hand I do not accept the heritors' plea that once they placed a fence round the Glebe they are relieved from all further obligation to keep it up. This plea cannot possibly hold good when the fence has disappeared as this one has done.

However in order that I may get the good of my grass as soon as it is ready and to save the heritors the trouble and expense of holding a meeting to dispose of the matter – which I shall have to call unless we reach some satisfactory agreement – I am willing to propose as a mutual arrangement, and without prejudice to the lawful rights or obligations either of the heritors or of myself – that if the heritors rebuild the dyke with the stones which remain I shall erect the necessary wires and posts to complete the fence and undertake to keep up the whole during my incumbency provided that when I die or leave Lumphanan the posts and wires shall be my property and not the heritors'.

I hope the heritors will see their way to accept this offer which I think is very reasonable and is as far as I can possibly go to meet them.

There is no further documentary evidence on this subject among my father's papers, but about 1925 the road authorities put up a substantial new fence in exchange for what was by then a pile of stones.

The 'rushes' field continued to defy all attempts over the years to make it good arable land. During the second war government subsidies made it more worthwhile to grow crops. In February 1941 my father received from the Maintenance of the Ministry Committee such a part refund; the accounts, approved by Kirk Session and Presbytery, relate to work done by Arthur Watson, Peelbog, first on 4-5 December 1939 examining drains (12 hours at tenpence an hour) then in May 1940 138 hours' work (at a shilling an hour) opening and clearing old drain and laying new drain, this work being paid for by my father at the end of May. The new drain pipes (288 3-inch, 120 4-inch) cost £3.17, a discount of 7/7 being allowed by Scottish Agricultural Industries Ltd for prompt payment. In December 1940 a bill was paid for work later that year carried out by John Cadger, Ashfield – but evidently not eligible for a refund – which included 'cutting rushes and draining'.

As his retirement approached, my father prepared to leave the glebe in order for his successor; after the ploughing and sowing of the east field, he had let the west field for grazing. The previous year the east field corn

crop was in August 1953 'rouped to Cloak' for £38, there being no need to
keep any of it for winter feed, all livestock being – or about to be – sold.
On 2 January 1954 John Stewart, drainer. was paid £19.12.6 for drainage work
in the west field 'as per arrangement with Board of Agriculture', a rebate
from the latter of £7.18.10 being secured. A year earlier Stewart had been
paid £3.7.6 'for lifting and clearing drain in East Field' and in March 1954
£4.5 'for deepening drain in East Field to connect with a deepened drain cut
by County Road Dept. across public road in to Lumphanan Burn'. All of these
expenses totalling £24.9.4 were repaid to my father by the General Trustees
at 30 March 1955. Against this was set the crop account for 1954: (The
notional share of glebe as part of Stipend had been noted in 1950 as £6.10
less owner's rates at 4s.4d.)

Grazing and Grain Crop on Lumphanan Glebe 1954

West Field let to Alex Esson, Shepherd	£15.0.0
East Field in Oats, rouped by Aberdeen and Northern Marts. less £1.1 Commission and £1.4 for Advertising Sale	18.15.0
	£33.15.0
Less ploughing [November 1953] by W. Rose £8.2.0	£25.13.0

There was a footnote to this: '1½ qr. oats for seed at 70/- per quarter –£5:5–
was a gift from Mr. Jas. Leslie, Farmer, Whitehouse'. Of this 1954 total my
father, retiring on 31 March, reckoned that he would receive £9.17.4; the
Maintenance of the Ministry Fund (31 weeks of the Vacancy) £15.5.10; and the
incoming minister 9s.10d. (one week). the year being calculated from 11 November
1953.

A typical harvest in our time was that of 1945. It began on Monday
3 September when Arthur Watson began scything the corn in the afternoon. For
the next nine days the weather was mostly fine and only essential parish duties
were performed while my father dealt with the sheaves, Arthur coming to cut
in the afternoons and Wendy helping in the afternoon and evening. By 8 September cutting was finished, the diary noting 'A.W. clyack' that Saturday

night. Monday 10th was dull, with some rain; my father made sheaves in the morning, after dealing with the joiner who was working in the wash-house, and making one sick-visit. Later he swept out the wash-house, then started stooking. Tuesday was fine again; the plumber was at the wash-house and my father went to the village to inquire after the invalid who was having an operation, then from 11 a.m. to noon 'leading' began, our pony Saligo between the shafts. This continued in the afternoon and early evening when Wendy joined in. My father then had a meeting of the Parish Hall Committee. During the night it was windy and on the 12th it was 'very fine'. Leading went on all morning; in the afternoon Wendy helped and they had tea in the field. That evening they finished a large stack - just in time. During the night there were thunder and lightning. It was then wet, off and on, until the end of the month. Then it was fine again and on the afternoons of 1st and 2nd October they stacked the last of the stooks. On 6 December ('slight snow, cold') the first sheaves were fed to the ponies. The sheaves were gradually brought from the stack into the steading; there is a note on 9 March 1946 'Sheaves all in'.

The term 'minister's grass' in glebe lore assumed that the incumbent would use horse transport, as did the provision of stabling and cover for a trap, whether in closed or open shed. (We used to be told of my father's explosion of horror the first time a motor car had the temerity to drive up his carefully kept approach road.) Dr Paul of Banchory Devenick comments on the coming of the railways and the turnpike roads, with public conveyances (i.e. stage-coaches) on the Deeside and Skene routes. In the early 1920's the first motor bus from Lumphanan via the Skene crossroads to Aberdeen, covering many areas not accessible from the railway, was operated from Torphins by Mr A. Davie, in partnership with Reid's garage. It was a long dark red vehicle with a tourer hood. If on the return journey from town there were only one or two passengers left, - the terminus was at The Pole, Lumphanan - these would be transferred to a car at Torphins and delivered even to their doors, complete with shopping parcels etc. 'Very obliging' was Mr Davie. He was succeeded by Mr Cormie and a cream-coloured bus with hard top, entry at the side rear, but before long his business was taken over by William Alexander's 'Bluebird' company of Camelon, Falkirk. The drivers and conductors were by then half local, half from Aberdeen.

The only alternatives to horse-transport in earlier days were walking or cycling, and my father was always a great walker. He still had, too, the bicycle on which in earlier days he had gone from his home at Auchindoun to holiday with a relative whose husband was grieve at the farm of Wester Delnies ('a five-pair place' as he recalled when nearly ninety) west of Nairn. About 1918 he acquired a new B.S.A., but apart from short local journeys and longer trips mostly involving main roads, he found driving the trap, or later riding the bigger ponies he bought, more suitable. There was generally a stable into which the pony could be put during a prolonged visit. When a brief diary was kept it generally included continuous statistics of the mileages he walked, drove, cycled or was motored (sometimes by an elder or other parishioner) on parish business - this in days when there was no question of driving grant or refund of expenses, although his Income Tax return occasionally showed a claim for a taxi-fare. He also noted numbers of parishioners (not other individuals) interviewed or visited at home or in hospital, and numbers attending services and classes.

For only one year, 1946, are the statistics of movements complete; in 1943 they are nearly so. But it is possible to compare part of a pre-war period in 1939, when his choice of transport within the parish (as opposed to rail or bus further afield, or the occasional motor sent to fetch him for a funeral or wedding) was limited to horse or bicycle, with part of 1940 and of 1943, the whole of 1946 and part of 1947. His auto-cycle features from late 1940, and in October 1950 Wendy purchased a second-hand Austin 10 car of 1934 vintage

from the merchant at the west side. She passed her driving test in Aberdeen
first time, not being in the least nonplussed by the question 'What would you
do if you met a flock of sheep in Market Street?' Whereat my father was inspired to try his auto-cycle test for the second time, and duly passed. The
first time he had failed to stop at a 'major road ahead' sign in Ballater;
thereafter one of his L-plates had been eaten by Donald Dunbar's goose at
the Waulkmill.

Table 1

Year	10-week Period	Total Mileage	Parishioners seen	Walked	Drove	Rode	Cycled	Auto-Cycled
					N/R = not recorded			
1929	Ap-June	150	141	N/R	N/R	-	N/R	-
1932	Jan-Mar	127	135	N/R	N/R	-	N/R	-
"	Mar-May	155	122	N/R	N/R	-	N/R	-
1939	May-Jul	239	71	66	83	90	-	-
1940	Jan-Mar	335	270	161	3	133	38	-
1943	Jan-Mar	581	257	78	8	75	97	323
"	Ap-June	738	400	65	46	16	119	592
1944	Jul-Sep	723	326	48	45		-	635
"	Sep-Nov	474	249	32	4		-	438
1945	Jan-Mar	236	225	186	84		-	16
"	Ap-June	424	213	123	5		-	296
"	Jul-Sep	795	210	41	34		-	720
"	Sep-Nov	529	246	98	-		-	431
1946	Feb-Ap	362	229	172	3	52	-	135
"	Jun-Aug	676	283	90	84	18	-	484
"	Aug-Oct	588	267	110	64	-	-	414
1946/7	Nov-Jan	384	224	161	10	-	-	213
1947	Jan-Mar	209	230	171	-	9	-	29
1950	Jan-Mar	206	264	155	-	9	39	12
"	Mar-May	219	213	82	4	7	126	-
1954	Jan-Mar	114	328	N/R	N/R	N/R	N/R	N/R

It is difficult to produce evidence of an average year which would be
statistically meaningful: always there was some particular circumstance that
militated against this, and one can only be grateful for the detail supplied
even in the most abbreviated diary entries which explains any apparently

unusual transport statistics. For example, we have figures for ten weeks during the summer of 1939 - end May to end July - which show a less than average number of pastoral calls (71) but a total of 83 miles driving and 90 miles riding. The walking total - 66 miles - was low. That was the period when the union of the two Lumphanan churches was being brought to a successful conclusion, beginning with the joint Communion service in May. But it also covered part of the duration of the summer afternoon Sunday School, then held at Home Farm, Camphill, in quarters provided by Mr and Mrs James Wilson. Besides making visits to 'round up' the children (a maximum of 24 attended) my father took the opportunity to see other people in the area and on the way home. On one occasion, before setting out for Camphill, extra mileage was involved in driving the bellman home after lunch; the latter had fainted in church that morning. One Saturday in June was a complete day off, on the occasion of the Choir Drive: they went by private bus to Braemar and Glenshee, on to Pitlochry, Killiecrankie, Dunkeld and Crieff, home by Perth and Brechin: three hundred miles not included in the tally. The previous day had had only one parishioner interview and one mile of walking; it was very hot and two swarms of bees were dealt with, although in the interval of capturing and hiving the latter - at 11.30 p.m. - my father had called a Presbytery meeting, duplicating the letters on his cyclostyle, and done some planting.

One might attempt to compare this with ten weeks in the winter of 1940, January to March, when 270 calls were made, despite eight days' illness in January and a journey south towards the end of the month. Wendy was ill in London, I was ill at school, Esdaile being evacuated to Ancrum House, Rox-burghshire (this involved 12 miles' walking not included in the week's total). Over the period he walked 161 miles, rode 133, cycled 38 but drove only 3, riding being warmer. Except for two or three days there was snow and frost all the time, but my father's bronchial cold was caught in the manse, writing letters in a north-facing room. There was a lot of illness around especially among the older people, and many visits were to say goodbye to servicemen

posted south. The 36 miles of cycling included 32 to Towie and back on
2 March (frosty but fine) to call on the relatives of an elderly ex-parishioner, Miss May McHardy, whose funeral he had taken a few days earlier. (A
car had been provided for this, thirty miles away on Donside). This was my
father's custom after a funeral. Some years before he had helped Miss McHardy
over her brother's affairs when he died: James had been a flockmaster at
Auchtavan (pronounced "Auchtivian") on Upper Deeside; she, formerly a cook
at Invercauld, had lived for many years in Torphins and been visited there.
Wishing to give my father something on that occasion she had asked if he
would care to have her brother's 1901 edition of Chambers's Dictionary, and
this he gladly accepted as ours had become distinctly tattered. The book
was then pungent with peat-reek and remains a treasure-house of information.
Another time she gave him her family's halberd, carried at the Lonach Gathering.

Almost half of the 1943 driving totals quoted in the table were in
connection with the Loanend monthly evening services as my father first picked
up Mattie McDonald who was playing the organ. Twice he took Aileen Irvine out
for a drive: now an invalid, she enjoyed these outings, being regaled en
route with tales of old Lumphanan. Twice too he drove the cart to Auchlossan
for oats and seed-corn. The overall travelling total was increased on account
of a vacancy in the Presbytery. The record number of calls from April to June
included repeated visits to particular invalids. The most noticeable factor
in the 1943 transport statistics is of course the auto-cycle, which did 150
miles to the gallon. Petrol was rationed and occasionally was not immediately
obtainable; on application to the County Buildings in Aberdeen my father
could collect an allowance of coupons. By that year the auto-cycle was
beginning to give trouble: late in April it was 'in G'[arage] at Aboyne, and
twice that autumn had a broken spring, as well as having various minor repairs.
The winter weather of early 1943 was not so very severe that it could not be
used continuously. Its one great disadvantage - apart from sudden mechanical
failure - was that on longer cold-weather journeys the rider required much

protective clothing. My father discovered the ideal headgear in a marine outfitters in Aberdeen, and his black leather and astrakhan bonnet with 'lugs' became a familiar feature. (Once in Dorset he was taken for a bishop.) There was some difficulty over supply during the war as it was regarded as a per-quisite of those who went to sea. Once on the overnight Aberdeen to London train I met in with Miss Thomson, well-known to generations of students and other readers as the presiding genius of the Reference Department of Aberdeen Public Library. She knew me quite well by sight, but only on this occasion realised that I came from Lumphanan. 'And you've still got Mr. Donald,' said 'Tommy'; 'puir man, he comes in wi' his...' and here she pulled an imaginary 'bonnet' over her head.

The table shows a considerable increase in the mileage walked during the early months of both 1945 and 1946. In both cases the auto-cycle was laid up untaxed until late March; in 1947 it was available but hardly used. There was much snow in all three winters. More will be written presently about the hard winter of 1946-7. My father also walked more in early 1950 but not on account of snow: he paid many visits on foot to elderly invalids, one living alone and isolated, another having legal matters to be attended to. The record mileage from July to September 1945 - mostly by auto-cycle - reflected the fact of my mother's death on 27 June after a protracted illness; during this time rather fewer visits than usual had been paid although up to the last day various parishioners at a distance within the parish were still cared for. Of the post-June total one visit of 75 miles was to the widow of a former Presbytery minister. Mileage was also increased by Presbytery business in connection with the union of Logie Coldstone and Cromar with Migvie.

The walking total for November 1946 to January 1947 included ten miles driving the sheep to Coull for the winter on 31 December. It is not clear why during March to May 1950, when it tended to be windy and wet, my father suddenly took more to cycling, even on an expedition to Logie Coldstone. In the latter case he may have recalled a previous expedition thither when the auto-cycle had broken down and had to be retrieved later.

On the whole the auto-cycle was fairly reliable and performed some impressive journeys, but - like any car - it did occasionally let my father down in awkward places. A good journey to Aberdeen - 25 miles - could be done in 65 minutes, ten minutes quicker than the bus. But when on a Sunday in February 1943 my father used it to get to a 3 p.m. meeting at Logie Coldstone, on the return journey, after doing 58 miles, it broke down at the Crossroads (the junction of the Tarland turnpike and the road to Lumphanan) entailing a walk pushing the auto-cycle of some three miles home. He then used the 'push-bike' to get to the evening service at Loanend at 7 p.m. Two days later, after some attention at the local garage, my father rode the auto-cycle to Aberdeen for hospital visiting, but it stopped on the way home at Garlogie and had to be repaired by the blacksmith at Cullerlie, a mile away. Once safely back at Lumphanan there was a call to be paid on the family of a patient just seen at the Infirmary. Two months later a round journey of 75 miles was accomplished to Braemar, but three days afterwards en route for Aberdeen the auto-cycle 'cracked' at Raemoir, and my father had to walk to Banchory to get a bus to Aberdeen and a Synod meeting. The following evening he cycled ten miles to Raemoir to retrieve the auto-cycle (missing a dramatic performance at Lumphanan: Cobblers Luck) but putting in a visit to Miss Agnes Cameron at Campfield, no doubt receiving a welcome cup of tea. Two days later he had to take the bus to Raemoir to retrieve the 'push-bike', cycling the ten miles home. Occasionally during the war it was the petrol that ran out in awkward places. The high driving total June-August 1946 appears to have been because the auto-cycle was temporarily out of action. On Sunday 21 July, for example, my father drove the pony to Birse (a total of 18 miles) for a special service; he was away from 2.30 to 9.30 p.m.

But in the autumn of 1947 there was a wonderful holiday tour in Inverness-shire, Morayshire and Banffshire of 560 miles on $3\frac{1}{2}$ gallons of petrol with only one broken spring on a bad road in Glenurquhart, repaired by the blacksmith at Dingwall. He visited many old friends, from ministers to shepherds, both above and below ground: in all nineteen churchyards. Little did he think he was to end his days in Inverness, unconscious between a former shepherd from Drumnadrochit and a minister of Resolis.

About 1920, after two unsuitable horses had been tried, the first complete 'turnout' was acquired, the Iceland pony Dandy, dun with black mane and tail, along with harness and trap (actually a well-bottomed gig). I think the whole cost £40. There was one long seat facing forward with corduroy-covered cushion which could seat two adults and a small child. Two other children could be sat on a facing wooden plank. The waterproof apron was lined with pseudo-leopard skin. The bridle had DANDY in fine Gothic beadwork, black on pale-blue. Dandy was ten hands - too small for riding except by children - but was a prodigious trotter in the trap. 'Passing Dandy' used to be our phrase for describing rapid movement. Dandy was with us for a quarter of a century, having come from the parish of Kincardine O'Neil; on an early outing in that area my father was surprised to find the trap draw up of its own accord and stop outside the local hostelry. Dandy was a great favourite of Mrs Arthur Watson who had only to appear on her bicycle, coming from shopping in the village, for Dandy to 'nicher' and trot up to the fence at the corner of the Burnside road where a sweetmeat was duly received. The ceremony ended with 'Now kiss me Dandy!' and the latter duly raised her nose and complied. Gradually by the mid-thirties Dandy grew less able for her tasks, although the vet's prediction that she would not survive the winter of 1936 proved over-pessimistic. Some trouble with her feet then necessitated poultices of hot porridge inside sewn-up old trouser-legs. After some further years as a pensioner Dandy was found, one day in March 1944, lying dead in her stall, and my father went for Arthur Watson to help bury her in the garden field.

A Welsh chestnut of rather fiery disposition was purchased about 1934.

We called him Ginger although he is diarised as 'Trot'. Less durable, he was by 1940 being treated by the vet for stiffness,being dosed with salts and later with worm powders. That was the year he and Dandy were occasionally taken out riding by two Glasgow evacuees from the village, brothers, by way of reward for unusually good behaviour. By 1943 Ginger had been sold and the pony was Saligo, a gentle, undemonstrative grey of great character but – inexplicably at first – rather nervous. He was purchased at Kittybrewster Auction Mart in November 1942, shortly after I had been posted away from a radar station at Saligo Bay on Islay to one near Aberdeen. We later discovered the possible cause of the nerves: the occupant of a passing car who had paused to look at the grey in the field asked 'Wasn't that the pony that was in the stramash at the Bridge of Don?' Saligo had a horror of tractors and had obviously been 'down' at some point, but nevertheless after the war when the agricultural shows were being revived and seeking support, he once won a third prize at the Tarland show. He was ridden there by Violet Calder of Cairnton who had shampooed him first with Drene. In 1951 I showed him at Banchory, but this time it was again Violet's mount, the newer dun and black and very placid pony Gretel, acquired in March 1949 (unplaced at Tarland) which was 'highly commended'. On this occasion, amid all the fun of the fair, Saligo took exception to the crawling board of a vendor of white mice. Nevertheless when both ponies took part in the Lumphanan contribution to the Pageant of Deeside at Aboyne Castle in 1949, with all its noise of battle and pipe bands, Saligo didn't move an untoward muscle, entering apparently into the youthful spirit of the occasion.

He was much loved by Craig's daughter Rosemary; when at the age of four she unexpectedly got rather close to him in the stable he merely looked round inquisitively. A week or two later she was allowed to ride him: 'I'm on Saligo!' Twice, when in wartime and post-war conditions it seemed he could manage without a pony, my father took him back to the mart at Aberdeen; twice he brought him home again. On the first occasion I recall my mother saying

that when, a few minutes after the homeward train had passed she heard the
stable door opening and hooves on the cobbles she was 'real glad'. At the
beginning of the winter before my father retired both ponies were sold, unfortunately not together. Gretel found a good home and was later repurchased by
Wendy. Saligo also found a kindly buyer at Kittybrewster Mart who wanted him
for his children. But shortly afterwards one cold day after another horse
sale this purchaser, dropping in to Cameron's Inn in Little Belmont Street,
told Mrs Mitchell there that he had been looking for another pony: he had
bought one not long before — a nice grey — from a minister, but it didn't
settle, had kept racing round the field, took pneumonia and died. Mrs Mitchell,
who with her late husband had many years earlier had the Lumphanan hotel and
remained a generous supporter of the church, replied 'I think I knew that pony'.

Only one of my father's diaries actually lists the costs of keeping a
horse for a year, from November 1942 to October 1943; even this makes no allowance for harness, saddlery, upkeep of gig etc., — a very occasional expense.
This particular year — halfway through a wartime phase of rising prices — may
not present an acceptable average assessment for 1913-54. Fortunately, however,
as regards comparison with keeping a horse, my father for approximately the same
twelvemonths meticulously noted his expenses for running an auto-cycle, although
with no estimate for depreciation. (See Tables 2, 3 and 4 page 7-17). But
with petrol at $2/1\frac{1}{2}$ a gallon and oil at one and sixpence a quart these are now
only of historical interest.

Even in the autocycle period, from December 1940, (the 'small car' my
father had visualised at the union with the Stothert Memorial Church in 1939
quickly receded into the mists of wartime economics) a horse remained a useful
standby. Lumphanan weather has remained unchanged over the years: this week
(February 1980) I hear from Miss Maggie Macgregor that although she has seen
more snow in her time at Moss-side, 'no car will get across our road [from the
Tarland turnpike at the Parkhill end] for hard packed snow and ice below'. In
January 1974, on the day before my father's funeral, Craig and I hesitated to

Table 2

Cost of horse November 1942 – October 1943

Purchase of pony	£26 : 0 : 0		
Railway horse-box	15 : 0		
Bruised oats	2 : 4 : 0		
Straw for bedding	5 :12 : 6		
Corn crop			
Drain work	11 : 0		
Ploughing	3 :10 : 0		
Seed	3 :12 : 0		
Help			
Sowing	12 : 6		
Reaping	1 : 0 : 0		
Leading	16 : 0		
Blacksmith	1 : 0 : 0		
Total	45 :13 : 0		

(Without cost of pony and horse-box: £18 :18: 0)

Table 3

Cost of auto-cycle 1943

Two tyres	£ 1 : 1 : 0
Road license	17 : 6
Driver's license	5 : 0
Tools	13 : 6
Petrol (18 galls.)	2 : 0 : $4\frac{1}{2}$
Oil	10 :11
Replacement parts and service	6 :10 : 0
Telephone calls re service	5 : 8
Travel by other means involved	10 : 3
Total	£12 :14 : $2\frac{1}{2}$

Table 4

Auto-cycle total mileage Dec. 1940 – Dec. 1946

Dec. 1940 – June 1941 : 1809
June 1941 – June 1942 : 4400
June 1942 – Dec. 1942 : 1791
Dec. 1942 – June 1943 : 1758
July 1943 – Dec. 1943 : 1012
Jan. 1944 – Dec. 1944 : 1074
Dec. 1944 – Dec. 1945 : 1333
Jan. 1946 – Dec. 1946 : 1330

risk a hired car between Parkhill and Moss-side. The approach from Lumphanan
village - 'the back o' the hill road' - has for years been merely a pedestrian
or tractor precinct. Even in 1937 my father records a journey there on horseback on Christmas Day - a Saturday - to see Maxwell Mearns, then aged 79:
'Deep snow melting on old road. Wreath at Moss-side up to G[inger]'s belly'.
The weather was 'Fairly mild - frosty later'.

'Minister's grass' of course, could support a horse or a few sheep out
of doors for perhaps only five or six months of the year. From early November
and sometimes until mid-May the horse was fed mostly in the stable. In 1951
the ponies were put out to grass by day only from 3 May, but on 7 May were
'not out'. If a corn crop had been grown that season, the sheaves were stacked
and gradually brought in for feed, although more straw for bedding would be
bought, often being fetched in our own small cart from a local farm. Threshed
oats or bruised was bought always for horses or hens. Horse transport came in
very useful for carrying passengers and goods. At one time any member of the
family travelling from Aberdeen by train would at least be fetched on return,
particularly if carrying parcels. Latterly we used the bus more for eastward
journeys, as it was cheaper and passed the manse. Bus travel did not however
agree with my mother. In the earlier days she would often go visiting with
my father in the trap and very occasionally drove herself. Also on the credit
side: there was always plenty of farmyard manure for the garden, although of
course this entailed regular 'mucking out' of the stables: these were adjacent
to the dung-court.

We children regarded a visit to the blacksmith's as a special treat.
Older habitués treated the smithy as a social centre. Writing of a post-
retirement sojourn in Lumphanan in 1960 my father reported: '... looked in on
the Smith and the usual Smithy callers'. My 1951 diary records: 'Took
Saligo to Smiddy: chatted to people while waiting'.

But the family classic on smithy-visiting was six-year-old Craig's essay
written in two parts in May 1921 for Lumphanan school, the two closing

sentences being particularly quoted:

> On Saturday I went to the blacksmith. I saw two anvils and two
> fires. I also saw two bellows one big and one small one. There were
> bicycle brakes, a saw like the butcher's and a rod of iron. The place
> where the horses get shod is very clean. The floor is very smooth. All
> the panes of the window were cracked. My message was for three hoops
> and three cleeks. The blacksmith put the iron into the fire then took
> it out and hammered it on the anvil. Then he put it into a pail of
> water to cool and harden the metal. On the roof there are horses' shoes.

> I went to the blacksmith on Saturday. I saw him shoe three pair
> of horses. There were a lot of men in charge of the horses. My message
> was for my father's lawn mower. When the mower was ready I took it
> home. I saw a donkey with long ears. The dam is beside the blacksmiths.
> For sale there were a lot of axes and one scyth. I also saw a lot of
> iron. I stayed four hours at the blacksmiths. I wont be to the
> blacksmith for a long time.

At this time the blacksmith may still have had an assistant; there certainly

was one in 1913, described in my father's first visiting list as 'shoer to

Collins'; he was a Unitarian. This forge was in the village; there was also

a blacksmith, 'Smith' Nicoll then, at Marywell, a member of the United Free

Church.

My father does not appear to have worked out even for one year the

economics of keeping sheep on the glebe, although he had them for most of his

41 years at Lumphanan. To begin with he had Leicesters, and scored some

successes with them at the Tarland Show. We have a silver medal inscribed

'Jubilee Show, Tarland 1920: Best Leicester Sheep, won by Master and the Misses

Donald, The Manse, Lumphanan'. (I cannot share the credit for this.) But

Leicesters needed better pasture than the glebe could afford, and in time he

switched to Blackface, which were less demanding. Mostly these overwintered

with another hill flock, returning when the worst of the winter was over to

be given extra feeding as the lambing season approached. We children thought

it was nice to have the first lamb on my mother's birthday, 19 March, but

this was in fact rather early in our climate. Generally lambing was from mid-

April to early May. Sometimes even then a new-born lamb had to be brought

indoors, put by the fire in a box and fed milk out of a bottle. In the fifties

the ewes wintered at home, a ram being borrowed from Alex Esson, Bankhead.

They were then occasionally driven to fresh pasture locally, for example at the Peel Ring, in the field known as 'the Irrigation', and would otherwise when required be fed on hay, corn and later turnips, cut up on our own machine into wire baskets. This involved much extra work, often in freezing weather.

My father's main argument for working the glebe was that the minister might have more in common with his parishioners, although originally it was no doubt also for subsistence. The wider sheep fraternity into which we were admitted stretched further, over Upper Deeside, and was particularly congenial. Dr Paul of Banchory Devenick relates how a former minister asked a very successful Fetteresso cow-cowper why he didn't try horse-cowping. 'Eh na, sir. I couldna venture wi' that, it's some sair for the saul [soul]'. My father had reservations about some of his horse transactions, but very rarely had reason to complain of sheep folk. (There was one disastrous incident of a Leicester ram which died; and once he overheard a relatively prosperous sheep-farmer at an Aboyne sale whispering encouragement to a suspected 'wheeler': 'It's a' richt. It's the minister's biddin'...') We all came to enjoy a day at Michael Fair, that ancient institution at Aboyne in October, and certainly did not expect to witness 'wheeling' there. There would on the other hand be a sympathetic response to an auctioneer's appeal: 'Come on, now, these are the shepherd's', that is, the personal property of a shepherd employed by a flockmaster, thus deserving of encouragement. On the sale catalogue would recur the resonant names ... Auchallater, Ballaterach, Bush Crathie ... (we appeared as 'Glebe, Lumphanan') and round the ring would be many familiar faces. A kenspeckle figure, generally standing just inside the ring, was Rob Aberdein. On one occasion two rather small lambs - an odd lot - were knocked down by the auctioneer to an unwitting Rob at six shillings apiece; voice from the crowd: 'Pit them in yer pooch, Bob!'

When our sheep first went to Aboyne, customs had hardly changed from

the old 'drove road' days: as the days for the sales approached the routes
would become alive with moving flocks accompanied by darting black and white
sheepdogs. At one time ours would be driven half-way the previous day by
my father or Craig to Albert Nicoll's at Tillybreen; they would then continue
together on sale day. In later years the sheep were driven first over the
hill to Bonnyside, where Jamie Sherriffs (later at the Bush, Crathie) would
add them to those he was taking to Aboyne next day. Latterly sheep would
be transported in ever-larger motor floats which would line up outside the
mart. On one occasion early in the last war my father, trying to fit in a
few days' holiday at the Kildrummy hotel, then kept by Mr and Mrs John Watt,
late of the Hillock, deputed to me the task of preparing the lambs for the
float early on the morning of the sale. This involved bringing ewes and
lambs in from the field into one of the stables and marking the lambs with
keel. The driver, 'Johndie' Milne, and his mate then handled them into the
float. At the receiving end were 'herds' (for whose services sixpence would
be deducted from the sale payment) who were very skilful at sorting the
sheep into separate pens.

After the sale the sheep would again be removed by float to their new
destination. In earlier days there would have been special sheep-trains
with two locomotives on the Deeside Line after Michael Fair. As children we
would draw aside the nursery curtains after dark to watch one of these
labouring up the incline opposite the manse.

The same routine had to be followed each year from the time the lambs
were born: cutting the lambs' tails early in June, clipping the ewes - with
hand clippers - in June or July. Help was occasionally employed for this -
early on by the Sherriffs family; from 1944 Alex Esson would do most of the
clipping. Dipping took place twice-yearly supervised by the Torphins policeman who would call in advance to notify the time and place. Craig recalls
dipping at Wardhead in James Grubb's time. Later on it was done by Alex

Laing in the village. latterly either by Peter Ferries at Cairnbeathie
or by Robert Silver – and then by William Emslie – at Wardhead. My father
would collect any 'pet' lambs that Mrs Sherriffs had at Burnside and take
them along with his. Once when my father had taken the sheep to Wardhead
I had to follow later with pony and trap so that he could go on to make
some calls in the west side while I drove the sheep home. In July and August
if the weather was hot the sheep had regularly to be examined for maggots, and
treated if necessary. Their hooves also needed regular attention and the
application, if indicated, of footrot ointment. There is one cryptic entry
by my father in a diary of 28 September 1931 (the royal train had just passed):
'Saw Queen. Sheeps' feet'.

The autumn sales were the climax of the year. A few sheep might also
be sent for slaughter to the mart at Torphins. At some point the wool
broker, Robert C. Dick. would supply the vast hessian wrapping into which
we would pack the fleeces, to be sent by rail to Aberdeen. The wool merchant
would actually add interest at $3\frac{1}{2}\%$ if payment were delayed. During and after
the second war such individual names as remained in the trade appeared under
the heading of British Wool Marketing Board or Ministry of Food – Meat and
Livestock Control.

It is possible to calculate the sheep market account for the year 1952;
but not the costs of very occasional hired labour. winter feed. and incidental
expenses such as renewal of fencing and transport. (See Table 5 page 7-23).
The sale prices then reflected wartime and postwar inflation; for example.
before the war average lambs might fetch 26/- (our cross hogg's two lambs
might each fetch 30/-). On the occasion when I took the lambs to Aboyne the
price was 49/3. Actually on my return home by bicycle on this occasion I
found my father there; he had cycled back from Kildrummy to fetch his fishing-
rod – or so he said; it was with some delight that I quoted the price.
This then rose until the late 1940's (in 1947 lambs fetched 82/6. ewes 102/-)

Table 5

The main figures for 1952 are as follows:

6/7 Oct. <u>Sold</u> 11 greyface lambs at 65/-
(less 9/7 commission, 6d. for herd)   £35 : 4 : 11
4 blackface wedders at 91/-
(less 4/7 commission, 6d. for herd)   17 :18 : 11

            Total   £53 : 3 : 10

<u>Bought</u> 11 Blackface ewes at 63/-   £34 :13 : 0
6 Blackface hoggs at 44/-   13 4 : 0

            Total   £47 :17 : 0

         Balance in hand   £ 5 : 6 : 10

27 Oct. <u>Sold</u> 17 ewes at 36/-
(less 15/9 commission)   £29 : 16: 3
         Balance in hand   £35 : 3: 1

31 December <u>Sold</u> 2 bales (58lb) wool
at 54 pence lb.   £13 : 1: 0
plus 3½% interest to date   3: 0

            Total   £13 : 4: 0

         Add balance   £35 : 3: 1

         Total from sales   £48 : 7: 1

Note: There is no record in 1952 of sheep being sent to the fatstock market but in December 1951 7 fat ewes of varying quality had there realised £17 : 5 : 10.

but seemed to ebb a little in the early fifties, not always necessarily
in accordance with quality. For example, in October 1943 my father bought
10 4-year-old ewes from Auchallater for 37/- each; eight years later
he bought 17 ewes at Michael Fair for 60/- each and sold them at the late
October sale in 1952 for 36/-: 'a terribly slow sale' I noted.

From 1920 until at least 1932 poultry was kept on a semi-commercial
basis, to the extent that eggs were sold to Andrew Collie & Co., or to Gordon
& Smith, grocers in Aberdeen, the former with a branch at Braemar. The fact
that some statistics were kept in 1920 and scrappily in 1932 is useful to
the extent that they indicate the reduction in profitability (it might be
more true to say the increase in commercial loss) over this period. My
father initially failed to impress the Aberdeen folk with the desirability
of having a supply of guaranteed fresh eggs, for which it was worth paying
a fractionally higher sum: to the Aberdonians eggs were eggs.

He began in 1920 with three hens, 12 pullets and two cockerels, costing
a total of £8.5s. That year he sold 149 dozen eggs for a total of £21.12.5,
not mentioning carriage. There was a specially constructed wooden crate for
despatch of these by train or bus. The average price per dozen was 5/- in
January, dropping to 2/6 for March to June, going up to 3/- in July and to
4/6 in October. This alone, when compared with the 1932 figures for April:
$10\frac{1}{2}$ pence per dozen, and May: $9\frac{1}{2}$ pence, explains why the whole venture was
abandoned. But 1920 figures for expenditure on feed (maize meal, bran, white
sharps and shell grit) totalling £17.7.10 and indicating a loss for the year
of £4.0.5 on egg sales, suggests that even then keeping hens on this basis
was hardly profitable. The large hens' food bucket was stirred up each morning
in the kitchen. Other factors can be taken into account: with a family of
five - later six - plenty of eggs and the occasional fowl (both featuring
also as acceptable gifts) were great assets. Also, the details of the 1920
feed bill suggest, as might be expected, that the number of birds kept duly

increased over the year. I recall that small chickens were fed with oatmeal
from our own girnel. The accommodation initially necessary was there. At
first they roosted and laid in a place off the midden which was eventually
converted into a stable with loose box. About 1924 more spacious quarters
were arranged in the barn, which opened on the east side on to the field
where the hens could scrape for themselves, on the west into the midden,
and on the north into a narrow roosting house with boxes for laying, formerly
the tool shed. On the north wall of the original henhouse was a ledge where
my bantam hen liked to lay and hatch out her tiny brood. An irascible beast,
she and the cock had been a gift from Miss Craib, then at Rowan Cottage,
Burnside, whom I visited sometimes on Sunday evenings. Later I got a present
of a cock from Mr Copland, Redstone, Tornaveen, who thought I might 'like a
change'.

The hens' feed was kept dry in the old 'chaumer' — known as the workshop. About 1924 my father acquired an incubator (housed in his study where
at least the lamp would give some welcome warmth) and as a consequence bought
two brooders and a wire chicken run. The varieties thus hatched were Rhode
Island Red, White Wyandotte and Exchequer Leghorn. The incubator was eventually lent around the parish while the wire run was splendid for drying shallots,
one of my father's garden specialities. We continued during the thirties to
keep a few hens producing eggs for home consumption only. In October 1942
my father bought six pullets at the 'Kitty' Hatcheries in Aberdeen, and these
would have consumed a small quantity of the oats which appear in the stable
statistics for that year, but were mostly fed on scraps and what they could
find, plus the occasional up-turned head of kale. The eggs would have supplemented the wartime diet most acceptably. In later years eggs were bought;
small quantities of fresh eggs could be acquired on a neighbourly basis.

No accounts have been kept for the bees: two or three hives were there
from the first, my father having been accustomed to dealing with them at his

home. For some years there were four hives, with in summer as many ruskies, but very much as a sideline. What was not required for winter feeding for the bees was used at home or given away; this was in sections, but occasionally 'rusky' combs would be strained in a cool oven into a 'crock'.

Craig took a great interest in the bees when he was at home, and once read a paper on the subject to the Mildmay Society at Emmanuel College, Cambridge. At my request he has produced a note on the art of 'drumming' a rusky, necessary when a surplus swarm has been kept in the 'skep' in which it was taken:

> I quite often 'drummed' a rusky. One smoked the rusky which one wanted the honey from, turned it upside down, and fixed an empty one above it with two cleeks [i.e. at an angle of some 45 degrees, open side downwards] and with two sticks quietly beat the sides of the lower one. After about 15 minutes the bees all had moved up, especially after the queen moved (this was done in September—October so that there was no incentive to the bees to fly away). The lower rusky was then left empty of bees, and one thumped the top of the other one by the entrance of another hive, and the bees ran in (all this was done in the early evening) and the two queens were presumed to fight it out as to which would rule.

From 1945 Wendy went to evening bee-keeping classes at the school and shared in their management. The hives had to be well protected in winter, old wool blankets being folded under the roofs. We also had wild bees in the space under the manse roof, but did not trouble about them.

CHAPTER EIGHT

<u>At all seasons, serving the Lord</u>

Manse and parish; baptisms, marriages, funerals; hospital
visiting; churchyard management; severe winters; the
Presbytery.

Chapter 8

I don't think it ever occurred to us children when young to wonder what our parishioners thought of us: we certainly didn't take too seriously my mother's occasional admonition to good behaviour 'Remember, your father's the minister'. We took a tremendous interest in the people, and they still call us by our first names. We were of course at (the old) Lumphanan school with many of them. Craig was and remains the most highly regarded. A typical incident occurred when during the war he ran into a Lumphanan man in Cairo who told him that another was also within reach. The three of them spent the evening together: it happened to be Craig's birthday. One of these men, John Merchant, returned from the war, Sandy Sutherland did not. Betty, very 'ladylike' with her hair 'up' at seventeen - she just missed the era of casual clothes - would have said she was regarded with less respect: she once recalled with delight on returning from a pre-Sale of Work tour of the parish with a 'guess-the baby's-name' doll someone saying: 'It's sure to be something quite common; we'll just put down "Betty".' Wendy was greatly loved by all unpretentious people. My status can be illustrated by an interview in 1953 after I had happened to broadcast for two minutes on the BBC's morning 'Programme Parade'. Next day I was shopping in the village where a young assistant (he was all of sixteen years of age, descendant of a long-established family) asked me 'Well, Heather, have you got over your speechifyin'?' He described the scene at breakfast the previous day: 'Ma grannie said to me "That's Heather!" "Canna be," I says...'

From an early age we children tackled any church or parish work that chanced to come our way; the former might include anything from lighting the church lamps or furnace to ringing the bell, deputising at the organ (a harmonium from Guelph, Ontario), or teaching in Sunday School. Craig was quite expert at the bell; I tried it only once. One Sunday morning when the bellman was unable to come my father had rung the 10 a.m. peal when half-seriously I offered to ring the next. To my astonishment he replied: 'All right, then, twenty-five past eleven, - and don't "tit" at the rope or you'll get it all snarled up', and off he went out to the Sunday School. I had never even untied the rope, and it was all I could do to get the bell to move at all: a most uncertain sound. Old Mr Grewer from Quithelhead Cottage, formerly the local representative for Singer sewing-machines, a kenspeckle tweedy figure on his bicycle, looked round the corner: 'I thocht there was somebody new at the bell the day'. Wendy - then keeping house at the manse - was the only one of us who actually conducted a service. It was the day for the monthly evening service at the West End hall, but after the morning service my father had completely lost his voice. Wendy - who would in any case have been playing the organ there - volunteered to go and have a community hymn-singing session. This was much appreciated, the people choosing what they would like to sing. My father used to have reservations about introducing an unfamiliar hymn: 'The folk won't know it...' but on this occasion Wendy reported that one or two of the requests were for hymns not normally sung in our church - including 'Work for the night is coming'. The Revised Church Hymnary had been introduced in 1928, and for many years after, when a hymn was given out, the number in both old and new books would be quoted.

Mainly, however, we children helped in dealing with callers on their various missions. I find that one Saturday evening in July 1949 I have noted in my diary 'Did flowers in church and Wendy saw to an old man who wanted a shirt, and then I weeded'. We had no telephone until March 1946, and then only on account of Presbytery business. Dealing with the vacancy at Coull, before the union with Tarland, in January 1951, my father must have fully appreciated this means of communication: 'Jan. 10 Wed. Snowfall 1 ft. No drift. Frost at night. Forenoon phoned Col. Lilburn, Miss M., P.M., Wood. Lamond. Coull K[irk] S[ession]. Afternoon Coull K.S. Coals came. Waggon stuck in hedge'. My guess is that having thus called the meeting, he then telephoned for motor transport: no 'taking over the hill'.

My father was frequently out visiting in the afternoon and evening, returning late when in the more remote areas of the parish - and in those days four miles away was remote, and dwellings were scattered. Sometimes lying in bed we could hear the sound afar off of the pony's willing homeward trotting. We were early trained to note names and take coherent messages. We knew that proclamation of marriage banns necessitated paying particular attention to the parishes in which the bride and bridegroom resided: boundaries were not always very well known.

Proclamations were altogether a delicate affair, and intending grooms were by no means always anxious to divulge their business to anyone but the minister. We would, of course, spot a 'proclamation' a mile off: or at least by the time the groom, in his best blue suit on a weekday, accompanied by his best man similarly attired, had parked their bicycles (after, perhaps, some preliminary to-ing and fro-ing) against the garden wall or by the steading. Once, when older, I was suddenly involved at a later stage. One post-war Sunday when my father was away, (Auntie Bee had just died at Bath), having left with me an intimation of banns which appeared to be in code, the preacher duly alighted from the bus; he was a well-known retired Deeside minister. When I gave him the 'proclamation' he confessed he had forgotten exactly what to say: would I write it out for him? This was no trouble, but it had - fortunately earlier - occurred to me that some certificate was customarily collected by the bridegroom on the following Tuesday. Having no idea what the form was for this, I had looked up 'Cox'. There it was: I copied it out, and the elderly minister duly signed it without comment. It was only later, when my father saw it at the wedding, delivered via the registrar, that it transpired that our 'Cox' was rather out of date, and I had used a rather archaic - but still perfectly legal - form of words.

When quite small I once dealt with a former parishioner who had settled elsewhere and wished to 'lift his lines'. I wrote down his name and new address. He then asked if there was anything to pay. I had no idea and said so: I only knew that proclamation of banns attracted (for the minister if doubling as session clerk) a fee of half-a-crown. This sum was immediately forthcoming - and I imagine later repaid - but my father awarded me the first one for my albeit hesitating enterprise. For many years my father acted as session clerk, and this half-crown fee was always given to my mother; after her death and until the end of the day Wendy and I got it alternately: she would even send my share to me in London, - sometimes with a piece of the wedding-cake.

The senior Divinity Professor at Aberdeen when my father was a student was Henry Cowan D.D., D.TH., D.C.L., of the Chair of Church History. Ordained in 1869 and appointed to the Chair in 1889, he obviously did not take too narrow a view of his responsibilities. A notebook of my father's contains his summaries of Professor Cowan's lectures on the marriage, baptismal and funeral services. While these contain much history - procedures are based on The Directory for the Public Worship of God, agreed upon by the Assembly of Divines at Westminster (1645) - there is also some very practical advice. For example, recalling that until the mid-eighteenth century church marriages were common, whereas ceremonies were then (say 1911) generally held in houses or hotels, a service in church should be encouraged for many reasons, not least because it might be accompanied by a smaller entertainment, therefore less expense. The Directory now advised against Sunday marriages on account of the labour and festivities involved; Cowan added 'railway journeys'. He believed that both parties should agree to be 'dutiful', having reminded them what these duties were, including being an influence for good on each other. Among 'Incidentals' he recommended that gown and bands be worn (adding 'Always take the cab offered'), that recitation of the service was better than reading. A last piece of advice: 'don't drink whisky at the toast' (a principle quite apart from that of total abstinence).

In the early days wedding ceremonies took place either in my father's
study, in the bride's home or in a hotel. If in the manse, tea was served
after the ceremony, which my mother attended; our three-tiered mahogany
cakestand would be placed within the half-circle of chairs. My mother always
offered 'best wishes' to the bride and 'congratulations' to the bridegroom.
The first wedding I can recall taking place in the church - about 1932 - was
that of Olive Stephen, whose mother then lived at Rowan Cottage, Burnside;
Olive was a sister of Mrs Charles Dunn, East Kincraigie, and of Mrs John Watt,
Hillock. She also married a Dunn and they lived at South Footie, Torphins.
I can remember how pretty she looked in bridal white, carrying flame-coloured
sweet-peas. Over thirty years later, newly-married ourselves, my husband and
I met them in the Edinburgh hotel where we all were staying for the Assembly.
Theirs was a summer wedding; when church weddings became more popular, even
in winter, it several times fell to my father to clear a path for them through
the snow. A week after the Coull meeting referred to above, the diary
includes: 'Sanded roads to manse and church for wedding 2 hours. Afternoon
P[ost] O[ffice] Banns. [David K. Moir, then postmaster, was also registrar]
St. Finan's wedding Alfred Craigmyle. 4-7 Hotel'. Wendy had played the organ.

This had been a Wednesday; generally weddings took place on a Saturday,
and on Sunday there would be the 'kirking', with bride and bridegroom,
bridesmaid and best man, in a row in church. A day or two earlier my father
would have visited a local bride with a gift of a Bible. Marriages at home
would be followed by a reception in the 'best room' - or perhaps in a farm
'loft'. A tale used to be told of my sister Wendy as a small child being
taken to such a wedding; the table groaned with all sorts of home-made
delicacies but Wendy declined everything. When asked what she would like she
said: 'Could I please have a bit of oatcake?' My mother was affronted but
came the ready response: 'Surely! There's plenty in the kitchen drawer!'
After tea and the cutting of the cake (as well as a portion at table, guests
would receive a pretty crepe-paper bag with a piece to take home - and perhaps

dream on?) my father customarily proposed the health of the bride and then withdrew, leaving the company to its less inhibited celebration. My mother obviously enjoyed these occasions. She was disappointed at the thought of missing Lizzie Grant's wedding at East Mains on 27 December 1922, writing to my father from hospital after a hernia operation: 'I think I will be just as well at home with my own wee Heather ... Much as I would like to go and "Hum" a mouse again with Mr. J.G. I think I had better refrain!!' Among my father's collection of photographs is a smiling snapshot taken of him in formal dress against a farmyard background. On the back he had written 'At Minew'. Recently I asked Annie Cockie (Mrs Alex Forbes) for an explanation of this: was there a wedding there? Back came the reply: 'That was our wedding, 48 years ago'.

Once, on regaining the pony-trap after a Mearns wedding in the Moss-side area, he found he had left his woollen gloves in the house. He returned indoors just in time to hear the bride's uncle James Ingram assuring everyone 'It's a' richt, the minister's awa'!' My father was heard to say 'No, he's not away yet, Jamie, but he's going now!' James Ingram, for long employed on the Dess estate, was in poor health when my sister Betty died, on 29 November 1934, and my father was disturbed to see him at her funeral, on a cold December day. Shortly afterwards the laird of Dess, Walter R. Davidson, came over to visit Ingram at Perkmoss; he called at the manse on the way and found a small notice on the door 'Back at 4 o'clock'. He duly returned to find me alone; I had been out collecting subscriptions for the District Nursing Association. Mr Davidson thought my notice a splendid idea. I then got the latest news of James Ingram, whom my father and I had ridden up to see some days earlier - Mrs Ingram entertaining us to glasses of fresh milk, 'straight from the cow' and Abernethy biscuits. (Those who kept cows knew that my father preferred this to tea.) My father's last visit to Ingram was on a sleeting Sunday afternoon early in January; six days later Jamie was buried.

It was only latterly that any public celebration of the special wedding

anniversaries took place. Silver weddings would tend to be of couples my
father had married: for example that of Alex Wood, for many years the cheerful and willing servant of the public in the capacities of souter, motor
engineer, taxi-man and garage proprietor providing float-transport. He
married Hilda Milne, one of the musical bakery family. Alex was then an
'incomer', a veteran of the 1914-18 war. At their silver wedding my father
recalled the past: Lumphanan was very proud of its gifted girls at the bakery;
first to marry was 'Fluffy' - 'well, well, that was all right, we all knew
Willie Dawson...' (of the family then at Upper Tillylair) - but who was this
newcomer? For all of us gathered at this occasion at the Northern Hotel in
Aberdeen there was really no need to expatiate on 'Widdie's' quarter-century
of public service.

I recall my father's attending at their home on the Findrack estate the
ruby wedding of Mr and Mrs Torrie, coming home with a bouquet of ruby-red
roses for the church. Some years before he retired there was the golden
wedding of Mr and Mrs George Buchan, married with three of a family before
his induction in 1913. Both played an active part in local life, particularly
when in charge of the Parish Hall. A part-time tailor, George was also a
barber, and green-keeper to the golf-course. Mrs Buchan was the first president of the Lumphanan W.R.I. Her sideline was fortune-telling from playing-
cards: sometimes extraordinarily accurate. She recalled to me once with
some horror her wedding outfit of purple velvet.

In January 1955 my father was invited to the golden wedding of Mr and
Mrs Andy Burnett, late of Bogerfoul, Lumphanan, of Tillybirlock, ('Birley')
Midmar, and of Burnside, Echt. Andy was a cousin of my Aunt Janet's second
husband David. Writing to my father some time later Mrs Andy (she wrote
marvellous letters, generally beginning 'My dear Friend and Minister' and at
some point 'burn this long story') enclosed an Aberdeen Press cutting about
the parish of Kinkell, including the rhyme:

> Oh! sic a parish, oh! sic a parish!
>> Oh! sic a parish is that o' Kinkell!
> They hae hangit the minister,
>> droun'd the precentor,
> Dung down the steeple, an' fuddl'd the bell.

- a series of calamities evidently founded on fact. She observed that the stones of Kinkell church were now to be used to repair her childhood's church of Keithhall: 'Our kirk when we were young, and all the folks walked long distances - that was in Dr. Donald's time. He used to often sing "Days and moments quickly flying" and we sang without a thought about the days...'

I think my father never actually attended the golden wedding of anyone he had himself united in marriage. In 1966 he bought in Edinburgh and addressed a golden wedding card for Mr and Mrs John Merchant of the Gallowfield family, then at 6 Perkhill Road, Lumphanan, but before it was posted evidently found he had mistaken the date; the event had been celebrated in 1965. John Merchant died the following year; it was their son John whom Craig had met in Cairo.

In my father's time at Lumphanan baptisms generally took place at home, rather than in church, or if in church then after the service. Unfortunately Finan's font - the oldest Christian relic on Deeside, it is thought, restored to Lumphanan as described in Chapter 3, - had now become a historical monument only, and babies were sprinkled out of my mother's Crown Derby bowl, or later out of a silver one from Cyprus sent by Craig, as a silver wedding present to our parents. The practice of home baptisms is now frowned upon, perhaps by those who have never witnessed the genuinely holy atmosphere of even a crofter's kitchen prepared for this ceremony. Certainly the public celebration of the sacrament - perhaps with virtually a queue of babies of different families lined up - has not prevented the national decline in family life which all deplore, whether in the home or in the larger family of the church. The solemnity of the occasion, as I remember it, all interest focussed upon one child, with perhaps two or three older generations of the family present, was equal to anything I have seen in a city church. Certainly it involved

more travelling for the minister. I recall one Sunday afternoon seeing my
father - at this time over 70 - dressing to go out, his auto-cycle at the
ready; I asked him casually where he was going. He was about to travel
many miles to christen the illegitimate grandchild of a former parishioner;
the local minister had declined to do so. Once in late October, when the
evening service at the Tornaveen meeting-house had been cancelled by those
locally responsible, because of bad weather, my father still set out because
he had arranged to take two baptisms in the area, one at Balmannocks, the
other at Mains of Findrack, on the Sunday afternoon, Sometimes when the
christening was the occasion for several generations to be present the baby's
parents no longer lived in the parish, and might indeed - especially after
World War II - be home on holiday from England or elsewhere. But there was
justification in the meaningfulness of the ceremony being performed by the
same minister who had baptised their parents. We children were all christened
in the manse; Craig's and Betty's baptisms have already been referred to;
Wendy was christened by the Reverend J.D. Mackenzie, Aboyne, I by the Reverend
Alexander McKenzie, Coull.

Altogether there was, I think, undeniable virtue in the presence of the
minister in the homes of the parishioners one might say from birth to burial.
In an age when the experts take over on most occasions - social workers,
probation officers, lawyers, welfare officers, health visitors - the phenomenon
of the parish minister who on occasion wore each or all of these hats in
addition to his own explains a good deal in connection with present-day social
malaise. People used to say in Lumphanan 'If there's ony trouble, the
minister's aye there'.

Professor Cowan, in his lectures, had certainly recommended baptism in
church, or if administered privately that gown and bands should then be worn.
He may have been thinking more of city charges: whatever trouble the minister
took in bringing the sacrament into people's homes, this would have been simpler
than bringing the baby and relatives to the church in areas where transport

was difficult if not non-existent. There is evidence, in stray extracts which my father made from our church records of the eighteenth century, of the occasional church christening then. Professor Cowan referred to the need hurriedly to baptise dying children; unbaptised infants were in olden days buried as near to the church walls as possible. He also, practical as ever, adjured his students 'Do all you can to prevent the infant crying' - almost certainly more a feature of church baptism.

In the nature of things, deaths could sometimes be foreseen and sometimes were the sudden result of some accident or other tragedy. Even after an illness the end might be sudden, and entail much emergency activity. Once after a death it happened that the lady who would have been available to do the 'laying out' could not be found, and my father asked Wendy, who had had nursing experience, if she could do it. She did - despite the fact that although she had been taught the procedure she had never actually carried it out on her own. On another occasion, my father being out visiting, she was called upon to help break the news of his accidental death to the wife of a contractor whose tractor had overturned, trapping him underneath. Tractor accidents became the modern equivalent of falling off a hay-cart. One Sunday evening when my father was taking his monthly service at Tornaveen and Wendy had driven him there, perhaps also playing the organ, two brothers - former parishioners with a long family connection - came to the manse where I was alone. The elder - we had been in the same class at school - broke the news: 'I've just run over my boy with the tractor'. It was clear, as we drank coffee and waited, that the father had suffered more than the son. He and his wife emigrated to Australia. There was the occasional suicide; sometimes this tendency seemed to run in families.

Despite progress in preventive medicine, - no longer a case of cowpox matter straight from the byre - quite serious epidemics were not yet unknown. In 1934 a boy of 7 and two little girls aged 6 and 5 had died. At that time the hospital at Aboyne was a 'fever' - isolation - institution. The

War Memorial Hospital at Torphins in these years had the occasional long-stay patient, otherwise operation cases (surgeons would come out from Aberdeen when necessary) and other short term sick, but not as a rule maternity cases. But an increasing number of sick parishioners went into Aberdeen hospitals: the Royal Infirmary (first at Woolmanhill, then after 1935 at Foresterhill), the City ('Fever') Hospital, the Sick Children's Hospital, Woodend or the Royal Mental. A few other patients might have to be visited at nursing-homes. My father's pocket notebooks would have lists of people to see at any or all of the main hospitals. Latterly the head porter at Foresterhill, Mr Petrie, was a Dufftown man who would sometimes tell him on his way in of an old acquaintance who had been admitted there. Other patients with only slight connections would be called on - for instance a guard on the Deeside Line. Hospital visiting in Aberdeen would in earlier, and again in later days be combined with attendance at County Education and Further Education Committee meetings, while the District Education Committee at Aboyne would similarly afford an opportunity for hospital or pastoral visiting there.

But in the earlier days of my father's ministry most patients were still treated at home - if only because there was so little in the way of curative treatment that could be offered, and in minor ailments more traditional remedies in the folklore. The Banchory doctor - at this time Dr Cran - would sometimes drop in at the manse for a cup of tea on his rounds. Once, after the tea had been drunk, my mother showed him one of her fingers which had been damaged and was festering painfully. 'Oh, Mrs Donald, that is a sore finger!' was Dr Cran's response, whereupon my mother felt so much better that further treatment is not recorded. Psychological medicine may be older than one thinks.

On reading a draft of this chapter my brother Craig, whose memory goes back eight years further than mine, remarked that I had said nothing about old-style farm funerals. On being invited to make his own contribution, he sent the following:

Death tended to be accepted philosophically, except where there was some tragic circumstance, and (possibly partly due to my father's preaching) in the Christian belief that it was a prelude to a better life. The funeral began in the home, the minister standing in the open doorway, with the family behind him, and facing the mourners in a semi-circle outside. The latter would be almost entirely male, in dark clothes - in some cases a frock-coat - with a tile or bowler hat. Immediate neighbours and friends had on previous days 'paid their respects' to the corpse, lying in an open coffin in 'the room' across the doorway from the kitchen, and commenting on how peaceful the deceased looked. At one time the custom was to touch the forehead or pat the crossed hands. Other close acquaintances would follow this ritual on arrival at the funeral, moving quickly but deliberately in and out, others merely joining the semi-circle and being greeted by the senior male family representative. The service consisted of readings from Scripture and prayers, and the coffin was then borne by near relatives or friends to the hearse, horse-drawn or motor, or if the distance was comparatively short, carried to the churchyard as the church bell tolled. A procession then set out at walking pace as the majority would be on foot, for a journey of possibly up to three miles, the cortege being on occasion as much as half a mile long.

The committal service followed conventional lines, the coffin being lowered into the grave by the nearest relatives, the senior at the head and the next senior at the foot, and two more on either side. After the committal the coffin would be covered with a mattress and a certain amount of soil, planks laid across the opening with wreaths on top, the gravedigger removing his cap to indicate that the ceremony was complete, the mourners then filing to take leave of the senior relative.

As with marriages and christenings, Professor Cowan had practical advice about funerals. Regarding the length of the service, if this were in church and accompanied by singing, it could go to half an hour; but when in the house, with mourners waiting outside in the cold, a quarter of an hour must suffice. Where accommodation was small, the service might be held ten minutes before the arrival of mourners; in this event the latter must be notified of the time 'for service or for "lifting"'. Prayers at the grave should be short, especially if cold. It looked bad to see hats on. (In practice, elderly men could retain these: others sometimes tended towards the compromise of holding hats to one side.) Professor Cowan recalled one occasion where on a very bad day he had only pronounced the Benediction at the grave. In such event an extra prayer was added at the house.

The philosophical acceptance of death was well illustrated in the readings ('not long, but a series of short extracts') recommended by Professor Cowan. It might be noted that most of these appeared both in 1909 and 1928

Order Books; an exception (which my father had added to his 1909 book) was
John 14: 'Let not your heart be troubled: ye believe in God, believe also
in me. In my Father's house are many mansions...' This applied also to
1 Thessalonians 4: 'But I would not have you to be ignorant, brethren,
concerning them which are asleep, that ye sorrow not, even as others which
have no hope...' For the funeral of a child, the Professor recommended
2 Samuel 12 (also in the 1909 book): the story of the death of David's child,
ending 'I shall go to him, but he shall not return to me'. In the 1909 book
only was Isaiah 40, v.11: 'He shall feed His flock like a shepherd: He shall
gather the lambs with His arm, and carry them in His bosom'. Both books had
Mark 10, vv. 13-15: '...Suffer the little children to come unto me...'

Professor Cowan favoured 'with limits' some personal references, and
this became my father's custom. Only latterly - I think after his retirement -
would he have made a note of what he was to say. For example, at the funeral
of Mr Grewer, late of Quithelhead Cottage, he said: '... And now we remember
before Thee those who are here this day sorrowing over the death of Thy
servant. Grant that they may look back now to all that he was to them in
life - his long years of faithful service, his fellowship with those who knew
him and amongst whom his life was spent. We remember those who ministered to
his needs in his latter days, and especially we remember her [his daughter
Theo] who has come so often from distant lands to visit him and succour him.
May the memory of these errands of mercy and of love bring comfort to her
in the days and years that lie ahead'.

The other note I have was for the funeral of John Riddler, Greenburn,
originally a Free Church member, who died twelve years after my father's
retirement:

> The grave has closed over another of our elders - a pillar of this
> particular church and a strong pillar of the Kingdom of God in his own
> immediate surroundings. Mr Riddler was not widely known - for he was
> modest: one of those who would never come forward unless asked and
> even when bidden reluctantly. But those who did know him (his neigh-
> bours) held him in the highest respect. Over 20 years since, a near

neighbour chanced to say to me – 'Mr. Riddler is a good man' – and those who knew him most intimately would agree that he could not have been better described.

Industrious, unassuming, peaceloving and gentle in his ways he spent a full life and died as he had expressed a desire to do in harness.

We shall miss him for he loved his church and served it well. Regular in attendance, he carried home the spirit of worship and lived as he had learned at the throne of Grace and now has passed peacefully to his rest. He has earned the reward 'Well done good and faithful servant – come up higher here'.

My father might have added that John was a faithful member of the choir, attendance at St Finan's entailing an extra mile and a half on his bicycle. Like my father he wore solid black leather leggings. As mentioned earlier, he played the fiddle in Maggie Macgregor's band.

I myself can recall only one occasion on which my father made a reference during the Sunday church service to someone who had just died. In fact he mentioned then that this was not his custom, but that 'Mrs. Copland was a very special person'. The wife of James Copland, then one of our senior elders and choir members, and the local representative of Scottish Agricultural Industries, she had virtually taken over the role of Mrs John King (Chapter 3) in her cheerful readiness to serve church and community. After my father's pulpit tribute he gave out the closing hymn: 'The King of Love my shepherd is'. We sang this at his funeral.

Funerals were by no means always straightforward ceremonies where people living locally were laid to rest with their forebears in the 'old' churchyard, in the adjacent cemetery, in the new cemetery at Craigton or at the Stothert Memorial. In some cases my father would travel quite a distance to a funeral elsewhere. When he came to Lumphanan, the gravedigger (also bellman) was 'old' George McDonald, living at the Cairnbeathie Cottage up the hill, who had held office since 1895. His predecessor as grave-digger, from 1870, was Alex Stevenson, Broomhill, whose record of interments had been lost. Accordingly, when McDonald resigned in 1914, my father and he went over the churchyard, the latter detailing all the interments made by himself and adding what he

knew of those made previously and of appropriate future tenants. He had a
useful knowledge, too, of obstructions - large stones - likely to preclude
burial. They came to the conclusion then that there were about 46 spaces
likely to be available, some never having been used, others unopened for
over 25 years and unlikely to be claimed by former parishioners. (At this
time there was no charge for a lair.) My father did not then realise that
there existed locally some prejudice against the use of 'tenantless' lairs
i.e. not used in living memory, therefore containing the dust of the unknown:
this apparently emerged at a Kirk Session meeting early in 1919. Until 1929
the heritors were responsible for the churchyard - even to approving proposed
monuments - the Parish Council making representations on behalf of their
'constituents'. In 1915 the Kirk Session had recommended that the heritors
take advantage of the 46 'vacant' lairs while at the same time improving the
surface and approaches; this last was rejected 'because of the war'. By
1919 some of the elders were pressing for an extension, and by 1923 six
heritors' meetings had been called at the instance of the Parish Council
without positive result, partly owing to the Council's own uncertainty as to
appropriate action. The minister, incidentally, had no official standing in
these matters; the heritors, however, appreciated his interest. Recently
some graves that had been opened had contained vestiges of early burials.
The Parish Council already had jurisdiction over the extension known as the
cemetery, originally feued by the Parochial Board in 1884, and by November
1923 had agreed to make available a few spaces there hitherto reserved for
'poor persons' until new ground was arranged. Meanwhile my father had proposed
that a portion of glebe be feued for the purpose, if agreed by the Presbytery,
enough for immediately foreseeable requirements, although at the same time
Court of Session authority should be sought to feu a larger space when such
might be required, perhaps in sixty years' time. This, however, gave rise
to legal difficulties: it was a case of feuing all of this larger space or
none, in the former case drastically reducing the glebe, although the Parish

Council were prepared to rent it back, and affecting access to the rest.
A modified proposal was put to the Presbytery.

By this time the new 1925 Act (or at least the Bill) governing church
property after the 1929 Union was in print, foreseeing the management of
churchyards handed over from heritors to parish councils. Moreover the
Lumphanan Parish Council sought virtually complete secular jurisdiction over
an insulated piece of church land. As my father put it, 'for all time coming
the minister's or his tenant's cattle gain access to water and pasturage at
the goodwill of the Parish Council'. He did not see how he could declare
before the Court of Session that such a bargain was for the Good of the
Benefice. The Council considered also that the 'green road' - the footpath
right of way from the Aboyne road - should be fenced off to keep back the
minister's sheep. 'Who', he asked, 'will cut the grass and otherwise maintain
the road?' The following year - 1925 - he proposed to the Parish Council that
they purchase instead a north-south strip, 70 feet wide, of the west portion
of the garden, with direct access from the main road. This met an enthusiastic
response. It was found, however, by the Presbytery on taking legal advice,
that a minister could not thus dispose of a part of his garden 'except under
very exceptional circumstances which did not exist in the present case.' In
the end the Parish Council bought instead the site between Craigton and the
village where the 'new cemetery' was attractively laid out.

George McDonald was succeeded, as gravedigger only, by James Emslie,
Woodside, who in turn, after an interim period when Alex Sherriffs, Kirkbrae,
took on the task, was followed in June 1917 by Maxwell Mearns. Then, after
Tom Mearns as interim, came 'The Good Companions' as we called them: John
Cadger, Ashfield, and George Maitland, retired from the post of gardener at
Auchenhove and living in the village. There being then three graveyards to
tend, two men were necessary, and they certainly kept them beautifully, the
grass always neatly mown and unturfed gravespaces edged. They took a pride
in their work and seemed to enjoy it, keeping up meanwhile what sometimes

seemed a hilarious line in conversation. 'Oh, John, John! ... Oh, man,
George!' we would hear. John Cadger was also village lamplighter when we
acquired our first (paraffin) street lamps – the last at the end of the
churchyard road. Electric street lighting came in September 1950. The Good
Companions were the last of the line, as was Pipe-Major John Stevenson, of
the U.F., who had cared for the Stothert Memorial graveyard as well as being
bellman there. The Parish Council had been abolished and the County Council
took over the care of graveyards, sending a 'flying squad' to maintain these,
and one or two men as required to dig graves and attend at funerals. On at
least one occasion, in July 1947, it seemed no-one was available for grave-
digging at St Finan's; my father noted in his diary: 'Forenoon: dug grave'.
In May he had helped to dig one at the Stothert. During the second war,
incidentally, all iron railings were removed for war purposes.

The County squad certainly kept the graveyards for many years at a
standard all too seldom seen nowadays. All graves were grassed over for ease
of mowing with modern machines. But once they carried out an order which on
aesthetic and historical grounds can only be called preposterous. My father
returned from a Synod committee meeting in town one day in March 1952 to hear
from Wendy that all our cherished table gravestones had been laid flat, their
supports removed. Very upset indeed, my father returned to town next day,
consulted a lawyer and saw the County Clerk. He also spoke to Lord Aberdeen,
then chairman of the education committees of which my father was a member.
The Act of 1925 had provided that any person proving to the satisfaction of
the new churchyard authority that they had a legitimate interest in any
tombstone would be entitled to provide for the preservation and maintenance
of the same. His one hope was to interest the Aberdeen family in one table
stone commemorating Malcolms, kin of Dr John Malcolm Bulloch, author of The
House of Gordon. But all to no avail. Later my father found that the supports
had been thrown over the Falls of Dess, shattered. Now the edges of the flat
stones (already we had a few very old ones whose inscriptions were barely if

at all legible) are being worn by machinery, and at funerals – where sometimes
there is no choice but to walk on them – feet are wearing down the lettering.
In fact, it is probably no easier than before to keep neat edges, while weeds
under the tables could readily have been discouraged; already there was
gravel underneath. The act of official vandalism has detracted from the
gracious picture once presented by the plain but pleasing intermingling of
shapes.

Even before the 1939 union of the two Lumphanan churches the dead were
not necessarily segregated according to their church membership or connection;
burial was more of a parish than a congregational concern. Severe winters
could present difficulties of transport and access, although hardly reaching
the proportions once experienced in North America: a Lumphanan emigrant to
Canada once told me that his first job there was to bury corpses that had had
to be kept in cold storage until the snow cleared and the ground defrosted.
He happened to be standing that spring by an open window counting his first
week's pay when a gust of wind came and blew the notes away.

My mother used to tell how at the first snowfall young Frank Glenesk
from the Craigton would harness their grey Meggie to the farm snow-plough and
sweep down the hill and round the access roads to churchyard and manse. In
later days my father often had to cut 'roadies' with a shovel in advance of
any official action, main roads having priority. I can just remember the old
fashioned ornate glass hearse with horses. The last horse to carry a coffin
over the snow was I think in January 1936 the 'miller's auld grey' bringing
the bellman's wife, Mrs Robert Emslie, down from Newton Croft on a sledge
draped with a tartan rug, to the churchyard gate.

During the severe winter of 1946-47 a typical situation developed over
the deaths of a well-loved couple. Mr and Mrs Charles Esson were farming
Glenshalg, up the 'old road' behind the U.F. Church, when my father came in
1913; to the end of the chapter Charlie, a cheerful, not to say convivial soul,
was known as 'Glen'. His wife was a sister of James Cockie of Mill Farm.

They moved about 1930 to Futtie, the low-lying farm near Camphill House.
(Mrs Esson used the local pronunciation of 'Camf'll') and there for some years
the 'barn' Sunday School was held in summer, with tea for teacher and organist
afterwards in the kitchen. The last time I recall seeing 'Glen' was at a
morning service at the Stothert Memorial. During the sermon a child who had
fallen asleep began a regular snoring. At lunch afterwards I remarked on
this. 'Oh,' said my father equably, 'I thought it was Charlie Esson'.
Eventually the Essons retired to Upper Deeside, and on the afternoon of
7 January 1947 – very cold, but not yet snowing – my father set off on his
auto-cycle (a round trip of 36 miles) to call first at the old school-house,
Inchmarnoch, half-way between Dinnet and Ballater, then at Ballater hospital
where Mrs Esson was lying with a broken leg. He had spent the morning mending
a fence whence a few sheep had been escaping into Henry Keith's turnip-field.
He had driven the main flock to winter at Coull on 31 December – a sunny,
almost spring-like day, although later the roads were very icy; the odd ones
were fortunately sold on 8 January. The last diary note for 7 January was
the familiar 'Gealed'.

On 28 January ('V. cold. snow') my father went by train to Ballater to
see Mrs Esson. Thereafter the snow began in earnest. Mrs Esson died on
8 February. On Sunday 9th, ('more snow – drifting..wild night. S[unday]
S[chool] 3. St.F[inan's] 4 no service') arrangements were made by telephone
with the County Council Roads Department for the grave to be prepared at the
Stothert Memorial churchyard. On Monday 10th ('v. cold day. deep drifts')
the grave-digging began, complicated by a big stone; my father 'cut roads'.
Meanwhile an old lady living alone in the village supervised by a neighbour,
had had a heart attack and was taken to Aboyne hospital. Mrs Esson was buried
on Tuesday 11 February. On Wednesday 12th ('More snow – cold') my father
'cut roads' at the manse, then was away from 11-6.30, having walked 10 miles
and travelled 28 by train and bus. First he went to Aboyne to see the Welfare
Officer (then W.G. Ironside, formerly at Lumphanan, not yet succeeded by Jack

Forbes) about the lady who had been admitted to hospital there, then to
visit the latter. Then on to Inchmarnoch to see Charles Esson whom he found
to be ill. On the way back he called on the minister at Dinnet. Next morning ('More snow. cold') he cleared snow for three hours, made three visits
in connection with these two invalids, and went by train to Banchory to
visit a third: the lady who in her youth rode a motor-cycle. On Friday 14th
(again more snow and cold) he cleared snow. The telephone rang: Charlie
Esson was dead. He telephoned in turn the undertaker and the Road Surveyor.
There followed a spell indoors while he addressed envelopes to church members
and duplicated church balance-sheets on his cyclostyle in preparation for a
congregational meeting. Then to the Stothert ('roads') and to make arrangements for the reception of 'Glen's' coffin that evening at the Hall. 'Evening:
At Hall to wait corpse 9-11'.

There was now some respite - no more 'onding' on Saturday although he
cleared snow for two hours in the morning ('New shovel') and 'cleared Church
path' for the two Sunday School children and ten of a congregation who turned
up on Sunday morning. On the Sunday afternoon there was a baptism at the
Hilton, and in the evening a sick-visit at Kincraigie (six miles walking in
all). A telephone call gave news of the death of the lady in Aboyne hospital.

On Monday morning, 17 February, - 'still cold' - in the north-facing
ground-floor lavatory the wash-basin taps were frozen - my father set off to
the village, posted the circulars to the congregation and went on to the
Stothert Memorial churchyard to check on Charles Esson's grave. Back at
St Finan's he cut a road to the churchyard there for the other funeral which
would be on Tuesday. ('Back sore'). At 2 p.m. 'Glen' joined his wife at the
Stothert. Next day my father cut roads again and helped when the coffin
came from Aboyne for the funeral at St Finan's at 2 p.m. There followed some
hospital and other visiting at Torphins.

This winter of 1946-47 was severe, but on the whole, for Lumphanan, not
unusually so. (My father had yet to quote on 26 December 1950: 'Slipper

extraord^r. Worst ever here' and for 22-28 December 1952: 'Ice on front Manse approach worst seen here by me'.)   In contrast to the spring, summer and autumn activities in garden and glebe, to quote further entries from this winter diary gives a fairly good idea of typical preoccupations at that season. The approaching Church At Home - and this one was to coincide with a Quinquennial Visitation by representatives of the Presbytery - necessitated visits or telephone calls concerning the entertainment as well as the usual pastoral visiting. Being in Torphins on Wednesday 19 February he called on the tailor, the well-known fiddler Alexander R. Henderson, to ask him to play for us. On Thursday 20th - still cold; taps still frozen - he cut roads in the snow from 9-12 o'clock, then after seeing the church treasurer about Quinquennial Visitation schedules set out on horseback for the Tornaveen area, riding nine miles in all. Next day there was more snow (and a report from the plumber), and after the congregational meeting in the evening 'Drifting'. There was more snow again on Saturday - more clearing of paths - and a funeral at Torphins. As was becoming customary, my father lit the church furnace - prepared by the beadle - but on Saturday night instead of early Sunday morning; 'very frosty'. Sunday 23rd was 'not so cold'. There were 5 at Sunday School, 12 at Church, but 15 in the evening at Bible Class, for which he had lit the church lamps, after an afternoon sick-visit.

Monday 24 February was frosty but sunny; after three hours of 'sticks and snow' my father took the 1 o'clock bus to Aberdeen and did a round of hospital and other visits. On Tuesday after an hour of snow-clearing ('hard frost: bright sun') he set off in the Cushnie direction. He got a lift with the local Scottish Agricultural Industries representative, Douglas Mutch, to Wester Foulis, walked from there to Wark, on to the school with the Alford butcher's van, and paid half-a-dozen other visits before walking home. ('V. hard frost'). On Wednesday 26th it was drifting again; after dealing with 'pipes and snow' he spent the day writing, going out only to the Post Office with a letter to or about one of the hospital patients - still 'drifting'.

In the evening 'Read and rested - some tired'. He was then 65. By Thursday 27 February there were 'deep drifts and drifting' to be dealt with. He paid two calls in the morning (probably connected with snow-clearing) on elderly ladies living alone at Burnside, then apart from a Post Office visit spent the day cyclostyling Presbytery circulars - the questionnaire on manses - and rested. 'More drift: deep wreaths' on Friday; three hours clearing paths, and later 'more paths' after dealing with the manse questionnaire.

Saturday 1 March brought 'yird drift': loose snow being blown off the top of more solid wreaths. After a visit to the west side - more drifting - my father telephoned around calling off both service and Bible Class for the following day, although the latter entailed a visit on Sunday afternoon, after calls on John King at Knappyround and at the Hillock. In the evening he called on an old lady in the village. On Monday 3 March, after the clearing of a path to the drying-ground for Wendy to hang out washing, there was more hospital visiting in Aberdeen, travelling by train: presumably the bus was off the road. On Tuesday ('V. frosty - sunny') he spent three hours cutting a path to the garden, and delivered the mail to Burnside. Later he 'cleared Wendy Villa': the corner inside the garden gate at the angle of the churchyard and garden walls. overhung by a canopy of ivy, furnished by then with two large elm logs for seats; it caught the sun and was sheltered even in winter. Then there were two visits in the village. Next day after three hours cutting paths my father set off on foot up the Perkhill, going as far as 'Johnnie' Laing's, then up to Helen Troup's at Woodbine and down past Ferniebrae. On Thursday 6th ('V. Frosty - softening later') he cut a path to the church, then took the train to Aboyne, calling on the Welfare Officer and on two former parishioners. After lunch at an hotel he took a bus to the Cambus O'May area, calling on three more ex-parishioners. Returning by train, he paid another call in the village. Besides other transport he had walked 10 miles.

There was more snow on March 7, with three hours of 'paths and overflow pipe'. He paid a call in the village and went up to Leyhead to settle our

butter account. In the evening he wrote to the 'Fuel overseer'. (They
were evidently short of coal; I had telephoned that evening from Aberdeen
but getting no reply assumed they had retired to bed to keep warm.) Saturday
8th brought hard frost; 'cleared snow from walls'. After a call in the
village two young people called about a wedding; on 28 March he was to clear
the road to the church for this ceremony on the 29th. Another parishioner
came to report an invalid. There was no Sunday School on the 9th but 6 turned
up to church and 16 in the evening for Bible Class. (Two weeks later this
had risen to 20). Monday 10th was 'fresher. Sleet, snow, drift'. After
clearing paths he took the 1 o'clock bus to Aberdeen. Before visiting two
patients in the Infirmary he called on T.B. Huxley-Jones of Gray's School of
Art with the list of names for the two War Memorial tablets, one in stone for
St Finan's, one to be executed in wood by Jones's wife, Gwyneth Holt, for the
Stothert. The last entry for the day is 'Booked Jas. E[mslie]'s Band' -
for a forthcoming Old Time Evening on 4 April. The following day, apart
from calling on the wife of one of the hospital patients, the day was spent
on 'paths'.

Path-clearing continued on Wednesday 12 March ('drifting') then from
4-9 p.m. he was at Torphins Church on a Quinquennial Visitation by a Presbytery deputation. He took the opportunity again to ask Alex Henderson to
play at the Old Time Evening and to visit a patient at the hospital there.
On Thursday ('more drift') it was 'V. cold in house'. There was some question
of an old lady being admitted to hospital, and that evening he visited her
in the village after seeing the Welfare Officer and another ex-parishioner
at Aboyne. On Friday 14 March 'on-ding ceased', and he cleared paths in the
morning and in the afternoon while awaiting a telephone call from the Welfare
Officer. The old lady was not to go into hospital and he visited her that
evening. Later a young man called about a proclamation of marriage. It was
milder with snow showers on Saturday, but there were still paths to clear
morning and afternoon, and two visits, one pastoral and one to collect seed

potatoes. Shopping in the village I noted that everyone seemed to be rushing about with capacious sledges drawn by cart-horses: with the glare of the snow it was a scene such as I was to see a year or two later in a similar community in southern Manitoba. In the evening my father lit the church furnace. The roads were still bad on Sunday evening; when I returned to Aberdeen the bus – normally taking an hour and a quarter – took two hours, with much jolting, and was later five hours on the return outward journey. Yet on 12 April it was really warm; we had tea out in the Wendy Villa, the bees coming after the honey.

In traditional clerical diary style my father made occasional mention of familiar birds seen and heard. It may be significant that prior to that hard winter of 1946–47, robins were singing from 25 August to 2 September, and by 5 September he recorded 'robin in stable'. In 1942 robin was not in the stable until 14 October, and was singing from 25–27 January 1943 in changeable, sometimes spring-like weather. Crows were reported on trees on 4 December 1942 (very cold) and on 6 January 1943, 'flying out' on 8 January. On 3 January 1946 ('Colder. wind. frost') 'Crows at home'. Crows went home on 6 December 1950, when after snow and hurricane it turned milder; they were 'on trees' on 26 November 1952. After the winter of 1946–47 two swallows were seen on 7 May: they used to haunt our cart-shed. In 1949 they appeared on 2 May, in 1950 on the 4th, and in 1952 one swallow on the 7th, more on the 9th, and on the 15th were seeking nests. Lapwings were noted on 2 March 1946 and a water wagtail on the 3rd and 17th; in 1950 four wagtails on 17 February, on 18 March 1952 one was seen. Seagulls – generally seen inland following the plough – were on 20 January 1945 noted on the dam (presumably at Faburn) when there was 'frost and more snow'. Larks were heard on 3 March in cold, hard weather. After some signs of spring on 6 February 1951 pigeons were cooing. We used to hear the first cuckoo from the Cairnbeathie wood, repeated by the echo which was a feature of our walled garden underneath the church, but this event does not rate a mention.

So far I have written very little about my father's work as a Presbytery

clerk, sole clerk to the Presbytery of Kincardine O'Neil before the 1929
Union, after the death of Mr McKenzie, Coull; joint clerk for correspondence
to the Presbytery of Deeside from the Union until 1942, thereafter until his
retirement clerk for records in succession to the Reverend J.M. Carlisle,
Torphins South. The minister at Coull, the Reverend R.H. Richmond, then
took on correspondence, being succeeded on his death by the Reverend David
Hamilton, Aboyne. Until 1929 the Presbytery met three times a year for
normal business, summoned by cyclostyled notices of agenda. After 1929 there
were five meetings a year, raised to six in 1933. At times the clerk was
involved in a good deal of coming-and-going besides, for example in the event
of vacancies. It might be appropriate to end this chapter on a philosophical
note, giving some indication of my father's general approach.

I have written earlier of the influence on my father of the Reverend
Dr Adam Semple of Huntly in theological matters. This extended also to
practice and procedure in the church, not so much in the sense of interpreting
church law as in bringing about its felicitous application, particularly when
it came to settling such questions as vacancies, such as now come under the
heading of union and readjustment. Concord would be achieved 'through the
substitution of wisdom and consecrated common-sense for the rule of law and
ecclesiastical domination'. My father was moved to put pen to paper on the
subject following the General Assembly of 1948, when the customary 'distinguished visitor' from H.M. Government, on this occasion Sir Stafford Cripps,
Chancellor of the Exchequer, 'seemed to consider it his duty to impress upon
the Assembly the need for the cultivation of the spiritual freedom of the
individual in an educated democracy. One wonders why the Church, now freed
from State control, should need to be counselled by the State to cherish
freedom. However, several recent decisions in Church Courts and the general
atmosphere of last week's meetings would appear to indicate that the Chancellor's advice is neither inappropriate nor unnecessary. May I illustrate
my theme by a story from Strathbogie?

Shortly after the abolition of Patronage [1874] a vacancy occurred in that region. The congregation, now free to elect their minister, naturally desired to take full advantage of this new freedom, and a thorough-going contest ensued between the radicals of the village and the more Tory-minded rural folk. The farmers won. Their man, the young assistant at Huntly, was elected.

But a flaw was discovered in the procedure towards the election and a protest was lodged with the Presbytery. The Presbytery, foreseeing trouble, met the vacant congregation. The Moderator, [of Presbytery] an old-time authority on procedure, called upon the objectors, and the village shoemaker, producing a bulky manuscript, began to read a detailed account of his objections. The Moderator, testy and impatient, interrupted the speaker more than once, demanding that he keep to the point; but these interruptions tended only to irritate the souter and render him even more loquacious.

Observing the course of events Adam Semple [since 1875 minister at Huntly] rose to pour oil upon the troubled waters. Remarking that Edinburgh Counsel had assured the Border farmer, Dandie Dinmont, that he preferred hill-folk to tell their story in their own way, he begged that the Presbytery should hear the speaker out and then proceed to judgment.

A glance of gratitude was flashed to the peacemaker by the souter who was confident that he had now a friend at court. Noting this signal of alliance, immediately the speech was ended and before the opposition rose to reply the minister asked leave to put a question.

"I have noticed, Sir, that your objections have been directed chiefly against alleged irregularity in the election procedure. Have you any objection to the minister elected - who, I think you know, is my assistant?"

"Na. Nane. Except we thocht him raither young for this important charge". "A mending fault, Sir. But have you no other objection to him?" "Na. We hae naething against the lad. In fac' we raither liket him in the poopit. He was sae modest-like".

"In that case might I warn you that were your objections sustained and this election overturned an even younger man might be voted in at next election? I would, therefore, suggest that, having done your duty to the parish by pointing out these alleged flaws in the committee's procedure, you might now, for the sake of harmony in the congregation, consult with your supporters whether you might now accept the young man elected and sign the Call".

The souter, not blind to danger in the future, with a sweep of his arm beckoned his supporters to the vestry - whence they soon emerged. "Well", said the Moderator, "Have you made a decision?" "I wad like a word wi' Mains first". And approaching the Convener, [of the vacancy committee] the souter accosted him. "Weel, Mains, ye ken ye're wrang. But we've decided that if you an' me shak' han's here i' th' Kirk, there'll be nae mair aboot it".

Mains, also scenting danger and desirous of maintaining prestige, replied, "Aye, Souter, ye say I'm wrang, bit fan ye invoke the Presbytery is it no' the Moderator's business tae pronounce the sentence? However, ye say, Souter, that if we shak' han's here there'll be nae mair words aboot it".

"Surely, Mains, surely. Is't a bargain?"

"Here's ma' han', Souter, an' you an' me for the good o' th' Kirk,
an' as brother elders, will back the young man an' guide him till he
gaithers sense".

Hands were shaken and the bargain sealed. Thus, not only was peace
restored in this hill-foot congregation, but from that day on a new
spirit breathed throughout Strathbogie ... this formerly rather
notorious Presbytery [in which the young man lived to celebrate an
honoured Jubilee.]

There is something in this tale suspiciously reminiscent of Dr William
Alexander's Johnny Gibb of Gushetneuk, first published in 1871, four years
before Adam Semple went to Huntly. Indeed my father had, many years before
writing the above, and following an intervention in the Assembly just then
past, lent the book to the Reverend (later Doctor) A.J.H. Gibson, joint
secretary of the Church and Ministry Department with particular responsibility
for the Maintenance of the Ministry Committee. Acknowledging a letter from
my father while on holiday at Findhorn in August 1931, - and doing so in a
distinctly admonitory tone - Mr Gibson then laid aside his official hat and added:

As to Johnnie Gibb. I have read it all with great interest,
pleasure, amusement often and appreciation always. To shew my appreciation I have taken the liberty of handing it on to my wife's
sister's husband, who is a farmer near here, and a great reader...
His wife was over here this afternoon and happened to say that she is
getting "bits of Gushetnook" read to her. Her husband is enjoying
it greatly...

My father himself succeeded in bringing about a very similar consummation
in a Deeside vacancy controversy, which ended happily with one side crossing
the floor to shake hands with the other.

CHAPTER NINE

Whatsoever thy hand findeth to do

Assembly time: manse children's tasks; garden and
grounds; recreations; the minister's wife; condition of
manses; dependants' grants: award and withdrawal.

Chapter 9

The fact that the General Assembly of the Church of Scotland met in Edinburgh towards the end of May presented problems for a country minister who still had a large garden and grounds, particularly if he worked the glebe and kept livestock. In our time there was no longer even a bachelor 'minister's man' resident in the chaumer with its adjacent dry closet which opened on to the dung-court, let alone a man with a family in a cottage across the road. Fortunately, by the time my father as a Presbytery clerk was attending more regularly, his children were old enough to keep things going at home. Over the years his became a familiar face in the Assembly Hall, his role often that of critic of the establishment as represented by those recently referred to in a Life and Work article as the 'mandarins of 121'. On the whole the latter did not hold this against him, and relations were amicable. Supplying information for his own brief biography for the Record of the Arts Class 1901-1905 (University of Aberdeen) published in 1951 to celebrate their Bajans' Jubilee, he included among his minor recreations 'Upholding the rights and privileges of the private member in General Assembly contra bureaucracies and circumtabular confederacies'. The British Weekly, reporting on the 1938 Assembly, said 'Mr. Donald is not to be cowed by official frowns, and the Assembly "insisted on fair play" for him generously - with less portentous assumption of the rebel's rôle he might become one of our best and most welcome debaters...'

As he grew older my father habitually carried a knobkerrie, its inlaid 'knob' carved by an invalid parishioner, James Burnett, Bogerfoul, who died after his parents, Mr and Mrs 'Andy' Burnett, moved to Tillybirlock, Midmar. Once during an Assembly debate my father had been using it to emphasise a point. There was a jocular intervention from the floor: was it permitted to brandish a lethal weapon in the Assembly Hall? My father's lightning response was 'This is not a lethal weapon. It is the mace of the Presbytery of Deeside'. Some years later, during his retirement, he was lunching with my husband and me in an Edinburgh hotel when an ex-Moderator, the Very Reverend Dr Roy Sanderson, happened to pass our table and paused to say 'I see you've still got your stick!' 'Oh, I never go anywhere without it.' His last speech was in the Assembly of 1963, representing the then Presbytery of Deeside and Donside, when the Moderator was the Very Reverend Professor James S. Stewart. The Report of the Inter-Church Relations Committee had emphasised promising advances from both sides in relations between Protestants and Catholics. Having been brought up in a partly Catholic area, my father – then in his eighty-first year – rose to support this trend, speaking of the neighbourliness experienced in his youth. In contrast, he deprecated such anti-Catholic manifestations as the slogan daubed on the fences of an Edinburgh football ground : 'Down with the Pope.' Here he was 'buzzed': he had exceeded his speaking time. Relating this afterwards my father added with a twinkle 'Of course Stewart is chaplain to the Hearts'.

In the early days we children would be asked what we would like him to bring us from Edinburgh, as reward for our efforts. In 1927 when I was barely five years old, not yet at school, my sister Wendy, aged 10, wrote to my father on 26 May at his Edinburgh hotel:

> I am writing this letter for Heather. She says this. 'I would like an exercise book for drawing girls on and a pencil. I have done all that you told me to...'

Two days earlier Wendy had written:

> Heather was very pleased with her instructions she got from you. She told me when I came home from school she had watched the chickens carefully and gathered sticks... The chickens are fine they are getting feathers on their wings and jump out into their sitting-room themselves but there was one tonight that you took out of the egg some sick kind. I took it into the fire and warmed it then I took it out to the brooder and is a little better. I can not see the one with the bad foot so I think it must be all right. I have filled their trays three times tonight so I hope that will do them until the morning. The tempeture (sic) is between eighty and ninety. One chicken caught a fly tonight and I saw it eating it up. I sprinkle some egg shell in the sitting-room floor and they eat it up as quick as anything.

These were newly-hatched chickens which had been transferred from the incubator to a two-compartment brooder in the field next the steading. At one end of this a lamp burned continuously; the chickens huddled round it at night but during the day moved down a tiny staircase to the 'sitting-room' next door. Later, when the chickens were stronger, the wire-netting 'run' would be placed next the brooder.

In the later letter of 26 May Wendy had also written on her own behalf, first reporting on the chickens:

> Today it has been a little cold in the morning. It was just like frost when I went to feed the chicks so I did not open the glass. Yesterday Mamma gave them a worm, they were all frightened at it but one took it in its mouth then the others chased after it and soon they ate it up. None of the chicks have died yet but there is a little white one that is not very fit... I shall be glad to see you home again on Saturday. I would like you to bring me a chubby umbrella and I will give you what I have saved up when you come home. Betty would like a Reaves (sic) paint-box. She thinks you might get it cheaper in Edinburgh ... Boysie [Craig: not yet at Fettes and with Betty going by train to school at Banchory] got a paper from Mr. Marr tonight about train fares and you can travel first class for five and eight [to Aberdeen]. Boysie does not want anything just now from Edinburgh...

On the back of this my economical mother had written:

> Just give children the money and I will spend it - perhaps blazers or something for Wendy and Heather Eh? They would need to be big. Everything all right. We will not go Stonehaven this week. Chicks need dinner...

Her elderly parents were then living in Stonehaven, and sometimes she would take one of us with her to visit them on a Saturday, giving my Aunt Ann a day off. For the young visitor my grandfather always produced a shilling: practically the only pocket-money we acquired, although a weekly sixpence for each was deposited in the school's War Savings scheme. Not only the livestock had to be looked after during my father's absence. My mother added a note on a parishioner who was ill: 'Mr. C. improving. Betty went last night and told Mrs. C. you were writing asking...'

During the 1935 General Assembly Wendy and I had rather different pre-occupations, mainly garden-planting and three sheep requiring special attention; one had lost its own lamb and was not too willing to accept a substitute. I seem to recall one Assembly when I had to milk such a ewe morning and evening, before and after school. Wendy wrote first to my father:

> The sweet-peas arrived with the carrier this evening about 8.30
> so if it keeps fine Heathie and I will plant them tomorrow... Dandy
> etc. have been behaving very well. She is always ready to come in
> at nights. Heather's sheep has not been behaving just the best. I
> have had to tether it again as it always walked away from us and some-
> times ran so that the lamby would not have got a drink but however I
> put the corn in the trough and all three sheep came to eat so I caught
> hold of it and then after some condoodles we got it securely fixed.
> Heather had a job with it in the morning and she had not very much time
> to waste with it but it will be alright for tomorrow. I will shift it
> to fresh pieces of grass. Heather and I have got the seeds safely
> sown...

I in turn wrote from bed on the night of 22 May:

> We have planted everything except Beet. There are some eruptions
> on the carrot plot which look like worm holes. Will I tramp them down?
> We have had some disagreements with the <u>sheep</u> (singular!) It would not
> come, even to Wendy, so we have tethered it. Since then, in careering
> round it has caught me with the rope and landed me on my back, and has
> lassoed Wendy's ankle, which is blue now. We hope to be more successful
> tomorrow.

Apparently I then dropped off to sleep but continued:

> <u>Thursday morning</u>: We shifted the sheep (plural) last night, the
> Football Field ones into the Churchyard Field. I have been giving them
> corn at 5 o'clock. Is that all right?...

Letters, of course, travelled quickly in those days, so that any reply would

arrive timeously.

Two years later we were at it again. Wendy wrote to my father on 19 May

1937:

> I have now planted all the potatoes. I had to get 5lbs. extra so
> with that I had just 4 left over. The ones Heather brought weren't so
> far sprouted as our own ones. H. is bringing sweet-peas this evening
> so I'll get them in tonight and probably I'll get the lettuces sown
> too... I mowed the lawn next football field yesterday. Miss Robertson
> [her former teacher at Lumphanan School, sometimes a stormy relationship]
> came along the road on her cycle in the evening and cried up if I was
> coming too, so I told her I would come for a short distance if she
> finished the lawn for me. This she did willingly... This morning I fixed
> the wirenetting of the cornfield and put wire netting up at the top gate
> which is now quite secure and I barrowed the other gate to its place.
> ...The corn has not appeared yet but everything is ready now. I'll shift
> the cross hogg etc. from the football into the rushes field for a while
> this evening and give them an eat on the way...

The cross hogg merited special treatment; as earlier noted she always

produced two splendid lambs. My letter to my father of 20 May 1937 announced

'There is one new lamb — that makes 14 and all the ewes lambed now'.

Garden planting depended a good deal upon the weather. In 1932 three rows of shallots were planted on 24 February, a fine, windy day; yet the first of April was very stormy with snow. After the severe winter of 1945-6, with snow and sleet until after mid-March, my father was planting shallots on 26 March ('mild, sunny. Weather gaw'.) and sowing lettuce and parsley next day. The following year both March and April were very cold, with occasional frost and sleet; on 4 May there was snow and sleet but four or five days later it became suddenly warm and sultry and after a thunderstorm it was very hot on the 11th. Sowing and planting that year began with peas and shallots on 15 April and was completed at intervals by Assembly time except for late potatoes. Yet in 1948 the shallots and peas were in on 12 March. Again in 1951 after another stormy spring most of this work was done at the last minute: my father left the garden at 3.30 p.m. on 21 May and caught the 4 o'clock bus for Aberdeen and so to Edinburgh. Carrot and beetroot seed went in early in June, swedes and late potatoes after that.

All work in the garden and grounds and on the glebe was done with fairly conventional tools until in the last few years a farmer who prepared the land and sowed the crop brought his own machinery - this was sometimes on the large side for our approaches. Lawn grass was cut with a small mower that required pushing; rough grass and thistles with a scythe; hedges with secateurs and hand-shears. Perhaps the most revolutionary tool acquired was a flexible grass rake. For trimming the lawn edges we were latterly permitted to borrow the finer sheep-shears, instead of using grass-shears. The progress in machinery by 1937 is indicated in the post-script to Wendy's letter of 19 May; during the cycle run with her former teacher 'Miss Robertson told me she had seen men demonstrating a new way of planting potatoes. They had a chute thing with a hole at the foot which went into the earth and the potato was put in at the top and slid into the earth itself. This saved bending down'. But it says a good deal for the quality of our garden tools that those which my father retained when he retired to Edinburgh (for many years he kept the garden

at the Retired Ministers' Residence) are still in use. We still grow
sweet-peas, too, on the frames which came from my grandfather's garden in
Larbert about 1920: we four children were photographed in front of them
about 1925.

In our days at Lumphanan, although certain fruits and vegetables could
be bought or picked wild locally, or from the vans which circulated, it was
assumed that most people grew their own basic quota of the better known
varieties. Our first fresh tomatoes, still quite a novelty, came with the
Aboyne butcher's van. I recall my mother describing the reaction of her
father Alexander Reid, an expert gardener, often a prizewinner at horticul-
tural shows in the Mearns and in Aberdeen, to the first tomatoes he grew:
he tasted one in the garden and promptly spat it out on the ground, whereupon
a scattering of fresh seedlings duly popped up. Once we grew a few tomatoes
in the south-facing sunny windows of our linen-room.

As a rule, hired labour in the garden - as distinct from the glebe and
grounds - was used mainly for the spring digging; in later days when less
family help was available some paid labour was devoted to planting, or hoeing
paths. Until after the 1939-45 war this cost a shilling an hour; afterwards
one and sixpence. The other basic expenses, once the tools were acquired,
were seeds, plants (mostly brassicas - these tended sometimes to be 'eaten
by rabbits') or the occasional renewal of berry bushes or strawberry plants,
some fertiliser to supplement horse-dung and leaf-mould, wire-netting for peas
and the maintenance of mower and shears. My father specialised in shallots
and would perhaps sell a few: he notes getting twenty shillings for an unspeci-
fied quantity of these in 1947. In 1942 the surplus was $22\frac{1}{2}$lb. There was
always a demand in Aberdeen for our Christmas roses, and boxfuls of blooms
would also be posted at Christmas to friends. Fairly typical is the tally of
expenses noted (perhaps not complete) for 1946: £2.16.3 for seeds and plants,
£2.5.0 for labour. In 1947 £4.1.10 went for seeds, plants and 17 currant and

18 gooseberry bushes, but the nurseryman at Banchory, Mr Petrie, gave my
father 34 sweet-pea plants 'as a luck-penny' when he went to pay his bill.
(Such bills were generally paid in person; my father seldom used his cheque-
book.) Labour that year came to £1.5.6. As to tool maintenance, in 1952
the village blacksmith, George Ellis, charged 3/6 for covering the mower-box,
sixpence for sharpening the hand-shears and 12/- for the new grass rake. The
mower was latterly sent by train to Aboyne to be sharpened.

In her letter of 26 May 1927 Wendy had reported to my father on the
garden flowers, including the blue violas which 'make a pretty corner'. These
had been developed by my grandfather, and several parishioners still have
them, as do Craig and I in our gardens. Almost forty years later, when Wendy
was in hospital in Aberdeen and one of the surgeons attending her, Mr James
Philip, had a country home at Lumphanan, he was setting off for town on a
Monday morning when his neighbour, Mrs Fred Christie, came running up with a
bunch of the blue violas: 'You'll just take these in to Wendy'. They were
personally delivered. Latterly Wendy specialised in carnations. A feature
of the garden was the old-fashioned climbing and rambler roses against the
high stone walls, including a Gloire de Dijon and a La France, at their
base long stretches of violets, some purple, some white. Chrysanthemums
had to be taken indoors in full bloom before the first frosts in October;
these wintered in the wash-house, as did scarlet geraniums. In what we called
'Mama's garden' - the plot under the wall to the left just inside the garden
gate, she grew Lady Gay roses, Lily of the Valley and Japanese anemones.

As has been noted, the minister's garden was by statute regarded as
possessing a particular sanctity, being surrounded by a stone wall which the
heritors had to maintain. 'Grounds' - in our case the area directly in front
of and around the house, - meeting with the approach to the church - required
a good deal of maintenance while not qualifying for any special protection.
Yet trees therein were sacrosanct in that they could not be felled without

permission. Some of the difficulties met with before our grounds attained
the high standard which they rapidly lost after my father's retirement have
already been suggested in my second chapter.

For the first year or two after 1913 the winding 'carriage road' up from
the iron gates through the lawn to the house was maintained; my mother once
recalled her brother George working on it. hoeing weeds, stripped to the waist
during the hot summer of 1914. Later the lower lawn was fenced off as pasture,
the driveway there disappearing. Surrounded on two sides by the hawthorn
hedge which, initially cut down drastically, thickened and, with a low fence.
provided a secure barrier for animals, this area still contained, among others,
the more ornamental trees considered appropriate to a 'gentleman's residence':
two arbor vitae, an Irish yew and a rather special elm which still defies
the 'Dutch' disease. With its top removed to admit more light it spread
umbrella-like in a large circle, particularly beautiful in autumn when the
leaves turned pale gold. Three sycamores there were cut down early on, the
stumps for long afterwards producing new shoots with young leaves. These
small forests were inexplicably named by Craig and Betty in their infancy the
Kangagongs. Betty when tiny succeeded in climbing right to the top of the
central arbor vitae tree, known thereafter as 'Betty's tree'. A regular task
here at the end of the year was the raking of leaves, removed in a deep wheelbarrow to mature for leaf-mould.

Before he retired my father planted a row of spruce at the bottom where
an L-shaped patch extending up the east side had been levelled during the
1914-18 war for growing potatoes. Later there was an attempt to make a bad-
minton court there for my mother: this proved impracticable because of the
perennial drainage problem. Water tended to run down off the public road, and
it was many years after a drain was laid within the grounds parallel to the
road that it was discovered why it had been ineffective: an over-anxious
labourer had carefully placed each pipe right up against the next one. Writing

to advise me about drainage on our Dorset patch my father warned me to leave a space between the pipes the width of two (old) pennies. Further up, in the north-east corner of the lower lawn, my father planted a rowan tree to mark the coronation of Queen Elizabeth in 1953. Here and there in the lower lawn clumps of daffodils, single and double snowdrops, one jonquil plant and a scattering of crocuses came up each spring.

In 1931 the area round the house was gravelled with pink granite chips from the gravel pit at Parkhill where William Mearns, Mosshead, supervised the operation. I can recall at school one of the 'boarded out' boys at Mearns's remarking that he had just spent Saturday working on 'our' gravel. This was very effective in keeping weeds down. Then one Sunday afternoon, the first of August 1948, a deluge of rain which caused the Lumphanan burn to flood all along its course from Shalgsyde to Dess (a local boy was alleged to have picked up a trout in the street) swept away much of this good gravel. Its replacement never looked so well, the new gravel being more finely ground.

A recurring problem on the top lawns, kept neatly mown, was molehills. Over the years various remedies were resorted to. Once Craig, home from abroad and planning to go fishing with his small daughter, discovered that his jar of carefully gathered worms had been purloined in this cause. Also to be mown were the small grass plot east of the house, continuing round the north side to the clock golf course at the back with its central half-coconut, replenished from the coconut-shy at the Aboyne Games.

At the corner of the west top lawn was placed in our time the sundial made by 'Postie' Lawson, a virtually accurate timepiece. We left it in situ. The pair of matching white pots, one in the centre of each circular plot on the top lawns, were annually filled with scarlet geraniums and dark blue lobelia, the plots with red dwarf dahlias and yellow calceolaria. By the garden gate, under the ivied churchyard wall, was a border of perennial flowers: crimson peonies, deep pink old-fashioned bush roses with behind them the blue delphiniums and at the gate a white bush rose. And from 1933,

on the slight mound at the curve of the west lawn, Finan's font. At the
north-east corner of the east front lawn, by the gate in the hedge (always
called the blue gate although it was repainted brown in 1929) at my mother's
instigation my father had planted a shapely sweet-briar rose. Another was
trained against the wall at the gates of the dung-court; their rose-hips in
autumn were as colourful as the flowers. In the hedge opposite this grew a
tiny pale pink rose, very prickly.

The last storm in our time to cause some damage in our grounds was the
hurricane of January 1953. Friday night 30-31st was wild, the wind accompanied by snow and later frost. Our telephone was cut off, the wire down.
By Sunday morning the wind was subsiding, but the trail of devastation in
woods still standing after the war had spread far and wide on Deeside. At
the manse the main task was clearing fallen branches and twigs. A storm
which about 1930 affected mostly the back of the house, the church approach
and the churchyard, might be noted in passing for the record. My father
wrote a note for the local paper:

> During the thunderstorm of Saturday morning a fireball struck the
> Manse of St. Finan's, Lumphanan, damaging the rain water pipes and
> roof lead gutters. Only at one point however did it enter the Manse
> doing small damage. [Some paintwork was scorched] The lightning seems
> to have been attracted by the metal water piping, passed along and down
> same into the rain water drain pipe which is completely shattered. After
> passing a short distance underground the flash emerged through the gravel
> of the Church approach which in a circle of two feet diameter is rendered
> soft and porous. From this point it leaped through the churchyard gate
> tearing up surface turf for several yards and slightly damaging two
> grave railings. The bark of a tall larch tree growing in the churchyard
> [later cut down] has also been peeled off and scattered in all directions.

My father generally took upon himself the responsibility of 'keeping'
another part of the 'policies', officially a cart road to the glebe but also
- as mentioned in Chapter 2 - a right of way for a footpath from the Aboyne
road to the church on the west side of the garden boundary, entered by the
gate of the 'rushes' field under the beech tree. At the church end a tall
iron gate gave access to a flight of steps up into the churchyard. This
path was known as the 'green road' and was neatly cut - sometimes even rolled

and the edge trimmed. On a Saturday night any animals in the field would
be moved elsewhere, the sheep often into the fenced-off lower lawn, adding
to the peaceful eve-of-Sabbath 'sheep may safely graze' aspect of the neatly tidied grounds. Similarly for the most part he kept the churchyard approach
from the Burnside road, where early on my mother planted snowdrops. In his
last years my father put in spruces and an arbor vitae hedge on the west side,
filling the gaps between the rather rambling hawthorn trees. Even trimming
the grass edges there and in the front approach took a good deal of time.

We each, when still at home, or back on holiday, had our particular
tasks in garden, grounds and glebe, all taking a share in cutting grass, raking gravel or leaves, weeding and picking fruit. Once when the elder children
were very small my father offered them a penny per hundred for picking dande-
lion heads, but soon he perceived that he was likely to be bankrupted, and
called a halt to the enthusiastic campaign. But he obviously imagined that
manse children were worth the Dependants' Grants which began to be paid during
the first war and were cut off in 1929. Craig specialised in pruning the hawthorn hedges; one year he gave me the wherewithal to purchase two tuppenny
ice-cream sliders for gathering up the prunings. He also scythed thistles
on the glebe. Both these tasks I inherited for a period. Wendy liked planting flowers: when wild primroses were still plentiful in places she put them
here and there, and she transplanted daffodils and double snowdrops to the
bank by the church approach. At the end of the day, when my father was retiring, a regular churchyard visitor to the grave of her small boy came panting
up the back road: 'Oh Wendy, Wendy! If I could just hae some o' the double
snowdrops!' and was willingly given a plant or two.

We had our recreations, too, the grounds and glebe — not to mention the
burn which bordered the latter — furnishing various favourite spots. The
burn was not well enough stocked with trout to permit of frequent fishing, but
after heavy rain one could be reasonably sure of catching something. Craig was
the best fisher — although my father notes getting ten trout over two days,
Saturday and Monday 10 and 12 August, in 1946. We did not, of course, have

exclusive fishing rights. I tried only once by myself and was so excited when I landed a small trout that I rushed up to the house with it straight away. The postman, Alex Fraser, chanced to be there and hooked it on to his sliding scales: it registered four ounces. My mother cooked it in oatmeal for my tea. The burn offered other delights including a small pool by a waterfall, and a lilac tree. At the bridge under the chestnut tree the school-children on their way home (from the old school) could play the game immortalised by A.A. Milne as 'Pooh-sticks'.

In winter we tobogganed either in our nursery field which sloped very steeply to the burn, or in Cairnbeathie's field to the south where one got a longer run. My father had made two large sledges with steel runners, and there was also a small American-style toboggan which I suspect came from Auntie Bee, the source of many of our toys. My father's — and later Wendy's — winter sport was curling, the local pond being part of the moat at the Peel Ring. Craig also had skates. The girls had skipping-ropes, and the hoops ('girds') made by the blacksmith.

In summer there was croquet and cricket, clock golf and pony-rides, and Wendy had a bow and arrow. We had a swing either under the spreading elm or on the top lawn in the copper beech, similarly decapitated for the sake of light and become a spreading umbrella. Only briefly were we all together. We used to get a holiday from Lumphanan School on the day of the Aboyne Games, but we did not attend this event until we were older. Instead we drove up to Quithelhead and had a picnic tea in Miss Helen Kemp's garden at the cottage. Blaeberry picking would also be an excuse for a picnic, perhaps on the Glenmillan hill or in the Craigton wood. When Auntie Bee came to stay in August we would hire Mr Jamieson, the hall-keeper, to drive us in his car up Deeside, returning with quantities of heather which was made up into small individual posies for the children in Auntie Bee's orthopaedic hospital.

But the gardening instinct was not to be subdued: the elder three each had a small wheelbarrow, and there were miniature garden tools. Craig, on

being shown a fine array of toys by a small contemporary he had been taken
to visit, surveyed them all and then put the question: 'But what do you
dig in the ground with?' I acquired a bucket and spade when on the first of
two holidays at my grandfather's in Stonehaven before he died in 1933. Wendy
had had similar childhood sojourns but on the whole did not care to stay away
from home. Yet it was with sadness that she wrote from Stonehaven that Auntie
Bee had taken them to church where the minister had said there would be no
more sea.

Indoors we had a modest number of good toys: Dobbin, a wooden horse
that could be pushed; (the rocking-horse at Lumphanan manse described by
Amy Stewart Fraser belonged to our predecessors.) There was also a small
dappled grey horse called Mollie; wooden locomotive engines: Wendy, accustomed to seeing 'Gordon Highlander' and 'Andrew Bain' passing on the Deeside
Line, called hers 'Mary Carmichael': Craig's grandchildren play with it; a
navy-blue tin Rolls-Royce, about six inches long, complete with chauffeur;
Mother's wooden toy cradle with her doll inside — china head and white kid
limbs and body; Craig's Meccano set. I collected and inherited a number of
dolls, furry animals and gollywogs (some home-made) which would be perched
at one end of the nursery sofa 'all higgledy-piggledy' as Dr Argo once remarked.
Earlier Betty had a French doll sent by Auntie Bee named Noël Badweather.
There was a miniature upright piano and a cardboard Noah's Ark. We had ping-
pong, blow football, various board and card games, including two editions of
Happy Families, bricks for building, chessboard, bagatelle and later Corinthian
bagatelle. Tops made out of cotton reels were duly replaced by yo-yo's. At
one of the nursery windows hung an Aeolian harp known as the 'toy-toys'.
Betty and I liked drawing — although Wendy was a better artist than I (she
once produced a classic version of The Wreck of the Hesperus as a weekend
exercise for Banchory School) — and we made paper dolls: Dolly Dimples.
We read The Rainbow, which my father would bring from Aberdeen on Thursday
after attending an Education Committee meeting, and The Children's Newspaper,

obtained then at the railway bookstall at Banchory, later locally. My

mother never cancelled the order for the latter, read it with interest and

passed it on to the boys who for a time brought the milk from East Kincraigie.

Craig went off to Fettes in 1928 and just before his first summer

vacation, when I was newly seven years old, I wrote to him: (evidently my

father was then in Edinburgh at some meeting)

> Dear Dumpledum,
>
> I got such a surprise last night when your letter arrived. I was
> through in the nursery playing with my Dolly Dimples when Mama cried
> me through then she told me that it was a letter from Dump. I hope
> you are enjoying vourself at Edinbura. We are coming down to the
> station to meet you. The girls say that they are getting on very well
> without you but I don't... I said to Betty that Daddy would be writing
> a letter to ask what we would like to bring home from Edinbura. I
> would of siad Dumpledum. [The spelling and grammar now deteriorate]
> I was out side picking buttercups and daysies in the morning and in
> the afternoon for the black boll. There is a bird in the wall beside
> the meel barl it has been very sunny today and you can amagon who many
> logers is at burnside. there has been boys fishing in our burn .. we
> had Mrs king's boy here today.
>
> Much love From little Dump.

The 'black bowl' - wide and shallow - was always in the centre of the

dining-room table. The original one was of glass, but one winter it was

cracked by frost and was replaced by a pottery - much inferior - article.

Small flowers were floated in it, or perhaps a single red rose. My mother

would leave forget-me-nots to wilt slightly before putting them in the black

bowl; they would then sit up very straight. One of these arrangements was

once much admired by Joseph Farquharson, then laird of Finzean and by then

promoted from A.R.A. to Royal Academician. A print of his 'Highland Raiders -

The Grouse at Home' hung on one wall of the dining-room. Our cousin Neta

(Kemp) Hamilton has told us how Joseph would fare forth in an Inverness cape

and set up his easel in the Finzean snow.

We girls were taken in turn by our parents to Founder's Day at Fettes,

my turn coinciding with my eleventh birthday. This was Craig's last year

when he took several prizes. Only parents attended the luncheon; I was

thrilled to be left in Craig's study with Eiffel Tower lemonade and sandwiches.

In August 1934 our parents actually were on holiday together. My father had not been in good health and my mother joined him for a long weekend at Cullen, where they stayed at Cathay House. They visited Cullen House gardens and also saw something of our old Burnside neighbours Mr and Mrs James Anderson, whose son, an Inspector on the railways, used to wave to us from the guard's van of the royal train. I think our Aunt Ann was with us, but we four were in charge of the parish. It was Betty, then nearly nineteen and on vacation from the University of Aberdeen, who wrote to my father:

> We all hope you and Mama had a fine weekend. We got on fine. The people had the baptism after the service on Sunday. When I saw the crowd of people – 3 men and 3 women and the two babies – I was frightened there wouldn't be enough seats in the study – but there were. Mrs. J. of Camphill and her son called yesterday – Boysie received them ... Mrs. C. was apologising for not coming to the church and occupying the Camphill pew but she is an Episcopalian. I'm sorry I didn't notice your P.S. about the cat till a good while later in the day because directly Mama left I caught it, skinned it and made soup of it – it was good soup – everyone enjoyed it...

This alleged culinary triumph on her part was of course pure nonsense. I can remember my mother's return: she was on the afternoon 'school' train when Wendy and I joined it at Banchory, and I recall noticing how white her hands were after a few days' absence from the kitchen range and other fire grates. When going out to some special occasion she would look at her hands and say 'I'll just wash a tea-towel': this meant soaking it in Hudson's Powder. When first married she had had a maid ('with streamers' Auntie Bee once told me) – or rather a succession of maids – but they didn't stay for any length of time, partly because, she said, they didn't like being left alone in our rambling house. One result of this was that small children might be taken with her, perhaps to a wedding. One of the maids, who stayed at least long enough to 'join the church', is next heard of working in a hospital in Morocco. An indication of the wages expected by a good maid was

given in a letter my mother wrote to my father when in December 1922 — six
months after I was born (we were all born at home) she was in Aberdeen
Royal Infirmary recovering from a hernia operation. She had been chatting
to the maid in charge of the doctors' residence: 'I had Lizzie thro' seeing
me this morning. She would like to come to my Baby!! If only we were that
we could have a gem like her but never mind something may happen some day —
if only we are all well meantime we will manage... I would imagine nothing
less than £40 [a year]...' We never did have another maid. The average nett
stipend over the years 1913-21 had been £200.16.5. She had been occupying
part of her unaccustomed leisure in planning how to reorganise her housekeep-
ing: '...I believe after all a stove would save some kitchen work sometimes —
if it even helped Sunday to be more Sunday and restful... There will be
plenty ways for all your odd coppers so we must be careful. By the time
everything is settled there won't be much left... We will need to get steps
before the Summer clean up as I am constantly stretching to corners taking
down cobwebs. That reminds me you might remove the feather duster from the
corner at the kitchen door — put it upstairs else it gets so damp...' We
did, in fact, acquire a three burner Valor Perfection paraffin stove, with
an oven over two burners, and a pair of household steps.

She expected to be home the following weekend: 'If Nurse could stay
'till Sat^y· that would be all right. You have no Sunday School Sunday so
I would not have an early start and I would not need to hurry as there would
be no visitors that day. Then there would just be 3 days schooling after
that so I could have a lazy time...' Nurse Durward, a diminutive local lady
known as 'Maggie Durra'd', had been left in charge of the household, an
arrangement to be complicated by the fact that Wendy, aged five, originally
sent to stay with our Aunt Janet Burnett, by then removed from Finzean to
Easter Ardoe, Banchory Devenick, had been homesick and had to be brought back.
'Poor wee Soul', wrote my mother, 'She would be happy last night with her
Baby'. On the contrary, one of Nurse Durward's preoccupations was keeping

Wendy out of Craig's Meccano set. I recall in 1935 my mother sending Wendy out to attend Nurse's funeral in the old churchyard at St Finan's, where she is commemorated, along with her mother and sister, by a small granite heart inscribed 'Mother, Mary, Maggie'.

My mother's reference to visitors showed that by that time contact with parishioners was well established, and indeed she wrote from hospital of a constant stream of visitors there from Lumphanan. In those pre-National Health Service days patients provided a good deal of their own nourishment '...I have plenty of eggs I am sure so don't worry sending. I can ask Auntie J. if I need...' She was thinking ahead to Christmas: '...We can send eggs to the Bruces [Edinburgh friends who used to holiday with the Kings at Knappyround] and chickens to the usual people. It is the plucking that is the business...'

Although evidence that survived from my mother's pre-1913 days was mostly of an artistic nature - she painted in oils either on canvas, on pottery plaques or, as was the fashion then, on mirror glass, later framed in plush - her later leisure activity (if such it could be called) took the form of carpentry or furniture restoring. My father once gave her a small saw for her birthday (which, naturally, we still have). For her, latterly, the day of a Presbytery meeting was almost a day off; earlier it was a chance to scrub the old cement floor of the kitchen, replaced by composition, which could be polished, in 1929. For this she would plan what she called some 'nefarious business': perhaps the rubbing down and treating with oil and turpentine of a good piece of furniture that had been crudely varnished. This was more satisfying than the everyday chores of a rambling non-electric house. Her treadle Singer sewing-machine was mostly used for repair work, but crumpled in one of its drawers was her sampler ('Mary J. Reid 1893') which she used purely for reference when numbering new linen or embroidering initials on tea-cloths, towels, table-napkins or other smaller items. The flower motifs were copied also - until the fashionable wave of 'lazy daisies' overtook such

painstaking detail. She would make her own tea-cloths, finished with open-
work hemstitching or with the addition of some lace border made in her youth.
On the plainer side she also, of course, made by hand my father's flannel
'linders' and knitted or re-footed socks. I still find the treadle machine
more suited to my own capabilities than the faster-moving electric equivalent.

Before her marriage my mother had done very little cooking or baking,
but certainly by the time I was conscious she was expert at the plain fare
on which we normally lived. This was typically Scottish: excellent soups
based on 'a pound of spaul and a bone' from the butcher's van, or on one of
our own fowls, and vegetables from the garden; (when small I was once sent
out for a bunch of chives and returned with a posy of purple flowers); stews
done in a large steel saucepan on top of the range, similarly steak mince;
steamed suet pastry dumpling filled with beef or mince; (steak pie would be
sent direct from butcher to baker to be covered with puff pastry: this was
a favourite entertaining dish); occasionally a milky rice soup, or a marrow-
bone stock to which a tin of tomatoes, shallots and some sago were added;
baked white fish, or herrings fried in oatmeal or 'soused'; various 'made-
up' dishes such as galantine or salads; in season we would receive gifts
of game or sometimes salmon. As there was no refrigeration, only the south-
facing larder with stone shelves and wire mesh over the window, some dishes
would be repeated, perhaps with variation, until finished. All meat was of
good quality and certainly relatively cheap, although my mother tended to
compare things with pre-war prices. I think we enjoyed the boiled beef as
much as the occasional gigot of mutton or roast beef. We had all kinds of
milk pudding, sometimes sponge pudding or roly-poly with jam, and fresh fruit
in season, with on Sundays the special treat of tinned peaches - perhaps
arranged as 'Melba' - or trifle.

My mother was an excellent self-taught baker. She seldom made cake, but
her girdle or oven scones, crumpets or oatcakes were certainly the best I have
ever tasted. Before I was of school age I would play in the kitchen while

she was busy with the girdle on the range: there was a low cupboard fitted
into the window, where the indoor paraffin apparatus was kept, and on top
of that I could set out the various buttons from the button-box kept in the
press. The box was a former tea-caddy, with portraits on either side of
Princess Mary and the Earl of Harewood. When finishing a bowlful of crumpet
batter my mother would call me over and a last batch of tiny circles would
be dropped on to the girdle: 'This one's for Peter Rabbit...' I then scraped
out the bowl. If it were oatcake day I liked to tidy up the board on which
she rolled them out: this I imagined was 'a meal'. Then there might be
shortbread, made in the round baking tins I still use with their raised
inscriptions PAISLEY FLOUR. The oblong tins for oven scones were/are
inscribed WATSONS BUTTERMILK TOFFEE. For special occasions cherry cake
would be purchased by the pound from the Home and Colonial Stores in Aberdeen,
although of course the local bakery and the Torphins baker's van supplied us
with bread, buns and biscuits.

A proforma reporting on the condition of manses in the Presbytery of
Deeside in 1947, completed in typescript (I have the carbon copy) from information supplied by ministers, shows that eleven manses out of eighteen still
had oil-lamps. This excluded three redundant manses which were let, at least
one of which, the Stothert Memorial manse at Lumphanan, still had no electricity. 'Assessment points against' manses averaged nearly 7; Lumphanan
manse had 9 points against, as had Birse; Braemar East (about to be sold
following the 1946 union) and Coull (subsequently sold) had 10; worst was
Logie Coldstone, with 11. A typed footnote stated 'All manses appear to be
burdensome for the stipends received'. Thirteen complained of large grounds,
ten were 'difficult to work'. Against Lumphanan my father's comment had been
'Rambling but could be reconstructed'. He had proposed this at the time of
the 1929 Union. The printed proforma had a note 'N.B. All over 7 points
against are suspect, too large and out of date'. But for the war, electricity
at least would have been available earlier - at a price. I seem to recall

that the Grampian scheme's original charge was tenpence a unit. Only the
cost of heating a minister's study could in time be set against income tax.

At least paraffin lamps gave out a modicum of heat, and were much used
in frosty winters at strategic points to prevent water-pipes from freezing.
The forty-gallon paraffin drum in the coal house would be replenished at
intervals by the oil company's tanker-lorry: we latterly had a local Shell-Mex
station. My mother would amuse us when small by her report 'Ethyl was here
today. She didn't knock, she just walked in'.

As a child the phrase 'many mansions' meant to me only a vision of piles
of red tins on a polished floor. We went through many tins of Mansion Polish
in our time, particularly over our fifty yards of linoleumed passages. In
one of the 'blank-for-notes' pages in one of my mother's cookery books was
a recipe in her writing: 'Floor Polish (Mr. Park's)': the retired minister
of Deskford still cared for the floors of the amply-proportioned house at
Torphins which had been bought to fit the manse furniture. The recipe demanded
equal quantities of Linseed oil, Turpentine, Methylated Spirit and Paraffin.
'Shake well'. At twelve I took over Betty's polishing tasks when at home;
Wendy preferred 'scullery' work, as our school syllabus had it. I had the
advantage, for a term, before leaving Lumphanan school, of Miss Elma Robertson's
course for the higher grade girls in basic cookery and scullery work, since
that year - 1933 - the Aberdeenshire schools changed over at Easter, while
Banchory kept to the autumn date. Naturally the course included cleaning the
flues of a kitchen range and operating a Valor Perfection stove; we did our
school cooking on the latter: semolina pudding, cornflour shape, English
stew, Irish stew, Toad-in-the-hole, apple balls, girdle scones, pancakes and
oatcakes, porridge and curried eggs, shortbread and syrup dumplings.

Chapter 2 records the installation in 1913 of a new iron and steel kitchen
range and hot water system in the manse, the latter serving the bathroom and
the one small kitchen sink. In 1929 we had two deep porcelain sinks as well
as a new small one installed in the scullery section of the now subdivided

kitchen, which also afforded three walk-in cupboards and one for hanging coats where was once the door opening into the cellar (now the vestibule at the new front door). Scarcely was this achieved when the 1913 range boiler burst. Until a new tiled range was put in during the second war our hot water came only from the boiler built into the small reception room - whimsically named 'the lounge' - made out of the former pantry opposite the new front door. One or two black iron kettles generally sat by whichever fire was on; my mother named these after the characters in 'Watty and Meg'; they were required particularly in the evening to fill the stone hot water bottles - in winter sometimes twice over before bedtime.

A major wash-day therefore often still involved the lighting of the wash-house boiler with preliminary soaking in cold water of the two wooden tubs to swell the wood and prevent leakage over one's feet into the open drain under-neath: these tasks my father would perform. The water ran away into a drain under an adjacent cold tap. At first the hot water from the old boiler was lifted out with a zinc dipper with a wooden handle. In 1929 an iron boiler with a tap replaced the vast bricked-up model. The wash-house was used also by the church cleaner when before the twice-yearly Communion the church floors were scrubbed. Between the wooden tubs a wringer was fixed, and the washed sheets (flannelette for cold bedrooms) and towels would be put through this before being hung out, with other items, on the clothes-lines by the hedge. If they did not dry outside they would be transferred to the drying loft over the wash-house which had wooden louvred windows on three sides. (An amateur archaeologist once insisted that this loft was a resurrection tower, used in the early 19th century to spot 'resurrectionists' engaged in grave-robbing. It predated this activity.) White pillow-slips, or perhaps pieces of lace, would after treatment with a 'blue-bag' be spread on the lawn to bleach. Once some pieces of lace disappeared, to be found lining the nest of a blackbird in the ivy of the churchyard wall.

When dry, sheets and towels would be folded, stretched taut and put through the mangle, and other things ironed with a box-iron, the heaters being taken red-hot by poker from the open fire. The kitchen table, or half the large nursery table, would be covered with an old folded blanket and cotton sheet, the iron set on its ornamental iron stand. This was of course a procedure being followed in many contemporary country homes, some boilers even being out-of-doors with an open fire below. Most farms and many manses had domestic staff to do it.

Dr A.J.H. Gibson, therefore, in his book Stipend in the Church of Scotland, published in 1961, wrote of ministers' wives: 'Collectively they have won for themselves a unique place in the love and esteem of the people, and this continues even although modern conditions governing domestic help make home duties much more exacting for the minister's wife than they used to be'. I think that perhaps this glosses over an element of criticism which might not have existed at all had not a certain pride prevented the fact from being generally realised that sometimes 'the lady of the manse' hardly enjoyed a 'lady's' life. Even now one might hesitate to write of this, but the discipline of the trained historian militates against the concealment of evidence; besides, one owes it perhaps to many who in their day had to play the roles of both Martha and Mary at one and the same time. Quite recently I read in Life and Work of the indignant reaction of one of our overseas missionaries, whom we all admire, who on a furlough tour of Scotland was unintentionally made aware of the extra domestic work she had caused a harassed country minister's wife. As the daughter-in-law of a former industrial missionary in Kenya, I know only too well the disadvantages of such a career and way of life: in earlier days at least these did not include lack of domestic help in either house or garden.

In retrospect we can but marvel at our parents' achievement not only in bringing us up in such a civilised (if not always comfortable) manner but in presenting altogether such a good front on such extremely limited resources. There was always enough both for us and to offer simple hospitality, at least until wartime rationing became a factor. I recall returning to University

after the second war and finding that a small fee was payable for the retrieval
of a class certificate not collected in 1942; the official at Marischal
College, however - a nephew of a lady in the parish - waved away my proffered
half-crown: 'That's all right: I once had a very nice cup of tea from your
mother'.

It was, of course, not unusual for my father to return from a round of
visiting with a bottle of fresh cream. Once, after the final session of a
class for intending communicants, a farmer's wife in a remote area produced
a parcel: her daughter, a member of the class, had said to her 'The minister's
been so good, you'll just make him a kebbock'.

I think my mother only once, in May 1938, accompanied my father to the
General Assembly, this partly in order to attend the special entertainments
at this time arranged for the Lord High Commissioner and Moderator at Esdaile,
where I was completing my first year. She was, I think, rather embarrassed
by my father's reviving the subject in Assembly of Dependants' Grants: at
this date less of a personal issue. But another minister's wife to whom she
spoke (from the Presbytery of Dalkeith, formerly in a charge in Orkney) left
her in no doubt as to the support he had, at least from a significant minority
on the distaff side.

What originally prompted my father in 1931 to bring up in Assembly the
question of Dependants' Grants was probably not so much personal considerations,
which were then pressing, as the apparent move by the General Trustees to
appropriate certain funds which accrued to the Maintenance of the Ministry
Committee, formed in 1920. Mostly laymen, the General Trustees had been
appointed in anticipation of the 1925 Act to deal with the financial issues
following the new relationship with the heritors after the 1929 Union of the
churches. Ministers who had been receiving teind stipend could choose, after
the Union, either to continue on this basis or to have their victual stipend
standardised, calculated according to the average victual stipend paid in each
parish - based formerly on the fluctuating value of grains - over the years

1873-1922 plus 5 per cent. Ministers who opted for the old basis, as it seems my father did for some time, probably until 1935, could later switch to standardised stipend. On a vacancy occurring, the stipend was automatically standardised. Dr Gibson notes that at Martinmas 1960 the number of teind stipends remaining unstandardised was nine. It might be noted here that what the 1911 Year Book called the 'serious diminution' of grain prices was the direct result of farming developments in North America in the wake of railway-building and consequent immigration. It was this situation which prompted Lord Mount Stephen, at the turn of the century, to set up the Trust which bears his name to add £100 to the stipends of certain parishes, mostly in his native Banffshire. While this indirectly benefitted smaller livings elsewhere whose stipends were supplemented from headquarters, it could mean that some 'Mount Stephen' parishes were taken out of the 'smaller living' category. The subsequent temporary increase in the price of grain during the Great War, inflating some stipends, gave rise to the original idea of Dependants' Grants, as will presently be put in context. Meanwhile, the claims of the General Trustees on part of the Maintenance of the Ministry Committee's funds at a time when these Grants had ceased, seemed to my father inappropriate.

Prior to the 1930 Assembly, which he could not attend, he had briefed another member to speak on this subject. The Maintenance of the Ministry Committee's 1930 deliverance had included the following:

> 4. The General Assembly empower the Committee, in accordance with
> the Plan of Union, to undertake the whole administration of all funds
> collected for stipend. They empower the Committee to confer with the
> Finance Committee with a view to sharing in a scheme by which the
> expenses of the General Trustees may be met.

But the proposal to omit the second sentence of this paragraph was not seconded, despite the very moderate tone of the member's speech, which ended 'he would be glad to withdraw his motion if an explanation was given'. No explanation was forthcoming. The sum involved – to meet the expenses of the General Trustees – was £2,500, enough to give, say, 62 ministers of 'smaller livings' with four dependant children, each a grant totalling £40.

The history of Dependants' Grants was outlined by my father at the 1931 Assembly when during the Maintenance of the Ministry debate he proposed that the Committee report to the next Assembly on the principle of Dependants' Grants, giving reasons for and against:

It had been a principle in the old Church of Scotland. [i.e. pre-1929.] During the war, and because of it, the incomes of certain ministers rose, while the incomes of others remained stationary. [In Aberdeenshire, meal and barley which in 1915-16 had been 21/8 and £2.9.9 a boll respectively, were in 1919-20 42/2 and £5.7.4. Further south prices tended to be proportionately higher. By 1930 these Aberdeenshire prices had fallen to 13/2 and £1.2.5.] Now the former, in a very Christian spirit, agreed to contribute of their surplus to help their poorer brethren, and a large sum was raised. How was it disposed of? It was agreed that it should be on the principle of Dependants' Grants, that was, instead of giving a surplus to every minister on the minimum level, a distinction should be made between those with children and those without. This went on till 1920, when that Fund came to an end, but in 1920 the General Assembly remitted to the Committee to consider "whether in estimating a minister's stipend allowance could be made for children dependent on him", and in 1921 the Committee unanimously recommended that special consideration should be given to the minister of a small living parish who had dependents, and the General Assembly approved of the recommendation. In 1924 the report was on these lines – "There are very few ministers of small living parishes whose means are such as to enable them to dispense with grants for their dependents, and there is no doubt that these grants afforded essential and timeous help to those who received them"; while in 1927 the report ran – "The grants have proved to be very great boons to ministers who have families to rear and educate. Without them it would have been impossible for many a small living minister to have carried on"... In 1928 the Assembly adopted the following deliverance:- "The General Assembly rejoice to hear that a grant of £10 has been provided for each dependant up to the limit of £300 [stipend minimum]". He contended that what was a matter of rejoicing in the Tolbooth - (laughter) - should not of necessity cause sorrow on the Mound. Finally, he would quote to them the last word of the old Church of Scotland on this matter, namely, the deliverance of the General Assembly of 1929 – "The General Assembly authorise the Committee to make payment of dependants' grants over and above the minimum of £300 and a manse, provided that the minimum of £300 and a manse has first been secured". Ministers of the old Church of Scotland had taken that as the last word of their Church on that particular principle... That was the reason why, speaking without shame, for himself and for others in a similar situation, he asked that this matter be taken into serious consideration... He quite realised that there were reasons against it as well as for it. Mr Whitelaw [Vice-Convener, Maintenance of the Ministry Committee] had written in the previous month a very excellent article in Life and Work, (laying down the principle) that in amalgamations such as theirs the best features of both sides ought to be retained in the united organisation...

This was seconded by another Deeside minister, the Reverend William Sawers, Dinnet, a widower with no children. In response the Vice-Convener 'said that

the speech which Mr. Donald had just delivered made him realise the danger
of drafting reports, writing articles, or making speeches. (Laughter.)
Everything that he had quoted up to a point had been said when the limit was
£300 and a manse'. The Committee were now aiming at a minimum stipend of
£400 and a manse. 'That of course changed the situation...' But 'there was
no reason why the Committee should not consider the subject anew, and he was
willing to accept the motion. (Applause).' The question was in fact virtually
allowed to lapse, partly perhaps in deference to the economic climate which,
incongruously, must have greatly assisted, with its cheap prices for many
goods, in making a minimum stipend go further. But the principle of dependants' grants was certainly unpopular with the later 'mandarins of 121', unfamiliar, perhaps, with the realities of life in remote places, or conscious
that ministers' children, enjoying an apparently rarified existence, already
came in for quite enough popular criticism. Seven years later the minimum
stipend rose to £305, the manse at Lumphanan remaining large as life. After
the union of the two Lumphanan churches my father received an allowance for
his extra responsibilities, initially £20.

When in 1939 the two Lumphanan churches were on the point of uniting,
my parents went to look at the U.F. manse with a view to deciding where they
would prefer to live. The fact that this house, although compact, has only
recently been brought to what is recognised as a comfortable condition, and
I think in 1939 did not fulfil the official minimum as to accommodation,
explains their reservations at that time. I was present and I well remember
the 'last straw': my mother opened the door of the lavatory, darkly tucked
underneath the stair, and shook her head: no, she really couldn't be doing
with that. There was, of course, no electricity, although I think calor gas
was used. For some years the U.F. manse was let, and the tenants made many
complaints.

My father had always maintained that the St Finan's manse had possibilities, given some imaginative reconstruction; he himself drew up possible

plans; the architect laird of Dess produced three different schemes. This
was on the eve of the second war, when there seemed a possibility of the
Grampian electricity scheme reaching our area. Eventually, a year or two
before my father retired, the Kirk Session offered to electrify the manse;
I don't know what my father's actual response was; my sister Wendy, as
housekeeper, probably weighed the advantages against the possibility of an
upheaval, at this late date, such as she could recall from 1929. They
declined it, and although electricity was installed during the next vacancy,
it was eventually found impracticable to heat the house adequately; dampness
resulted and the house at the Stothert Memorial became the manse. Even then,
double glazing was later resorted to. The coal ration in 1951 (including an
allowance for the study) appears to have been about six tons, costing just
under £30. Part of this would be 'nuts' for the new kitchen range. Paraffin
in 1949 cost a shilling a gallon. In addition, we used a fair quantity of
wood, and once in January 1950 my father bought a load of peat from a passing
merchant. The study fire was by no means regularly lit, my father doing his
winter reading or paperwork wherever the fire happened to be. even in the
church where it was relatively warm after a service. I recall searching for
him one Sunday afternoon and finding him sitting in a pew, a book in his
hand. It was <u>Alice in Wonderland</u>, which had been suggested as a suitable
gift for his grand-daughter Rosemary. He was sound asleep.

CHAPTER TEN

———————

<u>The defence shall be prepared</u>

1939-1945: Evacuees; Home Guard; parishioners on
war service; casualties; German prisoners of war.

Chapter 10

The Second World War really began for us on Friday 1 September 1939 with the arrival of the Glasgow evacuees. My father had been appointed billeting officer, and some days earlier had circularised the parishioners (a survey of the accommodation notionally available had already been made) notifying each of the number of evacuees provisionally allotted to them:

Evacuation of Glasgow Children

288 children and over 20 adults are due to arrive here any day. I have been asked by the County Convener to arrange for spreading these equitably over Lumphanan Civil Parish. This work has not been easy, but it has been done as fairly as possible. The Census of houses taken some time ago was <u>voluntary</u>. Events have changed this and Billeting is now done under Act of Parliament.

This will necessitate inconvenience to many, but our troubles are small compared with the risks of bombardment and death which will face the parents of these children at home or with the forces.

These are meantime the nation's children. They must get bed and board when here. Some alteration in numbers taken in or exchange of boys for girls <u>may</u> be possible later, and after one <u>week</u> from their arrival I shall be at home from 9-10 a.m. to discuss this. Meantime I must ask you to take the numbers noted below for the <u>first week</u>.

There is difficulty re providing mattresses and blankets as previously arranged for. Only about 1/3 of that asked for is available. Will those who really need these please let me know <u>at once</u> and I shall try to supply them when needed.

St. Finan's.	Fr. C. Donald.
Date <u>as postmark</u>.	Billeting Officer.

Bed and Board _____ children

House Room only _____ do.   _____ adults.

There began a constant stream of callers at the manse: so-and-so from the city would be coming to stay if there were a war... After some attempt to cope with this a line had to be drawn. Fortunately the number which came on 1 September (several more followed later) totalled only 133: 6 helpers, 18 mothers, 63 accompanied children and 46 unaccompanied.

They were expected any time after 5 o'clock to arrive by train at Lumphanan station. Craig, home on his first leave from Cyprus, stationed himself on the railway bridge with camera, all set to record the historic occasion. Up at the

Parish Hall refreshments were being prepared for the newcomers. Time passed:
darkness fell; still no train. Craig gave up and went to the hall to help.
About 10 p.m. they arrived, weary, hungry; a party mostly of young children,
some mothers with babes in arms, one or two schoolteachers and other helpers.
The hall was packed, rather like a slave market. The atmosphere was such
that my father's spectacles got so steamed up he couldn't see. The so-
carefully-planned schedule of so many to each house was discarded. Each householder knew what their quota was supposed to be: they were invited to pick
their own guests.

My mother had previously stated that she didn't care to have a teacher,
who, she supposed, would require or expect superior service which she was not
able to provide: 'Just some fine wifie with children...'. We had prepared
two rooms downstairs with several beds, and they were to have the use of the
ground floor lavatory with washbasin. Near the end of the day my father spied
a 'wifie' still with three boys, one in his mother's arms; their sister had
already found a home, and the mother was looking worried. 'It's all right:
I have a place for you'; he sent them off to us in one of the delivering cars.
They elected all to sleep in one room - our old 'nursery' - where a fire was
kindled. As long as they were there my mother cleaned and remade their fire
each morning and provided a cooked dish for dinner: not the sort of fare they
were used to, I think, but the boys liked it. Their mother, I was told,
missed her morning cup of tea. They used the front door which was directly
accessible, along the passage. Even after five years of polishing the passage
linoleum and the composition floor of the vestibule it was a novelty for me to
finish up actually perspiring. The eldest boy was at one point recruited by
Craig to herd the sheep but was soon dismissed. We did have some quite jolly
evenings round the piano - still in the nursery: the mother's favourite was
'The Old Rugged Cross'.

As promised in his circular, my father did indeed make himself available
the following Friday to hear complaints, and a note of his activities on

8, 9 and 11 September shows that he was engaged on the 8th from 7.30 a.m. to midnight, on the 9th (Saturday) from 6.30 a.m. to 8 p.m. (thereafter spending two hours preparing his Sunday service: he 'slept sound') and on Monday 11th from 8 a.m. to 9.30 p.m. on the various tasks connected with the evacuees. These included not only touring the homes and sorting out difficulties, but keeping meticulous accounts of all expenses involved, from transport (a hired car was permitted) to telephone calls, and of course dealing with payment vouchers. But this process began, in fact, on the day following the evacuees' arrival. A telephone call to the County Council on the question of splitting families (as we had no telephone, this meant going to the village) was followed by fifteen miles in a hired car, both lunch and tea (3/6 and 1/6 respectively) being taken en route. Each visit was noted: address, names of evacuees with ages of boys and girls, their Glasgow address, and comments: 'Pleased at date'; 'no children' [wanted]; 'settled'; 'Happy'; 'Will do best'; '?'; 'wild'; 'lice'; occasionally details of a switch of billet. Disorientated mothers tended to congregate in the village (especially on 'buroo' days when allowances were claimed) no doubt comparing notes and complaints. My mother was sometimes left literally holding the baby.

It was not by any means simply the fault of the evacuees that they had difficulty in settling. In their Glasgow environment they might have lacked fresh air, sunlight and wide-open spaces, but they had no doubt enjoyed 'mod. cons.' such as instant power for lighting and heating which the war itself ensured were still further postponed in Lumphanan. The comparative isolation of most of our homes, too, must have been disconcerting for families accustomed to stairheads and 'steamies', noisy streets with clanging tram-cars and shops nearby. Going round receiving complaints my father could understand the diffi-culties in adjusting to primitive facilities, - but not the dissatisfaction expressed about a house in the centre of the village which in the days of summer lodgers had been good enough for Dr Peter Giles, Master of Emmanuel College, Cambridge. (He had, of course, been brought up in Strichen: 'a guid blacksmith spoilt'.)

The most successful arrangements were perhaps those where a single child was billeted with a family and virtually adopted for the duration. An eight-year-old boy was taken by a couple whose family were grown up and away – all except the only boy who had died young and whose picture hung always over the fireplace. This evacuee stayed for over four years; on his return to Glasgow he wrote to my father:

> I am writing you a little note to let you know I am getting on fine.
>
> I hope you are all well at the Manse. Everybody that saw the Bible you gave me said it was a very good present to get and I thank you very, very much.
>
> My mother said it was very good of you to come down to the train with us.
>
> I hope I will hear from you soon.

A large percentage trickled back almost immediately. By the end of September 1939 sixty-two remained: 7 mothers, 22 accompanying children, 32 unaccompanied children and one helper; at the end of November there were 27 in all: 2 mothers with 5 children and 20 unaccompanied children. It may be recalled that the heavy bombing of Clydeside came just over a year later in the spring of 1941.

A household which took unaccompanied children was paid 10/6 for one, 17/- for two, 25/6 for 3 and 34/- for 4. For an adult with one child (presumed to supply their own food or to pay the householder for doing so) 8/- was paid; with two children 11/-, three 14/-, four 17/-, five 20/- and with six children 23/-. The mother at the farm where the billeting officer had been told the farmer's wife would 'do her best' wrote to my father after she and her four children had returned to Glasgow on 21 October:

> Dear Mr. Donald,
>
> I am awful sorry I could not manage up to see you. I got a wire from my husband to go home and I had to pack. We haven't got the money Mr. Donald to carry on with. You see I am paying £2 a week with Mrs. C – for our food and I just can't stand up to it, and all the kids needs so much and having to keep our home up too in Glasgow and my husband wrote and told me I must come home. I have rent to clear gas bills Electric bills and goodness knows where its going to come from. I wish I had never put in for this Evacuation at all it's just set me all wrong from the very start and its not that I am going to get much benefit 10/- will not keep six of us its not that we dont

like up here or discontented its just I cant see my way out
and sorry Mr. Donald.

Yours sincerely
Mrs K —

Meanwhile from the beginning of the evacuation rumours had been percolating back to Glasgow of the horrors encountered in these country districts. One of the teachers who had been temporarily seconded for the initial stage and had returned to Glasgow, Miss Mary Brander, wrote to my father on 12 September acknowledging a letter he had sent for delivery to the Director of Education, his student contemporary R.M. Allardyce. The teachers, Craig recalls were rather surprised that the minister of a remote country parish should be on such familiar terms with the Director. The latter was found to be 'overwhelmed' with evacuation work: 'the number of "complaints" from all over the country was legion, and usually without just cause'. Miss Brander continued:

> Today I visited a large number of parents whose children were, or still are, in Lumphanan. I was so glad to be able to tell them the truth, as they had been listening to wild stories, brought back by some of the discontented mothers. They showed obvious relief, when they knew their fears were groundless.
>
> I have asked those I visited to tell everyone concerned to call at Kennedy Street School, where I shall be only too pleased to furnish them with correct information. Yours has been a thankless task, but I can say without hesitation, that you spared no effort in your endeavour to accomplish it satisfactorily ....

Many years later, discussing this with a Scottish Office official of this period, I gathered that at St. Andrews House the war was expected to come to a swift and sudden end: the evacuation would be a short-term expedient. This seems the only explanation for what, on a long-term basis, was a pretty impossible scheme.

Not everyone who came was unhappy or a misfit, as has been indicated. Two other boys at least appreciated aspects of country life. My father's diary for 1940 contains more than once the apparently cryptic entry: 'A & B Kelly w. Trot'... 'A & R Kelly - ponies'. This being interpreted meant that the Kelly brothers, having been unusually well-behaved for a time, were rewarded by being allowed to ride, first, our chestnut pony Ginger, and then each to have a pony.

After forty years it is good to be able to confirm that gangsterism, in the wake of 'the evacuation', did not take serious hold of Lumphanan youth. A document of 1940 survives:

<u>Red Cross Gang</u>

A. Howden	)	
A. Irvine	)	Pass word
G. Gauld	)	<u>Bacon and Beans</u>
G. Paterson	)	

<u>Rules</u>

Anyone breaking into the money box is to be fined 6$^{\underline{d}}$ or put out. Any fighting the one who is to blames is tortured. Each member has to pay a 1$^{\underline{d}}$ per week for the funds or finded 6d. Each fortnigh their will be as feat.

Singed By
Red Cross Gang
13th May 1940

(The first-named gangster was the dismissed shepherd. The other three were 'locals'.)

Typically, my father adopted the incomers - even when they had returned to Glasgow - as parishioners. Snatching a brief vacation on his auto-cycle from 18 to 26 December 1941 he visited some of their homes in Glasgow on Christmas Eve. Wearing his customary auto-cycling headgear - not unlike a **biretta** - he was on some stair-heads thought to be a Catholic dignitary.

.   .   .   .

1939 had already been an unusually busy year. Much negotiation had preceded the union of our two Lumphanan churches. On Sunday 21 May there had been a joint Communion service; the Reverend George M. Park, late of Deskford, joined my father in the pulpit. On 2 July, following the dispatch of circulars to all parishioners, there was the formal Union Service at 3 p.m. attended by the Reverend John Ross, Kincardine O'Neil, the Presbytery representative officially in charge of the operation. A month later some new elders were ordained.

When local people were asked to volunteer as Air Raid Wardens my father was inclined to be sceptical. Agreeing with the sentiments of aul' Meg Mill of <u>The Muckle Spate</u> :

> The days hev come fan Scriptur' says
> The fouks in toons fa be,
> Sall leave their hames an' wor'dly gear,
> An' to the mountains flee...

he rather thought that if Lumphanan were to be bombed the only hope was to make for the wood. He wasn't actually around on the day that I saw a German aircraft, black crosses on its wings, swoop low but innocuously over our beech-tree at the top of the back road. At all events my mother announced that if he wouldn't be a warden then she would. She duly registered, and was taken aback to be outfitted with smart navy-blue waterproof and (not so smart) felt hat: such extravagance, quite unnecessary . These she carefully hung in her wardrobe (they emerged, I think, only once when I insisted on photo-graphing her in them) and proceeded to fit gas-masks for her neighbours dressed in mufti. The local banker, James M. Irvine, was in charge of A.R.P. (Air Raid Precautions). He, or one of his members, had to sally forth when an air-raid warning came and blow a whistle in certain areas, while one of the railway surfacemen would patrol the line.

When, however, on 15 May 1940, two weeks before the retreat from France, the call came over the radio for Local Defence Volunteers, my father was first at the recruiting station, the Police Station at Torphins. The form, as he filled it in, was as follows :

ABERDEENSHIRE CONSTABULARY

Local Defence Volunteer Corps

I apply for enrolment in the above Corps.
Name   Francis Cantlie Donald.
Address   The Manse, Lumphanan.
Present Occupation   Parish Minister.
Date of birth   2 Oct. 1882.
Any previous military service (give particulars)
        Private   6 VBGH [Volunteer Battalion
    Gordon Highlanders] 2 years
        Private to Sergeant 4th Gordons 4 years.
        Sergeant 6 Gordons 1 year.
Whether familiar with firearms - rifle, revolver or shotgun?
        Shotgun and Rifle. Had N.C.O. Course at Hythe Sept. 1905
        passed 3rd in order of merit in Class.
Whether prepared to serve away from home?
        Wish to keep within reasonable distance from Home.

The Home Guard, as it was called from 31 July, was by no means a novelty in the history of Aberdeenshire, nor was it anything new for such a body to be

led by the parish minister. In the book <u>Old Aberdeenshire Ministers and</u>
<u>Their People</u>, compiled from the literary remains of the Rev. John Davidson,
D.D., (Aberdeen 1895) his son notes that his father was for many years
chaplain of the 4th V.B. Gordon Highlanders and took a lively interest in
volunteering. Dr Davidson himself wrote of Benjie Mercer, minister of
Kildrummy, who died in 1815 aged 81, that he 'was one of many pastors who
organised their parishioners when the first volunteer movement was got up
to meet the threatened invasion of Napoleon. "Lods", he said, "I'll gae wi'
ye mysel'. Od, fan I was a laddie, I was a terrible craiter for fechtin'."'
Mr Mercer is also mentioned by Dr Paul of Banchory Devenick: 'In the prospect
of the invasion of this country by the French about the beginning of this
century, Mr Mercer was applied to by the neighbouring landed proprietors to
endeavour to induce his parishioners to join a corps of volunteers which was
being formed in the district. He consequently called a meeting of the young
men of the parish, and, after an address to stimulate their patriotism, laying
"Liowes" [his staff - a corruption of Lewis where he had been schoolmaster]
upon his shoulder, he urged them to follow him to the place of <u>rendezvous</u>,
saying, by way of encouragement, "Come, lads, follow me, for I aye delichtit
in fechtin'". Dr Paul also notes that at this time Mr Dawson the schoolmaster
at Dunottar - also a preacher - was chaplain to a corps of volunteers.

In Lumphanan there had been a Militia Club at least since the beginning
of the nineteenth century. A document setting out the revised rules of 1810
(the Club afforded an arrangement whereby any member called up for military
service at an inconvenient time in the rural year could be 'bought off')
includes the names and addresses of the members of that time. It would have
been usual for the schoolmaster to list those eligible for service between
the ages of 19 and 23, and later annotations are in the handwriting of his
daughter, Eliza Birnie, who married John Don, blacksmith at Peelbog from 1827.
There is no mention there of the then minister - the Rev. Wm. Shand was then
aged 70 - although notices concerning the Club were read on Sundays 'from the
latron'.

The history of the Home Guard of 1940 is rather more reminiscent of much earlier days. A short history of the Aberdeenshire Militia written by Colonel Thomas Innes in 1884 to mark the occasion of what became known as the Wet Review (the visit in drenching rain of the Prince of Wales and Princess Alexandra to present new colours to the Third Battalion, Gordon Highlanders) indicates that since 1314, the year of Bannockburn, the military spirit in Scottish people had been kept alive by the constant sense of danger from an antagonist of superior force. The Sovereign was in fact empowered by statute to require that 'all fencible men between the ages of 16 and 60 years should be ready to resist invasion, furnished with proper arms according to their condition, and ready to march with so many days' provisions'. By 1424, under James I, these arrangements were becoming even more comparable to those of the Local Defence Volunteers of 1940, although the battle-dress of the latter was very much simpler. Even the new Scottish National Dictionary fails adequately to interpret the 'hat, gorget... pesane with wambrasseris and reirbrasseris,... gloves of plate, pans and leg splents...' which were the basics demanded in 1424 'or gif him likes, better'. For both defence forces regular target practice was obligatory. In 1424 the statute decreed that 'all men busk them-selves to be archers frae they be twelve years of age; and that in ilk £10 of land there be bowmarks, specially near to paroche kirks, quarin upon hailie days men may cum, and, at the least, schute thrise about, and have usage of archerie...' In 1940 they were rationed to one shot each: there was no longer, however, the minatory provision that 'wha uses not, the said archerie, shall raise of him a wedder.' In fact, the early statute seems never to have been enforced, although during the Napoleonic wars - witness the Lumphanan Militia Club document - precautions were revived.

On 29 May 1940 Major Cook of Asloun called at the manse to ask if the minister would organise the Lumphanan Section of the L.D.V. A meeting of volunteers was called for Wednesday 5 June being intimated from the pulpit

the previous Sunday, both at the Stothert Memorial and at the West End Hall.
Meanwhile my father interviewed a number of local men of varying ages, from
William G. McRobbie, veteran of the 'Wet Review', through several 1914-18
ex-servicemen to one still at school. He looked out his own binoculars and
telescope and 'considered Plans'.

There was a large attendance for enrolment at the Parish Hall on 5 June.
Captain Spence came from Huntly as well as Major Cook. Next day Captain
Harold M. Ireland, a Canadian D.F.C. of the First World War who had been
running a silver fox farm at Tullochvenus, was booked to give a lecture on
aeroplanes and parachutes. The station-master, Robert Moir, and the keeper
of the level-crossing at Auchlossan, George Forbes, were to take care of
telephonic communications. An arrangement was made with the local Shell Mex
petrol store; later the police came in on the question of immobilising petrol
pumps. Men were nominated to ring both the church bells if such warning
were required. In the event of an imminent or attempted invasion the bells
would be rung continuously for five minutes; if enemy parachutists or airborne
troops had actually landed, the nearer bell would be tolled at short intervals
of a few seconds. It must be realised, especially in view of Lord Alanbrooke's
later edict on the subject, that in a scattered parish with little or no
telephonic communication, this was the only practical method of alert.

To use the church bells as an alert meant that no longer were they pealed
on Sundays. A letter to my parents from Mrs Andy Burnett refers to this and
also to the fact that on 17 October 1943, just before morning service, part of
the ceiling at St Finan's Church had fallen. This meant no further services
there for a considerable time. Mrs Burnett, after thanking my parents for
'a lovely day' she had spent with them, 'something to look back on. I wish
there were more like you two in this world', continued 'I hope the Church will
soon be open again and you all back to our usual Sabbath Day. I am like
Mrs Dunn. "I like to hear the Sabbath Bells".'

On 8 June Colonel Nicol of Ballogie and Captain Mills of The Firs, Torphins, (son-in-law of the late John Glenesk, Craigton) called at the manse to intimate the transfer of the Lumphanan Section of the Home Guard to the Deeside Area. On 10 June the recruits were addressed by General Sir James Burnett of Leys.

Now came the all-important business of arms supply and training. On 13 June my father collected two rifles from an Aberdeen depot and the local joiner constructed a practice target. More rifles were brought by Captain Mills, and on the evening of 17 June some men paraded at the Hall for rifle drill, some at the range for target practice. One volunteer was detailed to clean the rifles. At 9.15 p.m. at the Hall they had a lecture on the capitulation of France. Later two more shot-guns were offered locally; at one point the manse began to look like an arms dump, bayonets piled beside the John Gartly clock in the front vestibule. Some ammunition was concealed about the glebe. (Already the barn and toolshed were piled with great rolls of newsprint belonging to the Aberdeen Press and Journal.) A small revolver appeared on my father's dressing-table; no ammunition for it was ever forthcoming.

Meanwhile for my father there had been the routine of visiting homes where someone was about to leave for service in the armed forces; if possible he would go to see them off at the station. As was mentioned earlier, a number of our local men had joined the regular forces in the 1930's; others had joined the Territorial Army and had quickly been called up for active service. After that there was always someone - of either sex - going off or returning on leave. On 19 May 1940 our first casualty, Robert Geddes of the 6th Battalion, Gordon Highlanders, died in France. He was buried at Etaples Military Cemetery, not very far from the grave of another Lumphanan twenty-year-old, John Keith, who died in 1918. I best remember Robert coming with his sister Barbara to the 'barn' Sunday School at Futtie.

On 6 February 1940 my father's diary, resumed only temporarily in January after and before more interruptions, noted 'P. Sim Jr. leaving tomorrow.' At the end of the month Peter was on embarkation leave for France. About the same time my brother Craig, back in Cyprus for some months, having been forbidden to join a local regiment while on leave, went into camp at Polemedia with the newly formed Cyprus Regiment. He expected to be in France before long with a Pack Transport unit. Came Dunkirk and the Regiment was diverted to Egypt and Abyssinia.

In the Dunkirk evacuation, begun on 31 May 1940, nearly all our surviving local men got away from France. Some time later word came that they would be returning home on the forenoon train from Aberdeen. My father went down to the station where a number of people were waiting, including Peter Sim, Senior. The train came in, there was a flurry of arrivals - but where was young Peter? Nobody seemed to know. Someone remembered seeing him on board one of the 'little ships'... the rest was confusion. For two months there was no news of Peter Sim, a sapper with 706 General Construction Company, Royal Engineers. Then on 6/7 August 1940 the troopship Mohamed Ali El Kebir was torpedoed and sunk off the coast of Ireland. It transpired that Peter had been on board. Most of the troops on board were saved but Peter was washed ashore and buried at Kilcar, County Donegal. Craig recalls this wartime troopship as one of two small passengers ships of the Egyptian Khedival Mail Line which plied between Alexandria and Marseilles.

More fortunate was Jimmy Cromar (mentioned earlier in Chapter 3), captured with the 1st Gordons at St Valery. In 1960 he was referred to by name in a television programme by General Sir Brian Horrocks (printed in The Listener of 14 January 1960) as the first to escape by the Comet Line into Spain.

On Wednesday 3 July (early closing day in the village) at 12.30 p.m. came an alert to the Home Guard: 'Man posts in relays'. My father posted village men and called in 'landward' men by messenger. All turned up and at 5.45 p.m. came 'All clear'. This was a trial run. From then on the post at Highland Park was manned from 11 p.m. to 5 a.m. each night; my father arranged the rota and habitually set the watch, sometimes remaining for quite some time as well as doing his own turn. To a certain extent, I suspect, this was a form of pastoral visiting. There was, as a rule, very little traffic during these night watches; each passer-by was halted. On Saturday night 13 July there was a dance on in the Hall and he made a note to arrange queues at the Home Guard post for interviewing car drivers and cyclists. The inspecting officer, Colonel Nicol, came along and ordered red lights to be used in future. Battle-dress uniforms with forage caps bearing the Gordon badge had been issued at an early stage, and short patrols were undertaken during the night.

My father himself undertook surveys of different parts of the parish in anticipation of parachute landings, noting potential observation points, and the men were given an exercise in judging distances. On 5 June the meeting on 'Paras' was held, and co-operation with the A.R.P. was pursued. (There was no sign, in Lumphanan, of the strained relations between A.R.P. and Home Guard mentioned in the official war history of Civil Defence.)

It was on Saturday night, 7 September 1940, that 'the invasion' came. Again there was a dance on in the village. I cannot recall now how the alert arrived at the manse (we had no telephone) but it wasn't long before John Cadger from Burnside was ringing our church bell. By this time my father was on his way to the Parish Hall where he broke the news to the dancers, and issued instructions to the Home Guard members present. Suddenly there came a knock on our back door. Wendy, on vacation from St Thomas's Hospital, London, had already armed herself with the unloaded revolver from my father's room and shouted 'Who goes there?' An unmistakably local voice answered and the opened door revealed Charlie Benton, son of Cairnbeathie's grieve. He had been sent to fetch more ammunition. While this was being produced Charlie was asked what the dance was in aid of tonight. Still slightly shaken by his bellicose reception he seemed uncertain: it was only afterwards that it trans- pired that he had actually organised the event. The Home Guard were out for most of the night scouring the different areas of the parish without result.

The 'invasion' warning of September 1940 turned out to have been the result of some confusion at GHQ Home Forces. One cannot help feeling, however, that even with hindsight it was perfectly justified. The official war history reveals not only that the Joint Intelligence Committee had observed that moon and tide on the south-east coast favoured a landing 8-10 September, that four Germans, self-confessed spies, had actually been caught landing there from a rowing boat, that no provision had been made for any stage of readiness intermediate between 8 hours' notice and 'immediate action' and that in fact at 7 minutes past 8 that evening the signal for immediate action was issued by a deputy from GHQ Home Forces to Eastern and Southern Commands and to other bodies in London and the south. Other Commands received the signal for information only whereupon 'In some parts of the country certain Home Guard Commanders, acting on their own initiative, called out the Home Guard by the ringing of church bells, thereby giving the impression that German parachutists were already descending on the countryside. Amidst the prevailing atmosphere of expectancy reports were received that parachutists had actually landed on and that fast German motor-boats were approaching the coast, but on investigation all were shown to be without foundation'. Even the Boy Scout motto 'Be Prepared' would have been apt.

London did, in fact, suffer an air attack that night. Even now it is not clear why Hitler changed his mind at this time about invading a very inadequately defended Britain. A German map of the country published in the relevant volume of the official history, and indicating the supposed disposition of Home Forces at 20 September 1940, notes that Aberdeen was 'bedingt verven-dungs fähig' - i.e. worth investigating. However, in his wisdom the C-in-C Home Forces, General Brooke, afterwards 'made it clear that church bells were to be rung by order of a member of the Home Guard only if he had himself seen at least 25 parachutists descending, and not because other bells had been heard, or on the strength of second-hand reports' ...

Next day, Sunday, there was the usual attendance at church. My father preached on the 23rd Psalm: in times like these it was refreshing to look back to an atmosphere of quiet trust and confidence in a Higher Power: not fleeting

as the powers of this world, a Power who can carry out His plans and purposes...
'Thou preparedst a table before me in the presence of mine enemies...' Around
us was war, strife, alarms; but even nearer was abundant evidence of a fruit-
ful harvest: 'The earth is the Lord's and the fullness thereof...' In the
midst of and in spite of alarms we had peace, beauty, the majesty of nature,
the works of God.

There was some disappointment when the minister suggested that as we
had all been up all night the planned Sunday afternoon picking of sphagnum
moss should be cancelled. These picnics' were much enjoyed by participants.
The roadmen's lorry would transport us to whichever moss was selected, and the
WVS (run locally by Mrs Irvine and Mrs John Copland) would have arranged for
tea. I recall splendid picnics at Moss-side (Maggie Macgregor's) and at Nether
Tillylair (Mr and Mrs William Christie's). Gumbooted, we soon had the lorry
loaded up with the starheaded sphagnum. This was subsequently picked over
by the WVS and used for field-dressings.

By July 1941 the Lumphanan Section, Home Guard, had opened a Savings
Account with the North of Scotland Bank. It was registered in the names of
the Rev. Francis C. Donald, St Finan's Manse, and Mr Alexander Fraser,
Boghead. In red ink was added, 'To be operated on by both or the survivor'.
Gradually the Home Guard became more co-ordinated, with rather more organisation of authority in the higher echelons and some weeding-out further down.
Two of the 'halt and maimed' whom my father had recruited, one possibly the
best shot in the parish, the other with a sound knowledge of off-beat routes,
were discharged. My mother had to deal rather brusquely one day with a
visiting officer who demanded to know what qualifications my father had for
his task. Specialities such as map-reading intelligence were hived off to
inter-parish groups, their meetings announced by post with only a map reference given for the rendezvous - generally to be interpreted as Torquhindallochy
in the parish of Birse. Regular lectures and training for other parishes
began to be held weekly in Torphins. There were occasional incidents such

as '1.45 (Lumphanan) Home Guard ambushed Torphins convoy at Den' on mid-summer's night 1942. On the night of 21 April 1943 guns were heard from Aberdeen at 10.30 p.m. : unfortunately these were the only defence made available that night; I was one of the RAF radar operators who plotted the 'hostiles' from the longest possible range in and out of the city.

By this time several younger members of the Home Guard had left for active service. The Air Training Corps had been founded in which Harold Ireland played a leading part. Most girls of service age had joined the Forces or were in munitions, or replacing men in other tasks. (On the Deeside Line we had two girl Guards from Aberdeen.) For the younger ones there was the Girls Training Corps, led by the local school teachers. My father's parochial duties had not lessened, particularly as in many homes there was anxiety and uncertainty about members of families overseas. Typically, the 'parish' extended to cover former parishioners. Often on visits to Aberdeen he had to see the local representatives of the Red Cross, the Far East Prisoners of War organisation or the Soldiers Sailors and Air Forces Association; he might also correspond with the London headquarters. Early in 1941 my mother had had a cancer operation, and although she at first made a good recovery, she later had to have further in-patient and then out-patient hospital treatment and by 1944 was quite ill.

On 28 March 1941 Jack Dinnie, a Radio Officer in the Merchant Navy, was lost at sea from the Norwegian m.v. Svenor. He was 19. I well remember his young (adopted) sister Jean coming to the manse with the reported news and clutching at a straw, discussing with my mother the meaning of the term 'amidships'. There was no doubt that it had been a direct hit. My father happened to be away at the time; later my mother set out walking to call on Mrs Dinnie but had to turn in the village and come home again, too weak to face the hill to Craig Cottage. In July 1942 Mrs Dinnie came with the news that George was a prisoner in the Far East; happily he survived. Jack's name is on the Merchant Navy Memorial on Tower Hill in the City of London.

Earlier in 1942 uncertain news had begun to come in of those of our men -
all regulars - who were in the Far East. Most had been with the 2nd Gordons
at Selarang Barracks, Changi, Singapore; one was with the 2nd Royal Scots in
Hong Kong, one with the 2nd Battalion Scots Guards. Until Pearl Harbour, it
had been hoped to avoid war with Japan, and our Far Eastern troops were unpre-
pared for what was to come. Once the Japanese had begun to move Southwards
it was clear that our regular bases on Hong Kong and Singapore could not hold
out indefinitely.

With the 2nd Battalion The Royal Scots at Victoria Barracks on Hong Kong
was William J. Ross, son of 'Tony' Ross, once a familiar figure in the parish
driving the baker's horse-van. At first it was reported, in September 1942,
that he was a prisoner of war. Only in January 1943 was it known that he had
died on 19 December 1941 during the final battle at the Wong Nei Chong Gap,
aged 29, a member of the gallant 'D' Company under Captain Pinkerton. He is
buried in the Stanley Military Cemetery, Hong Kong, the original military
cemetery of the island, disused for 70 years but extended for reburial of the
men who fell during the fighting of 1941 or died under the occupation. My
father, visiting the Rosses in November 1945, noted in his diary 'William's
grave'. Under the care of the Commonwealth War Graves Commission, Stanley
could not be more beautiful. 'The steep, grassy slopes are planted with
magnolia, gardenia, rhododendron, jasmine, and everywhere are casuarina
trees, coniferous with purple blossoms. In the headstone borders are pink
and red polyantha roses and perennial asters'.

Meanwhile in early 1942 had come the battle for Singapore Island. The
Japanese had overcome Malaya and landed on the island: this became known
on 9 February. Wavell, who had just visited Singapore, had emphasised the
desirability of fighting on as long as possible: this proved to be a short
period. The men of the 2nd Gordons there became prisoners-of-war. The
historical notes in the relevant volume of the Commonwealth War Graves Commission summarise the fates of all the British servicemen involved: 'Some

perished on Japanese transports which were sunk while carrying them to forced labour or to permanent prisoner-of-war camps elsewhere. A host of others died of illness, frequently of malnutrition diseases, during the years of captivity. Many were employed by the Japanese in the construction of the railway from Thailand to Burma'.

The line from Bangkok to Rangoon was completed in October 1943 after one year of intensive forced labour. Willie Calder, son of Andrew Calder, Cairnton, died on 19 October in Burma, aged 36. He lies in Thanbyuzayat War Cemetery there. A Company Quartermaster Sergeant with the 2nd Gordons, we used to call him 'Soldier Calder'. I can recall his handsome figure in uniform passing the manse when on leave in the thirties. Two brothers whom I also associate with those in the Kintocher area who attended the 'barn' Sunday School, Leslie and Harold Milne, died as prisoners-of-war. Leslie, with the R.A.S.C., died on 21 April 1943 aged 27 in Thailand; he was buried in Kanchanaburi War Cemetery. Harold was sent to Borneo, where he died on 20 November 1944, then also 27. He has no known grave and is commemorated on the Singapore Memorial. Two other Lumphanan names on this column which stands on the site of Kranji war cemetery are those of Edward Cockie, who died aged 28 on 12 September 1944, and Ronald McGregor, who died aged 29 on the night of 2/3 March 1942. Both were Gordons, Ronald being a Sergeant.

My father's diary, still kept only intermittently, became dotted with the abbreviation 'Jap. Post' as he visited all the houses where news might be expected. At Monyroads — also in the 'barn' Sunday School area — the two Christie brothers, both with the 2nd Gordons at Singapore, now to be separated, were reported prisoners-of-war. Donald, a Sergeant, was to be sent to Thailand, eventually to be freed by New Zealanders in August 1945. William (it appears) had been in Borneo: on 19 September 1945 he was with 'Aussies'. The Australian war history records that the diarist of the 2/12th Field Ambulance was writing at Kuching (Sarawak) on 17 September: 'that perhaps the most strenuous work yet done by the unit in all its campaigns was performed during three days when among other achievements with serum and blood transfusions it saved the lives of up to 50 sufferers from famine oedema'. George Dinnie, already mentioned, had been reported a prisoner-of-war in July 1942, as was John Anderson, Kintocher Croft, who also returned late in 1945.

Sandy Sutherland, late of Ardieraar, whom with John Merchant Craig had met in Cairo, was with the 2nd Battalion Scots Guards. News came in February 1943 that he had died in Iran. A Lance-Corporal then with the Royal Signals (Tenth Army Signals) he had died on 26 January, aged 26, and was buried in Tehran War Cemetery. His younger brother William, also with the Scots Guards, was reported missing in June 1942 but returned. On 15 July 1942 my parents came to see me off at Aberdeen Joint Station bound for service in the W.A.A.F.; my father had come into town by auto-cycle so that he could call on the way back at the Sutherlands' new home at Skene. Between 29 July and 1 August 1942 my father called on five families within the parish who had just had further news from the Far East, as well as making investigations in Aberdeen on 30 July at the S.S.A.F.A., the British Legion and the G.P.O.

On 27 January 1943 my father called at Mosshead; Harry was missing. On the Royal Naval Memorial at Plymouth is the name of Harry Cruickshank Merchant, Royal Navy, H.M.S. President the Third, lost in M.V. British Vigilance on 3 January 1943, aged 19.

Meanwhile George Rattray, Brankholm, had died in hospital while undergoing vaccination preparatory to service overseas. On the night of 2/3 August 1943 Flying Officer (William) Douglas Christie, Nether Tillylair, died in air operations over Germany. Aged 27, he was buried in the Municipal Cemetery, Heligoland. The following year young Pat Cameron, Glenmillan, was lost on air operations with the R.A.F., on 14 June 1944 aged 22. His grave is at Choloy in France. The two women on our war memorial, Valerie Kinghorn (F.A.N.Y.) and Mary Wyness (W.A.A.F.) died as the result of accidents.

Altogether almost a hundred parishioners and ex-parishioners were involved in the various theatres of war: their names, in most cases with photographs, are recorded in the 'Welcome Home' fund group in the Parish Hall. Most were overseas at some point: Europe, the Far East, Africa, the Middle East, Greece, Italy, Europe again - even Iceland. This represented a wealth of new experience and perhaps it was astonishing how they settled down again. In January 1943 Ed. Sherriffs, in North Africa, was 'satiated with oranges'; in October 1945 he was back at Michael Fair. Young William Brown, Wester Tolmauds, had been in Stalag XXI; returning soon after VE Day, in October 1945 he was home on agricultural leave. (During the war even Canadian army men in this country would spend a leave helping with the harvest.) Agriculture remained a vital operation. On the morning of VJ Day, 15 August 1945, when after the dropping of two atomic bombs the war with Japan finally ended, little Charles Drummond came to the manse with the milk from East Kincraigie announcing 'The hay 's a' in, and the war's over'.

At the Armistice Day service in November 1949, remembering the dead of both world wars, the new war memorial tablet in St Finan's Church was unveiled by Mrs William Nicol, wife of the gamekeeper at Findrack. They had lost two sons: David, a Private in the 2nd Battalion The Queen's Own Cameron Highlanders, died on 13 March 1942, aged 27, and is buried near Halfaya Pass in Egypt, between Sollum and Mersa Matruh - familiar names at that time. Ian, a Sergeant Flight Engineer in the Royal Air Force Volunteer Reserve, 76 Squadron, died on 13 June 1943 and lies in Reichswald Forest War Cemetery, Germany.

To some it must have seemed no time since the ceremony at the village war memorial after the 1914-18 war, especially when my father spoke of 'those who just turned the key in their chests and went...' The St Finan's tablet, in granite, was executed by T.B. Huxley-Jones of Gray's School of Art, Aberdeen; the carved wood tablet at the Stothert Memorial Church was by his wife Gwyneth Holt. The 'Welcome Home' fund provided a playing field in the village which did much to promote Lumphanan's excellent record in the football league.

In a recently published book Thresholds of Peace: German Prisoners and the People of Britain, 1944-1948, the author Matthew Barry Sullivan praises

particularly the attitude in Scotland towards the prisoners-of-war who came
to work in our midst. He attributes this to the 'first-class co-operation'
between Dr Golzen of the Y.M.C.A. and the Assistant Chaplain General of
Scottish Command. At first, fraternisation was allowed only in 'churches,
chapels and Meeting Houses'; by August 1947 intermarriage was permitted.
Out of 400,000, over 25,000 former prisoners elected, at first count, to stay
in Britain. In Lumphanan one or two attended my father's Bible Class, and
when the Church At Home came round they were assured that they would be
welcome to attend. I can recall on that occasion going through to the hall-
keeper's kitchen rather late in the evening to help with the final washing-up
and finding the policeman esconced in an armchair there. It was customary
for him to look in briefly at such gatherings, but he was generally to be seen
in the hall. On being asked why he wasn't there tonight he explained he
couldn't very well go in there with prisoners-of-war ignoring the curfew.
I don't know whether the minister had undertaken to keep an eye on them or
had merely forgotten this formality. At all events the 'Bobby' cheerfully
volunteered for washing-up duty.

CHAPTER ELEVEN

The things which make for peace

Education: Lumphanan school; evening classes; campaign
for secondary school on Deeside; entertainments; holidays;
Harvest Thanksgiving; Christmas.

Chapter 11

The Reverend Dr Paul of Banchory Devenick, in his Past and Present of Aberdeenshire (1881), comments on the improvement in education in the counties
of Aberdeenshire, Banff and Moray following the Dick Bequest. Learning by
rote began to give way to an 'intellectual system' under the guidance of an
elite of University trained teachers, supervised by the Trust's own inspectors.
James Dick (1743-1828), born in Forres, made his original fortune in Jamaica;
over a hundred thousand pounds was to be applied 'to the maintenance and
assistance of the Country Parochial Schoolmasters ... in the three counties
of Aberdeen, Banff and Moray, except the Royal Burghs: it being my wish to
form a fund for the benefit of that neglected though useful class of men, and
to add to their present very trifling salaries...'

Craig and Betty were sent off to Lumphanan School together in 1920: there
was only a year between them and my mother thought it a pity to separate them.
Craig has written of the schoolmaster of his day:

Mr. James McLean was regarded as an ideal headmaster. Tall and
erect, with steel grey hair and clipped moustache, and a superficial
appearance of severity which belied his kindly nature, he commanded
respect, and the good order which prevailed would be the envy of many
schools today. Pupils with academic attainments were not numerous,
but except for the inevitable few, everyone left with a thorough
grounding in letters, figures and good manners, standing them in good
stead in many different careers, but mainly agriculture.

He was fortunate in his assistants. Miss Bessie Gray (later the
wife of Mr. Alex. Christie, banker, Huntly) had a natural way with
children, who took to her immediately. Without apparent effort on
anyone's part, she initiated them quickly in the 3 R's – the multipli-
cation table being recited en masse every morning after break, ending
in a crescendo of 12: 12: 144 – with a liberal sweetening of Art and
singing.

From her children passed into the hands of Miss Margaret Blackhall
(later married to Mr. William Sharp, farmer of Broomhill, Tornaveen,
and Scurdargue, Rhynie), another born teacher, whose regime was
stricter but no less effective, and it was exceptional for anyone not
to be promoted automatically to the Qualifying Class under the Headmaster whence they might proceed to at least the first two of the
three 'Higher Grade' classes.

Miss Gray also played the organ in the parish church, thereafter – she
recalls – occasionally enjoying the 'Pleasant Sunday Afternoons' organised

at the Free Church Hall by Mr W.G. McRobbie. The Christies retired to Nairn, and she came to see my father, then at Whinnieknowe, on his 90th birthday. Miss Blackhall (Mrs Sharp, then for many years a widow living in Torphins) was at my father's funeral in 1974. Craig visited her last in 1977; she died a year or two later.

Craig has another memory of Mr McLean: in 1921, when six years old, he was hitched up on to the wall of the playground by Annie Esson of Heathcote (some eight years older) in order to see the great fire in the Forest of Glentanar, some six miles away. He was spotted by the headmaster, deserted by Annie and left clinging to the wall, and sent for afterwards to the 'Big Room' to be ticked off (wall climbing being forbidden) to the great amusement of all the pupils there.

We were all fortunate in our succession of schoolmasters and other teachers. The academic teaching was good, and took some fortunate pupils far. But our education went beyond that. A former pupil (a farmer who could hardly have been called unsuccessful in life) once remarked that he 'never learned onything at Lumphanan school; the dominie was owre busy teaching us to be good citizens'. Quite a recommendation and not necessarily at variance with the verdict of Ian Forbes in his autobiographical Squad Man: 'In later years I often looked back and gave thanks for having such a fine schoolmaster as John Mudie, who ensured that my comparatively short schooling was of real value to me'. The senior pupils of these days, aged 13 to 14, seemed remarkably mature. When I was in the infant room our teacher was away for a short time and two of these, Nonnie Milne and Norman Harper, were in turn given charge of the three classes there; the latter held our attention with some story of which all I remember is the repeated 'One at a time, gentlemen, one at a time'.

Successive schoolmasters had different styles. I recall as a junior our going through to the 'big room' for a singing lesson and the dominie's voice at the end of one item 'Hands up those who weren't trying!' One hand went up: it belonged to a boy who later embarked on a successful engineering career. On another occasion we joined Mr Mudie's seniors for a literary session. Not then cricketers we were introduced to Sir Henry Newbolt's <u>Vitae Lampada</u> with its 'breathless hush in the close tonight', then the transition to the battle scene in the sodden red sands of the desert where still 'his captain's hand on his shoulder smote: Play up, play up! and play the game!'

In Mr John F. Davidson's day we were treated to Charles Murray - 'Hamewith' - and a more familiar close: evening at the farm.

> The mason's mear syne he set up in the closs
> An' coupit the ladle fu' keen.
> An' roon the ruck founs wi' the lave o' the loons
> Played "Takie" by licht o' the meen.

Yet we did not neglect the earlier classics entirely. We must have been studying <u>The Slave's Dream</u> by Longfellow:

> Beside the ungathered rice he lay,
> His sickle in his hand; ...

when the schoolmaster asked the class 'Who knows what a sickle is?' In the ensuing nonplussed hush I raised my hand, and was invited to come and draw it on the blackboard, evoking the astonished chorus: 'A hyowk!' Occasionally in this later period (1930's) senior pupils would go across to the schoolhouse to listen to a radio programme for schools. And in the master's cupboard were copies of Arthur Mee's <u>Children's Encyclopaedia.</u>

We certainly grew up with a respect for The Flag. In the letter quoted earlier which Wendy wrote to my father in Edinburgh on 24 May 1927 she describes the Empire Day service at the school where there was a flagpole in the girls' playground:

> The flag was up at the school. After dinner-time we went into
> Mr. Mudie's Room. First we sang the hundreth psalm then Mr. Anderson,
> Milton, gave a speech then we sang a hymn. We then went outside and
> formed up in a line and all saluted the flag then formed up and sang
> God Save Our Gracious King...

In my time on one Empire Day I recall reciting in my turn a verse of Charles Wolfe's poem <u>The Burial of Sir John Moore at Corunna</u>: 'They buried him darkly at dead of night ... With his martial cloak around him'. After this ceremony we used to get a half-holiday; in fact we used to chant a rhyme:

> The twenty-fourth of May is the Queen's Birthday
> If we don't get a holiday we'll all run away.

We even had a half-holiday on the centenary of Sir Walter Scott's death in
1932. My classmate Mary Grace Nicoll, Tillybreen, came home with me for
lunch. I wonder, fifty years later, if she now recalls, as I do, my mother
telling her 'You'll always remember that on Sir Walter Scott's centenary you
had lunch with a girl called Heather Donald'. On Armistice Day, 11 November,
there would also be a service at the school, with a two-minute silence when
I would try hard to think of my Uncle George whom I had never known. Older
pupils would, on the previous Saturday, have been visiting different areas
of the parish with trayfuls of poppies. At that time several different styles
of poppy would be supplied. I can remember my mother, overhearing Mary
Harper and me, over lunch at the manse, discussing the various prices for
these, commenting 'I think you two don't know whether you're selling poppies
or collecting for the Earl Haig Fund'.

In our day the school was at the centre of the parish, between Knappyround
and the 'Comply' - the rough track which afforded a short cut for children
coming from the West Side past the smithy at Marywell. A substantial red
granite building with Schoolhouse adjacent, it had three large rooms with wide
windows - above desk level - and a smaller room known as the science-room where
cookery classes also were held. In the middle room (Standards 2 to 4) above
the open coal fire was a large picture frame containing a poster for the Cunard
liner Mauretania. On the north wall was a high closed cupboard which contained,
among other things, a few books which we were allowed to take down and read if
we had finished some task. I recall The Swiss Family Robinson. In the 'Big
Room', on either side of the wall clock with its pendulum, inscribed Tempus fugit,
there were two etchings of groups of political figures such as William Pitt.
On the adjacent wall were two coloured prints of Millet paintings, The Angelus
and The Gleaners. Behind the dominie's desk was a group photograph of earlier
pupils including my brother Craig. Alongside the glass partition with the

Middle Room was a large well-filled bookcase bearing an inscription to the effect that it had been presented by Sir William Brooks of Glentanar.

The younger children used slates for most work, except for writing in copy-books, or doing exercises which the teacher would take home to correct. We called our slate-pencils 'skylies'. For drawing lessons we were given pencils or coloured crayons and pastel paper. In the infant room also there were low blackboards along one wall on which we could scribble or draw.

Next to the infant room was a tiny staff-room which contained also the lending library; on Fridays we could take a book home for the weekend and also one for the grown-ups. For the children there were three cloak-rooms with cold-water sinks and hooks for coats. The toilets were separate, out-of-doors next the 'shelter-sheds' in the boys' and girls' playgrounds. Initially earth-closets, they were rebuilt in my time to afford three pedal installations and one flush-lavatory for seniors (key in the dominie's room). At least that describes the girls' ones. Next the shelter-shed with bicycle rack in the boys' playground was the soup-kitchen with its boiler. When we were small the soup was made by 'Granny' Duthie, Hawthorn Cottage, Burnside, a venerable, bent but jolly grey-haired figure, dressed all in black with a shawl over her head. When she died (the school-children contributed towards a wreath) her daughter Bella took over, and later Mrs Arthur Watson. These were also school cleaners. A new building for both cooking and serving school dinners was later built while the school was still on the old site.

Normally we each brought a packed lunch with perhaps a small 'piece' for 'little play' - our equivalent of 'elevenses'. I can recall Bella Newman, who with her sister Mary lived at 'Mearns's', announcing with delight one 'little play' 'I've got toast!' (the toasted heel of a plain loaf). Most children brought an enamelled flask of cold tea or a bottle of milk. Only in winter did we have the hot soup three days a week, cocoa twice; the former would be Scotch broth, potato or split pea in turn, served in the classrooms out of buckets into tin bowls. Farmers would contribute vegetables; the

beef and other ingredients would come from funds raised by the Childrens'
Interests Committee, particularly at the annual event known as the 'Tattie
Souper', a dance held in the West End Hall. Once, playing the organ there for
the monthly evening service, I glanced up at the pine panelling above the
organ where hung Curwen's Modulator and spied a small piece of graffiti:
'Tattie Souper 1927'.

In time the school acquired the adjacent field where the boys could play
football and the girls have their 'housies'; formerly the latter, with their
collections of broken crocks, littered the schoolhouse entrance. The annual
sports and picnic were then held there instead of borrowing a field at Cairnbeathie, Bogloch or Auchenhove to which the children marched under the leadership of the village pipers with at one time Mr John Scott, farmer, Cloak,
beating the big drum. Each playground had a water tap with iron drinking cup.
When it was discovered that some girls were joining the boys at football in
the field Mr Davidson bought us a ball of our own - which we subscribed to by
degrees, Lizzie Cockie acting treasurer - and we played on the grass patch
by the flagpole.

Mostly in the playground we had the seasonal games: rounders, (known as
'Glasgow housies'), hide-and-seek, 'takie' (southerners might call it 'tig'),
various 'round' games, skipping and sliding, and for the boys 'bonnetie',
in a version different even from the three described in the Scottish National
Dictionary. The various caps were set out in a row, one boy rolled a ball
towards one, and if it went in, the owner had to retrieve it and hit one of
the players - who had scattered - with it. If he did so, that player was 'out';
otherwise the thrower was: whichever it was had to remove his cap. School
headgear, incidentally, tended to be distinctive rather than uniform. The
boys, of course, had 'bools' (marbles), playing into small holes dug out of
the sandy soil; I seem to remember boys joining girls once for a snowball
fight. The skipping season might begin with two big girls turning the long
rope to the sound of

> All in together, frosty weather,
> All - jump - OUT.

Smaller groups might be heard chanting

> Evie, Ivy, turn the ropie over,
> Mother's at the butcher's buying some beef.
> Baby's in the cradle, playing with the ladle,
> One - two - three!

When it was possible to have a long slide in the playground one would hear

the exhortation 'Keep the pottie bilin'' as the line of children followed

each other along. In warmer weather one might see a circle of girls sitting

on the grass, one girl walking round the outside while all proclaimed

> I sent a letter to my love
> And by the way I dropped it.
> I dee I dee I dropped it.
> An old man picked it up
> And put it in his p-o-c-k-e-t POCKET.

Then, at a quickened pace, while the letter-holder speeded up:

> An' the doggie winna bite you, nor you,
> Nor you, nor you ... but YOU.

The singing games were perhaps traditional with local variations. The familiar

'In and out the windows' with its second verse 'Stand before your lover...'

might end up 'Go and tell the bobby...' We were quite uninhibited about

supplying names for the 'lover' games:

> The wind, the wind, the wind blows high,
> The rain comes dashing through the sky,
> - - says she'll die,
> All for the sake of the rolling sky.
> She is nice and she is pretty,
> She is the girl of the golden city,
> She has lovers one, two, three,
> Tell me who that one shall be.   (Consultation)

> Down in yonder meadow where the green grass grows,
> There - - bleaches her clothes,
> She sang, and she sang, and she sang so sweet,
> She sang - - across the street ...

Counting rhymes such as 'Eetle, ottle, black bottle, eetle ottle out!' might

be prolonged indefinitely to keep up the suspense, this one perhaps ending

with a 'dirty dish clout!' Occasionally someone from another parish might

import a new version of any of these rhymes.

At the school there were also winter evening classes, attended in the early days mainly by young people who had left school at 14: in fact, continuation classes. These might culminate in a dramatic performance: I recall The Rajah of Rajapore, the title role played by a farm servant from the West Side; Craig remembers that in an earlier year they tackled The Merchant of Venice with David Sutherland, Cairnmude, in the lead. Later these tended to be dress-making, first-aid or bee-keeping classes.

Another enterprise in Lumphanan in the thirties was a series of lessons in gymnastics run by James Morrice, virtually our local steeplejack, and a consistent prizewinner at the Highland Games. The course ended with a public 'P.E.' demonstration in the Parish Hall. This excellent event was well attended, so far as spectator-space permitted. But when at the end my father led a vote of thanks to the instructor, James was speechless. 'Mr. Morrice is a man of deeds, not words' was the minister's comment.

After about 1930 a period of gradual change set in, probably a national rather than a local trend. This can no doubt be traced in the Minutes of Education Committees, although local variations may be attributable to succeeding schoolmasters and teachers. For example, just as I had reached the Qualifying Class, where I think we sat the first 'Control' examination prior to entering the Higher Grade, the powers that be decreed that no longer would French be taught at Lumphanan. The custom had been for pupils taking French to arrive at 9 a.m. for half-an-hour's tuition before Prayers. Our new headmaster, Mr Davidson, thereupon announced that any 'Big Room' pupils who cared to stay after 4 o'clock could learn Latin instead. Four or five of us did so.

But the main issue in the twenties was the question of providing secondary education on Deeside, educating pupils up to University Entrance level. It was on 25 January 1922 that my father brought this up at a meeting of the Presbytery of Kincardine O'Neil. On coming to Lumphanan in 1913 he had been astounded to find that in the fifty-eight miles from Braemar to Aberdeen there was then no such school. In his native Banffshire, except between Aberlour or Dufftown and Tomintoul in the Upper Cabrach, no pupil was more than six miles distant from full secondary education; this was available at Banff, Macduff, Fordyce, Buckie, Aberchirder, Keith, Mortlach, Aberlour and Tomintoul. Aberdeenshire, three times larger and four or five times more populous, had then only eight such schools, at Fraserburgh, Peterhead, Strichen, Ellon, Inverurie, Kemnay, Turriff and Huntly..

County Education Authorities had taken the place of the old Parish School Boards when these were abolished by Act of Parliament towards the end of the first world war, four members being allocated to Upper Deeside, i.e. Glassel to Braemar, but three years had gone past without any change in the status of the schools there. My father therefore suggested that the Presbytery should approach the Aberdeenshire County Authority with a view to having this remedied. A committee of five was appointed to consider this: two ministers and two elders (one of these Mr William Duncan, Deecastle, Dinnet was himself a member of the Aberdeenshire Education Authority) with my father as Convenor.

It was hardly a propitious time for such a proposal, the 'Geddes axe' having just fallen on such expenditure. However, in due course the Presbytery committee were invited to meet the County Education Authority and put forward their case. My father has recorded a detailed account of the whole affair. A compromise solution was eventually arrived at: the Aberdeenshire and Kincardineshire Education Authorities co-operated to have full secondary accommodation and staff at Banchory while Aberdeenshire made a financial contribution towards the cost of their pupils' higher secondary education there. (In later years parents made a contribution if Deeside pupils also had the first three years Higher Grade at Banchory.) A new wing at Banchory Central Higher Grade School (as it was first called) was opened in June 1925; it was afterwards known for many years as Banchory Secondary School, later Academy. The headmaster in 1925 was Mr Thomas Menzies, affectionately known as 'Auld Tam'. (Young Thomas was to have a distinguished career in Army Medical Services.)

My father himself became a member of the Aberdeenshire Education Committee
in the 1920's, attending meetings monthly in Aberdeen. Later, in 1951, he was
appointed to represent the Synod on the Education Committee, becoming also
a member of the Further Education Sub-Committee, and one of the Education
Committee Representatives on the Deeside Area Sub-Committee. This involved
not only attending meetings but spending a good deal of time up to his
retirement in 1954 in preparatory reading and consultation.

Inevitably numbers at Banchory had increased in the thirties to such
an extent that, taking into account also the long distances travelled by
some pupils, not all of whom lived near rail or direct bus services, a movement was set afoot to have full secondary education made available also at
either Ballater or Aboyne. The train from Ballater to Banchory reached
Lumphanan at 8.22 a.m., which seemed early enough. But some pupils had come
first from Crathie to Ballater, for example, or from Coull to Aboyne. One
of the minister's sons at Coull, admonished one day by the physical education
teacher for having forgotten to bring his gym-shoes, patiently replied 'Miss -
if you had to leave home when I do in the morning you might forget more than
your gym-shoes'. During the General Strike of 1926 transport had been further
complicated when the trains stopped running. Craig had to take the bus to
and from Raemoir, walking the three miles between Raemoir and Banchory.

After being held up by the war of 1939-45 and the subsequent repetition
of 'axeing' expenditure, this scheme came to fruition within my father's
lifetime when Aboyne was chosen as the appropriate centre for another full
secondary school. This was recalled by the Reverend Dr Urie of Kincardine
O'Neil in his address at my father's funeral in 1974 when he mentioned the
part he had played in bringing this about.

By this time Lumphanan had a new school - but primary only - in the
village instead of at the centre of the parish. In these later days transport
would be provided for children living more than two miles away; ironically,
however, the closure of the Deeside Railway meant the loss of what would

have been the most convenient form of transport, to either Banchory or Aboyne,
for many scholars. At the same time the much improved road (locally known as
the motorway) from Hirnley to the Aboyne road brought many benefits. When
we were at the old school, children from Tillybreen or Hirnley on the West
Side, or from Mosshead on the east, were from the age of five walking up to
three miles each way, sometimes during our long winters through quite deep
snow. The fire-guard in the class room would be draped with damp garments.
The introduction of Wellington boots proved a great boon, provided they were
changed on arrival for slippers; otherwise lacing or button boots were the
rule. The early private bus-service would sometimes help, free of charge,
by carrying children at least part of the way westward while pausing at the
Pole for turn-around, and might thereafter take east-bound children as far
as the village. The shorter Burnside road would in winter tend to be
wreathed in snow, sometimes level with the dykes.

Altogether the minister spent a fair amount of time over school affairs.
In 1929, for example, my father's diary records between May and June a
meeting of the Children's Interests Committee, two evenings judging children's
work prepared for the annual exhibition, an afternoon at the exhibition
(combined with Prize Day) and one at the Picnic. Earlier in the year, besides
relevant committee meetings, there would have been the school concert in the
Parish Hall (taking the chair on one of the two nights) and in December the
Christmas Tree there.

Mr and Mrs Mudie collaborated to produce the school concert in their
time; we suspected that they even composed some of the items. It was largely
musical, the choral items mostly contrived to present some theme in which
numerous children could take part in appropriate costume. Our family supply
of sunbonnets and candlesticks were generally in demand. It might open with
'Come to the Fair', the stage full of sun-bonneted country folk, in the background some contrived merry-go-round, 'stalls on the green', a gypsy fortune-
teller with her songs: 'This is your fortune true' and 'Where my caravan

has rested'. There might be a Red Indian scene:

> In the wigwam on the prairie,
> Ladies' dresses never vary,
> In time of need
> We add a bead
> If we think it necessary...

At that time the stage curtain was becoming rather threadbare, and the Indians delighted, while it was still closed, in waggling their bare toes in the holes. (Some years later not only did we achieve a new crimson set of curtains in place of the worn green blanketing, but by 1952, in an interval in Kye amang the corn, presented by the Kildrummy Players, I reported how much I had enjoyed reading the new safety curtain.)

The infants might line up to sing 'Baby's sock has a hole in the toe: Who will mend it, I'd like to know? It won't be YOU (pointing) and it won't be ME (ditto), but I guess I know who the one will be'. A sonorous male soloist (David Milne) might sing 'A policeman's lot is not a happy one', or Charlie Maclean might lead the Toy Town Artillery, each in appropriate uniform. Norman Harper, in Chinese costume, alleged an improbable trade in 'lilly gillies'. Dolly Milne in sailor suit might push a pretty girl on a swing (there was no end to the ingenuity of the 'props') who responded with 'Swing me in the moonlight'. The entertainment would end, in alternate years, either with a fairy wedding or a bedtime scene. The former involved much pink and blue organdie and tinsel in the chorus – all the fairies carrying star-pointed wands – and a tiny bride and bridegroom in formal dress (perhaps Isobel Wood and Ackie Mitchell). In the background was the song 'Fairy bells are ringing tonight' with at one point 'Hark to the bells DING DONG' – here the brass school hand-bell would join in. For the bedtime scene the theme tune was 'Goodnight, ladies', the children in night attire parading with lit candles, and at a later concert Roberta Sim singing 'Christopher Robin is saying his prayers'.

At the old-style Christmas Tree, the short platform entertainment would be given by grown-ups. All eyes would stray to the tall tree at the right under the stage with its candles and a gift for each schoolchild and also for younger members of families. We had already at the school gone through the ceremony whereby an invisible Santa showered us with numbered tickets, each corresponding to a suitable gift on the tree. At the Hall there was tea with a 'poke' for each, and at the end a distribution of apples or oranges to take home. Santa would be played by one of the Committee. In later years senior pupils had a more elaborate Christmas party, with supper and dancing at the school. (I can recall Craig driving me in the trap, clutching a trifle on which I had misguidedly already placed the 'hundreds and thousands'.) Juniors still had a tree in the Hall. The Parish Church had no children's party, only a distribution of apples and book prizes for attendance. The Free Church children had a 'Soiree'. After the 1939 union my father would attend seasonal events at the Tornaveen meeting-house, and after the war both Lumphanan and Tornaveen schools liked to have end-of-term services, either in school or at church. The minister would also accompany a summer outing, perhaps to Aberdeen.

At Lumphanan in Mr Davidson's time the new honours of Dux and Primary Dux were introduced. Edith Morrice, West Mains, was the first Dux and I was Primary, receiving a calf-bound edition of Dickens' Tale of Two Cities, which I now value very much. At the time I preferred the school story I won for my wild-flower collection. We used to press about a hundred wild flowers, pasting them into blank books with their names and a note on where they were found, and the date. Betty was Dux at Banchory in 1932, receiving a gold medal and having her name printed in gold letters on the board in the central hall. She got a silver medal for mathematics and German. At the same time she was sports champion and was allowed to choose her own gift. A nice umbrella, she told my mother, navy blue with a yellow handle. When she brought it home it was in fact a No.2 Box Brownie camera. Prizes at the Lumphanan school picnic or sports were small coins promptly spent, as a rule, on ice-cream or sweets at the stall run by the ladies. Everyone got something.

There were other occasional breaks in the routine of school life at Lumphanan: the visit of a photographer, of a local political candidate, or of a temperance advocate with his tale of the doctor who advised a rather deaf patient to take 'a cup of claret three times a day', with unusually satisfactory results. At the doctor's next visit the patient reported that he had taken just what the doctor recommended, 'a cup of carrots three times a day'. Then there was the conjuror, dancing round balancing a plate on top of an opened parasol. Less welcome, perhaps, was the Inspector of Schools. We would be given warning of his visit and I recall meeting Mrs Arthur Watson on Reid's Brae who called out from her bicycle 'Are ye shakin'?' That day he made me - aged 8 - read a piece from near the end of our reading-book (which contained an extremely well made up selection) - a tale of French children at school in Alsace-Lorraine following the 1871 takeover by Germany, and of the boy who shouted 'Vive La France!' I stumbled over the pronunciation of Alsace, but 'Vive la' was no trouble to a little girl with a brother at Fettes.

In the later thirties, and again after the war, during the summer vacation the school might be lent as a holiday camp for young people from the town. First, I think, was Aberdeen's St Katherine's Club, run by Miss Walker and Miss Moffat for working girls. The young women gave us a splendid concert in the Parish Hall. Later campers tended to be younger; my father would visit them at the school and would I think perhaps ask them to choose a favourite hymn which would then be sung when they all came to church on Sunday. At one such service the rows of boys in the north gallery remained virtually silent until the last hymn, one not normally sung at Lumphanan: 'What a friend we have in Jesus'. They then nearly raised the roof.

Many years later I was to have further happy contact with St Katherine's Club. Back at University in Aberdeen after the war I was among those who, under the leadership of Nigerian Kenneth Dike, revived a pre-war club for overseas students where these could meet the natives. This became known as the International Club. My contact with it continued as long as I was in Aberdeen, partly because under its aegis we had formed a rumba band in which I learned to play the guitar which my parents had given me when I passed my 'Highers'. The St Katherine's Club had been giving some hospitality to overseas students and as a return for this we gave them a concert at the Club, in March 1950, at which the University Principal's wife, Mrs Thomas Taylor, took the chair. The programme consisted mainly of traditional East African Indian, West African and West Indian musical items, then still rather a novelty in Aberdeen. At one of our rehearsals at St Katherine's Miss Walker began to write down the programme ...'Calypso', she repeated, pencil poised. 'what is that?'

In those post-war days there were of course many more overseas students from different parts of the world than when my father was a student. Unless at the General Assembly, I doubt if he had ever met an African or Indian. During the war I once pointed out to him across Union Street the black figure of one of four such men we had on our radar station: 'You'd better go and speak to him then' was his reaction. I remember my mother telling me 'Now you must be specially nice to these black men. They've come a long way to help you'. After the war my father happened to be at King's College one morning trying to gain entrance to the Library, but forestalled by the end-of-lecture rush of students bound for the probably few available books just recommended for some essay. It was an African who noticed the elderly minister and paused to hold the Library door open for him. After that my father might report 'I was talking to one of your African friends on the bus today. He was telling me...' He assumed (probably correctly) that I knew them all. Later on, coming to visit me in London, he would assure me that he could easily find his way about the Underground: 'I'll just ask a black man'. His friendship with a Hungarian divinity student has been mentioned: it seemed appropriate that on my graduation day at Aberdeen - the first unusually large post-war occasion (we were sent up two at a time, which was later found to be

unconstitutional) when the supply of degree hoods proved inadequate - it was
a Polish friend who tapped me on the shoulder and anxiously asked if he
might borrow my M.A. hood; it was in fact my father's.

The music at our Church At-Home tended to be traditional, or more modern,
Scottish; or drawing-room ballads. No corn-kisters: these were deserting
the farm steadings but reappearing on gramophone records which were obtainable
at the Garage. There would, in earlier days, generally be a lady 'guest'
singer: sometimes a friend from beyond the parish, or a local newcomer, or
someone not often able to attend public functions. I can remember Nurse
Ethel Reid with 'The Songs my mother sang'; Mrs Albert Nicoll with 'Doun the
burn, Davie lad', and Mrs Cocker, Upper Tillylair, with a Scottish selection.
Perhaps our most regular male soloist after Alex. Reid's day was James Copland,
who might give us 'Bonnie Strathyre' or 'The Bonnie lass o' Ballochmyle'.
Andrew Low once gave us a song with the colourful refrain 'There were yalla'
an' purple, an' voilet, an' blue' - I can hear his voice now, but cannot think
of the title. Donald Dunbar followed in much the same tradition. I seem to
remember Lizzie Dawson singing 'Robin Adair', and later the next generation
of the Bakery family, Hilda and Nora Milne, and 'I canna leave the auld
folks now, I'd better bide a wee' and 'Caller o'u' or 'Aileen Alannah'.
Still later, a Milne grand-daughter, Isobel Wood, with Mattie McDonald, whose
father succeeded to the Bakery, once sang in duet 'Alice, where art thou';
both were soloists. Charlie Leslie, Whitehouse, with his wife, formerly
Helen Marr, daughter of the station-master and a gifted painter, once sang
together 'The Crookit Bawbee'. A popular trio was 'Old King Cole', perhaps
by James Copland, Albert Nicoll, Senior, (for many years our precentor,
cycling from Tillybreen), and Charlie Leslie. Another trio which included
George McDonald, Glen Villa, had a chorus 'A tall wife, ... a small wife, no
wife, no wife at all give me...'

My father would cyclostyle copies of the words of one or two well-known
songs from the Students Song Book for community singing, perhaps 'Will ye no'

come back again', 'Green grow the rashes oh!' or 'Ye banks and braes'. In
the thirties the banker, James M. Irvine, would give us one of the Doric
monologues of Dufton Scott (a professional entertainer before he became a
bookseller in Inverurie) or occasionally Craig would join him in one of the
Scott sketches. (It was at a W.R.I. open evening in the summer of 1939
that Craig, home on leave from Cyprus, gave a monologue, dressed up in 'drag'
impersonating a lady just learning to play golf, complete with tan and white
shoes. The text came from a very old copy of The Baillie.) Once at the
At-Home Betty recited extracts from The Muckle Spate, by David Grant, dressed,
and in fact introduced, as a survivor of the flood. She was a keen golfer
and my father had said he would give her a steel-shafted golf-club - then a
novelty - if she would do so. I was in the wings as prompter. The nine-hole
golf-course just outside the village was part of the Finzean estate: the club
used to pay a 'peppercorn' rent of a shilling a year.

At some point during the Church At-Home my father would give a brief
annual report on church affairs, and there might be a talk, with a few jokes,
by a neighbouring minister. During the first part of the evening in the
Parish Hall the audience sat facing the platform; then the long benches
were moved backward or sideways to clear the centre of the floor for the
service of tea and later dancing. The hall, built in 1895 and managed by a
local committee of which my father was a member, was then still heated by
ornate black wrought-iron portable stoves. The big wooden boxes of mugs
would be carried round, followed by trays of 'pieces' and ladies carrying
kettles of tea. Before dancing began, pink powder would be shaken lightly
over the floor to create a smother surface. On either side of the hall
would be pinned up a programme of dances. When the band struck up the music
for the Grand March my father, wearing his clerical frock-coat and patent
leather shoes in place of his customary boots, would approach the lady guest,
one hand behind his back, and lead off the procession round the hall, followed
by my mother in the company of a senior elder. After dancing the Circassian

Circle which followed he would then circulate among the people, returning

to the dance floor from time to time. A waltz country dance generally

followed. The rest of the programme varied between reels, quadrilles,

lancers, dashing white sergeant, with in between schottische or polka, with

perhaps a fox-trot, one-step or waltz. ('Do you reverse?') As midnight

approached there would be a Highland Reel, then Auld Lang Syne, everyone

in one circle with hands linked.

Writing to me some years ago Maggie Macgregor recalled these occasions

where in earlier days her band had played for the dancing: '...they used to

be a very friendly affair. A song, a dance, or a story was very much enjoyed

by everyone, - but then everybody was out to make it an hour or two of being

a very happy evening'.

At a smaller Choir At-Home members of the Kirk Session would entertain

the choir. Even my father, I think, would contribute a song such as 'A Capital

Ship' from the Students Song Book. The refreshments would include a few

delicacies such as bowls of oranges peeled and divided, and a neighbouring

minister and his wife would be asked to join us, perhaps the Rosses from

Finzean, later at Slains.

After the war, when the cost of repairs at St Finan's Church - including

the new ceiling - had severely depleted resources, more frequent old time

evenings were held, still attracting a full hall. These were less formal:

seats throughout the evening were arranged round the hall and, because of

rationing (which continued into the '50's) everyone brought a contribution

to the tea. On 31 March 1947, for example, my father sent out cyclostyled

circulars to parishioners as follows:

Church "At Home"

Another Old Time Evening will be held
in The Parish Hall on Friday first
the 4th April   - 8-12 p.m.
Arrangements for Tea Bread - Kettles,
Trays, Milk &c. & for serving, same as
in Feby. - Will each household kindly
bring to the Hall by 7.45 a few
Sandwiches or Tea Cakes.

He had already, on 12 March, arranged for the main guest entertainer, the fiddler Alexander R. Henderson, Torphins, who brought along Police Constable Alex. Garioch as accompanist. They gave us selections from William Marshall and Scott Skinner. Soloists were Mattie McDonald and Albert Nicoll jr. and for dancing we had James Emslie's band.

Although in later days some local arrangements were made by telephone, musicians and vocalists were as a rule called on personally - particularly some who lived at a distance, including former parishioners. In these immediately post-war years with more events than usual, we were fortunate in their ready response, and they in turn were warmly received. Our former organist Mrs Symon and her husband, also a singer, might come from Tough, members of the Nicoll family from Monymusk. The managers of the Co-operative company which had taken over Moir's Stores turned out to be talented, and a new generation of young entertainers was coming along. A certain informality even pervaded choir practices at this time. Although older members continued to sing on Sundays, or attended practices for special services, it was the younger members who regularly gathered in the church hall on a Saturday late afternoon. Alastair Irvine, fetched from the football pitch, would sit down at the organ, sleeves still rolled up. Jimmy Moir, Davie Riach, Leslie Grant ... Jean (Dinnie) Pearson in charge of the hymn-list: we had a lot of fun as well as making quite a good stab at the music, even on occasion a 7-fold Amen. Elizabeth Donald succeeded as organist. Later the practices returned to the church (when still warm on a Sunday evening) and first Mrs Thomson, West Mains, played the organ, then the railway signalman, Mr Garvock.

Another form of money-raising, which also changed its style over the years, was a Sale of Work. The first to be recorded in my father's diary - Craig recalls an earlier one opened by Mr Wight of Camphill - was in July 1929. A women's meeting in the manse in April made preliminary arrangements (my mother's silver tea kettle in evidence). The Sale was in the Parish Hall; I much enjoyed the Jumble stall and spent my pennies on a china cup 'A Present from Edinburgh', the stall-holder reminding me that that was where Craig was.

Neither of my parents were very keen on this innovation; my mother was

concerned over the painstaking needle-work which fetched very little.   In

post-war years a different style was adopted.   Contributions became more

practical and goods in short supply fetched quite high prices when auctioned,

amid a general spirit of bonhomie.   A new bicycle might be 'raffled'.   A

notice for a Sale in 1946 was as follows:

Lumphanan Church

A Free Gift Sale for a Church Fabric Fund to replace reserves
used to pay replastering Church Ceilings will be held in the Parish
Hall on Sat. 5th October.

The Sale will be opened at 2.30 by Mrs. Crabbe of Findrack.
Mr. Charles Leslie will afterwards roup the Gifts. Teas will be
served in the Hall.   Shooting, Putting &c. outside.   Dance later.

Elders or Members of Committee will call sometime during the
two weeks before Sale to arrange for collecting Gifts.

Farm or Dairy Produce or any article likely to be useful will
be acceptable.   On account of Bread Rationing each household is
asked to contribute some Sandwiches, Cakes or Biscuits for Tea Table.

23/8/46   Fr. C. Donald.

I overheard a telephone conversation my father was having regarding the

sideshows: 'What about Auntie Sally ... have you got the chalk? ... What's

that? - a fishing-rod and a bottle ...' (turning to me) 'have we still got an

old top hat?' Presently he drove in with Aunt Sally 'looking like St. Olaf .

Now she looks like a Saracen'.   Introducing Mrs Crabbe, a Roman Catholic

from the Province of Quebec, my father said 'Mrs. Crabbe is a member of the

Old Church'.

Many such events were followed by dancing in the evening - an art taught

only spasmodically at school in early days, generally being picked up by

attendance at the event.   But once there were two dancing classes held in

the Hotel hall - a senior and a junior session - by Mr Hugh Rose Wood, himself

a fiddler.   He began by canvassing from door to door, and I was sent to the

junior one.   There we learned the traditional Scottish dances and also the

Charleston.   At the end of the season there was a joint session of seniors and juniors together. I felt very grown up at being partnered by Lou Burnett, a farm servant at Loanend. My father, when young, had had much more intensive instruction in his native Mortlach, that home of superlative fiddlers. After his retirement I took him once on holiday to Port Charlotte, Isle of Islay, where the ceilidh, with dancing, singing and story-telling, was the traditional entertainment. When his turn came to contribute at an impromptu ceilidh in the hotel, he spoke of the dancing classes he had attended in his youth, which evidently culminated in a demonstration of carving a fowl. The different stages were carefully outlined, ending with the sudden exhortation 'Now gobble him up!' This was well received, and there was I think some surprise and admiration when this clerical septuagenarian 'took the floor' when the next dance was announced, with one of the lady guests.

As a family we were particularly fond of island holidays, perhaps as a result of hearing tales of my father's sojourn as a summer missionary on Swona from April to September 1909 (as mentioned in Chapter 5). My mother thought his memories of that island, situated in the Pentland Firth, splitting the main current of the stormy Atlantic tides - it is now uninhabited - would have been less euphoric but for the parcels she used to send him there, four years before their marriage. Craig, Wendy and I all spent holidays in Orkney and Shetland. I was briefly stationed - at my own request - near St. Margaret's Hope on South Ronaldshay before demobilisation in October 1945. The following year on Friday 23 August I sailed for Kirkwall on the St. Rognvald for a ten-day holiday. Wendy suggested that my father could join me from Monday to Saturday if he went by air. Nothing loth he did so, making his first-ever flight from Dyce, much enjoying the aerial view of his native Banffshire. One afternoon we went by coach, over the new Churchill barriers which in the recent war had sealed in Scapa Flow after the sinking there of the Royal Oak, to the Hope where we called on a younger member of an old Swona family. Noticing in the room a rather fine sideboard, my father couldn't resist asking 'Is that wood from the wreck?' He was long remembered

in Swona for his timely help in raising subscriptions towards the purchase
of a motor engine for a jointly owned boat, the major contribution coming
from Mr James Coats of the Ferguslie Thread Works, Paisley. Until then only
a rowing boat was available for either routine or emergency trips.

Had my father not returned home on that Saturday in 1946 he might have
revived other memories. On the Sunday, spending the weekend at the Hope, I
was invited by the local doctor, then near retirement and living in the hotel,
to join him in a visit to the Pentland Skerries lighthouse, where my father
had taken services when weather permitted access by rowing boat. A young
keeper was sick, and it happened also to be the day for the rations to be
delivered there. We set off in a rowing boat, being transferred in mid-ocean
to a motor-boat, which cut a smooth path between what seemed in parts to be
high walls of water. On Swona in 1909 land transport was by oxen; when we
landed on the Skerries a donkey called Prince awaited the rations. I was
shown over the lighthouse with its spotless Diesel shed and gleaming tool-
bench (and chipped glass where German bullets had hit the tower). The happy
light-keeper's wife opened her wardrobe and showed me her wedding-dress hanging there. Back at the Hope – the sick keeper was taken on by road to hospital
at Kirkwall – the doctor took me to see another of my father's old Swona
friends. Allens, Norquays, Rosies, Sabistons: the Rosie family were the
last to leave Swona. They were featured in a Press and Journal article of
3 June 1936. 'We've no such thing as unemployment', James told the interviewer,
'we've always plenty to do...I once read in a newspaper of people being lonely
in London. Now, what can you make of that?' Among my father's papers is a
letter 'From your loving friend Jimie' dated Swona May 23 1910:

> I sit down with pleasure to answer your welcome letter.. Well we
> are having glorious weather here just now and the grey fish is
> just come. We are done with the corn crop but we have not begun
> the turnips yet.. We were in at Scapa when the fleet was but they
> stayed very short. We were engaged with a man to drive his goods
> we had 1£ a day and we could run trips for ourselves between times
> ... but the weather was so rough some days it was hardly weather
> to leave the pier but we were out every day we were out when the
> other motor boats could not come around the pier head so that was

good for Swona. We were at Scapa last week with a cargo of scrap
iron.. came all the way with the motor it is a splendid engine...

When my father was over 80 Wendy took him on the round sea cruise of
Orkney and Shetland. For this they borrowed our anoraks, an Eskimo novelty
not earlier available in the family. Wendy alleged that my father even
slept in my husband's one.

So far in this chronicle nothing has been written of two special
services which, although of ancient origin, had in the Church of Scotland
been revived in my father's time: harvest thanksgiving and Christmas. My
father made a point of waiting until each farm had finished the grain harvest
before holding the Harvest Thanksgiving service; in time this became a case
merely of checking on those likely to be late. When he first came to
Lumphanan there were some very late harvests indeed: in 1915 the service
was on the last Sunday of December; in 1916 it took place on 17 December.
This may have been the result both of weather and of wartime shortage of
labour. By the 1950's, with more mechanisation, the grain, once ripe enough,
was quickly cut, and we had to make sure we had picked the bunches of oats
and barley which, in deep 'Rebecca' jars, decorated the church for the
festival, in good time. On 29 August 1952 my father noted that he had gathered
the oats, whereas in 1941 he had done this on 15 November, in 1942 on 5 October.

The silver flower vase normally used at services was a gift in 1931 from
the late Reverend Peter Dunn, D.D., minister emeritus of Dalmeny. A son of
James Dunn, East Kincraigie, he had left a legacy for the purpose of procuring
a set of silver Communion cups in memory of his parents and of his brother
James who had succeeded at Kincraigie and like his father was for many years
an elder in the parish. However, as noted earlier, shortly after my father
came to Lumphanan it had been decided to discontinue the use of pewter 'common
cups' - presumably because of the danger at that time of spreading infectious
diseases - and stands of individual glasses were acquired. Under the circumstances it was decided on consultation with Dr Dunn's executor that the flower
vase be purchased instead. It was dedicated on 6 September 1931.

Professor Cowan, in his lecture on the observation of Christmas, quoted
the 1645 Church Directory as saying that saints days were not to be observed:
the Church of the Reformation ignored these holy days, and it was not until
the Episcopal Church was revived after 1745 that observance of Christmas and
Easter was renewed. But it was still well over a hundred years before this
came about in the Church of Scotland. He connected the revival with the
reintroduction of instrumental music; in our time this often meant organs
donated by Andrew Carnegie. We as a family observed Christmas Day, although
aware that many in the parish substituted Hogmanay – New Year's Eve – as the
day of celebration. We used to decorate the church with holly, perhaps from
Glenmillan House gardens, and our own Christmas roses. On Hogmanay we would
listen for the voices which generally turned up outside the back door:

> Rise up, gude wife, an' shak' yer feathers,
> Dinna think that we are beggars,
> We're only bairnies come tae play,
> So up an' gie's oor Hogmanay!
> Oor feet's caul', oor sheen's thin,
> Gie's a piece an' lat's rin.

In later years the Bible Class would go carol-singing in the village at
Christmas time in aid of the Sick Children's Hospital in Aberdeen. My father
would deliver the proceeds to the Lady Almoner. Even after the introduction
of the National Health Service these contributions were welcomed for dis-
cretionary distribution.

By then there was quite an enthusiastic interest in choral music on
Deeside, partly under the leadership of Victor Mackeson, organist at Banchory
East, and special services would be held in various churches, several choirs
participating. On my father's last Christmas Sunday at Lumphanan, after a
normal morning service, one of these was held, the choir of 43 including
singers from Kincardine O'Neil, Birse, Torphins and Dinnet, the congregation
numbering 93. Writing to tell me of this (I was spending Christmas in Dorset
with my Aunt Ann) my father hoped he was not too late with seasonal greetings;
'I have been extra busy over this weekend and forgot that you English folk

keep Christmas and that there may be no post on Christmas Day... On
Sunday afternoon I was at Milton of Auchlossan with Communion for Mrs.
and Miss Bremner and George and Miss Cromar so by night I was somewhat
tired'.

From Monday to Wednesday of that week my father had been in Edinburgh.
Arrangements were being made for his transfer to the Retired Ministers'
Residence in Carlton Street; a recent legacy had enabled the Church to
double the available accommodation there by buying the adjacent house
which was being suitably adapted. My father wrote:

> I went down past Carlton Street but didn't go in. I saw a head
> whiter and balder than mine peeping over an arm chair comfortably
> esconced with his feet to the fire and the 'Scotsman' spread out
> in front of him and the sun shining on the head and the paper -
> apparently much at ease.

Envoi

Unto the end

Retirement 1954-1974.

Envoi

My father spent seventeen happy years at the Retired Ministers' Residence
in Carlton Street. These years were not by any means spent in an armchair
with his feet to the fire, congenial as the fireside circle proved to be,
sometimes including an old acquaintance or fellow-student. Many a lively
discussion took place, on current or academic topics. From 1965, towards
5.45 p.m., voices were hushed and all eyes were focussed on the television
screen and the children's series <u>Magic Roundabout</u>, (intended for the under-
fives). Visitors were made welcome, and might unexpectedly benefit from the
breadth of experience represented there, varying indeed from the sublime to
the ridiculous. On one of our visits my husband and I were talking about a
musical play which our London neighbour, Rosemary Linnell, was preparing
for the forthcoming Edinburgh Festival Fringe: <u>The Clock that Hanged Mac-
pherson</u>; the idea had come from a remark by an old Dufftown friend of my
father's 'Did you see we'd got a new clock?' One of the ministers round the
fire spoke up: 'When I was nine years old I was taken by my mother to Banff
to call on a Mrs Wood who lived in Wood Street. Just around the pend was
the house of Painted Effie: she it was who, when Macpherson was fleeing
from his pursuers, threw blankets from an upstairs window to trip him up'.
Painted Effie was duly included in the cast, and both my father and this
fellow-resident joined us when the play was presented at the Royal Arch Halls.

Inevitably some of the residents at Carlton Street were less mobile than
others, and my father would spend a certain amount of time caring for these,
perhaps reading aloud to one or two who were blind or nearly so. His daily
walk, when weather permitted, might be into town or round the neighbouring
park, perhaps feeding the ducks on the pond with oddments of bread acquired
from the kitchen. He got to know some of their neighbours on the Stockbridge
side: once we were walking there together when he paused to speak to someone,
catching up on me in a moment or two with 'That's a friend of mine, man

Mackinnon, great Catholic'.

As noted earlier, he cared for the garden for many years, latterly handing over the flower-beds to an even older resident while he did the grass
with a lawn-mower given by Wendy. He wrote to me on 1 September 1967 before
leaving for a week on Deeside which was to include a Presbytery reception
for the Moderator: '..I was busy all the week in the garden getting it
tidied up before going North ... and I have never seen it looking better.
Mr. Leslie does the surrounds so that I have now only the grass to attend to -
but have the edges all trimmed up and the lawns well mowed - making the whole
the tidiest plot in the garden area between us and Danube Street'.

At the Register House and other libraries he embarked on some research
into Gordon family history and other historical work. He never preached
again but enjoyed attending various Edinburgh churches, his favourite perhaps
being the Canongate where he found 'the folk' particularly congenial. For
a time Wendy was working in Rosehall parish and they went together to that
church. Both enjoyed concerts of Scottish music in the city and the
occasional horse-show or sale. (It was after catching cold at a show on his
eighty-first birthday that he grew a beard). Wendy would drive him down to
London and Dorset, and when Craig was home on leave from abroad, or later
when living at Malvern, they would go on tour to some place of historical
interest or to visit old friends.

Latterly the number of ministers applying for places dropped and it
was decided to close the Residence. The Arnotts who had been in charge for
some time were appointed Matron and Supervisor of the Eventide Home at
Whinnieknowe, Nairn, and my father joined them there. While often remarking
that his memory was failing he astonished us by recalling the Nairn he had
known as a boy. Driving him round on his second day there he could direct
me along the Inverness road to the farm of Wester Delnies, pointing out on
the way the nearby smaller holding of Easter Delnies, just opposite the school,

to which his relatives had retired ... one could walk from the farmyard down
to the shore. For the next two years he enjoyed motor-runs with Craig or
with Ian and me through Speyside or down to his native Fiddichside ...
'We'll just go to the top of the hill and take a look down into Glass ...'
Occasionally a former parishioner would visit him. Nearby at Forres were
William and Lucy Grant; at their house my father once met again his former
precentor William Harper: no hint of loss of memory on this occasion.

On the evening of 18 December 1973 we in London were making final preparations for Christmas when the telephone rang. At Whinnieknowe the residents
after tea had been preoccupied with a new colour television set and no-one
noticed when my father slipped out of the men's lounge, in his hand the small
parcel he had just received through the post, and mounted the stairs to put
it away. Up two short flights, along the landing, two more steps down to
the wing where his room was. Always particularly careful on the stairs,
counting as he went, for once his vigilance wavered. They heard the crash
down in the kitchen below: when they rushed upstairs he was lying unconscious.
The ambulance just managed to get to the Royal Northern Infirmary at Inverness before the road was blocked by snow; accompanying him was Miss Margaret
Macfarlane of the Home staff.

I set out for London airport early next morning; the pilot spoke to
the passengers outlining the prospects: there were five inches of snow at
Inverness airport and he doubted whether we would make it. We didn't, but
we got as far as Glasgow. I got a train to Perth, and thought of trying the
coast route via Aberdeen, hiring a self-drive car there. No use, someone
said, that was blocked. The telephones were all in use: journalists reporting the latest oilfield news. I got on the Inverness train. Soon it was
dark, and we crawled northwards between banks of snow, stopping at frequent
intervals to let the snow-plough go through. When we got to Inverness about
10.30 p.m. the station platform was covered in rough snow but I made my way

across the road to the hotel. A helpful hall-porter drove me to the hospital in his three-wheeler, along the banks of the Ness and over the bridge. I was to become very familiar with that stretch of water walking back and forth in the next four weeks. There was something majestic about the sheer volume of the swollen stream, the rocks of icy snow swirling towards the firth: the river of God is full of water, I kept recalling.

My father never regained consciousness. He became more relaxed, the bruises fading from his brow and eye, his hand responding to pressure but his eyes unrecognising. Ian came up for ten days to share my vigil. Gradually there came a sense of the rightness of it all: the stage could not have been more appropriately set for the last act: the threads were being gathered up and neatly tied. I only wished he could have been aware of his surroundings in this kindly place, among people such as he had gone amongst, cared for as he had seen them cared for. One heard the occasional Gaelic voice and Gaelic prayer. Across the ward lay the Free Church minister at Resolis, in the next bed an old shepherd from Drumnadrochit. Everyone made kind inquiries; one visiting minister paused, shook his head and could only say 'It's a job...' but his own minister from Nairn, the Reverend A. Cameron Gibson, M.R.C.V.S., prayed for my father as if he were fully conscious.

They were decorating the ward for Christmas. A Chinese male nurse from Hong Kong painted snowflakes on the glass door and then a huge robin redbreast, filling the panel. 'I wish my father could see that', I told him, 'he loved a robin'. On the wall over his bed, which was next the door and the nurses' office, were the Christmas cards he had received, including several from old parishioners. Mr and Mrs Arnott came to see him, and Lucy Grant. Outside the storm abated a little, though it was still bitterly cold. One could see salmon washed up on the banks of the Ness: everywhere one walked through wet, slushy snow. On Christmas Eve they wheeled a small harmonium into the ward and to the end of his bed, followed by nurses in

their red-lined cloaks. A slight flicker crossed my father's face as they
sang the hymn 'As with gladness men of old...' ending with the verse:

> In the heavenly country bright
> Need they no created light;
> Thou its light, its joy, its crown,
> Thou its sun which goes not down;
> There for ever may we sing
> Hallelujahs to our King.

After Christmas came New Year and the Hogmanay television programme
could not have been better chosen: Scottish fiddle music from various
sources - Macpherson, William Marshall, Neil Gow, Scott Skinner. I put the
headphone to my father's ear but he gave no hint of recognition. But in
moments of obvious discomfort he could still be calmed by the long verbal
journeys we took over the well-trodden paths of his earlier days. Starting
at 'the clock' in the centre of Dufftown I would name all the places we
passed, or could see, from 'Jeanie Lowrie's' Royal Oak down the hill towards
Auchindoun, up the left-hand side .. Clunymore .. Cauldhame .. to the top of
the hill (where we took a look down into Glass), back down the other side ..
Earnfold .. the castle of Auchindoun .. Keithmore .. Upper Keithock 'better
known as the Mutherton' .. on to the old school and the Mill of Auchindoun
.. We didn't notice that the mill wheel was no longer turning or that County
Council roadmen were busy cutting a new route, avoiding the Bridge of
Fiddich, through the garden of the old Post Office where he was born.

Or we would travel in various directions round the parish of Lumphanan,
from the manse to the Pole past Cairnbeathie Cottage (not noticing there was
no longer a railway over the cutting) between the Peel Ring on the right and
the battle stone on the left, over the stone bridge under which the truant
Jimmy Cromar hid from the dominie, on to Bogloch and Auchenhove, dividing
at the top of the Bothy Brae, one journey to the left leading to the Home
Farm, Mill Farm, Andrew Kemp's, Nether Tillylair, Hirnley, Tillybreen, over
to Bonnyside .. the other, to the right, with a detour to Marywell, on to
the Milton, North Mains, Wardhead and Loanend, over the hill to Coull; or

up the old drove road to Cairnbeathie and Ardieraar, on to the Oldtowns
and the Newtons, over the hill to Kincardine O'Neil; or up the Burnside
road to the Craigton, down again visiting all seven houses at Burnside,
on to the Peelbog and the Dons' old smithy, up to the Hillock and Brankholm,
on to Leyhead and Broomhill; back at the Peelbog we took 'Reid's brae' to
Roadside, called in at the Wattie Rosses' bungalow and past the school to
Knappyround, where John King still tended his begonias and told tall stories,
left to the gamekeeper's at Knowehead .. East and West Kincraigie ..
Blelack .. Whitehouse .. Wartle .. Tulloch; or further up the Poorshouse
brae to Woodend and Heathcote; or we would make for the village past Arnhall,
Ed. Donald's cycle shop with the gramophone still playing 'The Dying Plough-
boy', over the railway bridge, past the smiddy and the dam, the Parish Hall
and the War Memorial (pause); up to the Stothert: again a choice of route;
down to the left is the 'Rumbly Rush', where in the thirties a group of
schoolboys tried to build a dam to make a swimming-pool, little thinking
they were soon to be off to a war...

The end came quietly on Friday 18 January when I was out for lunch.
My father had been as usual that morning, except that quite suddenly at
one point, for the first time since his fall, a quite perceptible smile had
crossed his face, a smile as of recognition on unexpectedly meeting some old
friend.

The weather remained uncertain and we decided that the journey back to
Lumphanan should be made as soon as possible: on Monday for the funeral
on Wednesday. He would lie in his old kirk. Monday was almost a spring
day. As we took the road for Dufftown - we had asked that he should be
taken thus instead of by the coast road - the sun came out and the snow-free
landscape glowed with welcoming colour. Down from 'the clock', past Jeanie
Lowrie's and on over the old Bridge of Fiddich - we must have been amongst
the last to cross by the bridge before the new diversion came into use -

and on towards Huntly. As we neared Lumphanan in mid-afternoon, still in
sunshine, I suggested that instead of going down the Perkhill and through
the village we take the 'Poorshouse brae' with its magnificent panorama
reaching out to the distant hills. We thus reached the church, perched on
its knoll with the belfry against the sky, from the west, making the small
detour to enter by the northern churchyard approach, the manse by then being
in private hands. I didn't know that in the village, watching for our arrival,
was James Calder of Cairnton, waiting to come and receive us at the church:
he only saw the empty hearse returning north. So I unlocked the door of the
church - the key, as ever, being in the lock - and the men carried him in.
Among the few belongings to be picked up at Nairn I had asked for his stick -
the knobkerrie with the handle carved by young James Burnett: 'I never go
anywhere without it'. So we taped it on to the top of the coffin, under
the family wreaths, and came out and locked the door.

Next day Craig and I drove out from Aberdeen to meet the minister, the
Reverend Silvester Skinner, and make final arrangements. We met him again
with James Calder at the church, where also was Mrs Peter Ferries, Cairnbeathie (Doris Laing of the Mill of Kintocher) who had brought some flowers
for the service, as she had done for Wendy. The Nairn undertaker, familiar
with country customs, had brought up the question of who was to 'take a cord':
'Will we just wait and see who comes?' We weren't at all sure who was left
to come, and rather expected merely a token turnout. So we paid one or two
calls to ensure that this at least was taken care of. At Wendy's funeral
in 1967 a younger generation had taken part: this time we went further back
towards older associations, including James Calder and Henry. Approaching
the smithy at Marywell to ask James Emslie, Craig took it for granted we
would take the short cut but accepted what turned out to be the correct advice
to go round by the road. The house door opened: 'It's Craig and Heather'.
Soon we were settled with teacups in our hands while the smith recalled the

day Craig was born. Their neighbour John Urquhart had dropped in: he had
for a time been 'beadle' at the West End Hall services before taking the farm
of Quithelhead. The years began to roll away. 'Do you still play the fiddle,
Smith?' He pointed to where it lay, on the piano stool. We then called at
Auchenhove and returned via Burnside: we wanted our old neighbour, Edward
Sherriffs, now the laird, to take part. There was no-one at home but we
left a card on the doorstep, and next day he was there, one of those who
carried the coffin from the church.

The day of the funeral was bitterly cold but bright. The Arnotts came
from Nairn and the Grants from Forres, with Francis and Elsie Cantlie from
Nether Enoch in the parish of Mortlach. (It was Elsie who suddenly noticed
'It's his stick!') Francis was head of the family in this country, the other
being in Canada. We brought another Cantlie relative, Charlotte Walker, widow
of the Medical Officer of Health for Banffshire, from Aberdeen. Craig had
asked me early on 'What do you think about the service?' my reply being
'Keep it cheery', which had his full agreement. I said Father didn't care
for the tune Crimond, and Wiltshire tended to drag, so we settled for the
hymnbook version of Psalm 23: 'The King of Love my Shepherd is'. Laura Stuart
had offered to play the organ and we had asked that her brother, the Reverend
Alex. Stuart, then at Banchory West, should take part. The Reverend Dr D.M.L.
Urie of Kincardine O'Neil gave the address. At Craig's suggestion the
service concluded with Kilmarnock: 'Come let us to the Lord our God'.

Craig and I made a list afterwards of those attending in the crowded
church, the names still very similar to those of the 1913 Testimonial. The
ministers of the Presbytery announced themselves by the names of their parishes.
Among former Deeside ministers was the Reverend John Tennant, late of Finzean
and then Cluny, led by a friend because he was awaiting a cataract operation.
He recalled my father's concern for the families of chaplains such as himself
on service during the second war. Sometimes it was hard to associate familiar

features with the right generation or member of that generation, but many
helpfully mentioned both their names. Craig was momentarily thrown by 'It's
Lizzie' - a girl who had been in his class at school - but I was able to
fill the gap and to introduce her husband with whom I had picked tatties at
Cairnbeathie; I had been a witness at their wedding. Another old schoolmate
of Craig's, Alex Cockie, said to Craig 'You were in Cyprus..' His son,
serving in the 1st Gordon Highlanders, had died in the forest fire at Troodos
in 1956. William Davie III had flown up from Hertfordshire: 'The Davies must
always be there!' Norman Bruce, sheep farmer, had come up from the Lothians;
recalling their family holidays with the Kings at Knappyround, he remembered
my brother posting a notice on the chestnut tree by the burn to the effect
that 'Boysie' was in future to be known as 'Craig'. I was able to introduce
him to that other sheepman Ed. Sherriffs, the latter quoting my father's
admonition, as Ed. trimmed the feet of the manse sheep: 'Canny wi' the
knife, Ed., you'll bleed them!', Ed.'s opinion being 'But it's good for them,
ye ken!' adding 'My mother thought there was nobody like your father'.

Altogether there was at my father's funeral more of a sense of reunion
than of separation, and thus he joined his many friends in the churchyard.
It would seem appropriate to end with part of Dr Urie's address:

Friends and Brethren,

We are gathered together within these hallowed walls to thank
God for the life and work of a beloved friend and pastor, who in
the fulness of years has passed to his reward.

The strength of the Church of Scotland has always been founded
on her parochial ministry, and of that ministry Francis Cantlie
Donald was a shining example. For forty years he faithfully discharged the duties of his sacred calling in this parish, sparing no
pains, and counting no effort too great as he sought to fulfil his
ideal of the country pastor. And I do not exaggerate - for it is
the plain, unvarnished truth - when I say that the acceptance with
which he laboured among his people had no equal in this Presbytery.

But a minister may be a tireless visitor, an eloquent preacher
and an efficient organizer, and yet, at the end of the day, make
little or no impression. For no ministry can be truly successful
without that mysterious personal quality by which contact is made
at a deep, human level.

It was the possession of this quality that made Francis Donald the unique personality that he was. Taking his fellow mortals as he found them: working with people as they were willing to work with him: concealing his private sorrows – and they were not few – behind a cheerful countenance: he got through to the people of Lumphanan and forged a bond which every passing year strengthened. And knowing Lumphanan as I do, I know there are not a few in this gathering who will cherish to the end of their days, the remembrance of the help they received from their beloved pastor in their time of need.

*   *   *   *   *

And now we have come to the end of the story. And shortly we shall convey to the last resting place all that is mortal of our dear, old friend, followed by the affectionate remembrance of three generations. And as we go forth, our thoughts and feelings are surely summed up in the words of the Psalmist: "Mark the perfect man, and behold the upright: for the end of that man is peace."